MODERN HADITH STUDIES

MODERN HADITH STUDIES

CONTINUING DEBATES AND NEW APPROACHES

◆ ◆ ◆

EDITED BY BELAL ABU-ALABBAS,
MICHAEL DANN AND
CHRISTOPHER MELCHERT

EDINBURGH
University Press

Edinburgh University Press is one of the leading university presses in the UK. We publish academic books and journals in our selected subject areas across the humanities and social sciences, combining cutting-edge scholarship with high editorial and production values to produce academic works of lasting importance. For more information visit our website: edinburghuniversitypress.com

Edinburgh University Press Ltd
The Tun – Holyrood Road
12 (2f) Jackson's Entry
Edinburgh EH8 8PJ

First published in hardback by Edinburgh University Press 2020

Typeset in KoufrUni by
Servis Filmsetting Ltd, Stockport, Cheshire,

A CIP record for this book is available from the British Library

ISBN 978 1 4744 4179 7 (hardback)
ISBN 978 1 4744 4180 3 (paperback)
ISBN 978 1 4744 4181 0 (webready PDF)
ISBN 978 1 4744 4182 7 (epub)

CONTENTS

Figures and Tables	vii
Acknowledgements	viii
Note on Conventions	ix
Notes on Contributors	x
Introduction *Christopher Melchert*	1
1. *Kunnā nakrahu al-kitāb*: Scripture, Transmission of Knowledge, and Politics in the Second Century AH (719–816 CE) *Pavel Pavlovitch*	9
2. The History of the *Adhān*: a View from the Hadith Literature *Maroussia Bednarkiewicz*	27
3. Ibn al-Mubārak, Traditionist *Christopher Melchert*	49
4. Early 'Traditionist Sufis': A Network Analysis *Jeremy Farrell*	70
5. The Common Link and its Relation to Hadith Terminology *Ali Aghaei*	97
6. Hadith Criticism between Traditionists and Jurisprudents *Mutaz al-Khatib*	129
7. Hadith Criticism in the Levant in the Twentieth Century: From *ẓāhir al-isnād* to *ʿilal al-ḥadīth* *Ahmad Snober*	151

8. The Reception and Representation of Western Hadith Studies in Turkish Academe 171
Fatma Kızıl

9. Can Different Questions Yield the Same Answers? Islamic and Western Scholarship on Shiʿi Narrators in the Sunni Tradition 192
Michael Dann

Index 215

FIGURES AND TABLES

Figures

2.1 Chains of transmitters for C1 30
2.2 Chains of transmitters for *umira bilāl an yashfaᶜ* .. 33
2.3 Chains of transmitters for C2 34
2.4 Chains of transmitters for C3 37

Tables

1.1 The stance of al-Nakhaᶜī, Ibn Sīrīn, Qatādah ibn Diᶜāmah and al-Zuhrī on *al-kitāb* and the Umayyad punctuation and sectioning of the Qurʾān 17
2.1 Primary sources and the number of narratives they contain for each category 29
2.2 Structural comparison between C1 and C2 36
2.3 Lexical comparison between C1 and C2 37
2.4 General outline of C3's narratives 38
2.5 The formulae of the *adhān* and the *iqāmah* and their repetitions in the narratives of C3 43
4.1 Concurrence between traditionist Sufi and proto-canonical hadith works 83
4.2 Most 'central' *ḥuffāẓ* by *ṭabaqah,* arranged chronologically 83
4.3 Mean metrics of prominence and centrality among *ḥuffāẓ* 84
4.4 Variability in prominence and centrality in *ṭabaqah* 84
4.5 Comparison of traditionist Sufis with contemporary *ḥuffāẓ* (*fl.* third / ninth century) 85
4.6 Comparison of traditionist Sufis with contemporary *ḥuffāẓ* (*fl.* fourth / tenth century) 85

ACKNOWLEDGEMENTS

Most of the chapters in this collection were first offered for comment and criticism, in earlier versions, at the symposium 'Modern Hadith Studies between Arabophone and Western Scholarship', convened at Pembroke College, Oxford, 9–10 January 2017, thanks to a gift from Brian Wilson (d. 2019), Old Pembrokian and former civil servant with a special burden for Arabic and Chinese. This volume is dedicated to his memory.

NOTE ON CONVENTIONS

The editors have imposed spelling, citation style and other conventions of Edinburgh University Press on all contributions with two major exceptions, both in accordance with usual practice in premodern studies. First, Arabic and Persian are transliterated in full (after the Library of Congress standard). Secondly, dates are split, the year of the Hijrah preceding that of the Common Era (or, sometimes, the two overlapping years of the Common Era when the sources do not permit any more precision). In order to make them findable in multiple editions, hadith reports in the Six Books are cited by book (*kitāb*) and section (*bāb*) so as to be compatible with the numbering of A. J. Wensinck et al., *Concordance et indices de la tradition musulmane*, 7 vols (Leiden: Brill, 1936–69), referred to in Arabic as *al-Muʿjam*. They are also cited by the most nearly conventional number, usually that of Fuʾād ʿAbd al-Bāqī in one of his editions.

NOTES ON CONTRIBUTORS

Belal Abu-Alabbas is British Academy Newton International Fellow at the University of Exeter and Lecturer at Al-Azhar University in Cairo. He is also an Associate Faculty Member at the Oriental Institute in Oxford. He publishes in the fields of Islamic intellectual history, Islamic legal thought and the history of the hadith corpus.

Ali Aghaei is Postdoctoral Researcher at Berlin-Brandenburg Academy of Sciences and Humanities (Berlin/Potsdam). His current research focuses on philological, palaeographical and codicological analysis of Qur'anic manuscripts. He is a Member of the Academic Board for *Encyclopaedia Islamica*, contributing to the *Dāneshnāmeh-ye Jahān-e Eslām* (*Encyclopaedia of the World of Islam*).

Maroussia Bednarkiewicz is Postdoctoral Fellow at the University of Innsbruck. She earned her doctorate from Oxford University on her dissertation documenting the history of the Islamic call to prayer (*adhān*). Her current research focuses on the development of digital means to analyse large corpora of classical Arabic texts.

Michael Dann is Assistant Professor at the University of Illinois, Urbana. His research interests include Early Islamic history, medieval and modern Islamic thought, sectarianism, Sunnism and Shiᶜism, hadith, biographical literature, and modern Islamic historiography.

Jeremy Farrell is a doctoral candidate at Emory University. His scholarship integrates computational and textual methods in order to describe the formation of Islamic religious movements from the ninth to eleventh centuries CE with a focus on Sufism.

Mutaz al-Khatib is Assistant Professor of Methodology and Ethics at the Centre for Islamic Legislation and Ethics (CILE), Qatar. His research focuses on Islamic law, legal thought and ethics. He publishes in the fields of hadith criticism, Islamic interpretation methods and Islamic law.

Fatma Kızıl is Assistant Professor of Hadith at Yalova University, Turkey, and the editor of *Hadīth and Sīra Studies* journal. Her research focuses on Western hadith studies, *isnād-cum-matn* analysis and the history of hadith transmission. She is the author of *Müşterek Râvi Teorisi ve Tenkidi* (2013) and is currently working on source analysis of *Ṣaḥīḥ* al-Bukhārī.

Christopher Melchert is Professor of Arabic and Islamic Studies at the Oriental Institute, Oxford. His research focuses on Islamic movements and institutions in the ninth–tenth centuries CE. He publishes in the fields of Islamic law, hadith and piety.

Pavel Pavlovitch is Professor in Medieval Arabo-Islamic Civilization at the Centre for Oriental Languages and Cultures, Sofia University St Kliment Ohridski. He publishes in the fields of early Islamic history, hadith criticism and the methodology of studying Muslim traditions. His latest major publications include the monograph *The Formation of the Islamic Understanding of* Kalāla *in the Second Century* AH *(718–816* CE*): Between Scripture and Canon* (2016) and several entries in *Encyclopaedia of Islam Three*.

Ahmad Snober is Assistant Professor of Hadith at Istanbul 29 Mayıs University. His research focuses on the history of the hadith corpus in the Sunni and Imami traditions. He has several publications in Arabic on hadith criticism, *isnād-matn* analysis and back-projection in *isnād*s.

INTRODUCTION

Christopher Melchert

'*Ḥadīth*' means 'speech' in Arabic. Technically, it indicates a report or a body of reports (the Arabic word is used both ways, although there is also a plural, *aḥādīth*) of what the Prophet or some other authoritative teacher said. From hadith, Muslim jurisprudents infer the Sunnah, the pattern of behaviour that Muslims should follow. A hadith report normally comes in two parts, the *matn* ('main part'), which is what the Prophet or other authority said, and the *isnād* ('support'), the chain of authorities by which it has reached the present collector. The *isnād* is one's proof that this report was not made up somewhere along the way and projected backward onto a venerable authority of the past. In time, writers distinguished between *ḥadīth* going back to the Prophet and *āthār* (sing. *athar*) going back to other early Muslims, but the terms were interchangeable in the early centuries. (Hadith reports were once called 'traditions' in European languages, by analogy with preliterary oral reports of what Jesus said. 'Hadith' is now in standard English dictionaries, but 'traditionist' may still be used for someone who collects hadith.)

Here is an example of a hadith report going back to the Prophet:

> There related to us ^{c}Ubayd Allāh ibn Mūsá: there reported to us Ḥanẓalah from Sālim from Ibn ^{c}Umar from the Prophet: he said, 'It is better for one of you to have his insides filled with pus than with poetry.'[1]

Here is another (henceforward, 'there related to us', 'from', and so on will be abbreviated by a simple sign):

> Abū al-Walīd al-Ṭayālisī < Shu^{c}bah < al-A^{c}mash < Abū Ṣāliḥ < Abū Hurayrah < the Messenger of God: 'It is better for one of you to have his insides filled with pus than with poetry.'[2]

The above are from two of the most trusted Sunni collections of hadith. Here is one from a collection of weak hadith:

> Muḥammad ibn al-Ḥasan al-Baṣrī < ʿAlī ibn Baḥr < ʿĪsá ibn Yūnus < al-Aḥwaṣ ibn al-Ḥakīm < Khālid ibn Maʿdān < Abū al-Dardāʾ < the Messenger of God: 'It is better for one of you to have his insides filled with pus and blood than with poetry.'[3]

Plainly, the quotation was unexceptionable. The collector of this concludes his review of hadith from this man, al-Aḥwaṣ ibn al-Ḥakīm, 'There is nothing he relates that is disreputable, except that his *isnād*s are not matched by anyone else's.'[4] That is, he heard genuine hadith, invented chains of transmission leading up to him, and substituted them for the *isnād*s leading up to the men he really heard them from.

The foregoing examples of hadith have mainly concerned the life of piety, but the first two help to constitute Islamic law inasmuch as it includes recommendations, identifying actions that are encouraged but not required or discouraged but not forbidden. Many essential rules depend on hadith. For example, the Qurʾān continually refers to the ritual prayer and alms (*ṣalāh, zakāh*) as essential duties, but only hadith specify that the ritual prayer begins with raising the hands and saying *Allāh akbar* or that the required alms is one-fortieth of wealth above a certain level.

Hadith also supports Islamic theology, where definite knowledge is necessary. For example, Sunni collections quote the Prophet as saying, 'An adulterer does not commit adultery as a believer, nor does he drink wine when he drinks as a believer, nor does he steal when he steals as a believer.' The chief transmitter of the collection of al-Bukhārī (d. 256/870) glosses this report with the note, 'I have found in the handwriting of Abū Jaʿfar (Muḥammad ibn Abī Ḥātim, Bukhārī's copyist), "Abū ʿAbd Allāh (al-Bukhārī) said, 'Its explanation is that it is snatched away from him', meaning faith."'[5] This is to comment on a theological controversy of the eighth and ninth centuries. The Sunni position is definitely that correct belief, not outward actions, separates the saved from the perishing. Partly because there are many hadith reports that identify this or that misbehaviour as tantamount to unbelief, it was necessary to explain that the unbelief associated with wrong actions is a temporary state.

The authenticity question became paramount early on. Muslim jurisprudents, deciding which hadith reports were reliable bases for action and belief, had to decide which ones really went back to the Prophet. Part of the problem was normally imperfect transmission by dictation or copying of manuscripts. For example, al-Bukhārī six times quotes the Prophet as saying, 'Actions are only by intentions. Every man has only what he has intended. Whosever emigration (*hijrah*) is to a lower good for him to get, or a woman for him to marry, his emigration is to what he emigrated to.' Although the *isnād*s all go back to one man in the mid-eighth century, no two of them are exactly identical, differing as to details such as the word for 'marry' and whether 'intention' is singular or plural.[6] More seriously, the problem often went further, into outright contradiction. It is not rare for collections of hadith arranged by topic to have a section of hadith in favour of some rule followed by a section against; for example, successive sections provided by al-Nasāʾī (d. 303/915?) by which the Prophet did or did not perform a special prostration in the course of reciting Q. 53.[7]

Some thinkers cited contradiction as a reason to relegate hadith to secondary status below the Qurʾān and consensus as indicators of what law to follow.[8] The position that prevailed accepted a degree of uncertainty. One could not be certain that the hadith supporting one's juridical position (say, that it was proper to raise one's hands repeatedly in the course of the ritual prayer) accurately represented the Prophet's precept and example, but one might think that one's own practice (or, usually, one's school's rule) was the most likely to represent the Prophet's precept and example.

The authenticity question dominated hadith scholarship in the Middle Ages. Early specialist hadith critics tried to sort more from less likely versions of what the Prophet had said. Later specialists concentrated on cataloguing, reorganising and synthesising earlier scholarship.[9] By sheer numbers, the greatest activity seems to have taken place in Egypt. In the Early Modern period, India became the most active centre of hadith scholarship.[10]

Hadith scholarship by Muslims was challenged in the twentieth century by scholarship from non-Muslims, starting most notably with a survey by Ignaz Goldziher.[11] He proposed that hadith literature is so rife with contradiction that one's starting presumption has to be that any particular hadith report does not go back to the Prophet, rather, that it reflects the polemical interests of later Muslims. Joseph Schacht refined Goldziher's argument by detailing some specific mechanisms by which, he thought, contrary rules were generated in the course of the eighth century and corresponding hadith projected back into the seventh.[12] From the 1980s, G. H. A. Juynboll extended Schacht's work to identify particular traditionists whom he thought to identify, by comparison of *isnād*s, as the probable originators of particular reports.[13] For very different reasons, some Muslims also downgraded hadith in the twentieth century, preferring to rely for religious doctrine on the Qurʾān alone.[14]

Naturally, there have been counterattacks. Refutations of Schacht from Muslims have tended to fall back on what appear to outsiders to be dogma and special pleading.[15] The most prominent European critic of Schacht's line has been Harald Motzki, who combines *isnād* comparison with more trusting presumptions to vindicate most of the hadith he has examined as far back as the early eighth century (although seldom to the early seventh).[16] Herbert Berg has forcefully argued that the authenticity debate is deadlocked over initial assumptions, and Motzki also has acknowledged that initial assumptions are crucial.[17] There remain many other historical questions having to do with hadith but not particularly whether they constitute a reliable body of quotations from the early seventh century. This volume especially addresses some such questions.

European and American hadith scholarship has been relatively slow to develop. Islamic theology was addressed early on, partly one guesses because theology seems to Christians to be the natural starting point, partly because the Arabic literature the student of Islamic theology apparently needs to master is relatively limited. Similarly, the European and American study of Islamic law tended at first to concentrate on jurisprudence, *uṣūl al-fiqh*, partly again because the literature is not so immense as for discussions of particular rules, *furūᶜ al-fiqh*, also probably on the assumption that starting with the principles is a short-cut to understanding the whole. Hadith seems to be the last area to catch on as a subject of study on its own, and the nebulousness of hadith is surely one reason for that – nebulous in the sense that the literature to be mastered is immense, nebulous also in the sense that its boundaries are very uncertain. Earlier students also tended to start with synthetic, theoretical treatments of the High Middle Ages, such as the introduction of Ibn al-Ṣalāḥ al-Shahrazūrī (d. Jerusalem, 643 / 1245).[18] They are of lively intrinsic interest but as documents of their own time, not as transparent reproductions of an earlier literature, unchanged except as to ease of reference. To analyse the methods of ninth-century critics and collectors, it is imperative to examine surviving works of the ninth century itself.

Pavel Pavlovitch has recently established himself as the most thorough critic to date of Motzki's *isnād-cum-matn* method of *isnād* comparison.[19] In this volume, '*Kunnā nakrahu al-kitāb*: Scripture, Transmission of Knowledge, and Politics in the Second Century AH (719–816 CE)' proposes to uncover the changing sense of a genuinely early saying as the concerns of Muslims changed over time, in this case from distrusting a tyrannical governor's edition of the Qurʾān to accepting that traditionists should keep written notes, not trusting to their memories alone. In 'The History of the *Adhān*: A View from the Hadith Literature', Maroussia Bednarkiewicz investigates hadith about the form of the call to prayer. The Qurʾān itself refers to a call (although using another term, *nidāʾ*) without laying down a form. Bednarkiewicz' technique of associating different wordings with different traditionists clearly shows the influence of Motzki, and she shares with him the determination to find an original core story. However, her interest is not to correct her predecessors, rather to show how the demands of formulating and defending rules over time led to adjusting stories of the Prophet and his Companions.

Christopher Melchert, 'Ibn al-Mubārak, Traditionist', begins with a survey of modern scholarship concerning this prominent eighth-century traditionist, comparing treatments in Arabic and English. It goes on to review his personal position as to various controversies of his time, but also regretfully observes limits to our understanding of such early figures when so much depends on what later compilers quoted of them. Jeremy Farrell, 'Early "Traditionist Sufis": A Network Analysis', re-opens a scholarly debate over the intersection between traditionists and Sufis (and their renunciant predecessors) across the eighth to tenth centuries. Like many studies in the new discipline of Digital Humanities, Farrell's statistical analysis does not much modify what older methods suggest, in this case that some tenth-century Sufis were also significantly involved in networks of hadith transmission. Still, such confirmation is welcome, and one looks forward to further statistical work to address such questions as whether hadith circles were small, such that everybody knew everybody else, or large and dispersed, so that exchange among contemporaries was indeed restricted.

Ali Aghaei, 'The Common Link and its Relation to Hadith Terminology', compares modern and medieval scholarship. In particular, Aghaei addresses the controversy over whether the medieval technical term *madār* ('pivot'), meaning someone to whom lines of transmission for a particular report continually converged, was effectively equivalent to Schacht's term 'common link'. After examining the usage of *madār* and related terms, Aghaei tends to vindicate G. H. A. Juynboll's assertion that they were. Modern students of the Qurʾān have relied heavily on some techniques of literary analysis additional to those used by medieval scholars, such as rhyme and verse length. Modern students of hadith have mostly relied on the same techniques as their medieval predecessors, differing mainly as to initial assumptions. As Aghaei also observes, however, they do work with rather different objects in view.

Moving to the High Middle Ages, Mutaz al-Khatib, 'Hadith Criticism between Traditionists and Jurisprudents', compares and contrasts hadith criticism as practised by traditionists, specialists in hadith, and jurisprudents, specialists in inferring the law from revelation. The theory of ninth-century Traditionalists, sometimes called 'Hadith Folk' for their devotion to hadith, was that correct law and theology would clearly emerge from the sifting of sound from weak hadith; that is, accurate from inaccurate quotations of the Prophet and his Companions. They proceeded by comparing *isnād*s, discarding uncorroborated reports. On examination, it appears that jurisprudents proceeded rather differently, partly because their attention was focused on the *matn* rather than the *isnād*, partly because they often evidently began with a rule to be defended – there are good, practical reasons for wanting the law to be stable and predictable.

Ahmad Snober, 'Hadith Criticism in the Levant in the Twentieth Century: From *ẓāhir al-isnād* to *ʿilal al-ḥadīth*', shows that modern Arab scholars were for long equally inclined with European to rely on late-medieval syntheses of earlier hadith criticism. In recent decades, however, a subtler, more supple approach to hadith criticism has been developed, closer to that of ninth-century Sunni critics. The new approach has been promoted largely in connection with controversies tangential to hadith, such as the continued relevance of medieval jurisprudence and the proper role of Islam in politics. It remains a welcome advance and an instance of convergence between hadith studies in and out of the Middle East.

Fatma Kızıl, 'The Reception and Representation of Western Hadith Studies in Turkish Academe', surveys developments in the Turkish Republic, which has recently become another major centre of hadith scholarship. As in the Arab world, students of hadith have been involved in political controversy, both internally (different evaluations of Westernisation and secularism, also very much the continued relevance of medieval jurisprudence) and externally (defence against European scepticism). But Kızıl's account is equally hopeful with Snober's inasmuch as it documents increasing publication of serious scholarship.

Finally, Michael Dann, 'Can Different Questions Yield the Same Answers? Islamic and Western Scholarship on Shiʿi Narrators in the Sunni Tradition', surveys scholarship in English, French, German, Arabic, Persian and Turkish. The volume of scholarship in Middle Eastern languages is unsurprisingly greater and many studies more voluminous than treatments of the same topics in European and North American scholarship. Muslim scholars seem to be more or less affected by normative considerations, but likewise non-Muslim, inasmuch as they use the terms of competing traditions.

Although this volume designedly exposes new approaches to the study of hadith apart from the authenticity question, that controversy does lurk behind many contributions. Jonathan Brown has clearly laid out some of the main reasons that what he calls the Historical Critical Method necessarily leads to results uncomfortable for the religious tradition.[20] The Principle of Analogy is the axiom that all ages are equal, so that, for example, if people in the near past have demonstrably been influenced by material considerations, so must have been people in the distant. This poses particular difficulty for the Sunni dogmatic position that the Companions were impeccable, unlike any later generation of Muslims. The Principle of Dissimilarity suggests that when there are multiple accounts of something, the one that agrees with later orthodoxy is the most likely to be a back projection. If we find records that eighth-century Muslims advocated one sort of law, ninth-century Muslims another, the Principle of Dissimilarity makes it a strong presumption that ninth-century quotations of the Prophet in support of ninth-century positions are not a rediscovery of original Islamic law but a back projection of ninth-century conceptions. As Brown observes, these axioms were applied to the Bible before the Qurʾān and hadith, so the discomfort of Muslims with Goldziher and Schacht today is similar to an earlier generation of Christians' discomfort with Baur and Wellhausen.

An additional difficulty is the nature of research in the Western academy. First, tenure and promotion depend largely on publication of original research. Secondly, no scholar is lauded as a reinforcer of common understandings. Rather, a scholar gets kudos by shifting the way people conceive of a field, the greater the shift the more kudos. (Michael Dann refers to 'counter-narratives'.) One baleful consequence is the tediously many articles that begin by affirming that no intelligent person has ever treated the topic at hand before now, or by summarising the common understanding of the question (which the present article will overturn) by some inanity no one has actually enounced. Another consequence is that the more genuinely original scholars want to be, the more they will constantly probe for weaknesses in common understandings. Muslims who complain of hostility to their religion are missing the point, but it must be conceded that original scholarship is likely to be uncomfortable for believers. (Let it also be conceded that Western scholarship has its own protected orthodoxies, if not religious then, for example, the 'surprising' degree of women's agency in any past time and place.) And we would offer the present volume as evidence that Islamic Studies is a vital field in the Middle East as well as in Europe and North America, among Muslim scholars as well as non-Muslim.

Notes

1. Bukhārī, *Ṣaḥīḥ, al-adab* 93, *bāb mā yukrahu an yakūna al-ghālib ᶜalá al-insān al-shiᶜr*, No. 6154.
2. Abū Dāwūd, *Sunan, al-adab* 87, *bāb mā jāʾa fī al-shiᶜr*, No. 5009.
3. Ibn ᶜAdī al-Qaṭṭān, *al-Kāmil fī ḍuᶜafāʾ al-rijāl*, ed. ᶜĀdil Aḥmad ᶜAbd al-Mawjūd and ᶜAlī Muḥammad Muᶜawwaḍ, 9 vols (Beirut: Dār al-Kutub al-ᶜIlmīyah, 1418/1997), 2:117, s.n. al-Aḥwaṣ ibn Ḥakīm.
4. Ibn ᶜAdī al-Qaṭṭān, *Kāmil* 2:119.
5. Bukhārī, *Ṣaḥīḥ, al-maẓālim* 30, *bāb al-nuhbá bi-ghayr idhn ṣāḥibih*, No. 2475 (among other places).
6. Bukhārī, *Ṣaḥīḥ, badʾ al-waḥy* 1, *bāb kayfa kāna badʾ al-waḥy*, No. 1; *al-'itq* 6, *bāb al-khaṭaʾ wa-al-nisyān*, No. 2529; *manāqib al-anṣār* 45, *bāb hijrat al-nabī*, No. 3898; *al-nikāḥ* 5, *bāb man hājara aw ᶜamila khayran li-tazwīj imraʾah*, No. 5070; *al-aymān wa-al-nudhūr* 23, *bāb al-nīyah fī al-aymān*, No. 6689; *al-ḥiyal* 1, *bāb fī tark al-ḥiyal*, No. 6953.
7. Nasāʾī, *Mujtabá, al-iftitāḥ* 49, *al-sujūd fī* wa-al-najm, Nos 958–9, then *al-iftitāḥ* 50, *tark al-sujūd fī al-najm*, No. 960.
8. For example, Ḍirār b. ᶜAmr (d. *c.* 180/796–7?), *K. al-Taḥrīsh*, ed. Hüseyin Hansu and Mehmet Keskin (Istanbul: Sharikat Dār al-Irshād and Beirut: Dār Ibn Ḥazm, 1435/2014).
9. A good survey of hadith science in the High Middle Ages is Jonathan A. C. Brown, *Hadith: Muhammad's Legacy in the Medieval and Modern World*, Foundations of Islam (Oxford: Oneworld, 2009, 2nd edn 2017).
10. As documented by Muḥammad ᶜIṣām ᶜArār al-Ḥasanī, *Itḥāf al-qārī bi-maᶜrifat juhūd wa-aᶜmāl al-ᶜulamaʾ ᶜalá Ṣaḥīḥ al-Bukhārī* (Damascus: al-Yamāmah, 1987).
11. Ignaz Goldziher, 'The Ḥadīth Literature', in *Muslim Studies*, ed. S. M. Stern, trans. C. R. Barber and S. M. Stern, 2 vols (Chicago: Aldine Atherton, 1968–71), 2:189–251.
12. Joseph Schacht, *The Origins of Muhammadan Jurisprudence* (Oxford: Clarendon Press, 1950).
13. See esp. G. H. A. Juynboll, *Muslim Tradition*, Cambridge Studies in Islamic Civilization (Cambridge: Cambridge University Press, 1983), and G. H. A. Juynboll, *Encyclopedia of Canonical Ḥadīth* (Leiden: Brill, 2007).

14. For one angle, see Aisha Y. Musa, *Ḥadīth as Scripture: Discussions on the Authority of Prophetic Traditions in Islam* (New York: Palgrave Macmillan, 2008). For another, see Fatma Kızıl, Chapter 8, this volume, esp. at nn. 73–4.
15. The most extensive example is M. Mustafa al-Azami, *On Schacht's Origins of Muhammadan Jurisprudence* (Riyadh: King Saud University, 1985), much reprinted, on which see the critique of Harald Motzki, *The Origins of Islamic Jurisprudence*, trans. Marion H. Katz, Islamic History and Civilization, Studies and Texts, 41 (Leiden: Brill, 2002), 39–45.
16. See esp. Motzki, *Origins*; Harald Motzki, with Nicolet Boekhoff-van der Voort and Sean W. Anthony, *Analysing Muslim Traditions*, Islamic History and Civilization, Studies and Texts, 78 (Leiden: Brill, 2010), which includes several articles translated from German; and Harald Motzki, 'Dating Muslim Traditions', *Arabica* 52 (2005): 204–53. See also *Ḥadīth: Origins and Developments*, ed. Harald Motzki, The Formation of the Classical Islamic World, 28 (Aldershot: Ashgate / Variorum, 2004), a collection of earlier articles by European and American scholars, most, but not all, calling for less scepticism than Schacht and Juynboll.
17. Herbert Berg, *The Development of Exegesis in Early Islam*, Curzon Studies in the Qurʾān (Richmond: Curzon, 2000), ch. 2; Motzki, 'Dating'.
18. See Ibn al-Ṣalāḥ, *An Introduction to the Science of the Ḥadīth*, trans. Eerik Dickinson with Muneer Fareed, Great Books of Islamic Civilisation (Reading: Garnet, 2005).
19. Pavel Pavlovitch, *The Formation of the Islamic Understanding of* kalāla *in the Second Century* AH *(718–816* CE*)*, Islamic History and Civilization, Studies and Texts, 126 (Leiden: Brill, 2016).
20. Brown, *Hadith* (2009), ch. 8, esp. 200–3.

CHAPTER

1

KUNNĀ NAKRAHU AL-KITĀB: SCRIPTURE, TRANSMISSION OF KNOWLEDGE, AND POLITICS IN THE SECOND CENTURY AH (719–816 CE)

Pavel Pavlovitch*

Introduction

This chapter centres on Ibn Shihāb al-Zuhrī's (d. 124/742) statement, 'We were averse to writing down knowledge until these rulers forced us to (accept) it, and therefore we thought it best not to forbid it to any Muslim.' I argue that the tradition comprises two conceptual layers, bearing on specific historical settings from the late Umayyad and the early ᶜAbbāsid periods. The oldest layer, which I designate 'the scriptural concern', originally included the phrase 'We were averse to *kitāb* (scripture)' as a negative response to the redaction of the Qurʾān carried out in the reign of ᶜAbd al-Malik ibn Marwān (r. 65–86/685–705). The nub of the more recent 'equalitarian concern' at the *matn*'s end is the struggle of the non-Arab Muslims (*mawālī*) in the second half of the second century AH (767–816 CE) for an equal right with the Arabs to acquire knowledge of Tradition.

In a short but instructive report (hereinafter, 'the coercion tradition'), the renowned hadith collector Ibn Shihāb al-Zuhrī (d. 124/742) declares:

> (1) *Kunnā nakrahu kitāba al-ᶜilm* (2) *ḥattá akrahanā ᶜalayhi hāʾulāʾi al-umarāʾ* (3) *fa-raʾaynā an-lā namnaᶜahu aḥadan min al-muslimīn.*
> (1) We were averse to writing down knowledge (2) until these rulers forced us to [accept] it, (3) and therefore we thought it best not to forbid it to any Muslim.[1]

In modern scholarship, al-Zuhrī's words have been conventionally interpreted as expressing his discontent with an Umayyad initiative to record Tradition (*kitāb al-ᶜilm*). In a study of the coercion tradition by means of *isnād-cum-matn* analysis,[2] I developed the argument that, either partly or in full, it goes back to the first half of the second century AH (718–68 CE), and that clause 1 originally read, *kunnā nakrahu al-kitāb* ('we were averse to *kitāb*'). Insofar as the word *kitāb* connotes 'holy writ', I suspected that in its earliest form the clause implied a 'scriptural concern' that later transmitters glossed over in three different ways. Most of them substituted for the word *kitāb* the *iḍāfah*-compound *kitāb al-ᶜilm* ('writing down knowledge'); a few transformed the same word into the semantically straightforward *kitābah* ('writing') or replaced it with the obfuscating accusative pronouns *-hu* and *-hā*; that is, *nakrahuhu/hā* ('we were averse to it').

In this chapter, I argue that the text (*matn*) of the coercion tradition is an amalgam of conceptual layers, bearing on specific historical settings from the late Umayyad and the early ᶜAbbāsid periods. The oldest layer, represented by the statement *kunnā nakrahu al-kitāb*, embodies al-Zuhrī's negative response to the redaction of the Qurʾān that the governor of Iraq al-Ḥajjāj ibn Yūsuf undertook between AH 84 and 85 (703–4 CE) on the order of the caliph ᶜAbd al-Malik ibn Marwān (r. 65–86/685–705). The more recent layer includes the 'equalitarian concern' at the *matn*'s end, which alludes to the struggle of the non-Arab Muslims (*mawālī*) in the second half of the second century AH/767–816 CE for an equal right to acquire knowledge of Tradition.

Semantic Strains and Composite Structure

Given al-Zuhrī's amicable relationship with several Umayyad caliphs,[3] his negative stance on their policy to record Tradition is striking. If he embraced the writing of Tradition after having initially opposed it, as Schoeler and Cook interpret the coercion tradition,[4] is not he expected to assess the Umayyad initiative in positive terms, or, lest he be suspected of duplicity, to at least refrain from expressing an opinion altogether? To explain the semantic tension between clauses 1 (opposition to writing) and 2 (grudging endorsement thereof), Cook considered al-Zuhrī's reference to the rulers' coercion as an excuse betraying the original weakness of those scholars who upheld written transmission of knowledge against an oralist majority.[5] Schoeler raised the possibility that Maᶜmar ibn Rāshid, who disliked the Umayyads, may have ascribed clause 2 to al-Zuhrī.[6] Besides, Maᶜmar's editing of the *matn* may have been driven by a wish to erase the memory of al-Zuhrī's one-time friendship with the *ancien régime*, which certainly gave rise to ideological qualms during the early ᶜAbbāsid period. The latter two possibilities suggest that the *matn* of the coercion tradition may be an amalgam of political and scholarly concerns, some of which post-date al-Zuhrī.

Clause 3 is no less perplexing than the preceding two clauses. Forced to record Tradition (clause 2), al-Zuhrī finds it best not to forbid its knowledge to any Muslim (clause 3). How do these two clauses work together? Do they imply that oral transmission hindered the spread of knowledge, whereas writing would be conducive towards its wider dissemination? If so, al-Zuhrī comes across, once again, as an unblushing opportunist who first advocated oral transmission, although he knew that it prevented many Muslims from knowledge, then yielded to political pressure in favour of writing, but presented his currying of the rulers' favour as solicitude for the spread of knowledge among Muslims. In its present context, clause 3 would seem to betray a politically induced attempt to besmirch al-Zuhrī rather than impartially describe his opinion as to how and to whom knowledge should be transmitted.

Alternatively, as suggested by Kister, al-Zuhrī's action in clause 3 may have been his way of decrying the rulers' coercion described in clause 2.[7] But why would al-Zuhrī express his protest by encouraging all Muslims to write down traditions? Kister explained that a request to write for the caliph's sons possibly unreliable traditions serving Umayyad political interests irked al-Zuhrī, and he responded by encouraging people to record traditions with sound attribution to early Islamic authorities.[8] Such an interpretation, however, presupposes a ripe system of hadith transmission and criticism, based on the concept of uninterrupted chains of transmission (*isnāds*) going back to the Prophet and his Companions, which was not in place during al-Zuhrī's lifetime.[9]

Our inability to explain coherently al-Zuhrī's motives and intentions points to a problem in the conventional understanding of the coercion tradition. The semantic difficulties stem from two factors: (1) the lack of attention to the *matn*'s composite structure; and (2) the questionable premise that it deals with the same episode in the early history of hadith science as a number of multifarious reports depicting Umayyad initiatives to record Tradition.

Ostensible Similarities

Three different Umayyad caliphs are reported to have bidden al-Zuhrī to codify either the entire Sunnah or some of its parts. In the present section, I take up six traditions that describe codification initiatives by ᶜUmar ibn ᶜAbd al-ᶜAzīz (r. 99–101/717–20) and Hishām ibn ᶜAbd al-Malik (r. 105–25/724–43). A report mentioning ᶜAbd al-Malik ibn Marwān will be treated in the next section.

1. Abū ᶜUbayd (d. 224/838–9?) cites a tradition in which ᶜUmar ibn ᶜAbd al-ᶜAzīz asks al-Zuhrī to write down the various aspects of the Sunnah concerning the alms tax.[10]
2. In a similar tradition, Ibn Abī Khaythamah (d. 279/892) presents ᶜUmar ibn ᶜAbd al-ᶜAzīz's initiative as an overarching project. The caliph reportedly ordered al-Zuhrī and other traditionists to 'collect [all] traditions' (*jamᶜ al-sunan*). They were written down in notebooks, which were dispatched to each province under caliphal authority.[11]
3. Ibn Saᶜd (d. 230/845) reports that Hishām ibn ᶜAbd al-Malik ordered al-Zuhrī to write traditions and dispatched scribes to record under his dictation.[12]
4. In a tradition cited by al-Fasawī (d. 277/890) and Abū Nuᶜaym (d. 430/1038), al-Zuhrī agrees that Hishām ibn ᶜAbd al-Malik may send scribes to record traditions during his lessons.[13]

5. Al-Fasawī also reports that al-Zuhrī dictated 400 traditions for Hishām's sons. One month later Hishām pretended that the traditions had been lost, whereupon al-Zuhrī dictated them anew. Upon comparing the two versions, Hishām found out that al-Zuhrī 'did not depart from a single letter'.[14]
6. Abū Nuᶜaym reports that Hishām ibn ᶜAbd al-Malik forced (*akraha*) al-Zuhrī to write hadith for the caliph's sons, whereupon others began to write.[15]

Traditions Nos 1 and 2 suggest that no later than the first half of the third century AH (815–65 CE), hadith scholars associated ᶜUmar ibn ᶜAbd al-ᶜAzīz with a project to codify the Sunnah, for which he enlisted the help of al-Zuhrī and, possibly, other scholars. Abbott may be right that tradition No 1, which limits al-Zuhrī's codifying activity to the alms tax, is earlier than tradition No. 2, which credits him with the grand project of 'collecting [all] traditions'.[16] Significantly, Ibn Abī Khaythamah states that ᶜUmar ibn ᶜAbd al-ᶜAzīz dispatched copies of the Sunnaic codex to the outlying provinces, a motif in which Schoeler recognised an echo of reports about the caliph ᶜUthmān's codification of the Qurʾān *c.* 30/650.[17] Note also that the expression *jamᶜ al-sunan* brings to mind the similar expression *jamᶜ al-Qurʾān* (collection of the Qurʾān) used to describe Abū Bakr's (r. 11–13/632–4) gathering of records of the revelation made during the Prophet's lifetime.[18] These correspondences may be pointing to an attempt on behalf of the originator of tradition No. 2 to assert the equal authority of the Qurʾān and the Sunnah as legal sources. If so, a third-century *Sitz im Leben* for this tradition would seem feasible,[19] in which case it is almost certainly later than tradition No. 1.

Despite the semblance of similarity, traditions Nos 1 and 2 differ substantially from the coercion tradition. Abū ᶜUbayd cites a long narrative, in which al-Zuhrī treats the issue of the alms tax, without appealing to earlier authorities. Even if al-Zuhrī based his exposition on a stock of memorised narratives, it hardly constitutes a 'writing of Tradition', due to the absence therein of any traditions in the conventional sense of the word. Ibn Abī Khaythamah speaks about *jamᶜ al-sunan*, which presupposes (not least because of its similarity to Abū Bakr's *jamᶜ al-Qurʾān*) the existence of written traditions that ᶜUmar ibn ᶜAbd al-ᶜAzīz ordered to be collected or transcribed on a different medium. According to this scenario, ᶜUmar's initiative would be different and, significantly, later than the initial instigation to write Tradition presumably referred to in the coercion tradition. And, for good measure, traditions Nos 1 and 2 do not include a coercion motif, explicitly or by implication, which further undermines the possibility of their bearing on the same historical circumstances.

Traditions Nos 3, 4, 5 and 6 name Hishām ibn ᶜAbd al-Malik as the royal champion of the writing of Tradition. Tradition No. 3 describes Hishām as having ordered (*amara*) al-Zuhrī to dictate traditions, which suggests a context resembling that of the coercion tradition. Nonetheless, the verb *amara* does not connote the compulsion and resentment inherent in the semantics of *akraha / kariha*, and al-Zuhrī is said to have dictated to Hishām's scribes. The latter detail is not present in the coercion tradition, which mentions al-Zuhrī alone and does not involve the said scribes.

Like Nos 1 and 2, traditions Nos 4 and 5 do not present al-Zuhrī as yielding to Umayyad pressure to write down hadith. One notes immediately that according to No. 4 al-Zuhrī was already teaching (willingly, it appears) to a considerable audience, signalled by the clause *idhā ijtamaᶜa ilayya al-nās* ('as people would come together with me'). Thus, tradition No. 4 depicts a setting of tranquil teaching strikingly dissimilar to the dramatic atmosphere in the coercion tradition where al-Zuhrī imparts his knowledge to the people after being forced to write. Arguably, No. 4 may have been a polemical response to the claims raised in the coercion tradition.

Tradition No. 5 aims at buttressing al-Zuhrī's veracity. This is clear from the trial topos, which is the crux of the narrative. The original disseminator of this tradition must have been a proponent of literal transmission (*al-riwāyah bi-al-lafẓ*), implied in the statement that the second dictation of al-Zuhrī's 400 traditions agreed *literatim* with his first dictation.

To the best of my knowledge, the earliest source to include tradition No. 6 is Abū Nuᶜaym's (d. 430 / 1038) *Ḥilyat al-awliyāᵓ*, which makes it too late to be representative of either al-Zuhrī's lifetime or the *Sitz im Leben* of the other three traditions.

The *isnāds* of the above six traditions witness to the meagre likelihood of their being a depiction of the same historical event referred to in the coercion tradition. These *isnāds* do not intersect at any level of transmission, and their association with al-Zuhrī is tenuous. In tradition No. 1, Abū ᶜUbayd cites ᶜUqayl ibn Khālid, who died between 141 and 144 / 758–62[20]; that is, at least ten years before Abū ᶜUbayd's birth in around 157 / 773–4.[21] Abū ᶜUbayd may have used a written source with ᶜUqayl's traditions, but, absent direct evidence, this possibility remains a hypothesis scarcely supported by biographical data.[22] One may argue that Abū ᶜUbayd, or, for that matter, al-Zuhrī, based his alms-tax exposition on a written document (*kitāb*) prepared by the Prophet and preserved by members of ᶜUmar ibn al-Khaṭṭāb's family. However, Abū ᶜUbayd's tradition to that effect (No. 936)[23] betrays a growth of the *isnād* whereby al-Zuhrī's personal effort to record parts of the Sunnah (Abū ᶜUbayd, No. 1850 = tradition No. 1 above) came to be portrayed as a document belonging to the idealised period of the Prophet's lifetime. *Pace* Juynboll, who tends to consider such taxation provisions as probably emanating from the lifetime of the Prophet,[24] I hesitate to date tradition No. 1 earlier than the year 170 / 786–7, when Abū ᶜUbayd reportedly set about studying hadith.[25]

Tradition No. 2 is carried by the *isnād* Ibn Abī Khaythamah > Ibrāhīm ibn al-Mundhir (d. 236 / 850–1) > Maᶜn ibn ᶜĪsá (d. 198 / 813–14) > Saᶜīd ibn Ziyād (d. ?). Saᶜīd ibn Ziyād is an obscure *mawlá* of the Zuhrid family,[26] who is not on record as having transmitted to Maᶜn ibn ᶜĪsá. Even if we assume the authenticity of the transmission above the level of Saᶜīd, this will lead us to the second half of the second century AH as the earliest period when tradition

No. 2 may have been put into circulation. This conclusion should be qualified with the results of our above *matn* analysis, which point to the last decades of the second century AH, that is, the later part of Ibrāhīm ibn al-Mundhir's lifetime, as the timeframe for the circulation of No. 2.

Tradition No. 3 is based on the *isnād* Ibn Saᶜd > al-Wāqidī (d. 207/823), reporting on the authority of al-Zuhrī's nephew Muḥammad ibn ᶜAbd Allāh ibn Muslim (d. 157/773–4?). Biographical reports about Muḥammad ibn ᶜAbd Allāh agree that he used to associate with al-Zuhrī traditions unparalleled by reliable auxiliary transmissions (*mutābiᶜāt*).[27] Muḥammad's alleged attendance of al-Zuhrī's lessons together with Hishām ibn ᶜAbd al-Malik's scribes may have been one of these suspect narratives; apart from Ibn Saᶜd, it is mentioned only by al-Mizzī.[28]

Tradition No. 4 is said to have reached al-Fasawī via ᶜAbd al-ᶜAzīz ibn ᶜAbd Allāh al-Uwaysī (d. ?), reporting on the authority of Ibrāhīm ibn Saᶜd (d. 182–5/798–802). Ibrāhīm ibn Saᶜd is a reliable transmitter, and if suspicion ever arose regarding his *isnād*s, it affected exactly those on the authority of al-Zuhrī, at the time of whose death Ibrāhīm may have been between fourteen and sixteen years old.[29]

Tradition No. 5 is based on the *isnād* Hishām ibn Khālid al-Salāmī (d. 249/863–4) > al-Walīd ibn Muslim (d. 194–5/809–11) > Saᶜīd ibn Bashīr (d. 168–70/784–7). The original disseminator may have been any of these three men, each of whom was active in Syria, but Hishām ibn Khālid and Saᶜīd ibn Bashīr, being described as *ṣadūq* (sincere),[30] are the most likely candidates. Hence, the tradition may be dated to either the period 125–70/742–86 or the first half of the third century AH (815–65 CE).

Abū Nuᶜaym's tradition (No. 6) is based on the *isnād* Abū Ḥāmid ibn Jabalah > Abū al-ᶜAbbās al-Sarrāj > Dāwūd ibn Rushayd (239/854) > Abū al-Malīḥ. As in Nos 1, 2, 3 and 4, the earliest transmitter in the *isnād* of No. 6 is its most problematic link. Our biographical sources know of two Abū al-Malīḥs who fit in the chronological framework of the report. First, Abū al-Malīḥ ibn Usāmah ibn ᶜUmayr, who was active in Basra, is said to have died in the year 98/716–17,[31] 108/726–7[32] or 112/730–1.[33] Only the first date allows unquestionably for Usāmah ibn ᶜUmayr's having witnessed, as he asserts, Hishām's coercion of al-Zuhrī to write down Tradition, which must have followed Hishām's ascension to the throne in 105/724. The possibility that Usāmah ibn ᶜUmayr is Abū al-Malīḥ from Abū Nuᶜaym's *isnād* is also undermined by the fact that none of the few biographers who include Usāmah in their dictionaries mention among his pupils a man by the name Dāwūd ibn Rushayd. The latter is known as a transmitter from another Abū al-Malīḥ – al-Ḥasan ibn ᶜUmar al-Raqqī (d. 181/797–8). Given that al-Ḥasan ibn ᶜUmar died fifty-seven lunar years after al-Zuhrī, it is highly unlikely that he had first-hand memories about the commencement of Hishām's policy to write down Tradition, which, for good measure, may hardly have occurred in the final few years of al-Zuhrī's lifetime. It is true that al-Ḥasan ibn ᶜUmar is said to have died at the age of ninety-four, or ninety-five lunar years, but I suspect that his longevity was a means to cast aside suspicion of the reliability of his transmission from al-Zuhrī.[34]

Our examination of the *isnād*s supporting the traditions that associate either ᶜUmar ibn ᶜAbd al-ᶜAzīz or Hishām ibn ᶜAbd al-Malik with the policy to write down Tradition shows that they are affected by similar reliability issues. In none of these *isnād*s is it possible to ascertain the historicity of the earliest authorities' witnessing of al-Zuhrī's ceding to Umayyad pressure to record Tradition. The *matn*s are similarly problematic. In five out of six traditions, the coercion element is absent; two different caliphs are mentioned as the initiators of the policy to write down Tradition, and the description of their initiative varies substantially from one report to another. These reports should be discarded as evidence about the *Sitz im Leben* of the coercion tradition, which is, it appears, in a class of its own.

The Scriptural Concern

In an isolated biographical report, Ibn ᶜAsākir (d. 571/1176) describes the events following an encounter between al-Zuhrī and ᶜAbd al-Malik ibn Marwān (r. 65–86/685–705):

> *Kharaja al-Zuhrī min al-Khaḍrāʾ . . . min ᶜindi ᶜAbd al-Malik fa-qāla: Yā ayyuhā al-nās innā qad kunnā manaᶜnākum shayʾan qad badhalnāhu li-hāʾulāʾ fa-taᶜālaw ḥattá uḥaddithakum.*[35]
>
> Al-Zuhrī came out from [the palace] al-Khaḍrāʾ . . . from the presence of ᶜAbd al-Malik, and said, 'O people, verily, we withheld from you something that we had granted to these [rulers]. Come forward so that I may tell you!'

This tradition is found in a late source, and the earliest transmitter in its *isnād* is the Syrian al-Walīd ibn Muslim (119–95/737–810/11), who was born too late to have met al-Zuhrī (d. 124/742). Admittedly, the *isnād* casts serious doubt on the association of Ibn ᶜAsākir's tradition with al-Zuhrī; its *matn*, however, includes unmistakable points of similarity to the *matn* of the coercion tradition. The verb *manaᶜa* and the demonstrative pronoun *hāʾulāʾ* are used in a context strikingly resembling that of clauses 2 and 3 in the coercion tradition's *matn*. The use of the verb *badhala* brings to mind a variant of the coercion tradition that Ibn Abī Khaythamah reports on the authority of Sufyān ibn ᶜUyaynah.[36] Granting that Ibn ᶜAsākir's tradition and the coercion tradition bear on identical historical circumstances, we may make two important conclusions. First, the coercion tradition describes events from ᶜAbd al-Malik's reign; and secondly, the object of al-Zuhrī's resentment was not the writing of Tradition. As much is suggested by Ibn ᶜAsākir's tradition, in which al-Zuhrī states, *fa-taᶜālaw ḥattá uḥaddithakum*, that is, 'come forward so that I may tell you' or 'transmit hadith to you'. In neither case does the context of the tradition suggest that the expression 'we withheld from you something that we had granted to those [rulers]' in the incipit of al-Zuhrī's statement and the verb *ḥaddatha* at its end imply his acceptance of written transmission of knowledge. Accordingly, al-Zuhrī's aversion to *kitāb* in the coercion tradition would appear to bear relationship to events from ʿAbd al-Malik's caliphate other than the writing of Tradition.

This hypothesis finds support in al-Dārimī's report that Ibrāhīm al-Nakhaʿī (d. 96/714) *kāna yakrahu al-kitāb*.[37] Al-Nakhaʿī died before the reigns of ʿUmar ibn ʿAbd al-ʿAzīz and Hishām ibn ʿAbd al-Malik, who are mentioned as champions of writing down Tradition (see section three above); he died after ʿAbd al-Malik, who is a central figure in Ibn ʿAsākir's tradition. Since neither al-Walīd ibn ʿAbd al-Malik nor his brother Sulaymān, whose reigns intervened between those of ʿAbd al-Malik and ʿUmar ibn ʿAbd al-ʿAzīz, is known to have dealt with the codification of Tradition, al-Nakhaʿī's aversion to *kitāb* most likely refers to the same events from ʿAbd al-Malik's reign that roused al-Zuhrī's aversion to *kitāb*. To this we must add that a number of traditions catalogue Muḥammad ibn Sīrīn (d. 110/729) and Qatādah ibn Diʿāmah (d. 117/735–6?) among those who *kāna yakrahu al-kitāb*.[38] In regard to the blind Qatādah, the word *kitāb*, no doubt, signifies 'book' not 'writing': Qatādah reportedly despised the sound of *kitāb* being put in front of him and would reach out a hand to push it away.[39]

If *kitāb* was somehow not to the taste of al-Nakhaʿī, Ibn Sīrīn, and Qatādah, and if they were responding to events from ʿAbd al-Mālik's reign, is it possible to establish the nature of these events? Is there a relationship between the aversion of these figures to *kitāb*, on the one hand, and al-Zuhrī's attitude described in the coercion tradition, on the other? Which aspect of *kitāb* bothered these scholars so much?

A major event in the caliphate of ʿAbd al-Malik was his project, supervised by the governor of Iraq, al-Ḥajjāj ibn Yūsuf, to prepare a uniform canonical codex of the Qurʾān.[40] Al-Ḥajjāj carried out the caliph's enterprise, which Omar Hamdan dubbed 'the second *maṣāḥif* project', in al-Wāsiṭ between the years 84 and 85 AH (703–4 CE).[41] The Umayyad undertaking elicited a negative reaction from renowned scholars,[42] including Ibrāhīm al-Nakhaʿī, Ibn Sīrīn and Qatādah ibn Diʿāmah, each of whom, it will be recalled, is known as someone who *kāna yakrahu al-kitāb*. Remarkably, these scholars' opposition to ʿAbd al-Malik's *maṣāḥif* project is cast in identical terms: *kāna yakrahu al-naqṭ*.[43] The word *naqṭ* may refer either to the diacritical points that distinguish between skeletally identical consonants in the Qurʾān (e.g., ـبـ, ـنـ, ـتـ, ـثـ)[44] or to the symbols of vertically (⁞) or horizontally (:::) aligned dots used as verse separators in early Qurʾān manuscripts.[45] According to our literary sources, both types of 'punctuation' were introduced in the course of the second *maṣāḥif* project.

That al-Nakhaʿī, Ibn Sīrīn and Qatādah may have resented an innovative arrangement of the Qurʾān is suggested by a peculiar tradition according to which Ibn Sīrīn and al-Ḥasan al-Baṣrī were averse (*kānā yakrahāni*) *awrād*.[46] Abū ʿUbayd (d. 224/838–9?) explains that the tradition refers to a practice of dividing the Qurʾān into large textual units (*wird*, pl. *awrād*) of equal length.

Each *wird* comprised several *sūrahs*, picked out regardless of their position in the established sequence (*taʾlīf*) of *sūrahs*. Abū ʿUbayd does not specify who introduced the *awrād*, but the mention of Ibn Sīrīn and al-Ḥasan al-Baṣrī as its opponents suggests, once again, ʿAbd al-Malik's *maṣāḥif* project as the likely trigger for the *awrād* scandal. Although never mentioned in relation to the second *maṣāḥif* project, al-Zuhrī also may have disliked ʿAbd al-Malik's innovations, which not only instituted the punctuation of the Qurʾān, but also may have resulted in the division of the initially integral text of scripture into individual *sūrahs*[47] and the delimitation of *āyah*s within each *sūrah*.

In sum, ʿAbd al-Malik's initiative to introduce *naqṭ* and, possibly, to effect an innovative sectioning of the Qurʾān (*awrād*) was dismissed by Muḥammad ibn Sīrīn, while Ibrāhīm al-Nakhaʿī and Qatādah ibn Diʿāmah shared with Ibn Sīrīn an aversion to *naqṭ*. These three scholars were also averse to *kitāb*. Understanding this word as 'scripture' will allow us to establish a logical connection between lines 1, 2, and 3 in Table 1.1: al-Nakhaʿī, Ibn Sīrīn and Qatādah, all of whom were active in Iraq, apparently rejected the recension of the Islamic scripture that the governor of Iraq, al-Ḥajjāj ibn Yūsuf, undertook at ʿAbd al-Malik's behest. Apart from 'scripture', *kitāb* in the present context seems to connote 'to conjoin', 'bring together' and 'sew'. These meanings of the verb *kataba*[48] bring to mind the notion of the Qurʾān's arrangement (*taʾlīf*). Al-Ḥajjāj ibn Yūsuf's *taʾlīf*, perhaps the first in the history of the Qurʾān, may be thought to have provoked Ibn Sīrīn's retort: 'Allāh's *taʾlīf* is better than your *taʾlīf*!'[49]

There are no extant biographical reports that elucidate al-Zuhrī's attitude towards the second *maṣāḥif* project, but one might reasonably think that it was negative as well. This much may be inferred from al-Zuhrī's unqualified use of the word *kitāb* in the locution *kunnā nakrahu al-kitāb* in the original version of the coercion tradition. Like other scholars of his time, al-Zuhrī perceived as coercion (*ikrāh*) the state-sponsored effort to impose the newly dotted and sectioned version of scripture as the only binding codex.[50] Notwithstanding his initial discontent, al-Zuhrī eventually acquiesced to the Umayyad codex, because it introduced a uniform text of scripture. As I have argued elsewhere, by the end of the first century AH the Qurʾān was transforming from

Table 1.1 The stance of al-Nakhaʿī, Ibn Sīrīn, Qatādah ibn Diʿāmah and al-Zuhrī on (1) *al-kitāb* and (2, 3) the Umayyad punctuation and sectioning of the Qurʾān

	Ibrāhīm al-Nakhaʿī (d. 96/714)	Muḥammad ibn Sīrīn (d. 110/729)	Qatādah ibn Diʿāmah (d. 117/735–6?)	Ibn Shihāb al-Zuhrī (d. 124/742)
1	*Kāna yakrahu al-kitāb*	*Kāna yakrahu al-kitāb*	*Kāna yakrahu al-kitāb*	*Kunnā nakrahu al-kitāb*
2	*Kāna yakrahu al-naqṭ*	*Kāna yakrahu al-naqṭ*	*Kāna yakrahu al-naqṭ*	n/a
3	n/a	*Kāna yakrahu al-awrād*	n/a	n/a

scripture used for ritual purposes into a canonical source of Islamic law.[51] The uniform reading had become a prerequisite for an effective exegesis of the Qurʾān, and al-Ḥajjāj's *kitāb* afforded the needed textual basis even for those scholars who initially opposed the Umayyad codification project.

The Equalitarian Concern

In the second section, I highlighted the semantic tension between al-Zuhrī's submission to the official demand to write down Tradition (clause 2) and his decision to share his knowledge with all Muslims (clause 3). This tension, as well as the possibility to remove clause 3 without opening a structural or semantic gap, indicate that this clause was a later addition to the original *matn*. But who may have been interested in asserting al-Zuhrī's eagerness? The key to answering this question lies in the 'equalitarian concern' in clause 3, most conspicuously articulated in al-Fasawī's version of the coercion tradition, in which clause 3 reads, *fa-aḥbabnā an nuwāsiya bayna al-nās* ('and we preferred to make the people equal').[52] Kister observes that clause 3 advocates a universal and equal entitlement to knowledge, notwithstanding social status or gender.[53] If extended to matters of descent and ethnicity, Kister's conclusion brings us to the status of the non-Arab Muslims (*mawālī*) and their bid for equality with the Arabs during the second / eight century.

By the beginning of al-Ḥajjāj ibn Yūsuf's office in Iraq (75–95 / 694–714), many non-Arabs had embraced Islam, abandoned their farmlands and settled in urban centres, where they sought both relief from taxation and an alternative source of income as, for instance, service in the conquest army.[54] The conversion of many *mawālī* to Islam for such fiscal advantages as avoiding the poll tax (*jizyah*), and also probably the land tax (*kharāj*), deprived the central government of significant proceeds.[55] To counter the decline of tax income, Umayyad officials hindered conversion to Islam and on many occasions continued to levy the same taxes on converts that they had been paying before embracing Islam.[56] During his short reign (99–101 / 717–20), ᶜUmar ibn ᶜAbd al-ᶜAzīz tried to redress the injustice, but his policy had no lasting consequences in the eastern part of the empire either because he died too early to supervise its full implementation or because this policy faltered in the face of the insurmountable resistance of the influential notables in the east. In any case, ᶜUmar ibn ᶜAbd al-ᶜAzīz's policy embodied a tendency to treat Arabs and *mawālī* on an equal footing in matters of religion and taxation. Now, al-Zuhrī's alleged call for equality in the knowledge of Tradition makes sense in the context of ᶜUmar ibn ᶜAbd al-ᶜAzīz's caliphate. Such knowledge could have been especially beneficial for those non-Arabs who embraced Islam and strove to assert their newly-gained rights in matters of taxation.

Might al-Zuhrī have advocated equality between Arabs and *mawālī*? As noted by Abbott, by the end of the first century AH the *mawālī* had entered an open economic and cultural competition with their Arab overlords, which had ramifications in the field of the emerging religious sciences, hence, the transmission of knowledge.[57] The rise of *mawālī* to social and scholarly prominence was not to the taste of the pure Arab al-Zuhrī: he is said to have been hostile to both transmission on the authority of *mawālī*[58] and alarmed by their presence in the provincial scholarly élites.[59] Thus, the equalitarian concern at the end of the coercion tradition would seem to refer to a *Sitz im Leben* other than ᶜUmar ibn ᶜAbd al-ᶜAzīz' policy of restoring justice to the *mawālī* converts deprived of due fiscal privileges. A transmitter other than al-Zuhrī would have formulated clause 3, with reference to social circumstances that only superficially resemble events from ᶜUmar ibn ᶜAbd al-ᶜAzīz' caliphate.

The remarkable expression 'and we preferred to make the people equal' in al-Fasawī's variant of the coercion tradition points to another way of interpreting the equalitarian concern. The root morpheme of the verb *nuwāsī* (*w-s-y*) aligns both phonetically and semantically with the corresponding morpheme of the word *taswiyah* (*s-w-y*) in the soubriquet *ahl al-taswiyah* ('the advocates of equality'), which was applied to the followers of the literary movement known as *shuᶜūbīyah*.[60] If clause 3 in the coercion tradition implies a *shuᶜūbī* tenor, it most likely refers to the early decades of the ᶜAbbāsid caliphate (*c.* 132–195/750–810), when followers of the *shuᶜūbīyah* were calling for equality between the *mawālī* and the Arabs.[61] Later on, perhaps in the wake of the civil war (195–8/810–13) between al-Amīn and al-Maᵓmūn, in which the latter's Khurāsānī forces defeated the former's Arab supporters, the *shuᶜūbīyah* took on a clear anti-Arab tinge and, as such, it may hardly be associated with the equalitarian undertone of clause 3. This chronology suggests that clause 3 was attached to the coercion tradition either by the *mawlá* Maᶜmar ibn Rāshid (d. 153/770?) or by his student, the *mawlá* ᶜAbd al-Razzāq al-Ṣanᶜānī (d. 211/827).[62]

Conclusion

In the second half of the second century AH,[63] ᶜAbd al-Razzāq al-Ṣanᶜānī put into circulation a composite tradition in which Ibn Shihāb al-Zuhrī complains that, for all his dislike of the written transmission of knowledge (*kitāb al-ᶜilm*), Umayyad *amīr*s compelled him to commit Tradition to writing. Usually interpreted as a witness to the transition from oral communication to written record of hadith, the evidence surveyed above suggests that this report nevertheless originally related to social and political circumstances that are immaterial to the modalities of hadith transmission.

The expression *kitāb al-ᶜilm* ('writing of knowledge') in clause 1 of the coercion tradition is a reformulation of an original *matn*, which included the word *kitāb* without additional qualifications. In this case the word *kitāb* most likely meant 'scripture'. This 'scriptural concern' arose *c.* 84–5/703–4, when ᶜAbd al-Malik ibn Marwān initiated a project to work out a textually fixed and conveniently sectioned version of the Qurᵓān. The caliph's undertaking, whose implementation was entrusted to the learned but high-handed governor of Iraq, al-Ḥajjāj ibn Yūsuf, elicited objections by al-Zuhrī and other scholars of his time. At first, they denounced the introduction of diacritical points (*naqṭ*) and, possibly, the division of the integral Qurʾānic text into previously unseen discrete units, *sūrahs* and *āyahs*. Ultimately, these early scholars endorsed, grudgingly, the results of ʿAbd al-Malik's initiative, insofar as it guaranteed the hermeneutical unity of scripture, which was of foremost importance for its use as a canonical source of Islamic law.

The unqualified use of the word *kitāb* in al-Zuhrī's statement became problematic once the short-lived opposition to ʿAbd al-Malik's *maṣāḥif* project had petered out, and al-Zuhrī's words, which at first meant 'we were averse to the scripture's dotting and arrangement', came to be understood as implying a now inscrutable aversion to scripture per se. To avoid this intolerable connotation, ʿAbd al-Razzāq, or his informant, Maʿmar ibn Rāshid, affixed the word *ʿilm* to the word *kitāb*, thereby asserting, in an anachronistic manner, that al-Zuhrī had in mind 'writing of knowledge'. This semantic shift entailed the re-contextualisation of al-Zuhrī's original expression, which came to be associated with the second-century debate on the legitimacy of transmitting hadith in writing. In the early ʿAbbāsid period, the reinterpretation of al-Zuhrī's words also addressed ideological concerns: it not only presents the Umayyads as oppressors who cow scholars into obedience but also offsets the opprobrium of al-Zuhrī's rapport with the unholy rulers.

The proposed reinterpretation of the coercion tradition leaves an open question. How does al-Zuhrī's opposition to ʿAbd al-Malik's codification of the Qurʾān relate to al-Zuhrī's pivotal role in the spreading of traditions about the earlier ʿUthmānic codification?[64] Conceivably, he may have considered the two codifications as chronologically separate and substantively different historical events. On the other hand, the ʿUthmānic narrative may have been al-Zuhrī's way of oppugning the Umayyad project before eventually condoning it.

Clause 3 of the coercion tradition implies the politically charged doctrine that all Muslims are equal with respect to the acquisition of knowledge. Mastery of hadith as a foremost source of legal norms could empower the non-Arab converts to Islam who demanded the same fiscal privileges as enjoyed by those – for the most part Arabs – who were born Muslims. I am inclined to think that this equalitarian concern, even if in tune with events in al-Zuhrī's lifetime, as, for instance, ʿUmar ibn ʿAbd al-ʿAzīz' policy to endorse the fiscal rights of the *mawālī* converts, was added to the *matn* after al-Zuhrī's death. As a pure Arab, he would not champion equality between *mawālī* and their Arab overlords. The *isnād* of the coercion tradition suggests ʿAbd al-Razzāq al-Ṣanʿānī or his teacher Maʿmar ibn Rāshid, both of whom were *mawālī*, as the originators of the equalitarian concern, which therefore goes back to the second half of the second century AH/767–816 CE.

To conclude the present study, I should note the epistemological advantage of combining *isnad-cum-matn* analysis with the examination of legal, political and exegetical concerns that often underlie the outward formulation of Muslim traditions. Whereas *isnad-cum-matn* analysis is a formal procedure to reconstruct the earliest formulation of a tradition and associate it with a common link, form-critical analysis delves into the semantic structure of the *matn*. Semantic strains between its constitutive parts, as well as evolution of concepts from vagueness to clarity of expression and allusions to specific life settings are all structural marks capable of affording glimpses into the murky chapters of the tradition's history from before its collection, redaction, and further transmission by the common link and the partial common links.

Notes

* I would like to thank Professor Gregor Schoeler and Professor Harald Motzki for their critical reading of an early draft of this chapter. All errors of fact or opinion are the author's sole responsibility

1. ᶜAbd al-Razzāq, *al-Muṣannaf*, ed. Ḥabīb al-Raḥmān al-Aᶜẓamī, 12 vols (Beirut: al-Maktab al-Islāmī, 1403/1983), 11:258. To facilitate the analysis, I divide the *matn* into three clauses.
2. Pavel Pavlovitch, 'Juynboll, al-Zuhrī, and *al-Kitāb*: About the Historicity of Transmission below the Common Link Level', in Petra M. Sijpesteijn and Camilla Adang (eds), *Islam at 250: Studies in Memory of G. H. A. Juynboll* (Leiden: Brill, 2020), 103–29.
3. For an excellent review of al-Zuhrī's relationship with the Umayyads, see Michael Lecker, 'Biographical Notes on Ibn Shihāb al-Zuhrī', *Journal of Semitic Studies* 41 (1996): 24–8.
4. Gregor Schoeler, 'Oral Torah and Ḥadīṯ: Transmission, Prohibition of Writing, Redaction', in Gregor Schoeler, *The Oral and Written in Early Islam*, ed. James E. Montgomery, trans. Uwe Vagelpohl, Routledge Studies in Middle Eastern Literatures, 13 (London: Routledge, 2006), 123–4; cf. Michael Cook, 'The Opponents of the Writing of Tradition in Early Islam', *Arabica* 44 (1997): 459–61, §§ 37–41.
5. Cook, 'Opponents', 486, § 96.
6. Schoeler, 'Torah', 123. Maᶜmar was also critical of al-Zuhrī's practices as a hadith transmitter (Lecker, 'Biographical Notes', 29).
7. Meir J. Kister, '… *Lā taqraʾū l-qurʾāna ᶜalā l-muṣḥafiyyīna wa-lā taḥmilū l-ᶜilma ᶜani l-ṣaḥafiyyīn* . . . Some Notes on the Transmission of *Ḥadīth*', *Jerusalem Studies in Arabic and Islam* 22 (1998): 159.
8. Kister, '… *Lā taqraʾū l-qurʾāna*, 158–9.
9. G. H. A. Juynboll, *Muslim Tradition* (Cambridge: Cambridge University Press, 1983), 17ff.
10. Abū ᶜUbayd, *Kitāb al-Amwāl*, ed. Muḥammad ᶜAmārah (Beirut: Dār al-Shurūq, 1409/1989), 686–8, Nos 1849–50.
11. Ibn Abī Khaythamah, *al-Tārīkh al-kabīr*, ed. Ṣalāḥ ibn Fatḥī Halal, 4 vols (Cairo: al-Fārūq al-Ḥadīthah, 1424/2004), 2:247.
12. Ibn Saᶜd, *al-Ṭabaqāt. Al-Qism al-mutammim*, ed. Ziyād Muḥammad Manṣūr, Silsilat iḥyā' al-turāth 6 (Medina: Maktabat al-ᶜUlūm wa-al-Ḥikam, 1408/1987), 453.

13. Al-Fasawī, *al-Maʿrifah wa-al-tārīkh*, ed. Akram Ḍiyāʾ al-ʿUmarī, 3rd edn, 4 vols, (Medina: Maktabat al-Dār, 1410), 1:632 (one scribe); Abū Nuʿaym, *Ḥilyat al-awliyāʾ*, 10 vols (Cairo: Maktabat al-Khānjī, 1932–8, repr. 1416/1996), 3:361 (two scribes).
14. Al-Fasawī, *Maʿrifah* 1:640.
15. Abū Nuʿaym, *Ḥilyat* 3:363. Ibn ʿAsākir (d. 571/1176) cites what seems to be a literarily embellished variant of the same tradition, based on an *isnād* that includes none of the transmitters cited by Abū Nuʿaym: Ibn ʿAsākir, *Tārīkh Madīnat Dimashq*, ed. ʿUmar ibn Gharāmah al-ʿAmrawī, 80 vols (Beirut: Dār al-Fikr, 1415–21/1995–2000), 55:333.
16. Nabia Abbott, *Studies in Arabic Literary Papyri, vol. 2: Qurʾānic Commentary and Tradition* (Chicago: University of Chicago Press, 1967), 32.
17. Schoeler, 'Torah', 124.
18. Ibn Abī Dāwūd, *Kitāb al-Maṣāḥif*, ed. Muḥibb al-Dīn ʿAbd al-Sabḥān Wāʿiẓ, 2 vols (Beirut: Dār al-Bashāʾir al-Islāmīyah, 1423/2002), 1:151–69.
19. I take for a *terminus post quem* the promulgation of al-Shāfiʿī's teaching that the Sunnah and the Qurʾān are two varieties of revelation, formulated in his *Risālah* towards the end of the second century AH. Given that Abū ʿUbayd does not seem to have been acquainted with this teaching, and that the *Risālah* as we know it may date to the third quarter of the ninth century CE (Christopher Melchert, 'Qurʾānic Abrogation across the Ninth Century: Shāfiʿī, Abū ʿUbayd, Muḥāsibī, and Ibn Qutaybah', in Bernard G. Weiss (ed.), *Studies in Islamic Legal Theory*, Islamic Law and Society, 15 (Leiden: Brill, 2002), 84–6, 96), Ibn Abī Khaythamah's tradition may have come into being about twenty-five years after Abū ʿUbayd's death.
20. Al-Mizzī, *Tahdhīb* al-Kamāl, ed. Bashshār ʿAwwād Maʿrūf, 35 vols (Beirut: Muʾassasat al-Risālah, 1983/1403), 20:245.
21. Estimated date of birth from al-Khaṭīb al-Baghdādī, *Tārīkh Baghdād*, 14 vols (Cairo: Maktabat al-Khānjī, 1349/1931), 12:416.
22. ʿUqayl preferred transmission from memory (*ḥifẓ*), but he also reportedly possessed a book with al-Zuhrī's traditions (al-Mizzī, *Tahdhīb* 20:244–5).
23. Abū ʿUbayd, *Amwāl*, 458, No. 936. At the end of tradition No. 1 above (= Abū ʿUbayd No. 1850), which does not mention the family of ʿUmar ibn al-Khaṭṭāb, Abū ʿUbayd states that it forms one *matn* with tradition No. 936, which asserts that the alms tax rules were part of a document preserved by ʿUmar's family. If the two traditions were one narrative unit, or even if Abū ʿUbayd tried to knit them together, this is a witness to an attempt to present al-Zuhrī's alms-tax tradition (No. 1850) as embodying a legal practice that had been established decades before al-Zuhrī's birth (No. 936). Note that tradition No. 936 has its match in the *Muwaṭṭaʾ* of Mālik, rec. Yaḥyá ibn Yaḥyá, *al-zakāh* 11, *ṣadaqāt al-māshiyah*, which, tellingly, adduces ʿUmar's letter about the alms tax without citing intermediate authorities and without associating it with the Prophet, as Abū ʿUbayd does. Schacht was certainly right to consider the latter tradition as an exemplary instance of spreading *isnād*s (Joseph Schacht, *Origins of Muhammadan Jurisprudence* (Oxford: Clarendon Press, 1950), 167; cf. Ignaz Goldziher, *Muhammedanische Studien*, 2 vols (Halle a. S., 1889–90), 2:51–2).

24. Juynboll, *Muslim Tradition*, 24–5.
25. I deduce this dating from reports that towards 179/795 Abū ʿUbayd had arrived in Basra, where, as noted by Gottschalk, he already behaved as a 'self-confident young scholar' (Hans Gottschalk, 'Abū ʿUbaid al-Qāsim b. Sallām. Studie zur Geschichte der arabischen Biographie', *Der Islam* 23 (1936): 269).
26. Even al-Mizzī, who meticulously collected biographical reports, produced only a few lines about Saʿīd ibn Ziyād (*Tahdhīb* 10:441).
27. Al-ʿUqaylī, *Kitāb al-Ḍuʿafāʾ*, ed. Māzin ibn Muḥammad al-Sarsāwī, 7 vols (Cairo: Maktabat Dār Ibn ʿAbbās, 1429/2008), 5:296–300. Ibn Ḥibbān describes Muḥammad ibn ʿAbd Allāh as someone who had a bad memory, committed many mistakes and erred when transmitting from his uncle (Ibn Ḥibbān, *Kitāb al-Majrūḥīn*, ed. Ḥamdī ʿAbd al-Majīd ibn Ismāʿīl al-Salafī, 2 vols [Riyadh: Dār al-Ṣumayʿī, 1420/2000], 2:258).
28. Al-Mizzī, *Tahdhīb* 25:558.
29. Al-Mizzī, *Tahdhīb* 2:92; Ibn Ḥajar, *Tahdhīb* 1:122.
30. Ibn Abī Ḥātim, *al-Jarḥ wa-al-taʿdīl*, 9 vols (Hyderabad: Jamʿīyat Dāʾirat al-Maʿārif al-ʿUthmānīyah, 1360–71, repr. Beirut: Dār Iḥyāʾ al-Turāth al-ʿArabī, n.d.), 9:57 (Hishām); al-Mizzī, *Tahdhīb* 10:350–1 (Saʿīd). About the negative connotation of *ṣadūq*, see Juynboll, *Muslim Tradition*, 183–8.
31. Ibn Ḥibbān, *Kitāb al-Thiqāt*, ed. Muḥammad ʿAbd al-Muʿīd Khān, 10 vols (Hyderabad: Maṭbaʿat Majlis Dāʾirat al-Maʿārif al-ʿUthmānīyah, 1393–1403/1973–83), 5:190; cf. al-Mizzī, *Tahdhīb* 32:318.
32. Khalīfah ibn Khayyāṭ, *Kitāb al-Ṭabaqāt*, ed. Akram Ḍiyāʾ al-ʿUmarī (Baghdad: Maṭbaʿat al-ʿĀnī, 1387/1967), 207.
33. Ibn Saʿd, *Kitāb al-Ṭabaqāt al-kabīr*, ed. ʿAlī Muḥammad ʿUmar, 11 vols (Cairo: Maktabat al-Khānjī, 1421/2001), 8:278.
34. According to Ibn Ḥanbal, Abū al-Malīḥ's transmission from al-Zuhrī was confused (*muḍṭarib*): al-Mizzī, *Tahdhīb* 6:282.
35. Ibn ʿAsākir, *Tārīkh* 55:333.
36. Ibn Abī Khaythamah, *Tārīkh* 2:251, No. 2728.
37. Al-Dārimī, *al-Musnad*, ed. Ḥusayn Salīm Asad al-Dārānī, 4 vols (Riyadh: Dār al-Mughnī, 1421/2000), 1:414.
38. About Ibn Sīrīn, see Ibn Ḥanbal, *Kitāb al-ʿIlal wa-maʿrifat al-rijāl*, ed. Waṣī Allāh ibn Muḥammad ʿAbbās, 4 vols, 2nd edn (Riyadh: Dār al-Khānī, 1422/2001), 1:245; 2:392. At 2:393, Ibn Ḥanbal adds the explanation that by *kitāb* Ibn Sīrīn meant *kitāb al-ʿilm*. The possible understanding of *yakrahu al-kitāb* as 'he was averse to (written/codified/a project to codify) scripture' bothered Ibn Ḥanbal no less than it bothered those transmitters of the coercion tradition who subjected it to the same change, without, however, acknowledging their intervention. About Qatādah, see al-Dārimī, *Musnad* 1:412. Al-Dārimī uses the expression *kāna yakrahu al-kitābah*, but in his next clause, *kāna al-Awzāʿī yakrahuhu*, the singular masculine form of the anaphoric referent *-hu* betrays that the original form was *kitāb*, not *kitābah*.
39. Al-Dārimī, *Musnad* 1:412.
40. Omar Hamdan, 'The Second *Maṣāḥif* Project: a Step towards the Canonization of

the Qurʾānic Text', in Angelika Neuwirth, Nicolai Sinai and Michael Marx (eds), *The Qurʾān in Context*, Texts and Studies on the Qurʾān, 6 (Leiden: Brill, 2010), 800, 807ff.

41. Hamdan, 'Second *Maṣāḥif* Project', 801.
42. For a list of opponents, see Ibn Abī Dāwūd, *Maṣāḥif* 2:521–5, Nos 445–60.
43. About al-Nakhaʿī, see ʿAbd al-Razzāq, *Muṣannaf* 4:322; Ibn Abī Dāwūd, *Maṣāḥif* 2:525, Nos 458–9; al-Dānī, *al-Muḥkam fī naqṭ al-maṣāḥif*, ed. ʿIzzat Ḥasan (Damascus: Dār al-Fikr, 1418/1997), 11. About Ibn Sīrīn, see Ibn Abī Dāwūd, *Maṣāḥif* 2:522–4, Nos 448–53, and al-Dānī, *Muḥkam*, 11. About Qatādah, see Ibn Abī Dāwūd, *Maṣāḥif* 2:524–5, Nos 454–7.
44. Hamdan, 'Second *Maṣāḥif* Project', 807–9.
45. Hamdan, 'Second *Maṣāḥif* Project', 817.
46. Abū ʿUbayd, *Gharīb al-ḥadīth*, ed. Ḥusayn Muḥammad Muḥammad Sharaf, 5 vols (Cairo: al-Hayʾah al-ʿĀmmah li-Shuʾūn al-Maṭābiʿ al-Amīrīyah, 1424/1984), 5:121.
47. Al-Ḥasan al-Baṣrī is credited with the introduction of the *basmalah* at the beginning of the *sūrahs* and the insertion of a dividing line between each two *sūrahs* (Hamdan, 'Second *Maṣāḥif* Project', 815–16). The evidence of Qurʾān manuscripts from the last decades of the first century AH, however, contradicts the message of the literary sources. For the most part, these manuscripts lack diacritics and orthoepic signs; even when used, such signs do not appear in places where they could alleviate difficult readings (François Déroche, *Qurʾans of the Umayyads*, Leiden Studies in Islam and Society, 1 [Leiden: Brill, 2013], 35, 71–2).
48. Al-Farāhīdī, *Kitāb al-ʿAyn*, ed. ʿAbd al-Ḥamīd Hindāwī, 4 vols (Beirut: Dār al-Kutub al-ʿIlmīyah, 1424/2003), 4:8, s.v. *k-t-b*; Lane, *Dictionary*, s.v. *k-t-b*.
49. Abū ʿUbayd, *Gharīb* 5:121.
50. Hamdan, 'Second *Maṣāḥif* Project', 823–4. About the existence of diverse records of revelation, some of which lay in the background of al-Ḥajjāj's recension while others were deliberately excluded from it, see Alfred-Louis de Prémare, 'ʿAbd al-Malik b. Marwān and the Process of the Qurʾān's Composition', in Karl-Heinz Ohlig and Gerd-R. Puin (eds), *The Hidden Origins of Islam: New Research into Its Early History* (New York: Prometheus Books, 2010), 204–5.
51. Pavel Pavlovitch, *The Formation of the Islamic Understanding of* Kalāla *in the Second Century* AH *(718–816* CE*): Between Scripture and Canon*, Islamic History and Civilization, Studies and Texts, 126 (Leiden: Brill, 2016), 368–75.
52. Al-Fasawī, *Maʿrifah* 1:633.
53. Kister, '*Lā taqraʾū*', 160–2.
54. Gerald R. Hawting, *The First Dynasty of Islam: the Umayyad Caliphate* AD *661–750*, 2nd edn (London: Routledge, 2000), 70.
55. Hawting, *The First Dynasty of Islam*, 80–1. The terms *jizyah* and *kharāj* were applied with considerable overlap in the first century, denoting a tax in general levied on the conquered population. See *Encyclopaedia of Islam*, 2nd edn (*EI*²), s.v. 'd̲j̲izya', by Cl. Cahen.
56. Vacillation between encouragement of local people to accept Islam and the need to keep a steady flow of revenue to the local and central authorities engendered

sustained social tension in the eastern provinces of the caliphate during the final decades of Umayyad rule (Hawting, *First Dynasty*, 85–6, 95). While acknowledging this fact, Juda has argued that ᶜAbd al-Malik ibn Marwān and ᶜUmar ibn ᶜAbd al-ᶜAzīz tried to prevent drying out of tax revenues by imposing a land tax (*jizyah, jizyat arḍ, kharāj*) on both Arabs and *mawālī* in Iraq and Greater Syria (Jamal Juda, 'The Economic Status of the Mawālī in Early Islam', in Monique Bernards and John Nawas (eds), *Patronate and Patronage in Early and Classical Islam*, Islamic History and Civilization, Studies and Texts, 61 (Leiden: Brill, 2005), 271–3).

57. Abbott, *Studies in Arabic Literary Papyri* 2:15–16. On the role of the *mawālī* in early Islamic sciences, see further John Nawas and Monique Bernards, 'A Preliminary Report on the Netherlands Ulama Project (NUP): the Evolution of the Class of *ᶜUlamāʾ* in Islam with Special Emphasis on the Non-Arab Converts (*Mawālī*) from the First through Fourth Century AH', in U. Vermeulen and J. M. F. van Reeth (eds), *Law, Christianity and Modernism in Islamic Society*, Analecta Lovaniensi analecta, 86 (Leuven: Peeters, 1998), 97–107; Harald Motzki, 'The Role of Non-Arab Converts in the Development of Early Islamic Law', *Islamic Law and Society* 6 (1999): 293–317; G. H. A. Juynboll, 'The Role of Non-Arabs, the *mawālī*, in the Early Development of Muslim *Ḥadīth*', *Le Muséon* 118 (2005): 355–86; 'P. Crone, 'Mawlā', *EI*[2]. Notwithstanding their disagreements, the authors of these studies clearly show that the *mawālī* played a significant role in the development of early Islamic sciences. About the tense relationship between Arabs and *mawālī* in the reign of Yazīd ibn ᶜAbd al-Mālik (101–5/720–4), see Christian C. Sahner, 'The First Iconoclasm in Islam: a New History of the Edict of Yazīd II (AH 104/AD 723)', *Der Islam* 94 (2017): 36.

58. Al-Zuhrī had a strong bias (*taᶜaṣṣub*) against transmitting on the authority of *mawālī* (al-Balkhī, *Qabūl al-akhbār*, ed. al-Ḥusaynī ibn ᶜUmar ibn ᶜAbd al-Raḥīm, 2 vols [Beirut: Dār al-Kutub al-ᶜIlmīyah, 1421/2000], 1:269). He would dispense with *mawālī* informants in favour of the children of emigrants and helpers (al-Fasawī, *Maᶜrifah*, 1:641).

59. Al-Ḥākim al-Naysābūrī, *Maᶜrifat ᶜulūm al-ḥadīth*, ed. al-Sayyid Muᶜaẓẓam Ḥusayn, 2nd edn (Beirut: Dār al-Kutub al-ᶜIlmīyah, 1397/1977), 198–9.

60. Goldziher, *Muhammedanische Studien* 1:146, 165; Roy P. Mottahedeh, 'The Shuᶜûbîyah Controversy and the Social History of Early Islamic Iran', *International Journal of Middle East Studies* 7 (1976): 164.

61. The history of the *shuᶜūbīyah* is difficult to follow in detail, but this chronology may be inferred from the floruit of the early *shuᶜūbīs* listed by Mottahedeh ('Controversy') and Susanne Enderwitz (*EI*[2], s.v. 'shuᶜūbiyya'), as well as from Goldziher's chronological references (*Muhammedanische Studien* 1:147ff., esp. 160–3, 195–207). See also Sarah Bowen Savant, 'Naming Shuᶜūbīs', in Alireza Korangy et al. (eds), *Essays in Islamic Philology, History, and Philosophy* (Berlin: De Gruyter, 2016), 171–6.

62. ᶜAbd al-Razzāq transmitted from Maᶜmar ibn Rāshid a tradition that served the interests of the Nabateans by stating that ᶜAlī himself was of Nabatean origin (Goldziher, *Muhammedanische Studien* 1:157). The *mawlā* al-Aᶜmash (d. 148/765?) is remembered as having reproached the *mawlā* Shuᶜbah ibn al-Ḥajjāj

(82–160/701–76) for teaching hadith to the masses with the words 'Woe to you, Shuʿbah! Do not hang pearls around the necks of the swine!' (Ibn al-Jaʿd, *Musnad*, ed. ʿĀmir Aḥmad Ḥaydar [Beirut: Muʾassasat Nādir, 1417/1996, repr. Dār al-Kutub al-ʿIlmīyah, 1417/1996], 129). Al-Aʿmash used the same expression to scorn a party (*qawm*) from al-Wāsiṭ who asked him to relate hadith (al-ʿIjlī, *Maʿrifat al-thiqāt*, ed. ʿAbd al-ʿAlīm ʿAbd al-ʿAẓīm al-Bastawī, 2 vols [Medina: Maktabat al-Dār, 1405/1985], 1:432). These reports suggest that disputes over the possibility of sharing hadith with wide audiences may have begun either towards the end of al-Zuhrī's lifetime or some time thereafter.

63. This chronology is based on the assumption that ʿAbd al-Razzāq received the scriptural part of the tradition from Maʿmar ibn Rāshid in the Yemen. Although Maʿmar's arrival in the Yemen cannot be dated with precision, the sources give the impression that he spent the last decade of his life there (Pavlovitch, *Formation*, 195, n. 53).
64. Harald Motzki, 'The Collection of the Qurʾān: a Reconsideration of Western Views in Light of Recent Methodological Developments', *Der Islam* 78 (2001): 28–31.

CHAPTER

2

THE HISTORY OF THE *ADHĀN*: A VIEW FROM THE HADITH LITERATURE

Maroussia Bednarkiewicz*

In most hadith collections, there are narratives concerned with the so-called beginning of the *adhān*, *badʾ al-adhān* or *badʾ al-nidāʾ*. They recount the introduction of the Islamic call to prayer and explain how Muslims, inspired by Jewish and Christian practices, developed their own ritual. The history of the *adhān* and its introduction raises numerous questions. Why and how was the Islamic call to prayer introduced? What role did Jewish and Christian rituals play? Was there a development phase or was it always the same set of chanted formulae? Who were the people interested in the history of its introduction and why did they narrate it?

Using close textual analysis and recent methodological development in hadith studies, I have reconstructed a potential common structure underlying all the texts, which I have called the 'proto-narrative'. The results of my research show that the narrators and transmitters used this proto-narrative to construct different narratives, variously intertwining historical facts with oneiric traditions, disguised political statements or religious claims. Often, we can identify the characteristics of transmission processes by certain narrators or collectors. Systematic analysis of the primary sources was performed with the help of network visualisation tools to produce data-dense graphs of transmission, unfolding in time and space. The results of the present research contribute to a better understanding of the birth of the Islamic call to prayer at the time of the Prophet and its cultural implications for the following decades. They also shed light on the mechanisms employed in some of the narratives to promote different viewpoints.

General Outline

When the narratives concerned with the introduction of the *adhān* are put together, it appears clearly that they all follow the same storyline despite their numerous differences: at some point Muslims felt the need to develop their call to prayer. They thought about, or used, the Jewish trumpet or the Christian *semantron*, before someone suggested a call to prayer consisting of chanted formulae. The accounts narrating the introduction of the *adhān* can be divided into three different categories in terms of content (*matn*) and chain of transmitters (*isnād*). The first category contains narratives attributed to Ibn ᶜUmar that are present in almost all the main hadith collections. Its peculiarity is the preponderant role it attributes to ᶜUmar ibn al-Khaṭṭāb. The second category encompasses narratives allegedly narrated by Anas ibn Mālik. It is present in only three collections of hadith and characteristically suggests lighting a fire to indicate the time of the prayers. It mentions the *iqāmah*, the second call to prayer, along with the *adhān*. The third category is more complex: its chains of transmission are divided into many branches and the story narrated displays more details, its distinctive feature being the description of a dream as divine inspiration for the establishment of the *adhān*. These categories will be called, respectively, categories 1, 2 and 3, also abbreviated C1, C2 and C3.

The Sources

The texts narrating the introduction of the *adhān* were extracted from hadith collections and historical treatises. In order to facilitate the presentation of the large amount of information obtained through the close analysis of this material, I have usually limited the sources presented here to the third / ninth century. However, I shall mention later materials as well when relevant. Table 2.1 lists the main primary sources and the additional later materials in chronological order, with the number of narratives they contain for each of the category C1, C2 and C3:

Category 1

The first category encompasses six reports gathered in the collections of ᶜAbd al-Razzāq, al-Bukhārī, Muslim, al-Tirmidhī, Ibn Mājah and Ibn Ḥanbal.[1] The reports are almost identical, with only slight lexical differences. The text below highlights these differences in bold, separated by slashes:

كَانَ الْمُسْلِمُونَ حِينَ قَدِمُوا الْمَدِينَةَ يَجْتَمِعُونَ فَيَتَحَيَّنُونَ الصَّلاَةَ، لَيْسَ يُنَادَى لَهَا/بها فَتَكَلَّمُوا يَوْمًا فِي ذَلِكَ فَقَالَ بَعْضُهُمْ
اتَّخِذُوا نَاقُوسًا مِثْلَ نَاقُوسِ النَّصَارَى وَقَالَ بَعْضُهُمْ]اتَّخِذُوا/بَلْ] بُوقًا/قرنا مِثْلَ قَرْنِ الْيَهُودِ فَقَالَ عُمَرُ أَوَلاَ تَبْعَثُونَ
رَجُلاً يُنَادِي بِالصَّلاَةِ فَقَالَ رَسُولُ اللَّهِ صلى الله عليه وسلم يَا بِلاَلُ قُمْ فَنَادِ/فأَذِّن بِالصَّلاَةِ

When the Muslims arrived at Medina, they used to assemble for the prayer, without there being any call **to/for** it [the prayer]. Once they discussed this. Some people suggested the use of a *nāqūs* like the *nāqūs* of the Christians, others proposed a ***būq/qarn*** like the ***būq/qarn*** [horn] used by the Jews, but ᶜUmar said, 'Would you send a man to call [people to gather] for the prayer?' Then the Messenger of God . . . said, 'Bilāl, stand up and **call/chant the *adhān* for prayer.**'[2]

Table 2.1 Primary sources and the number of narratives they contain for each category

Sources: third/ninth century	C1	C2	C3
Mālik ibn Anas, *Muwaṭṭa*ʾ			1
al-Ṭayālisī, *Musnad*			1
ʿAbd al-Razzāq, *Muṣannaf*	1		2
Ibn Hishām, *al-Sīrah*			2
Ibn Saʿd, *Kitāb al-Ṭabaqāt al-Kabīr*			3
al-Bukhārī, *Ṣaḥīḥ*	1	2	
Muslim, *Ṣaḥīḥ*	1	2	
Abū Dāwud, *Sunan*			5
Tirmidhī, *Jāmiʿ*	1		1
Ibn Mājah, *Sunan*			2
Ibn Ḥanbal, *Musnad*			3
Ibn Abī Shaybah, *Muṣannaf*			1
Dārimī, *Sunan*			1
Fourth–fifth / tenth–eleventh century			
Nasāʾī, *Sunan*	1		
Ibn Khuzaymah, *Ṣaḥīḥ*	1		
Ibn Ḥibban, *Ṣaḥīḥ*			1
al-Nuʿmān, *Kitāb al-Īḍāḥ*			1
Ibn Bābawayh, *Kitāb man lā yaḥḍuruhu al-faqīh*			1
al-Bayhaqī, *Sunan*	1	1	2

Chains of Transmission

I have displayed the transmission chains of these narratives in a diagram, taking into consideration time and space beside the transmission paths (Figure 2.1). Each horizontal stripe represents a lapse of twenty-five years. The transmitters are arranged according to the reported dates of their death. Transmitters who are linked to a specific city have been circled with a line representing their respective cities. Figure 2.1 shows that the story gained popularity from the first half of the third/ninth century onwards. This means that the main foci of the narratives are likely to reflect the concerns of the generations of these times. Speech bubbles have been added to indicate the lexical modifications introduced by ʿAbd al-Razzāq.

Starting in Medina with Ibn ʿUmar (d. 74/693–4?) and Nāfiʿ (d. 117/735–6?), the first category of narratives moved initially southwards towards Mecca (Ibn Jurayj, d. 150/767?) and then northwards mainly to Baghdad, where many of the transmitters were active: Ḥajjāj ibn Muḥammad (d. 206/821–2), Abū Bakr ibn Abī al-Naḍr (d. 245/859–60), Hārūn ibn ʿAbd Allāh (d. 243/858) and Maḥmūd ibn Ghaylān (d. 249/864?). We have here one of these complex cases that can fall into Haider and Sadeghi's category of accounts linked to multiple locations and without clear traces of

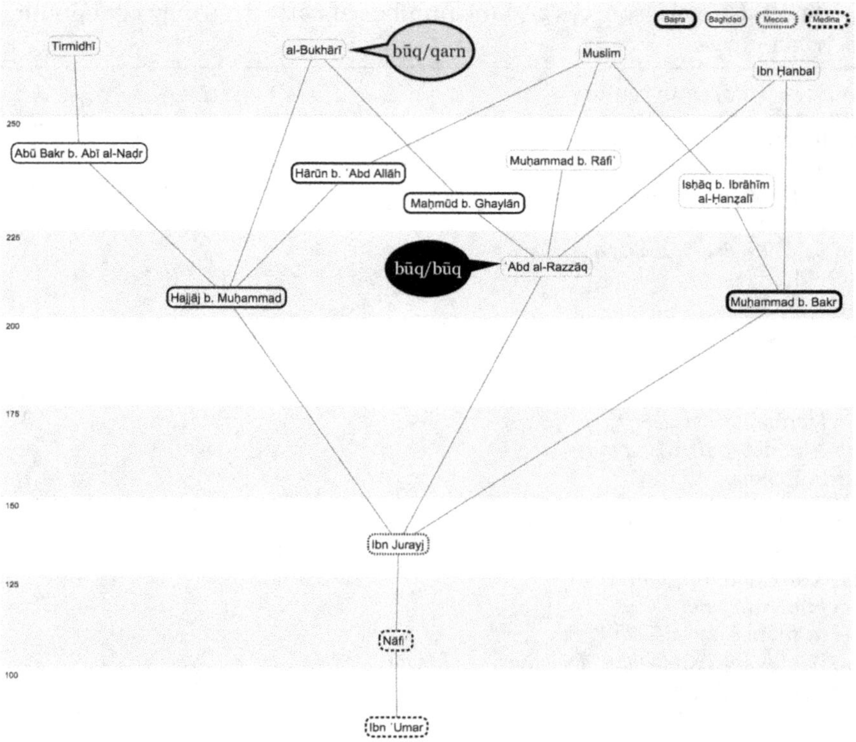

Figure 2.1 Chains of transmitters for C1

regionalism.[3] The lexical and thematic analyses below confirm the information provided by the *asānīd*.

Lexical Discrepancies

There are three kinds of lexical discrepancies in the narratives of C1:

1. insignificant differences without impact on the meaning;
2. *qarn* and *būq*;
3. *adhān* and *nidāʾ*.

The first lexical difference is between the prepositions *li* and *bi*, and may be explained either as a copyist's mistake, or simply the narrator or compiler's choice since the two prepositions in the sentence have the same meaning. The same may be said about the repetition of *ittakhidhū* in al-Tirmidhī's recension or the particle *bal* which is not present in Muslim's version. The repetition seems to be a rhythmic addition without consequence for the meaning. As for the particle, it adds a nuance, which could be translated as 'rather'. It may also be considered an empty word that can be ignored without affecting the general meaning of the sentence. Muslim is again the one narrating a different version without *bal*. Such lexical discrepancies highlight the fact that perfect *verbatim* transmission is rare and the following examples suggest that it might not have been a priority or major concern among transmitters.

The second kind of lexical discrepancies concern the Jewish trumpet. Since Jews were using different kinds of horns and trumpets, it was possible to confuse them. Nevertheless, most transmitters of C1 seem to be familiar with the Jewish instrument *qeren* (Hebrew קֶרֶן, Aram. *qəran* קרן *qarnā* קרנא, Arab. *qarn* قرن), as they use its Arabic equivalent without feeling the need to explain its meaning.[4] Also, the word *būq* (from the Greek βωχάνη or Latin *buccina*) does not appear to describe any of the Jewish horn-like instruments. The question is therefore where and why *būq* occurs in the recensions of ᶜAbd al-Razzāq and al-Bukhārī. I see three possible explanations: (1) a transmission error on written notes of the report occurred on the two final letters of *qarn* and *būq*: *rāʾ*/*wāw* and *nūn*/*qāf*; (2) ᶜAbd al-Razzāq aimed to avoid the Hebrew word or he was addressing an audience more familiar with *būq* than with *qarn*; (3) finally, language usage evolved in some regions and *būq* started replacing there the word *qarn*, as in the Yemen, where ᶜAbd al-Razzāq was active.[5]

This particular type of terminological discrepancy in a small set of hadith reports shows the precedence given to meaning over literality. Verbatim transmission was not only difficult, but also not the priority, and al-Bukhārī gives a clear example for that: he chose to create a hybrid version of the recensions he received from Ḥajjāj ibn Muḥammad (with the repetition of *qarn*) and Maḥmūd ibn Ghaylān (with the repetition of *būq*), but he did not deem it necessary to provide justification for his choice, probably because it did not affect the general meaning.

The last lexical discrepancy concerns the use of two different words to describe the call to prayer: *adhān* and *nidāʾ*. All the narratives except one contain the phrase *yunādī bi-al-ṣalāh*, 'to call to prayer'. The verb *nādá* is the Qurʾānic word used to describe the call to prayer.[6] It shows that the early Muslims called to prayer without having an official term and an established ritual for it. The word *adhān* also appears in Qurʾān 9:3 to designate an announcement from God through the Prophet. The evolution from *nidāʾ* to *adhān* reveals how a simple means to call to prayer was transformed into a divine announcement and thus a religious ritual.[7] This was helped by the influence of Jews and Christians, who possessed developed religious rituals and sacred sounds.[8] While the *adhān* was surely not introduced as such overnight, it must have come about before significant divisions split the Muslim community, so that all Muslims could agree on its definition and adopt a common name to describe it. That several narratives insist on a role played by ᶜUmar ibn al-Khaṭṭāb in the introduction of the *adhān* raises the question of whether or not he played a role in this process.

ᶜUmar's Role

In C1, it is ᶜUmar ibn al-Khaṭṭāb (d. 23/644) who introduced the new Islamic ritual to call Muslims to prayer. The narratives of the other two categories do not attribute such a role to ᶜUmar. This inconsistency suggests that ᶜUmar's involvement could have been apocryphal. Many people could have had reasons to create a strong bond between ᶜUmar and the *adhān*: his descendants during his caliphate (r. 13–23/634–44) to enhance his prestige as religious leader or later on, his supporters under the Umayyads in order to justify his position as religious and political authority, or under the ᶜAbbāsids as counter-propaganda against the new authorities.[9] Although there are no solid grounds to doubt ᶜUmar's involvement, it is likely that his role was exaggerated by certain narrators of C1. According to some sources, the caliph ᶜUthmān (r. 23–35/644–55) introduced modifications to the *adhān*.[10] It is therefore possible that his predecessor tried to harmonise the ritual, without success, and sought support in such narratives as C1's.

The Shiᶜi *adhān* brings forth one more argument in this hypothesis: its difference is more likely to have been a reaction to a Companion's decision than to a Prophetic tradition since the Shiᶜa only separated themselves from the rest of the community after Muḥammad's death. In fact, the *adhān* or the proto-*adhān* was probably introduced when the Muslim community had not split yet and could agree easily on a common ritual. After the disappearance of the unifying leader, several schisms occurred. As a result, it became increasingly difficult to establish new consensus between the different factions. The Shiᶜi *adhān* was likely to be a response to ᶜUmar's preference for a certain practice of the *adhān*. The narratives of C1, which are more concerned with ᶜUmar's role than with the formulae of the *adhān* for instance, must have started circulating during the reign of the second caliph or slightly after, at the time of Ibn ᶜUmar. Over time, it was certainly modified. The natural bias of any eye-witness, the bias of memories and 'memories of memories' as well as the actual purpose and the contemporary needs all partake in creating the narratives we have now.[11]

Category 2

The second category contains only four narratives from the collections of al-Bukhārī and Muslim.[12] Both collectors mention two recensions with the same single strand, which then spread out in different branches.

Al-Bukhārī 10/1.1
قَالَ ذَكَرُوا النَّارَ وَالنَّاقُوسَ فَذَكَرُوا الْيَهُودَ وَالنَّصَارَى فَأُمِرَ بِلاَلٌ أَنْ يَشْفَعَ الأَذَانَ وَأَنْ يُوتِرَ الإِقَامَةَ

Al-Bukhārī 10/2.2
قَالَ لَمَّا كَثُرَ النَّاسُ قَالَ ذَكَرُوا أَنْ يَعْلَمُوا وَقْتَ الصلوة بِشَيْءٍ يَعْرِفُونَهُ فَذَكَرُوا أَنْ يُورُوا نَارًا أَوْ يَضْرِبُوا نَاقُوسًا فَأُمِرَ
بِلاَلٌ أَنْ يَشْفَعَ الأَذَانَ وَأَنْ يُوتِرَ الإِقَامَةَ

Muslim 4/2.3

قَالَ ذَكَرُوا أَنْ يَعْلَمُوا وَقْتَ الصَّلَاةِ بِشَيْءٍ يَعْرِفُونَهُ فَذَكَرُوا أَنْ يُنَوِّرُوا نَارًا أَوْ يَضْرِبُوا نَاقُوسًا فَأُمِرَ بِلَالٌ أَنْ يَشْفَعَ الأَذَانَ وَأَنْ يُوتِرَ الإِقَامَةَ

Muslim 4/2.4

قَالَ لَمَّا كَثُرَ النَّاسُ قَالَ ذَكَرُوا أَنْ يَعْلَمُوا وَقْتَ الصلوة بِشَيْءٍ يَعْرِفُونَهُ فَذَكَرُوا أَنْ يَضْرِبُوا نَاقُوسًا فَأُمِرَ بِلَالٌ أَنْ يَشْفَعَ الأَذَانَ وَأَنْ يُوتِرَ الإِقَامَةَ

English translation (the parts that differ are in italic; the parts that are common are in bold): *When people increased in number they discussed the question as to how to know the time for the prayer by some familiar means.* **They suggested** that a **fire** *be lit or that a* ***nāqūs*** *be struck. They mentioned the Jews and Christians.* **Bilāl was ordered to pronounce the wording of the *adhān* twice and of the *iqāmah* once.**[13]

The narratives can be divided into two parts: the introductions, which vary from one narrative to the other; and the conclusion, which is the same for each narrative and is also found alone in other hadith collections (see in Figure 2.2 the links which are not in bold). The *asānīd* of the *aḥādīth* narrating the conclusion indicate that this part was circulating mainly in Basra.

Figure 2.2 gathers the chains of transmission of the four narratives under

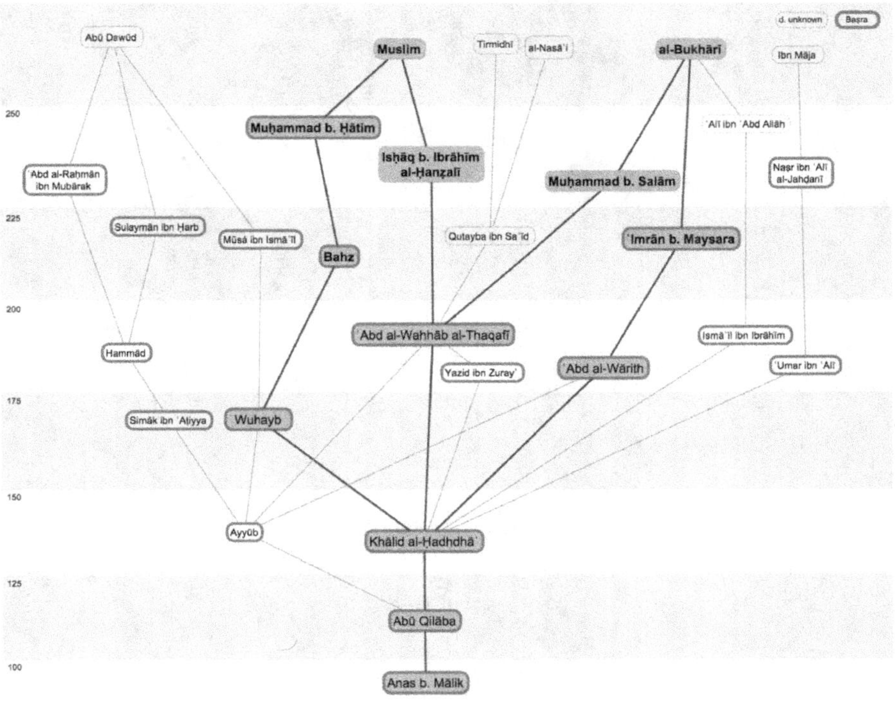

Figure 2.2 Chains of transmitters for *umira bilāl an yashfa*ᶜ …

examination here. Transmitters and links are highlighted in bold, while the other simple links lead to the other narratives containing the conclusion only. Transmitters from Basra are circled with a thick stroke. The *isnād*-chains do not reach to the Prophet but to Anas ibn Mālik (d. 93/711–12).[14] This might indicate that the narrative started at the time of Abū Qilābah (d. 104/722–3?), who relied on Anas as a Companion to address the issue of concern in these narratives: the right number of repetitions for both the *adhān* and the *iqāmah*, that is, a ritual or *fiqh* question.[15] The introduction narrating the historical development of the *adhān* has then been added by some transmitters in al-Bukhārī's and Muslim's versions of the narrative. In the black speech bubbles pertaining to the chains of transmissions of C2's narratives, Figure 2.3 shows which part was potentially added by which transmitter.

We observe here the creation of hybrid narratives which combine the historical introduction with the theological conclusion. This latter part reflects debates in Basra about the number of repetitions of the formulae in the calls to prayer. Abū Qilābah supported those defending two repetitions of the *takbīr* instead of the four advocated by others and adduced a maxim that he attributed to Anas ibn Mālik. Presumably, Khālid al-Ḥadhdhā᾽ merged the

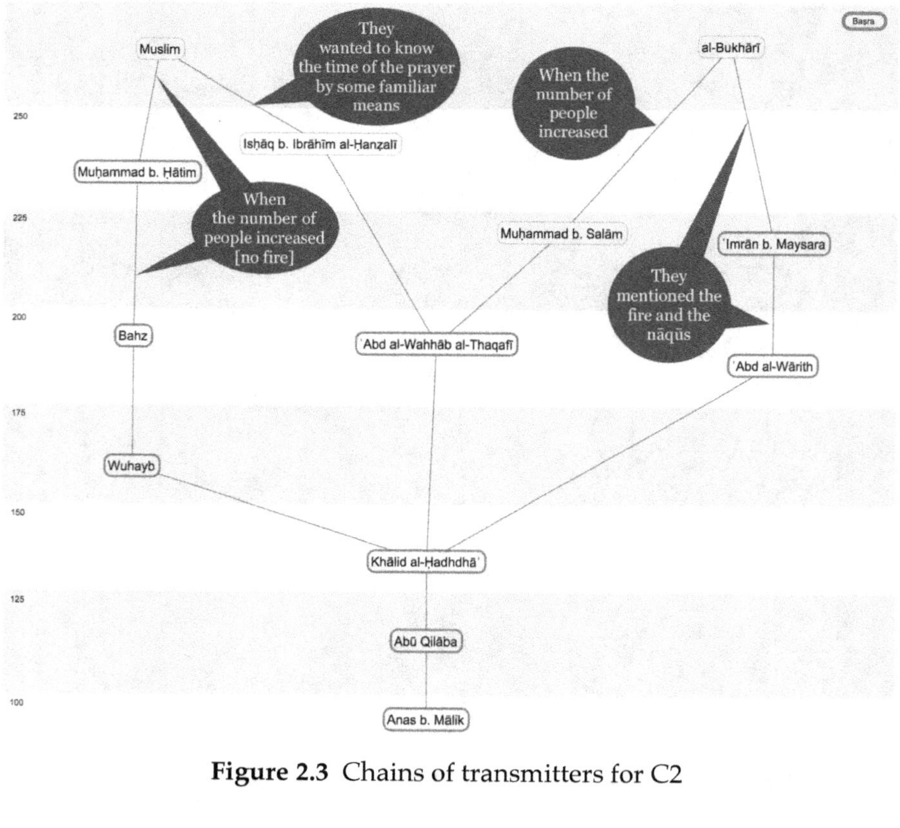

Figure 2.3 Chains of transmitters for C2

theological with the historical parts. Later narrators transmitted his hybrid version in their own way, probably orally if we consider the level of variations, rendering its gist more than its exact wording. One of the most striking variations is the mention of the fire.

Fire

I see three possible ways to explain the presence of fire in this second category:

1. Similar to *būq* and *qarn*, a lexical error occurred. A transmitter was unable to read the word *būq* and thought it was *nār*, or he misheard *nār* for *qarn*. The written proximity between *būq* and *nār* and the acoustic similarity between *qarn* and *nār* can explain the confusion, but they do not seem enough to build a strong case.
2. Some people suggested a visual call rather than an acoustic one. Medina was known for its numerous tower-houses, *āṭām*, sg. *uṭum*, which were apparently pulled down by ᶜUthmān ibn ᶜAffān (r. 23–35 / 644–55), after the introduction of the *adhān*.[16] *Al-nār* was often used as a signal.[17] We also have *manār* towers, which later became the famous *minarets*. A fire could have been lit in such towers to help worshippers locate the mosques. Thus, it was possible to think of the fire as a signal for the call to prayer. However, fire was convenient mainly at night; more importantly, how could a fire wake up people for the morning prayer? If the suggestion was indeed made, it must have been deemed impractical and rejected.
3. Finally, Ibn Ḥajar al-ᶜAsqalānī argues that C2's narratives were incomplete. He gives therefore a fuller version of the story:

   فقالوا لو اتخذنا ناقوسًا فقال رسول لله . . . ذلك للنصارى. فقالوا: لو اتخذنا بوقًا، فقال رسول الله [...] ذلك لليهود، فقالوا لو رفعنا نارًا فقال ذلك للمجوس

   They said, 'If we use the *nāqūs* (?).' Then the Prophet said, 'This [belongs] to the Christians.' [Then] they said, 'And if we use the *būq*.' Then the Prophet said, 'This [belongs] to the Jews.' [Then] they said, 'And if we set a fire.' Then he said, 'This [belongs] to the Zoroastrians (*majūs*).'[18]

In Ibn Ḥajar's interpretation, C2's narratives are truncated. Nevertheless, contrary to the *nāqūs* and the *būq*, the fire had never been a convoker for anyone, Zoroastrians or others. Consequently, it could have been added to localise the narratives and address a population that had more contacts with or included Zoroastrians. This version, which Ibn Ḥajar favours, adds the prophetic authority to condemn unequivocally the use of non-Islamic rituals or traditions.

What Ibn Ḥajar does not take into consideration is the possibility that the version he supports is itself a late variant as well. We notice that his interpretation is a back-projection that does not seem to match the initial meaning of the narratives discussed so far. It also reflects a clear hostility towards non-Islamic rituals, which seems to be a personal or later interpretation. In C1, the Prophet intervenes only to support ʿUmar, not to condemn the *nāqūs* or the *būq*. In C2, he does not appear at all. The first two categories give us an example of how hadith reports were used over time to address political and religious issues, how they were merged or truncated to fit the purpose, and how later scholars could still combine different versions and add the prophetic authority to serve their arguments. The third category continues to exemplify these points, although it contains much more elaborate and potentially later information.

Before turning to the third category, let us summarise our findings regarding C1 and C2. The two categories display a certain number of similarities. Their comparison allows us to start drawing the proto-narrative, which preceded the narratives of both categories and was then embellished: in the case of C1 to give a preponderant role to ʿUmar; in the case of C2 to clarify and fix two religious rituals, the *adhān* and the *iqāmah*. Tables 2.2 and 2.3 summarise the similarities and dissimilarities between C1 and C2 at (1) the structural level and (2) the lexical level, respectively. The similar structure of the narratives within the two categories reveals the proto-narrative that inspired them. Conversely, the lexical disparities in Table 2.3 stress the distance that separates the two categories in terms of geographical origin and purpose.

Category 3

The third category contains twenty versions of the dream story with more differences across their texts than in any narratives of the previous two categories.[19] This level of complexity is best illustrated by the chains of transmission. In Figure 2.4, tags have been added to the links between transmitters

Table 2.2 Structural comparison between C1 and C2

Similarities	Differences C1 vs C2
External factors lead Muslims to create the *adhān*	When the Muslims arrived at Medina vs when the number of people increased
Suggestion to use non-Islamic means to call to prayer, including the *nāqūs*	The use of the *būq* / *qarn* vs the use of *nār*
Bilāl's primary role as *muʾadhdhin*	ʿUmar, the Prophet and Bilāl vs Bilāl as only actor
Mention of the *adhān*	Mention of the *adhān* vs mention of the *adhān* and the *iqāmah*
General structure of the narrative	Semi-developed narrative vs summary-like or incomplete version

Table 2.3 Lexical comparison between C1 and C2

C1	C2
كَانَ الْمُسْلِمُونَ حِينَ قَدِمُوا الْمَدِينَةَ يَجْتَمِعُونَ فَيَتَحَيَّنُونَ الصَّلاَةَ، لَيْسَ يُنَادَى لَهَا/بها	قَالَ لَمَّا كَثُرَ النَّاسُ
فَتَكَلَّمُوا يَوْمًا فِي ذَلِكَ	فَذَكَرُوا الْيَهُودَ وَالنَّصَارَىقَالَ ذَكَرُوا أَنْ يَعْلَمُوا وَقْتَ الصلوة بِشَىْءٍ يَعْرِفُونَهُ فَذَكَرُوا أَنْ يُورُوا نَارًا
فَقَالَ بَعْضُهُمْ اتَّخِذُوا نَاقُوسًا مِثْلَ نَاقُوسِ النَّصَارَى	أَوْ يَضْرِبُوا نَاقُوسًا
وَقَالَ بَعْضُهُمْ بَلْ بُوقًا/قرنا مِثْلَ قَرْنِ الْيَهُودِ	
فَقَالَ عُمَرُ أَوَلاَ تَبْعَثُونَ رَجُلاً يُنَادِي بِالصَّلاَةِ فَقَالَ رَسُولُ اللَّهِ صلى الله عليه وسلم يَا بِلاَلُ قُمْ فَنَادِ بِالصَّلاَةِ	فَأُمِرَ بِلاَلٌ أَنْ يَشْفَعَ الأَذَانَ وَيُوتِرَ الإِقَامَةَ

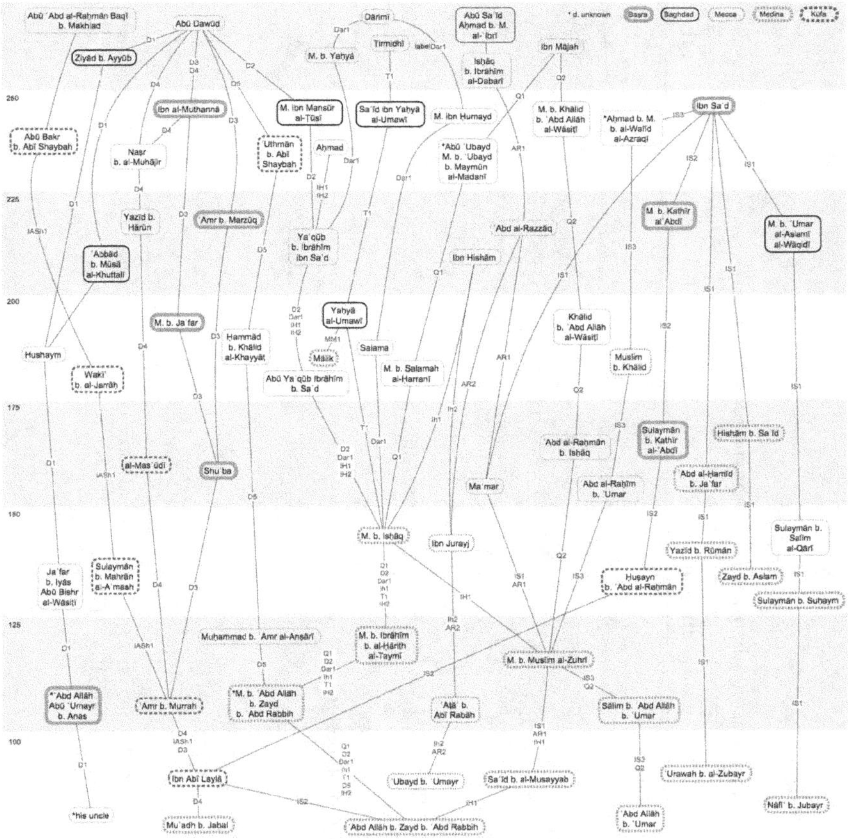

Figure 2.4 Chains of transmitters for C3

Table 2.4 General outline of C3's narratives

	Ih1	Ih2	AR1	AR2	D1	D2	D3	D4	D5	T	Q1	Q2	MM	IH1	IH2	IASh	IS1	IS2	IS3	Dar
introduction	x	x	x	x	x	x	x		x			x	x	x	x		x	x	x	x
būq	x		x		[x]						x	x					x		x	x
nāqūs	x	x	x	x	x	x	x				x	x	[x]	x	x		x	x	x	x
karihah	x				x							x		x						x
ᶜAbd Allāh ibn Zayd	x		x		x	x	[x]	x	x	x	x	x	x	x	x	x	x	x	x	x
the dream	x	[x]	x	[x]	x	x	x	x	x	x	x	x	x	x	x	x	x	x	x	x
– a man	x		x		x	x	x				x			x	x	x	x	x		x
– green garments	x						x				x			x		x	x	x		x
– *nāqūs*	x	[x]	x	[x]		x					x		x	x	x		x			x
– can I buy?	x		x			x					x			x	x		x			x
– something better	x		x			x					x			x	x		x			x
– *adhān*	x		x			x		x			x			x	x	x	x	[x]		x
– *iqāma*						x		x						x	x	x		[x]		x
Prophet's approval	x	x		x		x	x				x			x	x					x
ᶜUmar's dream	x	x	x	x	x	x	x			x	x	x			x		x	x	x	x
Bilāl	x	x	x	x	x	x	x	x	x	x	x	x		x	x	x	x	x	x	x

Abbreviations: Ih = Ibn Hishām; AR = ᶜAbd al-Razzāq; D = Abū Dāwūd; T = Tirmidhī; Q = Ibn Mājah; MM = Mālik; IH = Ibn Ḥanbal; IASh = Ibn Abī Shaybah; IS = Ibn Saᶜd; Dar = Dārimī.

to indicate which scholar transmitted to which recipients, thus solving the ambiguity otherwise present at common links. The diagram shows the quite even repartition of transmitters in different cities and throughout each epoch of twenty-five years. Only Medina holds a majority of transmitters over the first 150 years. The figure also highlights the spread of this version, which can be explained by the fact that it addresses directly the question of the right number of repetitions of the *adhān*, which became important when jurists started writing about the right practice of the *adhān*.

Outline of the Dream Story

The general outline of the narratives within C3 is identical to the one observed in C1 and C2, confirming the presence of the hypothetical proto-narrative at their basis. The main difference is the mention of a dream which distinguishes this category. Table 2.4 presents the detailed outline, which can be divided into three sections: (1) the introduction; (2) the dream; and (3) the conclusion. Each narrative is presented horizontally and the cells with an 'X' indicate the presence of the element in the corresponding narrative. The square brackets indicate a partial or truncated mention of the element in question. Finally, each text has been given an acronym with the initial letters of the collector's name and a number if he transmitted more than one narrative. The references are given in the table.

The Introduction

Three elements distinguish the introduction to the dream story from the introductions of C1 and C2's narratives: (a) the disagreement on the *nāqūs*; (b) the Prophet's disapproval; and (c) the uneven treatment of the trumpet.

The Disagreement on the nāqūs

Transmitters of C3's narratives disagreed regarding the suggestion of using a *nāqūs*. The words they employed indicate an absence of consensus about two main points:

1. Did the Prophet think of making a *nāqūs* or order it?
2. Was the *nāqūs* fabricated and eventually used or not?

Some stress the thinking process around the *nāqūs* or the wish to have a *nāqūs* which did not lead to any concrete actions. These narratives [AR1, AR2, D1, Ih2, IS1, IS2, IS3, Q2] contain the verbs *hamma* ('he thought'), *arāda* ('he wanted'), *iʾtamara* ('he deliberated'), *qāla* ('he said') or *dhakara* ('he mentioned'). Other narratives [D2, Dar, Ih1, IH1, IH2, IS1, Q1] state that the Prophet ordered a *nāqūs* with the verb *amara* ('he ordered' or 'commanded').

The last group of narratives [D3, Dar, Ih1, Q1] explains that the *nāqūs* was fabricated and chiselled ready to be used or indeed struck with the verbs *naḥata* (in the passive form: *nuḥita*, 'it was chiselled') or *naqasa* ('he struck the *nāqūs*').

This disparity between the narratives concerning only the *nāqūs* suggests that people disagreed about what really happened with the Christian instrument. It is possible that they did not remember properly and hence only partial memories were recalled and put together. Nevertheless, if the *nāqūs* was truly used at the time of the Prophet as a trial call to prayer, it is likely that some transmitters would try to hide this fact or would simply not believe it when it was narrated to them because imitating the Christians was already considered non-Islamic and the *nāqūs* became forbidden by prominent scholars.[20] After having conquered vast territories previously under Christian rule, Muslims had to develop a legal apparatus to regulate the life of Christians within Muslim territories. By doing so, they were forced to introduce rules that did not exist at the time of the Prophet and could even contradict his example. If some narratives were attesting the accepted presence of the *nāqūs* at the time of the Prophet, they were in contradiction with the evolving policies of the Muslim authorities. To reconcile past and present, certain narrators seem to have added clarifying elements to guarantee an interpretation of their narratives conformed to the rulings of their time. Another example of such 'clarifying elements' is the disapproval of the Prophet that appears in five narratives.

Karihah: *The Prophet's Disapproval*

The verb *kariha* is added to indicate that the Prophet disapproved of the use of the trumpet and/or the *nāqūs* [D1, Dar, Ih1, IH1, Q2]. Since it appears that the *nāqūs* was strongly associated with the introduction of the *adhān* in the collective memory, transmitters found ways to prevent their audience from interpreting the *adhān* narrative as a sign of the Prophet's endorsement of the Christian ritual. In fact, without the *karihah* clause, one senses an open attitude from the Prophet and his Companions towards non-Muslims' instruments. They give the impression of seriously considering using them. They might have manufactured and even used them. With the conquest of Christian territories throughout the seventh century and the increasing need for distinctions between Muslims and Christians, this permeability between the two faiths diminished. Some imitation of Christian practices even became forbidden. In this context, it was probably easier to adapt the narratives to the new social environment with the *karihah* clause, than to imply that Muḥammad let Muslims use a Christian instrument without condemning it. Some transmitters found other solutions as well: they replaced the *nāqūs* by a 'thing' [D5], or 'two pieces of wood' [MM], or they omitted it [D4, T].

This does not mean that these transmitters thought they were correcting the narrative. They might as well have considered that it needed to be clarified, mainly that the instruments were not adopted, and clarifications were needed to avoid confusion. What appears now as an addition could have been perceived by some as a clarification, a paraphrase. We observe here again the preference given to meaning over literal transmission.

The Trumpet

The Jewish trumpet is mentioned in seven narratives only. Most of the time, the word *būq* is used, which as we saw in C1 indicates a late redaction probably towards the third/ninth century. In one narrative [D1], we find *'qun*^{c} in the sense of *shabbūr'* (*al-qun*^{c} *ya*^{c}*nī al-shabbūr*). The same narrative also explains that a banner was suggested along with the other instruments. These lexical peculiarities come with an Iraqi *isnād*, which differs considerably from all other chains of transmission and does not share any common links with them. The elaborated text of the narrative implies again a late redaction and potential additions that did not belong to the proto-narrative. Yet it would be difficult to distinguish between the original elements and the later additions, which renders the reconstruction of the proto-narrative problematic. Nevertheless, the comparison of all the narratives in the present corpus has proven efficient in highlighting interests that may have influenced the making of the narratives. The *karihah* clause and the lexical discrepancies around the suggested instruments to call to prayer reflect such interests. Another – main – interest is also expressed in the dreams, the comparative analysis of which unveils the purpose of C3's narratives.

The Dream

The impression of disparity between the narratives that comes out of the analysis of the introduction only becomes more obvious with the investigation of the dream. The transmitters seem to disagree with each other in their narratives, and the divergences are greater than in the introduction, to the extent that few versions display enough similarities to be associated with each other. The present section briefly summarises this central part, giving the main elements of the comparative analysis. The study focuses first on the structure and then on the content.

Despite their differences, the various dreams have an identical structure. By comparing the narratives, a strong correlation between the chains of transmission and the content occurs. When the contents are almost identical, the chains of transmission are also similar, like in IH1–Dar and IH2–D2. Conversely, when the contents present only vague similarities, the chains of transmission also vary considerably, like in Ih1, Q1 and IS1. This latter type of narratives – slightly similar context with slightly similar chains of transmission – exemplifies the stress laid upon the meaning to the detriment of the form and the wording, which easily leads to variations in the content, even with similar chains of transmission, as we saw in C1. Finally, two methods of transmission emerge: the summarising method, applied by al-Dārimī to concentrate the narrative on a central topic, even though this requires the removal of some elements; and the merging method, applied by Ibn Saᶜd (IS1) to condense similar narratives into one single text, although this again required the removal of some elements.

While the structural comparison stressed the similarities between all the narratives, the analysis of isolated elements has highlighted rather the disparities between the versions and their regional or personal particularities. We see again in the presentation of the dream how priority is given to the meaning over the form and the wording generates differences. The main example is probably the addition or omission of a green garment worn by the stranger who taught the call to prayer. Its presence shows the will to shape the dream according to common dream patterns, but since it is not important to the core message of the narrative it is omitted by several transmitters.[21]

The treatment of the formulae of the *adhān* is also diverse. Some narrators [AR1, D2, D4, Dar, IH1, IH2, Q1] give the formulae in full, for it seems that their main concern is to promote the righteous practice of the *adhān* according to their belief. Table 2.5 summarises the number of repetitions of each formula presented by some of the narratives.

The existence of these different practices attests to the slow development of the *adhān*. The practice was probably neither uniform at the time of the Prophet nor was it established as an official ritual. It developed from a practical call to a ritual with a fixed set of chanted formulae. But the repetitions of these formulae varied from place to place and the Shiᶜah distinguished themselves by using a longer version.

The Dreamers

The main dreamer is ᶜAbd Allāh ibn Zayd (d. 32/652–3), a Companion, who is mainly remembered through his dream on the *adhān*.[22] He belonged to the Anṣār and came from the Banū al-Ḥārith from Najrān. The *adhān* was undoubtedly not introduced as such in one night, for this contradicts all the evidence we have from the hadith reports themselves. This does not mean that ᶜAbd Allāh did not play a role in the introduction of the *adhān*. As Savant notes, 'Muslims could not write history however they pleased. The past was not infinitely flexible, but it could be reworked within certain boundaries.'[23] Shiᶜi narratives also confirm in a way that ᶜAbd Allāh did play a role: according to them, he was unworthy to receive such a revelation, which came to the Prophet instead through an angel.[24] These narratives challenge contemporaneous memories regarding ᶜAbd Allāh, suggesting thus that these memories existed. ᶜAbd Allāh was undoubtedly remembered by many Muslims as the one who suggested the use of the voice to call to prayer.

How ᶜAbd Allāh took part in the introduction of the *adhān* is impossible to say. Nevertheless, it is clear that the dream is a tool to give authority to the positions that it advocates. It follows a visible pattern of Islamic dream, with

Table 2.5 The formulae of the *adhān* and the *iqāmah* and their repetitions in the narratives of C3

أذان	Ih1	Ih2	AR1	AR2	D1	D2	D3	D4	D5	T	Q1	Q2	MM	IH1	IH2	IASh	IS1	IS2	IS3	Dar
ٱللهُ أَكْبَر	4		2			4		2			4			4	4	(2)	1			4
أَشْهَدُ أَنْ لَا إِلٰه إِلَّا ٱلله	2		2			2		2			2			2	2	(2)	1			2
رَسُولُ ٱللهادمحماأَشْهَدُ أَنَّ	2		2			2		2			2			2	2	(2)	1			2
حَيَّ عَلَى ٱلصَّلَاة	2		2			2		2			2			2	2	(2)	1			2
حَيَّ عَلَى ٱلْفَلَاح	2		2			2		2			2			2	2	(2)	1			2
ٱللهُ أَكْبَر	2		2			2		2			2			2	2	(2)	2			2
لَا إِلٰه إِلَّا ٱلله	1		1			1		1			1			1	1	(2)	1			1
إقامة	Ih1	Ih2	AR1	AR2	D1	D2	D3	D4	D5	T	Q1	Q2	MM	IH1	IH2	IASh	IS1	IS2	IS3	Dar
ٱللهُ أَكْبَر						2		(2)						2	2	(2)				(1)
أَشْهَدُ أَنْ لَا إِلٰه إِلَّا ٱلله						1		(2)						1	1	(2)				(1)
رَسُولُ ٱللهادمحماأَشْهَدُ أَنَّ						1		(2)						1	1	(2)				(1)
حَيَّ عَلَى ٱلصَّلَاة						1		(2)						1	1	(2)				(1)
حَيَّ عَلَى ٱلْفَلَاح						1		(2)						1	1	(2)				(1)
قد قامت الصلاة						2	1	2						2	2	(2)				2
ٱللهُ أَكْبَر						2		(2)						2	2	(2)				2
لَا إِلٰه إِلَّا ٱلله						1		(1)						1	1	(2)				1

a stranger, dressed in green, teaching formulae to a pious person. The majority of narratives also affirm that ᶜUmar ibn al-Khaṭṭāb had a similar dream, bringing forth again the second caliph [Ih1-2, AR1-2, D1-3, Q1, IH1-2, Dar]. In this case, the dream legitimates not only the *adhān* practices but also the role of ᶜUmar.

Regional and temporal interests also emerge. In Mecca and, in the generation after Ibn Jurayj, in Baghdad too, ᶜUmar's role was the main concern. In most other cities, notably Basra, Wasit and Kufa, the focus seems to have been on the ritual's shape, a conclusion confirmed by the analysis of C2. Medina, which was probably the birth place of the proto-narrative, is represented by the main harmonising narrators who tried to reconcile all the versions, namely, al-Zuhrī and Ibn Isḥāq.

The End of the Third Category of Narratives

Various elements are again introduced in the conclusions of the narratives. Often, the dream is said to have received the approval of the Prophet, which might be a direct response to Shiᶜi criticism. Answers to the audience of the narratives appear as well. The *anṣār* may have wondered why ᶜAbd Allāh ibn Zayd was not given the honour of calling the *adhān* since he is the one who had the dream. To this, some replied that ᶜAbd Allāh did not have a strong enough voice, and others explained that he was sick. The Prophet is also said to have asked sometimes the reason why ᶜUmar did not narrate his dream before ᶜAbd Allāh. ᶜUmar usually justified himself by arguing that ᶜAbd Allāh was quicker than he was and he felt ashamed. These examples show how hadith reports were shaped by the audience, and the religious and political contexts as much as the transmitters.

Conclusion

The comparative analysis of the contents and the chains of transmission of this corpus of narratives has provided three kinds of information. With knowledge of the general context, it highlights first the interests at stake at certain times and places within religious, political and theological debates. Once the possible additions, omissions and modifications have been identified, it is then possible to point out the elements that triggered them or served as a basis for them. Finally, by observing these changes, it becomes easier for us to draw parallels between similar methods used by narrators to reach particular aims.

At the level of transmission, for instance, we have observed the priority given to the meaning over literality. Some transmitters seem to have been little concerned about a verbatim transmission, as long as their interpretation of the general meaning was preserved. This prioritising is applied by transmitters who produce a summary-like version. Ibn Abī Shaybah and Mālik in particular display a unique recension of the dream story that resembles a summary compared with the others. In both cases, the summary effect can be the sign of an old recension, the details of which would have been lost over the numerous generations of transmitters. It may also be a summary by one transmitter or collector who decided to give the general meaning without entering into the details of the story. This may be the strategy of a jurist, who wants to use the story as a basis for a ruling, contrary to a story-teller who might be more interested in entertaining his audience than lecturing them on the legal implication of the narrative. Indeed, Mālik and Ibn Abī Shaybah are both jurists, and they are more concerned about law-making than history.

A great variety of changes were applied on the *adhān* narratives, and yet the same structure common to the texts we have still appears behind all these changes and was brought to light by the comparative analysis carried out on this corpus. This structure, which I call the proto-narrative, reflects collective memories and was used by different narrators, transmitters, legal scholars or historians to serve their various interests. Modern technologies, in particular, the digitalisation of large numbers of sources, will allow us increasingly to analyse comprehensive corpora of similar narratives in order to extract more information on hadith genesis and Islamic history. The more pixels we have, the clearer the whole picture will appear.

Notes

* I would like to thank Christopher Melchert, David Taylor, Belal Abu-Alabbas, Azaher Miah, Álvaro Tejero Cantero, and Geri Della Rocca de Candal for their valuable comments.

1. Similar narratives belonging to this first category are also found in al-Nasāʾī, *Kitāb al-sunan al-kubrá*, ed. ʿAbd al-Ghaffār Sulaymān al-Bundārī et al., 7 vols (Beirut: Dār al-Kutub al-ʿIlmīyah, 1991), *al-adhān* 1, *badʾ al-nidāʾ bi-al-ṣalāh*, Nos 1590–1; Ibn Khuzaymah, *Ṣaḥīḥ*, ed. Muḥammad Muṣṭafá al-Aʿẓamī, 4 vols (Beirut: al-Maktab al-Islāmī, 1970), *al-ṣalāh, jimāʿ abwāb al-adhān wa-al-iqāmah, bāb badʾ al-adhān wa-al-iqāmah*, p. 219; al-Bayhaqī, *al-Sunan al-kubrá*, ed. Muḥammad ʿAbd al-Qādir ʿAṭā, 7 vols (Beirut: Dār al-Kutub al-ʿIlmīyah, 1994), 1:573–4, *al-ṣalāh, dhikr jimāʿ abwāb al-adhān wa-al-iqāmah, bāb badʾ al-adhān*, No. 1831.
2. ʿAbd Al-Razzāq, *al-Muṣannaf*, ed. Ḥabīb al-Raḥmān al-Aʿẓamī, 10 vols (Beirut: al-Majlis al-ʿIlmī, 1970), 1:356–7; al-Bukhārī, *al-Jāmiʿ al-ṣaḥīḥ*, in Ibn Ḥajar, *Fatḥ al-bārī*, ed. Muḥibb al-Dīn al-Khaṭīb et al., 13 vols (Cairo: Maṭbaʿat Muṣṭafá Muḥammad, 1979), 2:77, *al-adhān* 1, *bāb badʾ al-adhān wa-al-iqāmah*, No. 604; Muslim, *al-Ṣaḥīḥ*, ed. Muḥammad Fuʾād ʿAbd al-Bāqī, 5 vols (Cairo: Dār Iḥyāʾ al-Kutub al-ʿArabīyah, 1955), 1:385, *al-ṣalāh* 1, *bāb badʿ al-adhān*, No. 377; al-Tirmidhī, *al-Jāmiʿ al-kabīr*, ed. Bashshār ʿAwwād Maʿrūf, 6 vols (Beirut: Dār al-Gharb al-Islāmī, 1996), 1:233, *al-ṣalāh* 25, *bāb mā jāʾ fi badʾ al-adhān*, No. 190; Aḥmad ibn Ḥanbal, *Musnad*, ed. Shuʿayb al-Arnāʾūṭ et al., 50 vols (Beirut: Muʾassasat al-Risālah, 1993), 10:425. The translation into English is mine.
3. Behnam Sadeghi, 'The Travelling Tradition Test: a Method for Dating Traditions', *Der Islam* 85 (2010): 210; Najam Iftikhar Haider, 'The Geography of the *Isnād*:

Possibilities for the Reconstruction of Local Ritual Practice in the 2nd/8th Century', *Der Islam* 90 (2013): 318.

4. On the Islamic trumpet and the Jewish *qeren*, see Avinoam Shalem, *The Oliphant: Islamic Objects in Historical Context*, Islamic History and Civilization, Studies and Texts, 54 (Leiden: Brill, 2004), 54; John Arthur Smith, *Music in Ancient Judaism and Early Christianity* (London: Routledge, 2016), 112, 158, 158 n. 47; and especially the study of the root 'QRN' by Margit Süring, *The Horn-motifs in the Hebrew Bible and Related Ancient Near Eastern Literature and Iconography* (Berrien Springs, MI: Andrews University Press, 1980), 38–116.
5. On the evolution of the word *būq*, see *EI*², s.v. 'Būḳ', by H. G. Farmer.
6. Qurʾān, 5:58, 62:9. See Carl Heinrich Becker, 'Zur Geschichte des islamischen Kultus', *Der Islam* 3 (1912): 387.
7. This might reflect a very early stage of Donner's 'Qurʾānicization': see Fred M. Donner, 'Qurʾānicization of Religio-Political Discourse in the Umayyad Period', *Revue des mondes musulmans et de la Méditerranée* 129 (2011): 79–92.
8. By 'sacred sounds' I mean sounds that are part of religious rituals. The concept is used rather loosely in socio-anthropological studies and I have not found yet a thorough examination of the development of sound from secular or profane to sacred. It goes without saying that sounds are often more difficult to study than material culture from the perspective of historical development.
9. For the role of the Umayyads in promoting ᶜUmar's *sunnah*, see Avraham Hakim, 'ᶜUmar b. al-Ḫaṭṭāb: l'autorité religieuse et morale', *Arabica* 55 (2008): 21–3.
10. See how ᶜUthmān added a third call to prayer when the number of people increased in ᶜUmar ibn Shabbah, *Kitāb tārīkh al-madīnah al-munawwarah: akhbār al-madīnah al-nabawīyah*, ed. ᶜAlī Muḥammad Dandal et al. (Beirut: Dār al-Kutub al-ᶜIlmīyah, 1996), 958; al-Bukhārī, *Ṣaḥīḥ*, 2:393, *al-jumuᶜah* 21, *bāb al-adhān yawm al-jumuᶜah*, No. 912; Abū Dāwūd, *Sunān*, *al-ṣalāh* 217, *bāb al-nidāʾ yawm al-jumuᶜah*, No. 1087; al-Tirmidhī, *Jāmiᶜ* 1: 521–2, *al-jumuᶜah* 255, *bāb mā jāʾ fi adhān al-jumuᶜah*, No. 516; Ibn Mājah, *Sunān*, *iqāmat al-ṣalāh wa-al-sunnah fihā* 97, *bāb mā jāʾa fi al-adhān yawm al-jumuᶜah*, No. 1135.
11. Jan Vansina, *Oral Tradition as History* (Madison, WI: University of Wisconsin Press, 1985), 160. Also see the discussion of 'memories of memories' in Gregor Schoeler, *The Biography of Muḥammad: Nature and Authenticity* (London: Routledge, 2011).
12. A similar narrative is also present in al-Bayhaqī, *al-Sunan al-kubrá* 1:574, *al-ṣalāh, dhikr jimāᶜ abwāb al-adhān wa-al-iqāmah, bāb badʾ al-adhān*, No. 1832. Al-Bayhaqī quotes the version transmitted by Isḥāq ibn Ibrāhīm and mentions the version of al-Bukhārī without noting its differences.
13. Al-Bukhārī, *al-Jāmiᶜ al-ṣaḥīḥ* 2:77, 82, *al-adhān* 1, *bāb badʾ al-adhān*, No. 603, and *al-adhān* 2, *bāb al-adhān mathná mathná*, No. 606; Muslim, *Ṣaḥīḥ*, *al-ṣalāh* 2, *bāb al-amr bi-shafᶜ al-adhān*, No. 378. The English translation is mine.
14. According to Juynboll, such narratives as do not involve the Prophet (*mawqūf*) 'have a greater claim to being considered historically tenable': G. H. A. Juynboll, *Encyclopedia of Canonical Ḥadīth* (Leiden: Brill, 2007), 59.
15. Juynboll, *Encyclopedia*, 58.

16. Jonathan Bloom, *The Minaret* (Edinburgh: Edinburgh University Press, 2013), 46. Bloom also describes the construction of lighthouse towers between Kufa and Mecca: 'the early Abbasids also erected beacons and markers. As early as 752, the first Abbasid caliph Abu-al-ᶜAbbās had erected beacon towers (*manār*) and milestones (*mīl*) along the pilgrimage route from Kūfa to Mecca' (Bloom, *Minaret*, 56).
17. Some examples of 'fire signals' may be seen in Bloom, *Minaret*, 24.
18. Ibn Ḥajar al-ᶜAsqalānī, *Fatḥ al-Bārī*, ed. Muḥammad Fuʾād ᶜAbd al-Bāqī, 13 vols (Beirut: Dār al-Maᶜrifah, 1959), 2:80, *al-adhān* 10, *bāb badʾ al-adhān*, No. 604. The English translation is mine.
19. ᶜAbd al-Razzāq, *Muṣannaf*, 1:356; al-Tirmidhī, *al-Jāmiᶜ al-kabīr* 1:231–2, *al-ṣalāh* 25, *bāb mā jāʾ fī badʾ al-adhān*, No. 189; Ibn Mājah, *Sunan*, ed. Muḥammad Fuʾād ᶜAbd al-Bāqī, 5 vols (Cairo: ᶜĪsá al-Bābī al-Ḥalabī, 1952), 1:232–3, *al-adhān wa-al-sunnah fīhā* 1, *bāb badʾ al-adhān*, Nos 706–7; Abū Dāwūd. *Sunan*, *al-ṣalāh* 27, *bāb badʾ al-adhān*, Nos 498, 499, 506, 507, 512; Mālik ibn Anas, *al-Muwaṭṭaʾ*, rec. Yaḥyá ibn Yaḥyá, *al-ṣalāh* 41, *mā jāʾa fī al-nidāʾ lil-ṣalāh*, No. 1; Aḥmad ibn Ḥanbal, *Musnad* 26:399–403; Muḥammad ibn Saᶜd, *Kitāb al-ṭabaqāt al-kabīr*, ed. ᶜAlī Muḥammad ᶜUmar, 11 vols (Cairo: Maktabat al-Khānjī, 2001), 1:212–13; Ibn Abī Shaybah, *al-Muṣannaf*, ed. Ḥamad ibn ᶜAbd Allāh al-Jumᶜah and Muḥammad ibn Ibrāhīm al-Luḥaydān, 16 vols (Riyadh: Maktabat al-Rushd, 2004), 2:5; Ibn Hishām, *al-Sīrah al-nabawīyah*, ed. ᶜUmar ᶜAbd al-Salām Tadmurī, 4 vols (Beirut: Dār al-Kitāb al-ᶜArabī, 1990), 2:149–51; ᶜAbd Allah ibn ᶜAbd al-Raḥmān al-Dārimī, *al-Musnad*, ed. Ḥusayn Salīm Asad al-Dārānī, 4 vols (Riyadh: Dār al-Mughnī, 2000), 2:758–60. These hadith reports are also found in Ibn Ḥibbān, *al-Ṣaḥīḥ*, arr. Ibn Balabān, ed. Shuᶜayb al-Arnāʾūṭ and Ḥusayn Asad, 18 vols (Beirut: Muʾassasat al-Risālah, 1984–91), 4:541–3; and in the *Sunan* of al-Bayhaqī, 1:574–5.
20. For more on the question, see Salam Rassi, 'Justifying Islam in the Islamic Middle Ages: the Apologetic Theology of Abdisho bar Brikha (d. 1318)', DPhil dissertation, University of Oxford, 2016, 213–15. I also dedicate the final chapter of my doctoral thesis to the opinions of three Muslim jurists regarding the *nāqūs*.
21. See Pierre Lory, *Le rêve et ses interprétations en Islam* (Paris: Albin Michel, 2015); Elizabeth Sirriyeh, *Dreams and Visions in the World of Islam: a History of Muslim Dreaming and Foreknowing* (London: I. B. Tauris, 2015); John Lamoreaux, *The Early Muslim Tradition of Dream Interpretation* (Albany, NY: State University of New York Press, 2002); and, in particular, Leah Kinberg, 'Qurʾān and Ḥadīth: a Struggle for Supremacy as Reflected in Dream Narratives', in Louise Marlow (ed.), *Dreaming Across Boundaries: the Interpretation of Dreams in Islamic Lands* (Boston, MA: Ilex Foundation and Harvard University Press, 2008), 41; Leah Kinberg, 'Literal Dreams and Prophetic Hadith in Classical Islam: a Comparison of Two Ways of Legitimation', *Der Islam* 70 (1993): 282. Kinberg treats the legitimisation function of dreams in an earlier article, 'The Legitimization of the *Madhāhib* through Dreams', *Arabica* 32 (1985): 47–79, in which she shows 'the similarity between the dream and the hadith as literary means of expression. They both reflect ideas and tendencies prevalent in Islam, and both are used as means of legitimization' (78).

22. See al-Mizzī, *Tahdhīb al-kamāl fi asmā˒ al-rijāl*, ed. Bashshār ᶜAwwād Maᶜrūf, 35 vols (Beirut: Mu˒assasat al-Risālah, 1982–92), 14:540; Ibn Saᶜd, *Ṭabaqāt* 3:497; al-Ṭabarī, *Tārīkh al-rusul wa-al-mulūk*, ed. Muḥammad Abū al-Faḍl Ibrāhīm, Dhakhā˒ir al-ᶜarab 30, 10 vols (Cairo: Dār al-Maᶜārif, 1960–9), 3:121.
23. Sarah Bowen Savant, *The New Muslims of Post-Conquest Iran: Tradition, Memory and Conversion* (Cambridge: Cambridge University Press, 2013), 168.
24. See al-Qāḍī Abū Ḥanīfah al-Nuᶜmān, *Kitāb al-Īḍāḥ*, ed. Muḥammad Kāẓim Raḥmatī (Beirut: Mu˒assasat al-Aᶜlamī, 2007), 59–60; and Muḥammad ibn ᶜAlī Ibn Bābawayh al-Qummī, *Kitāb man lā yaḥḍuruhu al-faqīh*, ed. Husayn al-ᶜAlamī, 4 vols (Beirut: Dār Ṣaᶜb, 1981–6), 1:197–8. I would like to thank Kumail Rajani for these references.

CHAPTER

3

IBN AL-MUBĀRAK, TRADITIONIST

Christopher Melchert

Ibn al-Mubārak (d. 181/797) is most famous for two collections of hadith, *al-Jihād* and *al-Zuhd*. Two others attributed to him are the additional collections *al-Musnad* and *Kitāb al-Birr wa-al-ṣilah*.[1] He has been the subject of five monographs that I know of: four in Arabic, one in English. Ibn al-Mubārak also figured prominently in a 1975 article by Raif Georges Khoury, a 1996 book by Michael Bonner, a 2007 book by D. G. Tor, a 2009 article by Roberta Denaro, and a 2015 article by this author. The following chapter is mainly a review essay comparing Salem's book and the four earlier ones in Arabic, then some new research by me.

Arabic Monographs to Date

The earliest of the Arabic monographs is that of Muḥammad ᶜUthmān Jamāl, published in 1971.[2] To his credit, Jamāl covers the main aspects of his importance in chapters on 'Ibn al-Mubārak the traditionist', 'Ibn al-Mubārak the jurisprudent' and 'his Sufism'. On the other hand, he relies heavily on earlier synthetic scholarship, not discriminating between early and late sources. For example, he lists his shaykhs in hadith as named by Ibn Ḥajar, and then adds eleven named only by al-Nawawī.[3] He does not assemble names from the works of Ibn al-Mubārak (admittedly in manuscript as yet except for *al-Zuhd*). And he hardly indicates that any of what he relates is controversial, such as Ibn al-Mubārak's relation to Abū Ḥanīfah, which he characterises as the loyalty of a disciple to his master, citing works of the thirteenth–twentieth centuries.[4]

The next biography to have appeared is that of ᶜAbd al-Majīd al-Muḥtasib, published in 1972.[5] Like Jamāl, al-Muḥtasib quotes medieval biographical sources to establish the events of his life, his teaching and his reputation. He spends no time on the works of Ibn al-Mubārak himself. That of ᶜIṣām Muḥammad al-Ḥājj ᶜAlī, published in 1990, is an even shorter synthesis of the biographical literature.[6] Hence, for example, whereas Jamāl and al-Muḥtasib observe that al-Khaṭīb al-Baghdādī offers two dates for Ibn al-Mubārak's birth, 118 and 119, ᶜAlī offers only one, 118.[7]

The fourth in the series is by far the most substantial, from Muḥammad Saᶜīd ibn Muḥammad Ḥasan Aḥmad Bukhārī, published in 2003.[8] He relies heavily on the biographical literature, like his predecessors, but he comes up with more information. For example, his list of the works of Ibn al-Mubārak runs to twelve, although including mistaken citations, such as three manuscripts that are all just copies of the *Musnad*.[9] He also analyses the works themselves in various ways. For example, he tells us that *Kitāb al-Zuhd* in the recension of al-Ḥusayn ibn al-Ḥasan includes 411 items not from Ibn al-Mubārak, almost exactly a quarter of the book.[10] He supplements his list of Ibn al-Mubārak's most important shaykhs by telling us how often each of them is cited in each of the Six Books and the *Zuhd, Musnad* and *Jihād* of Ibn al-Mubārak.[11] (He does not include figures for transmissions in *Kitāb al-Birr wa-al-ṣilah*. It is extant in the recension of al-Ḥusayn ibn al-Ḥasan, who according to Bukhārī contributed 184 items out of 338, 60 per cent, from other shaykhs than Ibn al-Mubārak.[12])

The last of the monographs in Arabic is from Riyāḍ Aḥmad Ibrāhīm al-Dūrī, published in 2005.[13] Like the works of Jamāl, al-Muḥtasib and ᶜAlī, it is mainly a collection of material from biographical dictionaries. The special attention to *jihād* and history that al-Dūrī's title promises turns out to mean a long chapter, almost half the book, quoting hadith reports about the Prophet and Rightly Guided Caliphs with Ibn al-Mubārak in the *isnād*.

So much for monographs in Arabic. To generalise, they are all characterised by uncritical quotation of the biographical record. They are most obviously uncritical in ignoring the possibility that Ibn al-Mubārak's reputation should have changed over time, or from field to field (as between Sufi- and hadith-oriented biographers), so that a quotation from al-Qushayrī in the eleventh century or al-Dhahabī in the fourteenth has the same status as a quotation from Ibn Abī Ḥātim al-Rāzī in the early tenth century. More subtly, they tend to shy away from controversy, even where it is evident in the medieval sources. A notable example is Ibn al-Mubārak's relation to Abū Ḥanīfah. Al-Muḥtasib quotes liberally from ᶜĪsá al-Ayyūbī's refutation of al-Khaṭīb al-Baghdādī but concludes simply that after taking up with Mālik, Ibn al-Mubārak inclined towards him and away from Abū Ḥanīfah. Mālik's juridical programme was closer to his respecting the Sunnah.[14] ᶜAlī does no more than to list Mālik among Ibn al-Mubārak's most important teachers and to quote him as acknowledging a debt to Abū Ḥanīfah.[15] Bukhārī relates Ibn al-Mubārak's praise of Abū Ḥanīfah but nothing of his alleged repudiation. He says summarily that his greatest influences in jurisprudence were Sufyān al-Thawrī, representing the 'school' (*madrasah*) of hadith, and Abū Ḥanīfah, representing the 'school' of *raᵓy*.[16] Al-Dūrī complacently cites *Tārīkh Baghdād* to establish that Abū Ḥanīfah was his master in jurisprudence.[17] Al-Muḥtasib thus comes the closest to acknowledging controversy, but concludes on the basis of an anachronistic, dogmatic characterisation of early Mālikism.

Bukhārī's book is by far the best researched of these, and indeed furnishes substantial evidence of Ibn al-Mubārak's legal position, mainly eighty-six opinions attributed to him by al-Tirmidhī (d. 279/892?) in *al-Jāmiᶜ al-ṣaḥīḥ*. In this selection, at least, Ibn al-Mubārak agrees fifty-two times with Sufyān al-Thawrī, forty-six times with Aḥmad ibn Ḥanbal, forty-five times with al-Shāfiᶜī, forty times with Isḥāq ibn Rāhūyah, only sixteen times with Mālik and ten times with 'the people of Kufa'. On the other hand, he disagrees seventeen times with Aḥmad ibn Ḥanbal, fourteen times with al-Shāfiᶜī, thirteen times with Isḥāq ibn Rāhūyah and ten times with Mālik. (Al-Tirmidhī reports many more agreements than disagreements.) This apparently aligns him in law with Sufyān al-Thawrī (more on this to come). But I am the one who had to count: Bukhārī just quotes his sources. This piling up of quotations without analysis seems to be another recurring feature of Arabophone scholarship. Books in Arabic are often useful this way. 'It's like having a research assistant', a doctoral student recently observed to me. A basic difficulty, I would guess, is that these Arab authors apparently write partly to set up their subject as a model for emulation. Jamāl's title even makes this explicit. Discussing past disputes among Muslims is not helpful to such a project, at least within the Sunni camp.

Studies in European Languages

A major study in French is by Raif Georges Khoury, examining quotations of Ibn al-Mubārak's works in the *Iṣābah* of Ibn Ḥajar al-ᶜAsqalānī (d. Cairo, 852/1449).[18] Of forty citations of the *Zuhd* that Khoury has found in the *Iṣābah*, most quotations are close, if not identical, to passages in our text of the *Zuhd*. However, Khoury was unable to find seven or eight in our text of the *Zuhd*.[19] Similarly, he found thirteen citations of Ibn al-Mubārak, *al-Jihād*, in the *Iṣābah* but was unable to locate one of them in our text.[20] He attributes discrepancies to Ibn Ḥajar's having access to different copies of the text. Khoury takes it that both Ibn al-Mubārak and al-Ḥusayn ibn al-Ḥasan wrote books by the title *al-Birr wa-al-ṣilah*.[21] Khoury is notably optimistic about finding stable texts already in the eighth century.[22] It is conceivable that Ibn al-Mubārak assembled a collection of hadith reports on filial piety, later interpolated by al-Ḥusayn ibn al-Ḥasan; however, it seems more likely to me that al-Ḥusayn's material from Ibn al-Mubārak should be considered a part of what he took down from Ibn al-Mubārak's dictation, to which he felt free to add material from other notes just because the concept of fixed texts became established only around the end of his lifetime. Of course, I benefit here from a generation of scholarship not available to Khoury in the 1970s, especially the work of Gregor Schoeler.[23]

Here I shall review Michael Bonner, Deborah Tor and Roberta Denaro very cursorily. The first two are concerned with the politics of frontier warfare, which they conceive of as part of the wider shift of power from the caliph to independent ulema.[24] Denaro describes how the later biographical tradition developed some elements of his biography, among others how travel, trade and *jihād* kept him apart from ᶜAbbāsid power, while leaving alone others, notably the likelihood that he was celibate.[25] My own contribution to the study of Ibn al-Mubārak is an article written in 2011 but not published till 2015.[26] It mainly tries to fix the relation between Ibn al-Mubārak's works *al-Zuhd* and *al-Jihād*, more generally renunciation and the holy war, even renunciation and Islamic law at the end, where I contend that the terms *qitāl* and even largely *siyar* were eclipsed by *jihād* under the influence of renunciant piety. Notable shortcomings are neglect of earlier studies in Arabic, particularly Bukhārī's, neglect of Tor's study, neglect of an edition of *al-Birr wa-al-ṣilah*, and mis-statement of the number of hadith related by Ibn al-Mubārak in Bukhārī's *Ṣaḥīḥ*.

To generalise about these four studies, they obviously stress *jihād*. However, two of them are studies of *jihād* that incidentally discuss Ibn al-Mubārak, one is about *jihād* and other issues as presented in the biographical tradition, and the last tries to place Ibn al-Mubārak's doctrine of *jihād* in the context of his work in the fields of hadith and renunciation. By contrast with the Arabic monographs, they are all centrally concerned with change over time. For example, Bonner observes that feats of arms occupy increasingly much space in biographies of Ibn al-Mubārak.[27] I suppose this concern with change over time illustrates several outstanding tendencies of modern Western historical writing: scepticism of orthodoxies (here, the idea that current Sunni views express an unchanging, correct Islam), a critical attitude (here meaning to be on the lookout for history as propaganda for current views – to the dogmatically committed likely to seem cynical), and the imperative that scholars always say something new (the conventional view they must challenge being almost always to begin with what the tradition says about itself, so that here is where scholars will continually probe for weaknesses).

Most recently, in 2016, there appeared a monograph by Feryal Salem, a version of her 2013 PhD dissertation.[28] Salem prefaces her survey of the biographical sources with a mealy-mouthed critique of all attempts to confirm or disconfirm the veracity of medieval accounts. She concludes, 'it must be noted that even unverifiable historical narratives remain significant for the way in which the general corpus of these reports in the classical texts depict an ontological truth about how early Muslims themselves viewed Islamic scholars and their work' (8). This seems typically wordy (what, by contrast, would be a *non-ontological truth*?). Worse, Salem often refers as here to 'classical texts', implicitly denying change over time among Muslims reconstructing their past. On the contrary, there had to be changes, as Bonner has observed of Ibn al-Mubārak's feats of arms.

Salem makes limited and sometimes careless use of previous scholarship. She correctly cites Gregor Schoeler for the idea that books before the mid-ninth century typically have the nature of lecture notes, but ignores its relevance to the works attributed to Ibn al-Mubārak. If he is the source of only three-quarters of the items in *al-Zuhd* in the recension of al-Ḥusayn ibn al-Ḥasan, which she prefers, fewer than half of the items in *al-Birr wa-al-ṣilah*, then how much should we infer from their content and organisation about Ibn al-Mubārak's peculiar values? Salem cites Bukhārī as telling us that Ibn al-Mubārak transmitted from 539 scholars in the Six Books, but this figure is actually what Bukhārī got by combining numerous lists and, crucially, his own count of shaykhs in the *Zuhd, Musnad* and *Jihād* of Ibn al-Mubārak.[29] She endorses Nimrod Hurvitz' concept of 'mild asceticism', overlooking that his contrasting notion of extreme asceticism is based on one source only, ᶜAṭṭār from three centuries later; likewise, Leah Kinberg's neutralising reduction of *zuhd* to 'ethics', overlooking that it is almost entirely based on definitions from the Sufi period.[30]

Salem does not seem deeply familiar with the literature of Sufism. She says of Ibn al-Mubārak, *al-Zuhd,* that 'This book is strikingly similar in format to the *Risāla al-Qushayriyya*' (45). The first section of the *Risālah* is a collection of biographies, the middle one explains Sufi terminology, and the last reviews Sufi practice. In format, it is extremely unlike *al-Zuhd,* a topical collection of sayings from start to finish. Strange interpretations likewise betray lack of familiarity with hadith and its literature. Salem says of Ibn Lahīᶜah that, 'Ibn Abī Ḥātim and Abū Zurᶜa al-Rāzī are cited as having said, "His case is problematic. He wrote *ḥadīths* for [the purpose of] recognition', citing Ibn Abī Ḥātim, *Taqdimah* 5:147 (59). The book is actually *al-Jarḥ wa-al-taᶜdīl* (*Taqdimah* is the title of the introductory volume alone), the first quoted authority there is Abū Ḥātim, not his son, and the Arabic phrase is *yuktabu ḥadīthuhu ᶜalá al-iᶜtibār,* a common expression in tenth-century hadith criticism meaning that his hadith is worth recording for the purpose of corroboration.[31] She proposes that Ibn al-Mubārak, *al-Jihād,* is the earliest book in the *jihād* genre, other examples being Ibn Abī ᶜĀṣim and Ibn Ṭāhir al-Sulamī's books by the same title (n.43). But Ibn Abī ᶜĀṣim's book comprises almost entirely Prophet hadith that encourage one to fight, whereas Ibn al-Mubārak's book is mostly post-prophetic, while Ibn Ṭāhir's is mostly an exposition of Shāfiᶜi law. They plainly represent no particular genre. (How many pages of either did Salem read?) The poet Abū al-ᶜAtāhiyah becomes 'Ibn Itāhiyya' (89).[32]

Salem carelessly uses anachronistic terminology. She says of *al-Jihād,* 'a great many of the *ḥadīths* included in them [i.e., it] do not directly deal with combat or associated legal matters, but rather they discuss the so-called "greater jihād" of piety and ethical conduct' (75). The term *al-jihād al-akbar* does not occur in Shiᶜi sources until the early tenth century, and in Sunni not until the mid-eleventh.[33] She says that 'Isrāʾīliyyāt . . . were regarded as unreliable' (120), says a quotation of Jesus is 'one of the Isrāʾīliyyāt, perhaps transmitted through Christian converts to Islam' (n.122), asks 'What accounts for Ibn al-Mubārak's limited use of Isrāʾīliyyāt and Ibn Ḥanbal's willingness to include them?' (135), and so on, without hinting that the term was invented only much later, also without any census of stories from pre-Muḥammadan prophets reported by Ibn al-Mubārak – I count thirteen in *al-Zuhd* from Wahb ibn Munabbih alone, their most notorious purveyor.[34]

'ᶜAbdallāh b. al-Mubārak was known for his success as a merchant', Salem says, 'and his disapproval of ascetics who utilised the concept of *tawakkul* as a pretext for not striving to earn a livelihood' (37). Whether there were such insincere ascetics seems difficult for historians to determine – certainly, Salem attempts no demonstration. She returns often to Ibn al-Mubārak's being a trader to discredit any notion that he advocated a distasteful level of austerity but not to *al-Zuhd*, which says almost nothing to connect *tawakkul* and the legitimacy of living on alms (but more on this to come). It has plenty on the danger of riches; for example, 'He who has two dirhams will be judged more severely than he who has one' (Abū Dharr, No. 555).

I could go on. For a monograph, *The Emergence of Early Sufi Piety* is distressingly under-researched. It lowers my esteem for a section of the University of Chicago and for the book series in which it has been published, both of which should have called for repairs. Some of its faults evidently come of falling between two stools, in particular being aware of sceptical Western scholarship yet wanting to set up Ibn al-Mubārak as a model for emulation. It is plain that Salem is distressed by the impracticality of eighth-century renunciant piety, for example, hence her determination to find that Ibn al-Mubārak advocated something very different. From the point of view of historical scholarship, though, it appears to be a disaster, leading her to ignore what she sees and to avoid looking further. In some measure, perhaps, this is the hazard of determining one's results in advance as opposed to going wherever one's evidence leads, the latter course being at least the announced preference among scholars in the West today.

The Distribution of Ibn al-Mubārak's Shaykhs

To accomplish something more positive here, I propose to build on Bukhārī's book and my previous article to understand better Ibn al-Mubārak's work as a traditionist. Among other things, that article offers some comparisons among collections of hadith from Ibn al-Mubārak. They seem to be inconsistent with one another as to the geographical provenance of the hadith therein. I have now collected 227 hadith reports in al-Bukhārī's *Ṣaḥīḥ* transmitted through Ibn al-Mubārak. Considering different regions, most are from Syria, overwhelmingly Yūnus ibn Yazīd al-Aylī (d. 159/775–6?), from whom Ibn al-Mubārak is recorded as transmitting seventy-eight reports (34 per cent of the total). From Yemen, all from Maᶜmar ibn Rāshid (d. 154/770–1), come forty-four (19 per cent). From Basra come thirty-six (16 per cent), Kufa fourteen (6 per cent) and Iraq altogether 22 per cent. From Medina come thirty-nine (17 per cent), Mecca ten (4 per cent), the Hijaz altogether another 22 per cent. Egypt trails as the source of just five (2 per cent).

I have undertaken a parallel analysis of the 343 hadith reports in Aḥmad's

Musnad transmitted through Ibn al-Mubārak. From Syria, half of them from Yūnus ibn Yazīd, come 110 (32 per cent). From the Yemen, all from Maᶜmar ibn Rāshid, come thirty-one (9 per cent). From Basra come twenty-seven (8 per cent), Kufa twenty-four (7 per cent) and Iraq altogether 17 per cent. From Medina come forty-four (13 per cent), Mecca seven (2 per cent), the Hijaz altogether 16 per cent. By comparison, Basra is the source of a quarter of the items in *al-Zuhd*, Kufa almost a third, Iraq altogether a majority. About a sixth comes from the Hijaz, an eighth from Syria, less than half that from Yemen. When it comes to provenance, the big difference between Aḥmad's selection and al-Bukhārī's is that eighty-two in Aḥmad's *Musnad* come from Egypt, or 24 per cent of the total.

As for the topics of hadith reports transmitted by Ibn al-Mubārak, I have taken a rough list of categories from Muslim's introduction to his *Jāmiᶜ*.[35] The rank order is the same in al-Bukhārī, *al-Ṣaḥīḥ* and Aḥmad, *al-Musnad*: in diminishing order, *aḥkām* (rules), *al-targhīb wa-al-targhīb* (encouragements and discouragements), history, and rewards and punishments. Less common are hadith reports setting out devotions (such as prayers to repeat), *sunan al-dīn* (theology), eschatology and other things. However, a considerably larger proportion of the hadith in *al-Ṣaḥīḥ* deal with *aḥkām* than in *al-Musnad*, 44 per cent as opposed to 33 per cent, while a somewhat smaller proportion in *al-Ṣaḥīḥ* deal with *al-targhīb wa-al-tarhīb* (17 per cent as opposed to 26 per cent). Aḥmad's selection of hadith transmitted by Ibn al-Mubārak comprises less on *aḥkām* than *al-Musnad* as a whole, more on *al-targhīb wa-al-tarhīb*, which at least agrees on Ibn al-Mubārak's being identified as an author mainly with *Kitāb al-Zuhd*.[36]

Still, it appears that collectors such as Aḥmad and al-Bukhārī, separated from each other by about one generation, chose which of Ibn al-Mubārak's hadith to transmit according to their peculiar needs (including short chains between themselves and Ibn al-Mubārak's shaykhs) and the accident of what shaykhs they had met. Sufyān al-Thawrī is the jurisprudent with whom Ibn al-Mubārak most often agrees in the sample from al-Tirmidhī, besides being by far the most cited in *al-Zuhd* (189 times, as against ninety-four citations of Maᶜmar, the next most), yet Ibn al-Mubārak transmits from him only six times in each of the *Ṣaḥīḥ* and the *Musnad* (and from Mālik just once in the *Ṣaḥīḥ*, twice in the *Musnad*) – an example of how Aḥmad and al-Bukhārī bypass Ibn al-Mubārak at need.

I adduced geographical comparisons before in support of my contention that we should not consider the *Zuhd*, *Musnad* and *Jihād* as equally assembled by Ibn al-Mubārak and reflecting his preferences and emphases. Methodologically, I would now extend that to any eighth-century figure that appears in a ninth-century collection. First, we should assume that any ninth-century collection of Prophet hadith presents only a small sample of what was circulating a century earlier. Secondly, we should avoid any strong presumption that it is a representative sample. This much may count as common knowledge. Thirdly, I would now stress, we should also be reluctant to infer the general shape of a particular traditionist's knowledge from selective quotation a century later of the hadith he transmitted.

Ibn al-Mubārak's Juridical Tendency

As indicated before, the biographical sources themselves disagree as to Ibn al-Mubārak's relation to Abū Ḥanīfah. Juridical literature of the tenth century and later seems to indicate that he was moderately important to the Ḥanafi tradition. He is cited eleven times in al-Sarakhsī (483/1090–1?), *al-Mabsūṭ*. He is cited eighteen times in al-Jaṣṣāṣ al-Rāzī (d. 370/981), *Mukhtaṣar ikhtilāf al-ʿulamāʾ*: seven times transmitting Abū Ḥanīfah's opinion, ten times Sufyān al-Thawrī's, and once his own. He is cited eighteen times in Ibn Māzah (d. 616/1219–20), *al-Muḥīṭ al-burhānī fī al-fiqh al-nuʿmānī*: eight times transmitting Abū Ḥanīfah's opinion, once Sufyān al-Thawrī's, and nine times his own.[37] This weakens the credibility of ninth-century and later reports that he repudiated Abū Ḥanīfah late in life.

As for the earlier hadith tradition, al-Tirmidhī, *al-Jāmiʿ al-ṣaḥīḥ*, is apparently our most voluminous source for Ibn al-Mubārak's juridical opinions and, as reviewed above, seems to indicate that Ibn al-Mubārak was closest to a non-Ḥanafi tendency within the Kufan tradition. (Following Schacht, the presumption here is that there were identifiable regional traditions of Islamic law in the eighth century, within each region there being identifiable majority and minority positions.[38]) Al-Tirmidhī recounts at the beginning of *Kitāb al-ʿIlal*, the final book of *al-Jāmiʿ al-ṣaḥīḥ*, his sources for the juridical opinions he reports. Here are those from whom he has Ibn al-Mubārak's:

Abū Wahb Muḥammad ibn Muzāḥim (Marwazi, d. 209/824–5) < Ibn al-Mubārak;
ʿAbdān (ʿAbd Allāh ibn ʿUthmān, Marwazi, d. 221/836) < Sufyān ibn ʿAbd al-Malik (Marwazi, d. before 200/815–16) < Ibn al-Mubārak;
Ḥibbān ibn Mūsá (Marwazi, d. 233/847–8) < Ibn al-Mubārak;
Wahb ibn Zamʿah (Marwazi) < Faḍālah al-Nasawī (transferred to Marw) < Ibn al-Mubārak.

One oddity of the list is that ʿAbdān and Ḥibbān ibn Mūsá are major sources of Ibn al-Mubārak's hadith for al-Bukhārī (between them some 40 per cent of the total), whereas none of the others appears as a transmitter from Ibn al-Mubārak in either the *Ṣaḥīḥ* of al-Bukhārī or the *Musnad* of Aḥmad. Another is that al-Tirmidhī has ʿAbdān relating legal positions from Ibn al-Mubārak indirectly, whereas al-Bukhārī quotes him as relating hadith from him directly. Ibn al-Nadīm also attributes to Ibn al-Mubārak a book by the name of *al-Sunan*, most likely a collection of hadith on juridical topics. It is possible that ʿAbdān heard hadith from him directly, this book *al-Sunan* from him only indirectly; however, it seems equally possible that a link has been suppressed in ʿAbdān's relation of hadith. At any rate, the list of al-Tirmidhī's sources confirms that Ibn al-Mubārak's doctrine was collected especially in Marw.

Muḥammad ibn Naṣr al-Marwazī (d. 295/907–8?), *Ikhtilāf al-ᶜulamāʾ*, is another major early source for the juridical opinions of early figures outside the classical schools of law.[39] Unfortunately, Ibn al-Mubārak is not quoted here very often – fourteen times, by my count, as opposed to eighty-six times in al-Tirmidhī, *al-Jāmiᶜ*. In this sample, Ibn al-Mubārak apparently agrees most often with Aḥmad, Isḥāq and al-Shāfiᶜī, disagrees most often with *aṣḥāb al-raʾy* (probably the early Ḥanafīyah) and al-Shāfiᶜī's Baghdadi follower Abū Thawr (d. 240/854). However, the numbers are too small to look significant; for example, three disagreements with *aṣḥāb al-raʾy* are balanced by two agreements. A number of Arab scholars have collected the juridical opinions of various early figures from quotations in later works.[40] I suspect that not enough quotations of Ibn al-Mubārak survive to constitute a book (to reconstitute *Kitāb al-Sunan*).

Ibn al-Mubārak's closeness to Sufyān al-Thawrī, on the evidence of both Ḥanafi writers and al-Tirmidhī, is confirmed by an early Ḥanbali source that quotes him as saying, 'We do not choose anyone over Sufyān.'[41] Ibn Abī Ḥātim quotes Muᶜtamir ibn Sulaymān (Basran, d. 187/802–3) as saying that Sufyān al-Thawrī was succeeded as *faqīh al-ᶜarab* ('the jurisprudent of the Arabs') by Ibn al-Mubārak.[42] He also quotes Ibn al-Mubārak through Abū Dāwūd al-Ṭayālisī (Basran, d. 204/819?) as saying that when he was in Khurasan, he would sit with Shuᶜbah (Basran, d. 160/777?) and Sufyān, meaning, explains Abū Dāwūd, that he would inspect their books.[43] Muᶜtamir and Abū Dāwūd might be interpreted here as Basrans keen to appropriate a Kufan authority for their own centre. Present knowledge identifies Sufyān himself with a Kufan minority opposed to the predominant Kufan school that would survive in the Ḥanafi.[44] Even the Ḥanbali sources are ambiguous as to the connection between Ibn al-Mubārak and Abū Ḥanīfah. For example, he is quoted both as rejecting Abū Ḥanīfah's position as to raising the hands in the course of the ritual prayer and as saying, 'I used to go to him (meaning Abū Ḥanīfah) in secret from Sufyān and our comrades.'[45] Altogether, he seems to have followed the Kufan school of law (unsurprising for someone from Marw) without choosing decisively between the two leading tendencies identified (especially in the next century?) with Abū Ḥanīfah and Sufyān al-Thawrī.[46]

Ibn al-Mubārak on Voluntary Poverty

Salem relies heavily on biographies of Ibn al-Mubārak to make out that he was a staunch advocate of inward detachment from worldly goods without any outward abstention. The argument seems weak inasmuch as it does not draw on the early literature of renunciation, particularly Ibn al-Mubārak's own major contribution to it, *al-Zuhd*. However, this is admittedly not only Salem's idea, for Ibn al-Mubārak has been made out to be a major early opponent of *tawakkul* by none other than Benedikt Reinert, relying on *al-Zuhd* in manuscript and quotations in later Sufi literature.[47] This seems to be the sense of a quotation of Ibn al-Mubārak in Abū Naṣr al-Sarrāj (d. 378/988), *Kitāb al-Lumaᶜ*: 'Your acquisitions (*makāsib*) will not prevent you from turning over your affairs (*tafwīḍ*) and total trust (*tawakkul*; in God) as long as you do not lose them in your acquisition.'[48] That is, deliberate pursuit of gain may put one's proper dependence on God at risk, as by involving ethically dubious means, but not necessarily. Reinert also cites an earlier quotation in a Ḥanbali source, the book of al-Khallāl (d. Baghdad, 311/923) in favour of earning a living: 'I never saw any of them who was rational (*ᶜāqil*)', glossed as meaning the Sufis (*ṣūfiyīn*).[49] Al-Muḥāsibī names two Sufis who repudiated buying and selling, ᶜAbd Allāh ibn Yazīd and ᶜAbdak, perhaps in particular at the time of the Fourth Civil War (Amīn vs Maʾmūn, 195–8/810–13, much longer in Syria).[50] *Ṣūfiyat al-Muᶜtazilah* may have been particularly associated with *inkār al-kasb*, the repudiation of deliberate activity in pursuit of one's provision (trying to live on whatever God should send one's way, in effect probably alms), although al-Muḥāsibī attributes this doctrine especially to Shaqīq al-Balkhī (d. 194/809–10). Ibn al-Nadīm lists two Muᶜtazili writers he particularly identifies as Sufis. However, it is only a fringe member of their party, Ibn al-Rāwandī, to whom he attributes a book *Fasād al-dār wa-taḥrīm al-makāsib*, meaning 'the decadence of the House [of Islam] and the illicitness of gain'. This title sounds as if it is less likely to have enjoined living on alms as a pious exercise than to have lamented that all sources of income were by now so involved with illicit practices, especially the private appropriation of what should have been public lands, that it was impossible any longer to live purely.[51]

Whether it was particularly Sufis' reliance on alms that bothered Ibn al-Mubārak is uncertain. The previous item in al-Khallāl's book quotes ᶜAbd al-Raḥmān ibn Mahdī (Basran, d. 198/814) as saying more generally that some of the Sufis had been led to madness, others to secret unbelief (*zandaqah*), but then contrasting Sufyān al-Thawrī's taking along a pudding on the pilgrimage that included lamb, which perhaps makes the Sufis overly abstemious.[52] On the other hand, the next quotation has Mālik ibn Anas (d. 179/795) laughing uncontrollably on being told of some Yemeni Sufis who wore fine clothes but then did such-and-such – just what is not specified, but citing *tawakkul* as an excuse for refusing to earn a living is certainly not the issue.[53]

Reinert does not rely only on Sufi literature to characterise Ibn al-Mubārak's position, but cites a section title in *al-Zuhd* as the earliest expression of polarisation. Unknown to him, though, the title is *al-tawakkul wa-al-tawāḍuᶜ* ('putting one's trust [in God] and humility') in the recension of al-Ḥusayn ibn al-Ḥasan but *al-kafāf min al-ᶜaysh* ('sufficiency of livelihood') in the recension of Nuᶜaym ibn Ḥammād.[54] Moreover, the only one of the seven following reports to mention *tawakkul* is a version of something in the Sermon on the Mount: 'If you properly put your trust in God (*law innakum tatawakkalūna ᶜalá*

Allāh ḥaqqa tawakkulih), he will provide for you as he provides for the birds. They go out with empty stomachs and return with full' (No. 559; cf. Matthew 6:26).[55] This is not a refutation of *inkār al-kasb*, tending rather to endorse it.

Al-Khallāl makes it clear that *tawakkul* was an issue for Aḥmad ibn Ḥanbal (d. 241/855). He repeatedly quotes him against such practice of *tawakkul* as leads to dependence on alms; for example, denying that someone who goes on pilgrimage without any provision but in the company of others is actually *mutawakkil*, since he relies on their food sacks for his provision.[56] Besides the Prophet and Aḥmad, the person al-Khallāl most often quotes is Sufyān al-Thawrī, followed by Sufyān ibn ᶜUyaynah (d. 198/814) and (surprisingly, since he was supposedly Shaqīq al-Balkhī's master) Ibrāhīm ibn Adham (d. 163/779–80?). But he quotes Ibn al-Mubārak only once, without mention of *tawakkul*.[57] Neither, indeed, do Sufyān al-Thawrī, Sufyān ibn ᶜUyaynah or Ibrāhīm ibn Adham speak of *tawakkul*. On the evidence of this source, the association of *tawakkul* with *inkār al-kasb* was a development of the ninth century.

I do not question whether there was increasing distrust of austerity in the second half of the eighth century (as distinct from fear that outward austerity should be combined with inward worldliness, which must go back further). Sufyān al-Thawrī and Sufyān ibn ᶜUyaynah are both major sources of material in Ibn al-Mubārak, *al-Zuhd*, and I have myself cited both of them in connection with increasing distrust. To the contrary, still, are many praises of voluntary poverty quoted of Ibn al-Mubārak; for example, 'Increase of your Hereafter will come only by the decrease of your (share of) the world, while increase of your (share of) the world will come only by the decrease of your Hereafter.'[58] His own practice of austerity is mentioned, as when Ibn Abī Ḥātim quotes someone who saw Ibn al-Mubārak completely barefoot, shopping in the market for his needs.[59] Even in the Sufi literature, we find such quotations of him as this definition of *zuhd*: 'Renunciation is to keep trust in God most high while loving poverty.'[60] I have argued before that the most reliable picture of eighth-century renunciant piety is to be found in the literature of hadith, the least reliable in that of Sufism. In neither of them does Ibn al-Mubārak appear to be a favourite source of world-affirming sentiments. I would conclude he was at least no leader of the opposition to outward austerity itself.

Ibn al-Mubārak's Theological Tendency

The question of Sunnism against Shiᶜism was raised at the Pembroke conference. Ibn al-Mubārak was particularly associated with a hardening of attitudes in the later eighth century. This seems only weakly supported in the sources that I have surveyed. The creed attributed alternatively to Ghulām Khalīl (d. 275/888) and al-Barbahārī (d. 329/941) quotes Ibn al-Mubārak, 'The root of 72 fancies is just four of them. From these four branched out the 72 fancies: the Qadarīyah, the Murjiʾah, the Shīᶜah, and the Khawārij.'[61] Abū

Nu^caym relates two stories in which Ibn al-Mubārak takes a stand against association with unspecified heretics (*ṣāḥib bid^cah*).[62] Ibn Abī Ḥātim mentions that Ibn al-Mubārak said they had left (i.e., ceased to relate hadith from) ^cAmr ibn ^cUbayd (d. 144/761–2?) because he was an active promoter (*kāna yad^cū*), glossed as referring to *qadar* (anti-predestinarianism).[63] ^cAbd Allāh ibn Aḥmad makes him both more involved with ^cAmr and more disapproving: he was asked, 'Have you heard from ^cAmr ibn ^cUbayd?' He said, 'This much' with his hand, indicating a great deal. 'So why do you not name him, whereas you do name others of the Qadarīyah?' He said, 'Because this one was a chief (*ra^ɔs*).'[64]

Ibn al-Mubārak is sometimes quoted against relating hadith from Shi^cah; for example, 'Do not relate hadith of ^cAmr ibn Thābit, for he insults the early ones (*salaf*).'[65] On the other hand, there is al-Mizzī's list of 211 shaykhs from whom Ibn al-Mubārak related hadith: by my count, ten are identified by Ibn Ḥajar as Shi^ci, five as Qadari and four as Murji^ɔ (with some overlap; for example, ^cAwf al-A^crābī, Shi^ci and Qadari).[66] One who is oddly missing from al-Mizzī's list, ^cAbd Allāh ibn Lahī^cah (Egyptian, d. 174/790), was sometimes accused of Shi^cism.[67] Ibn Abī Ḥātim quotes Ibn al-Mubārak himself as saying he had given rise to doubts (*arāba*).[68] Yet Ibn Lahī^cah is the third most-cited of Ibn al-Mubārak's sources in Aḥmad's *Musnad*, second in *al-Zuhd*. Ibn Abī Ḥātim also quotes Nu^caym ibn Ḥammād as saying, 'Ibn al-Mubārak would not discard a man's hadith unless he heard something of him that he could not rebut.'[69] At least by this measure, whom he trusted to relate hadith, Ibn al-Mubārak does not seem to have led the way in rejecting sectaries.

The Works of Ibn al-Mubārak

I observed in my previous article that Ibn al-Nadīm attributes to Ibn al-Mubārak five works: *Kitāb al-Sunan* on jurisprudence (*fiqh*), *Kitāb al-Tafsīr*, *Kitāb al-Tārīkh*, *Kitāb al-Zuhd* and *Kitāb al-Birr wa-al-ṣilah*.[70] Of the first, presumably a collection of hadith on legal topics, no trace survives. Of the second, comprising Qur^ɔānic commentary, I observed earlier that later sources seldom quote either Ibn al-Mubārak's own opinion on the Qur^ɔān or Qur^ɔānic glosses with him in the *isnād*. However, I also observed that Aḥmad ibn Ḥanbal quotes ^cAbd al-Razzāq as recalling that Ibn al-Mubārak and Ma^cmar (ibn Rāshid) would recite *tafsīr* to each other.[71] In the *Tafsīr* itself, we have this report from ^cAbd al-Razzāq: 'I saw Ibn al-Mubārak reading *al-tafsīr* before Ma^cmar', probably referring to his reading or reciting from his notes for Ma^cmar's approval as to their accuracy.[72] A good two-thirds of ^cAbd al-Razzāq's own Qur^ɔān commentary is made up of glosses he relates from Ma^cmar. It therefore seems likely, I will now add, that Ibn al-Mubārak's *Tafsīr* was a similar collection of glosses from Ma^cmar with additions from elsewhere. I have little to add here of *Kitāb al-Tārīkh*, the third title on Ibn al-Nadīm's list. Bukhārī collects Ibn al-Mubārak's comments on the reliability of hadith transmitters but admits that he is not among the most prominent critics.[73] One occasionally runs across a quotation; for example, from Ibn Ḥajar, '(Sulaymān ibn Ṭarkhān) al-Taymī, on whom the people of Basra relied who had not heard from Abū al-ᶜĀliyah.'[74]

As for *Kitāb al-Birr wa-al-ṣilah*, Sezgin lists no manuscript for it and I reported in my previous article that I knew of no trace of it since Ibn al-Nadīm's citation.[75] I did observe that Ibn Khayr al-Ishbīlī (d. 575/1179) mentions having a *Kitāb al-Birr wa-al-ṣilah* from al-Ḥusayn ibn al-Ḥasan. I guessed that this was the title attributed by Ibn al-Nadīm directly to Ibn al-Mubārak, and that it comprised some combination, like *al-Zuhd*, of material from Ibn al-Mubārak and from other shaykhs. I have since remarked citations of *Kitāb al-Birr wa-al-ṣilah* by Ibn Ḥajar and al-Suyūṭī (d. 911/1505), both of whom knew it in the recension of al-Ḥusayn ibn al-Ḥasan.[76] What I found only on reading Salem's book is that there was a 1991 edition of it. As observed above, items related through Ibn al-Mubārak constitute only 40 per cent of the text. (Ibn Ḥajar also had a book from Ibn al-Mubārak not mentioned by any other source I know of, *al-Istiʾdhān*, presumably a collection of hadith on the etiquette of asking for entry to someone's house. It was apparently collected by Ibn al-Mubārak's leading disciple ᶜAbdān.[77]) It seems fair to consider *al-Birr* a work not by Ibn al-Mubārak but by al-Ḥusayn ibn al-Ḥasan.

Like *al-Birr*, the *Musnad* attributed to Ibn al-Mubārak survives as a unicum in Damascus.[78] Fuat Sezgin identifies the work as the recension of al-Ḥasan ibn Sufyān al-Nasawī (d. 303/916), which is based on the *isnād*s in the work. Nearly all of it is traced through him < Ḥibbān ibn Mūsā al-Marwazī (d. 233/847–8) < Ibn al-Mubārak, but a few items are rather < Ibrāhīm ibn ᶜAbd Allāh al-Khallāl < Ibn al-Mubārak.[79] Ḥibbān ibn Mūsá was also a major source of Bukhārī's for hadith from Ibn al-Mubārak. It was first edited by Muṣṭafá ᶜUthmān Muḥammad as part of his doctoral dissertation (al-Azhar, 1979), later published as a book.[80] It was independently edited and published by Ṣubḥī al-Badrī al-Sāmarrāʾī before Muḥammad's book version had appeared.[81] Both editions seem to be imperfect but Muḥammad's the better. It includes six hadith reports missed by al-Sāmarrāʾī (Nos 76, 86–9, 141), whereas al-Sāmarrāʾī's edition includes one report missed by Muḥammad's (No. 147 between Muḥammad's Nos 157 and 158). Al-Sāmarrāʾī's edition sometimes alters texts to make them congruent with better-known versions (for example, al-Sāmarrāʾī, No. 242, *lā mā ṣallaw*, as opposed to Muḥammad, No. 257, *ammā mā ṣallawu ʾl-ṣalāta fa-lā*).

Kitāb al-Zuhd is one of five works attributed to Ibn al-Mubārak by Ibn al-Nadīm.[82] Ibn Ḥajar apparently refers to it interchangeably as *al-Zuhd* and *al-Raqāʾiq*. The Alexandria manuscript of Abū Nuᶜaym's recension refers to it as *al-Raqāʾiq fī al-zuhd*, the Chester Beatty manuscript as *al-Zuhd wa-al-raqāʾiq*, the Leipzig manuscripts as *al-Zuhd*. Editor Ḥabīb al-Raḥmān al-Aᶜẓamī combined two manuscripts of the recension of al-Ḥusayn ibn al-Ḥasan al-Marwazī (l. Mecca, d. 246/860–1) with one of the recension of Nuᶜaym ibn Ḥammād (d. Samarra, 228/843?) to produce the first printed version under the title *Kitāb al-Zuhd wa-al-raqāʾiq*. He first presents the recension of al-Ḥusayn, then 436 items separately numbered found only in Nuᶜaym's recension. The editor says little of how the recensions of al-Ḥusayn and Nuᶜaym are related except for the extra items in the latter. It appears, however, that the first three-quarters of Nuᶜaym's recension is a fairly close parallel to al-Ḥusayn's, for al-Aᶜẓamī occasionally remarks where an item of Nuᶜaym's comes between two items in al-Ḥusayn's; for example, No. 203 from Nuᶜaym comes between Nos 793 and 794 from al-Ḥusayn, No. 206 from Nuᶜaym between Nos 822 and 823 from al-Ḥusayn. He also, as observed, points out where a section title in al-Ḥusayn's recension corresponds to a different one in Nuᶜaym's. Subsequent indexes refer to the items from Nuᶜaym alone as 'additions' (*ziyādāt*) and the Dār al-Kutub al-ᶜIlmīyah edition of 1419/1998 announces on the title page *Kitāb al-Zuhd wa-yalīhi Kitāb al-Raqāʾiq*, as if they were effectively separate books.[83] They look to me closer than that. (Also, I would reserve the term 'additions' for items inserted by al-Ḥusayn from shaykhs other than Ibn al-Mubārak – as observed, about a quarter of the extant text.)

I have recently inspected a microfilm of the Chester Beatty manuscript of *al-Zuhd* (as one might have expected Salem's dissertation supervisors to suggest her doing). It runs from No. 704 to the middle of No. 934, then (folios having been shuffled) from the middle of No. 616 to No. 700. That is, it intersects with a little less than a fifth of the Carullah (Istanbul) manuscript of al-Ḥusayn's recension. It reproduces the same chain of transmitters as al-Aᶜẓamī's manuscript, which plainly rules out using this chain to provide anything more than a *terminus post quem* for when either text was copied: in both versions, the chain of transmitters was evidently copied along with the manuscript. As for textual variants between al-Aᶜẓamī's recensions, the Chester Beatty manuscript usually agrees with the Carullah manuscript on which al-Aᶜẓamī relies against the Alexandria manuscript of Nuᶜaym's recension. Sometimes, however, Chester Beatty agrees with Alexandria; for example, in including an addition at the end of No. 721. It includes one additional item between Nos 786 and 787 not included in either the Carullah or Alexandria manuscripts, whereby Mujāhid (Meccan, d. 103/721–2?) gives the advice, 'When you (start to) yawn while reciting the Qurʾān, restrain it till it goes away.' It includes the same extra item as Nuᶜaym between Nos 822 and 823. It exposes an instance of homoioteleuton from No. 927 to No. 928, where al-Aᶜẓamī's edition apparently jumps from the middle of one item into the middle of the next. (As with several smaller discrepancies, the mistake here may have come from al-Aᶜẓamī rather than his manuscripts.[84])

In my previous article, I argued against supposing that the core of al-Ḥusayn's recension (that is, items he relates from Ibn al-Mubārak) was compiled directly by Ibn al-Mubārak himself, whereas Nuᶜaym's was his independent compilation. Al-Aᶜẓamī's notes suggest that Nuᶜaym's recension closely resembles al-Ḥusayn's except for al-Ḥusayn's interpolations from other than Ibn al-Mubārak and the last part of Nuᶜaym's, which continues where al-Ḥusayn's text leaves off. Comparison with the Chester Beatty manuscript confirms that some discrepancies between al-Ḥusayn's recension and Nuᶜaym's go back only to much later copies. We obviously need a new edition of *al-Zuhd* based on all the known manuscripts. My guess at this point is that not only the Chester Beatty but also the Carullah manuscript of al-Ḥusayn's recension is incomplete. The sources of the additional section of Nuᶜaym's recension are very similar to those of al-Ḥusayn's. In both, for example, the shaykh most often cited by Ibn al-Mubārak is by far Sufyān al-Thawrī, followed by Maᶜmar, then Ibn Lahīᶜah; in both, a little over half of all items come from Iraq. Altogether, the more similar these two recensions are, the more we should consider their contents and order to reflect Ibn al-Mubārak's priorities, not just those of his disciples. The *Zuhd* of Ibn al-Mubārak would then be comparable to its contemporary the *Muwaṭṭaʾ* of Mālik: extant in a number of recensions that vary somewhat in the number of items, their order and the exact titles under which they are classified but that must correspond roughly to notes from Ibn al-Mubārak and Mālik themselves.

Notes

1. Ibn al-Mubārak, *al-Zuhd wa-al-raqāʾiq*, ed. Ḥabīb al-Raḥmān al-Aᶜẓamī (Malegaon: Majlis Iḥyāʾ al-Maᶜārif, 1386, repr. with different pagination but the same item numbers, Beirut: Dār al-Kutub al-ᶜIlmīyah, 1419/1998); Ibn al-Mubārak, *K. al-Jihād*, ed. Nazīh Ḥammād (Beirut: Dār al-Nūr, 1971/1391, repr. with different pagination but the same item numbers, Beirut: al-Maktabah al-ᶜAṣrīyah, 1409/1988); Ibn al-Mubārak, *al-Musnad*, ed. Ṣubḥī al-Badrī al-Sāmarrāʾī (Riyadh: Maktabat al-Maᶜārif, 1407/1987), also ed. Muṣṭafá ᶜUthmān Muḥammad, with *K. al-Birr wa-al-ṣilah* (Beirut: Dār al-Kutub al-ᶜIlmīyah, 1411/1991). Ibn al-Mubārak, *al-Zuhd wa-al-raqāʾiq*, ed. Aḥmad Farīd, 2 vols (Riyadh: Dār al-Miᶜrāj al-Dawlīyah, 1415/1995), is a corrected version of al-Aᶜẓamī's that omits additions from al-Ḥusayn al-Marwazī and Ibn Ṣāᶜid as well as all items found only in the recension of Nuᶜaym ibn Ḥammād.
2. Muḥammad ᶜUthmān Jamāl, *ᶜAbd Allāh ibn al-Mubārak al-imām al-qudwah*, Aᶜlām al-muslimīn 1 (Damascus: Dār al-Qalam, 1391/1971).
3. Jamāl, *ᶜAbd Allāh*, 82–3.
4. Jamāl, *ᶜAbd Allāh*, 100–8, citing Ẓafar Aḥmad ᶜU̱smānī (Pakistani, d. 1394/1974), al-Nawawī (d. 676/1277) and Ibn Ḥajar al-Haytamī (d. 974/1567?).
5. ᶜAbd al-Majīd al-Muḥtasib, *ᶜAbd Allāh ibn al-Mubārak al-Marwazī (118–181 H.)* (Amman: Wizārat al-Awqāf wa-al-Shuʾūn wa-al-Muqaddasāt al-Islāmīyah, 1392/1972).
6. ᶜIṣām Muḥammad al-Ḥājj ᶜAlī, *al-Imām al-mujāhid ᶜAbd Allāh ibn al-Mubārak*, Aᶜlām al-fuqahāʾ wa-al-muḥaddithīn (Beirut: Dār al-Kutub al-ᶜIlmīyah, 1411/1990).
7. Muḥtasib, *ᶜAbd Allāh*, 7; Jamāl, *ᶜAbd Allāh*, 48; ᶜAlī, *Imām*, 55.
8. Muḥammad Saᶜīd ibn Muḥammad Ḥasan Aḥmad Bukhārī, *al-Imām ᶜAbd Allāh ibn al-Mubārak al-Marwazī al-imām al-nāqid* (Riyadh: Maktabat al-Rushd, 1424/2003).

9. Bukhārī, *al-Imām ᶜAbd Allāh*, 55–8.
10. Bukhārī, *al-Imām ᶜAbd Allāh*, 60.
11. Bukhārī, *al-Imām ᶜAbd Allāh*, 77–149.
12. Bukhārī, *al-Imām ᶜAbd Allāh*, 71.
13. Riyāḍ Aḥmad Ibrāhīm al-Dūrī, *al-Imām al-ḥāfiẓ ᶜAbd Allāh ibn al-Mubārak: mawāqifuhu al-jihādīyah wa-marwīyātuhu al-tārīkhīyah* (Beirut: Dār al-Kutub al-ᶜIlmīyah, 1426 / 2005).
14. Muḥtasib, *ᶜAbd Allāh*, 54–62. On ᶜĪsá al-Ayyūbī al-Malik al-Muᶜaẓẓam (d. 624 / 1227), his defence of Abū Ḥanīfah, and the first edition of *Tārīkh Baghdād*, see Ahmad Khan, 'Islamic Tradition in an Age of Print', in Elisabeth Kendall and Ahmad Khan (eds), *Reclaiming Islamic Tradition* (Edinburgh: Edinburgh University Press, 2016), 52–99, at 62–3.
15. ᶜAlī, *al-Imām al-mujāhid*, 58–9.
16. Bukhārī, *al-Imām ᶜAbd Allāh*, 322–3, 330–1.
17. Dūrī, *al-Imām al-ḥāfiẓ*, 67.
18. Raif Georges Khoury, 'L'Importance de l'Iṣāba d'Ibn Ḥağar al-ᶜAsqalānī pour l'étude de la littérature arabe des siècles islamiques: vue à travers l'example des oeuvres de ᶜAbdallāh ibn al-Mubārak (118 / 736–181 / 797)', *Studia Islamica* 42 (1975): 115–45.
19. Khoury, 'Importance', 123–7. The edition of *al-Zuhd* available to Khoury lacks an index. This want is now supplied by Yūsuf ᶜAbd al-Raḥmān al-Marᶜashlī, *Fihris* Kitāb al-Zuhd *lil-imām al-ḥāfiẓ shaykh al-Islām ᶜAbd Allāh al-Mubārak* [*sic*] *al-Marwazī*, Silsilat fahāris kutub al-sunnah 5 (Beirut: Dār al-Nūr al-Islāmī, 1408 / 1987), alternatively Muḥammad Muḥammad Sharīf, *Mawsūᶜat fahāris kutub al-zuhd* (Dammam: Dār Ibn al-Jawzī, 1413 / 1992).
20. Khoury, 'Importance', 128–9.
21. Khoury, 'Importance', 130.
22. Cf. Raif Georges Khoury, 'L'Avènement des Abbasides et son importance pour le développ[eme]nt de l'écriture en Islam', in Krzystof Kościelniak (ed.), *Prosperity and Stagnation: Some Cultural and Social Aspects of the Abbasid Period*, Orientalia Christiana Cracoviensia monographiae 1 (Cracow: UNUM, 2010), 63–85.
23. See esp. Gregor Schoeler, *The Oral and the Written in Early Islam*, ed. James E. Montgomery, trans. Uwe Vagelpohl, Routledge Studies in Middle Eastern Literatures, 13 (London: Routledge, 2006), and Gregor Schoeler, *The Genesis of Literature in Islam: From the Aural to the Read*, trans. Shawkat M. Toorawa, New Edinburgh Islamic Surveys (Edinburgh: Edinburgh University Press, 2009). See also Stefan Leder, 'Authorship and Transmission in Unauthored Literature: the Akhbār Attributed to Haytham ibn ᶜAdī', *Oriens* 31 (1988): 67–81, and Christopher Melchert, 'Aḥmad ibn Ḥanbal's Book of Renunciation', *Der Islam* 85 (2008): 345–59, for parallel cases of additions from other sources.
24. Michael Bonner, *Aristocratic Violence and the Holy War*, American Oriental ser. 81 (New Haven, CT: American Oriental Society, 1996); D. G. Tor, *Violent Order: Religious Warfare, Chivalry, and the ᶜAyyār Phenomenon in the Medieval Islamic World*, Istanbuler Texte und Studien, 11 (Würzburg: Ergon, 2007).

25. Roberta Denaro, 'From Marw to the *ṯuġūr*: Ibn al-Mubārak and the Shaping of a Biographical Tradition', *Eurasian Studies* 7 (2009): 125–44.
26. Christopher Melchert, 'Ibn al-Mubārak's *Kitāb al-Jihād* and Early Renunciant Literature', in Robert Gleave and István Kristó-Nagy (eds), *Violence in Islamic Thought from the Qurʾān to the Mongols*, Legitimate and Illegitimate Violence in Islamic Thought, 1 (Edinburgh: Edinburgh University Press, 2015), 49–69.
27. Bonner, *Aristocratic Violence*, 120.
28. Feryal Salem, *The Emergence of Early Sufi Piety and Sunnī Scholasticism: ʿAbdallāh b. al-Mubārak and the Formation of Sunnī Identity in the Second Islamic Century*, Islamic History and Civilization, Studies and Texts, 125 (Leiden: Brill, 2016).
29. Salem, *Emergence of Early Sufi Piety*, 45, citing Bukhārī, *al-Imām ʿAbd Allāh*, 80.
30. Salem, *Emergence of Early Sufi Piety*, 105–7; Nimrod Hurvitz, 'Biographies and Mild Asceticism: a Study of Islamic Moral Imagination', *Studia Islamica* 85 (1997): 41–65; Leah Kinberg, 'What is Meant by *zuhd*', *Studia Islamica* 61 (1985): 27–44.
31. On *iʿtibār*, see Shammāʾ Jamāl al-Asmar, *al-Iʿtibār fī ʿulūm al-ḥadīth al-sharīf*, Maktabat al-rasāʾil al-jāmiʿīyah al-ʿālamīyah, 39 (Damascus: Dār al-Nawādir, 1434/2013). It is glossed as 'consideration' by Jonathan A. C. Brown, *Hadith: Muhammad's Legacy in the Medieval and Modern World*, Foundations of Islam (Oxford: Oneworld, 2009), 93.
32. It is to her credit that Salem reproduces and translates poetry attributed to Ibn al-Mubārak. Oddly, she cites no source for any of it. I here compare Salem's version (*Emergence of Early Sufi Piety*, 89) with that in al-Qāḍī ʿIyāḍ, *Tartīb al-Madārik*, ed. Muḥammad ibn Tāwīt al-Ṭanjī and Saʿīd Aḥmad Aʿrāb, 8 vols (Rabāṭ, al-Muḥammadīyah, Tetouan: various, 1966–83), 3:47.
33. Melchert, 'Ibn al-Mubārak's *Kitāb al-Jihād*', 67.
34. See Roberto Tottoli, 'Origin and Use of the Term *isrāʾīliyyāt* in Muslim Literature', *Arabica* 46 (1999): 193–210.
35. G. H. A. Juynboll, 'Muslim's Introduction to his *Ṣaḥīḥ*', *Jerusalem Studies in Arabic and Islam* 5 (1984): 263–311, at 265.
36. On topics represented in Aḥmad's *Musnad*, see Christopher Melchert, 'The *Musnad* of Aḥmad ibn Ḥanbal', *Der Islam* 82 (2005): 32–51, at 45.
37. Figure from al-Sarakhsī based on Khalīl al-Mays, *Fahāris al-Mabsūṭ* (Beirut: Dār al-Maʿrifah, 1400/1980). Figures from al-Jaṣṣāṣ and Ibn Māzah provided by Salman Younas, 'The Ḥanafī School: a Study of its Social and Legal Dimensions, 189/805–340/952', DPhil. dissertation, University of Oxford, 2018, 77–8.
38. Joseph Schacht, *The Origins of Muhammadan Jurisprudence* (Oxford: Clarendon Press, 1950). For the current state of the question, see Christopher Melchert, 'Basra and Kufa as the Earliest Centers of Islamic Legal Controversy', in Behnam Sadeghi, Asad Q. Ahmed, Adam Silverstein and Robert G. Hoyland (eds), *Islamic Cultures, Islamic Contexts: Essays in Honor of Professor Patricia Crone*, Islamic History and Civilization, Studies and Texts, 114 (Leiden: Brill, 2015), 173–94.
39. Muḥammad ibn Naṣr al-Marwazī, *Ikhtilāf al-ʿulamāʾ*, ed. Ṣubḥī al-Sāmarrāʾī (Beirut: ʿĀlam al-Kutub, 1405/1985).
40. For example, Muḥammad Rawwās Qalʿah'jī, *Mawsūʿat fiqh Ibrāhīm al-Nakhaʿī*, Silsilat mawsūʿāt fiqh al-salaf 8, 2 vols (Beirut: Dār al-Nafāʾis, 1406/1986);

Muḥammad Rawwās Qalᶜah'jī, *Mawsūᶜat fiqh Sufyān al-Thawrī*, Silsilat mawsūᶜāt fiqh al-salaf 10 (Beirut: Dār al-Nafāʾis, 1410/1990).

41. Aḥmad ibn Ḥanbal (attrib.), *K. al-ᶜIlal wa-maᶜrifat al-rijāl*, ed. Waṣī Allāh ibn Muḥammad ᶜAbbās, 4 vols (Beirut: al-Maktab al-Islāmī, 1988), 3:480 = *K. al-Jāmiᶜ fī al-ᶜilal wa-maᶜrifat al-rijāl*, ed. Muḥammad Ḥusām Bayḍūn, 2 vols (Beirut: Muʾassasat al-Kutub al-Thaqāfīyah, 1410/1990), 2:276. References to the latter edition are henceforth in italics.
42. Ibn Abī Ḥātim, *Jarḥ* 1:262.
43. Abū Nuᶜaym, *Ḥilyat al-awliyā'*, 10 vols (Cairo: Maṭbaᶜat al-Saᶜādah, 1352–7/1932–8).
44. Schacht, *Origins of Muhammadan Jurisprudence*, 242. Hans-Peter Raddatz reviews Sufyān al-Thawrī's Kufan connections and remarks that three-quarters of the hadith in the extant *Kitāb al-Farāʾiḍ* attributed to him come from Kufan shaykhs. He also remarks some inclination away from Kufan Shiᶜism, towards relative rationalism, under the influence of the Basran tradition, especially through Ayyūb al-Sakhtiyānī (d. 133/751?) and ᶜAbd Allāh ibn ᶜAwn (d. 151/768–9?). See Raddatz, 'Frühislamisches Erbrecht nach dem Kitāb al-Farāʾiḍ des Sufyān aṯ-Ṯawrī', *Die Welt des Islams* 13 (1971): 26–78, esp. 25–8, 71–5.
45. Kawsaj, *Masāʾil al-imām Aḥmad ibn Ḥanbal wa-Isḥāq ibn Rāhūyah*, ed. Abū al-Ḥusayn Khālid ibn Maḥmūd al-Rabāṭ, Wiʾām al-Ḥawshī and Jumᶜah Fatḥī, 2 vols (Riyadh: Dār al-Hijrah, 1425/2004), 2:588–9; Ḥarb al-Kirmānī, *Masāʾil al-imām Aḥmad ibn Muḥammad ibn Ḥanbal wa-Isḥāq ibn Rāhūyah*, ed. Nāṣir ibn Suᶜūd ibn ᶜAbd Allāh al-Salāmah (Riyadh: Maktabat al-Rushd, 1425/2004), 426.
46. On the Ḥanafi presence in Marw, see Christopher Melchert, 'The Spread of Ḥanafism to Khurasan and Transoxania', in A. C. S. Peacock and D. G. Tor (eds), *Medieval Central Asia and the Persianate World*, I. B. Tauris and BIPS Persian Studies, 7 (London: I. B. Tauris, 2015), 13–30, esp. 14–15; also Wilferd Madelung, 'The Early Murjiʾa in Khurāsān and Transoxania and the spread of Ḥanafism', *Der Islam* 59 (1982): 32–9.
47. Benedikt Reinert, *Die Lehre vom* tawakkul *in der klassischen Sufik*, Studien zur Sprache, Geschichte und Kultur des islamischen Orients, ed. Bertold Spuler, 3 (Berlin: Walter de Gruyter, 1968), 143, 220, 257.
48. Al-Sarrāj, *The Kitáb al-Lumaᶜ fī 'l-taṣawwuf*, ed. Reynold Alleyne Nicholson, E. J. W. Gibb Memorial, 22 (Leiden and London: Brill and Luzac, 1914), 196, cited by Reinert, *Lehre*, 220.
49. Abū Bakr al-Khallāl, *K. al-Ḥathth ᶜalá al-tijārah wa-al-ṣināᶜah wa-al-ᶜamal*, ed. Abū ᶜAbd Allāh Maḥmūd ibn Muḥammad al-Ḥaddād, Bulūgh al-amānī min al-ajzāʾ wa-al-amālī 2, Masāʾil Aḥmad, 1 (Riyadh: Dār al-ᶜĀṣimah, 1407), 144, cited by Reinert, *Lehre*, 257.
50. Muḥāsibī, *al-Makāsib*, in *al-Masāʾil fī aᶜmāl al-qulūb wa-al-jawāriḥ wa-al-makāsib wa-al-ᶜaql*, ed. ᶜAbd al-Qādir Aḥmad ᶜAṭā (Cairo: ᶜĀlam al-Kutub, 1969), 212. On *inkār al-kasb* and early Sufis, see also Christopher Melchert, 'Baṣran Origins of Classical Sufism', *Der Islam* 82 (2005): 221–40, at 231–2, and Josef van Ess, *Theologie und Gesellschaft im 2. und 3. Jahrhundert Hidschra*, 6 vols (Berlin: Walter de Gruyter, 1991–5), 3:130–45, 4:88–94, on *ṣūfiyat al-muᶜtazilah*.
51. Johann Fück, 'Some Hitherto Unpublished Texts on the Muᶜtazilite Movement

from Ibn al-Nadīm's *Kitāb-al-Fihrist'*, in S. M. Abdullah (ed.), *Professor Muhammad Shafi*[c] *Presentation Volume* (Lahore: Majlis-e-Armughān-e-[c]Ilmī, 1955), 51–74, at 71, 73. One of Ibn al-Mubārak's Kufan contemporaries, Wakī[c] (d. 197/812?), had already come to a similar conclusion: 'If a man swore to eat nothing but the licit, wear nothing but the licit, and not walk except in the licit, we would tell him, "Take off your clothes and throw yourself into the Euphrates." . . . The purely licit we do not know today . . . The world has the status of carrion: take from it what will sustain you' (Abū Nu[c]aym, *Ḥilyah* 8:370). Similarly, Yūsuf ibn Asbāṭ (d. 195/810–11) said, 'If a man were, as to leaving the world, like Abū Dharr, Salmān and Abū al-Dardā[ʾ], we still would not call him a renunciant, for renunciation concerns only the purely licit, whereas the purely licit is unknown today' (Abū Nu[c]aym, *Ḥilyah* 8:238).

52. Khallāl, *Ḥathth*, 143–4.
53. Khallāl, *Ḥathth*, 143–4.
54. Ibn al-Mubārak, *Zuhd*, 197 *189*; cited by Reinert, *Lehre*, 143.
55. Also related through Ibn al-Mubārak in Tirmidhī, *al-Jāmi*[c] *al-ṣaḥīḥ*, *al-zuhd* 33, *bāb fī al-tawakkul*, No. 2344; through Ibn Lahī[c]ah in Ibn Mājah, *al-Sunan*, *al-zuhd* 14, *bāb al-tawakkul wa-al-yaqīn*, No. 4164. Another version quoting [c]Īsá, and closer to the New Testament, is at Ibn al-Mubārak, *Zuhd*, No. 848.
56. Khallāl, *Ḥathth*, 142. Confirmed by Ṣāliḥ ibn Aḥmad, *Masā*[ʾ]*il al-imām Aḥmad ibn Ḥanbal*, ed. Ṭāriq ibn [c]Awad Allāh ibn Muḥammad (Riyadh: Dār al-Waṭan, 1420/1999), 115, where Aḥmad is asked about a group who make no effort (*lā ya*[c]*malūn*) while saying they are practising *tawakkul*. He responds that they are innovators (*mubtadi*[c]*ah*).
57. See n. 48. Ibn al-Mubārak also appears in one *isnād* that I have noticed, relating Ibn Mujāhid's gloss of Q. 2:267, 'spend some of the good things you have acquired' as 'trade (*tijārah*)': Khallāl, *Ḥathth*, 70.
58. Abū Nu[c]aym, *Ḥilyat* 8:166–7.
59. Ibn Abī Ḥātim, *Jarḥ* 1:278.
60. Al-Qushayrī, *Al-Qushayri's Epistle on Sufism*, trans. Alexander D. Knysh, rev. Muhammad Eissa, Great Books of Islamic Civilisation (Reading: Garnet, 2007), 136, § on *zuhd*.
61. Ibn Abī Ya[c]lá, *Ṭabaqāt al-ḥanābilah*, ed. Muḥammad Ḥāmid al-Fiqī, 2 vols (Cairo: Maṭba[c]at al-Sunnah al-Muḥammadīyah, 1371/1952), 2:40 = ed. [c]Abd al-Raḥmān ibn Sulaymān al-[c]Uthaymīn, 2 vols (n.p.: al-Amānah al-[c]āmmah lil-iḥtifāl bi-murūr mi[ʾ]at [c]ām [c]alá ta[ʾ]sīs al-mamlakah, 1419/1999), 3:72; Louis Massignon, *Recueil de texts inédits concernant l'histoire de la mystique en pays d'Islam*, Collection de texts inédits relatives á la mystique musulmane, 1 (Paris: Paul Geuthner, 1929), 212–14 (excerpt from Ẓāhirīyah *majāmi*[c] 13). On the attribution of the creed, see Christopher Melchert, 'The Ḥanābila and the Early Sufis', *Arabica* 48 (2001): 352–67, at 361–2; Christopher Melchert, 'The Creeds of Aḥmad Ibn Ḥanbal', with Saud Al-Sarhan, in Robert Gleave (ed.), *Books and Bibliophiles: Studies in Honour of Paul Auchterlonie on the Bio-bibliography of the Muslim World* (n.p.: Gibb Memorial Trust, 2014), 29–50, at 49–50; and *Encyclopaedia of Islam*, 3rd edn, s.v. 'Ghulām Khalīl', by Maher Jarrar.

62. Abū Nuʿaym, *Ḥilyat* 8:168.
63. Ibn Abī Ḥātim, *Jarḥ* 1:273.
64. ʿAbd Allāh ibn Aḥmad, *K. al-Sunnah*, ed. ʿAbd Allāh ibn Ḥasan ibn Ḥusayn (Mecca: al-Maṭbaʿah al-Salafīyah, 1349), 131 = ed. Abū Hājir Muḥammad Saʿīd ibn Basyūnī Zaghlūl (Beirut: Dār al-Kutub al-ʿIlmīyah, 1405/1985), 149.
65. Aḥmad, *ʿIlal* 3:486 *2:278*. ʿAmr ibn Thābit was a Kufan client (d. 172/788–9) accused of *rafḍ*, on whom, see Ibn Ḥajar, *Tahdhīb* al-Tahdhīb, 12 vols (Hyderabad: Majlis Dāʾirat al-Maʿārif al-Niẓāmīyah, 1325–7, repr. Beirut: Dār Ṣādir, n.d.), 8:9–10.
66. Al-Mizzī, *Tahdhīb al-Kamāl fi asmāʾ al-rijāl*, ed. Bashshār ʿAwwād Maʿrūf, 35 vols (Beirut: Muʾassasat al-Risālah, 1413/1992), 16:6–10. On ʿAwf al-Aʿrābī (Basran, d. 147/764–5?), see Ibn Ḥajar, *Tahdhīb* 8:166–7.
67. Al-Kindī, *The Governors and Judges of Egypt*, ed. Rhuvon Guest, E. J. W. Gibb Memorial, 19 (Leiden: Brill, 1912), 369; al-Dhahabī, *Tārīkh al-islām*, ed. ʿUmar ʿAbd al-Salām Tadmurī, 52 vols (Beirut: Dār al-Kitāb al-ʿArabī, 1407–21/1987–2000), 11 (171–180 H.): 224–5.
68. Ibn Abī Ḥātim, *Jarḥ* 1:271, with the gloss 'His imperfection has become manifest (*qad ẓaharat ʿawratuh*).'
69. Ibn Abī Ḥātim, *Jarḥ* 1:274. There may also have been some element here of pious fear that aspersing traditionists amounted to *ghībah* (slander), on which, see Christopher Melchert, 'Early Renunciants as *Ḥadīth* Transmitters', *Muslim World* 92 (2002): 407–18, at 413–14.
70. Ibn al-Nadīm, *Fihrist, fann* 6, *maqālah* 6 = *Kitâb al-Fihrist*, ed. Gustav Flügel, with Johannes Roedigger and August Mueller (Leipzig: F. C. W. Vogel, 1872), 228.
71. Aḥmad, *ʿIlal* 1:272, 2:361 *1:114, 327*.
72. ʿAbd al-Razzāq, *al-Tafsīr*, ed. ʿAbd al-Muʿṭī Amīn Qalʿajī, 2 vols (Beirut: Dār al-Maʿrifah, 1411/1991), 1:105, *ad* Q. 2:225.
73. Bukhārī, *al-Imām ʿAbd Allāh*, 235–56 (men he counted trustworthy), 257–308 (men he aspersed), 309 (his prominence).
74. Ibn Ḥajar, *Tahdhīb* 4:202.
75. Sezgin, *Geschichte des arabischen Schrifttums* (*GAS*) 1:95, No. 4. The Ẓāhirīyah unicum does appear in Najm ʿAbd al-Raḥmān Khalaf, *Istidrākāt ʿalá* Tārīkh al-turāth al-ʿarabī *li-Fuʾād Sizgīn fi ʿilm al-ḥadīth*, Maktabat Niẓām Yaʿqūbī al-Khāṣṣah-Baḥrayn, Dirāsāt wa-buḥūth 1 (Beirut: Dār al-Bashāʾir al-Islāmīyah, 1421/2000), 84.
76. Ibn Ḥajar, *al-Muʿjam al-mufahras*, ed. Muḥammad Shakūr Maḥmūd al-Ḥājjī Umrayr al-Mayādīnī (Beirut: Muʾassasat al-Risālah, 1418/1998), 84, No. 233; al-Suyūṭī, *Anshāb al-kuthub fi ansāb al-kutub*, ed. Ibrāhīm Bājis ʿAbd al-Majīd, Taḥqīq al-turāth 31 (Riyadh: Markaz al-Malik Fayṣal lil-Buḥūth wa-al-Dirāsāt al-Islāmīyah, 1437/2016), 190.
77. Ibn Ḥajar, *Muʿjam*, 87, No. 251.
78. Sezgin, *GAS* 1:95, No. 3; Khalaf, *Istidrākāt*, 84.
79. Melchert, 'Ibn al-Mubārak's *Kitāb al-Jihād*', 54. I go on there to compare the approximately 350 hadith reports in each of Bukhārī's *Ṣaḥīḥ* and Aḥmad's *Musnad*. This estimate of 350 in Bukhārī's *Ṣaḥīḥ* is evidently erroneous. Sezgin's

numbers add up to 218, the modern author Bukhārī proposes 212, I would now say 227 based on paging directly through the *Ṣaḥīḥ*. Cf. M. Fuad Sezgin, *Buhârî'nin kaynakları*, Ankara Üniversitesi İlâhiyat Fakültesi yayınlarından, 13 (Istanbul: Ibrahim Horoz Basimevi, 1956), index; Bukhārī, *al-Imām ᶜAbd Allāh*, 178–9. Sāmarrāʾī continually points his name Ḥabbān ibn Mūsá, but I follow rather Ibn Ḥajar, *Tabṣīr al-muntabih*, ed. ᶜAlī Muḥammad al-Bijāwī, rev. Muḥammad ᶜAlī al-Najjār, Turāthunā, 4 vols (Cairo: al-Dār al-Miṣrīyah, 1964?–7, repr. Beirut: al-Maktabah al-ᶜIlmīyah, n.d.), 1:278.

80. Ibn al-Mubārak, *al-Musnad*, ed. Muṣṭafá ᶜUthmān Muḥammad, with *K. al-Birr wa-al-ṣilah* (Beirut: Dār al-Kutub al-ᶜIlmīyah, 1411 / 1991).
81. Ibn al-Mubārak, *al-Musnad*, ed. Ṣubḥī al-Badrī al-Sāmarrāʾī (Riyadh: Maktabat al-Maᶜārif, 1407 / 1987).
82. Ibn al-Nadīm, *Fihrist, fann* 6, *maqālah* 6 = *Kitâb al-Fihrist*, ed. Gustav Flügel, with Johannes Roediger and August Mueller (Leipzig: F. C. W. Vogel, 1872), 228.
83. See nn. 1, 19.
84. Some mistakes are identified in a master's thesis by Saᶜīd ibn ᶜAlī ibn ᶜAbd Allāh Āl Nāshiᶜ al-Asmarī, 'Kitāb al-Zuhd wa-al-raqāʾiq', Jāmiᶜat Umm al-Qurá, 1423 / 2012, 8–9 (accessed 11 April 2017, available at: http: / / libback.uqu.edu.sa / hipres / FUTXT / 13555.pdf). But this thesis covers only part of the text and compares only the Carullah manuscript. The two Leipzig manuscripts are described by K. Vollers, *Katalog der Handschriften der Universitäts-Bibliothek zu Leipzig* 2: *Die islamischen, christlich-orientalischen, jüdischen und Samaritanischen Handschriften* (Leipzig: Otto Harrassowitz, 1906), 82–5. The second is definitely the recension of al-Ḥusayn al-Marwazī, but Vollers' table of contents differs more widely from the printed version than the table of contents for the first, confirming that section titles are liable to be added and modified by copyists.

CHAPTER

4

EARLY 'TRADITIONIST SUFIS': A NETWORK ANALYSIS

Jeremy Farrell

Introduction

Roy P. Mottahedeh's *Loyalty and Leadership in an Early Islamic Society* articulates a widely cited model of societal cohesion during the late-ᶜAbbasid and Buyid periods, a time typified by rapid institutional segmentation and widespread sectarian antipathies.[1] In the broadest theoretical sense, *Loyalty and Leadership* examines how the conditions that engender group-level specialisation and differentiation motivate cooperation or competition. In a series of astute case studies, Mottahedeh highlights a pervasive ethos of 'negative loyalties' as a barrier to the success of various actors in building and maintaining collaborative ventures.[2] This chapter joins the debate over the dynamics of co-evolutionary social processes during the third and fourth/ninth and tenth centuries by examining the case of cooperation between hadith specialists and Sufis.

By the end of the sixth/twelfth century, mass participation in hadith transmission and Sufi ritual had become dominant features of the intellectual and practical landscape of Sunnism.[3] The later situation appears to contrast sharply with an earlier period when hadith specialists and Sufis are thought to have found little common ground.[4] This model of the diachronic development of relations between hadith specialists and Sufis, which I term the 'split–reconciliation hypothesis', has appeared in various forms; few have articulated its elements with the erudition of Christopher Melchert. In one study of the differentiation of these groups, Melchert echoes the negative-loyalties thesis in his contention that hadith specialists and Sufis achieved only a modicum of comity near the end of the fourth/tenth century, after 'ha[ving] been separated for more than a century'.[5] Even then, he is able to marshal only tacit evidence of shared orientations. Thus, whereas intensive time commitments were the norm for becoming a leading hadith expert or Sufi in the third/ninth century – memorising hundreds of thousands of reports or performing 'heroic' acts of worship, respectively – by the fourth/tenth century, 'it presumably became easier again to pursue both hadith and renunciation'.[6] In Melchert's view, this rapprochement occurred thanks to both the rise of 'authoritative' hadith works, such as the *Ṣaḥīḥayn* of Abū ᶜAbd Allāh al-Bukhārī (d. 256/870) and Muslim ibn al-Ḥajjāj (d. 261/875), and the widespread acceptance amongst the Sufis of a type of piety that prioritised an 'inward moral attitude'.[7]

This account sketches the principal components of the split–reconciliation hypothesis with admirable concision. However, this model of early hadith-specialist and Sufi conflict evinces several distinct weaknesses. The first is historiographical, given that Melchert draws his evidence for early Sufis' activity from prosopographical works that were composed in the late fourth/tenth century or afterward, such as Abū ᶜAbd al-Raḥmān al-Sulamī's (d. 412/1021) *Ṭabaqāt al-ṣūfiyah* and Abū Nuᶜaym al-Iṣfahānī's (d. 430/1038) *Ḥilyat al-awliyāʾ wa-ṭabaqāt al-aṣfiyāʾ*. While this lag should not automatically disqualify such material as unreliable, Melchert elsewhere admits that the choice of these sources is motivated by 'convenience' as much as historicity.[8] The nature of this evidence of a split, in turn, weakens the force of the arguments related to the alleged reconciliation. As for the motivation for a détente between the two sides, the assumption of widespread acknowledgement of the authority of the *Ṣaḥīḥayn* in hadith-specialist circles, much less among Sufis, cannot be taken for granted, as Jonathan A. C. Brown has persuasively argued in his seminal study of the 'canonisation' of these works.[9] Additionally, Melchert 'presumes', rather than demonstrates, that new developments such as the cultivation of an 'inward' piety induced the erstwhile opponents to combine their efforts. While none of these objections individually renders the split–reconciliation hypothesis untenable, it is equally true that consequential details of the relations between the hadith-specialist and Sufi communities that it presupposes remain under-substantiated.

Here, I propose an alternative, novel model of early collaboration between hadith specialists and Sufis. Over the past quarter of a century, fresh primary material that bears directly on the split–reconciliation hypothesis has become available with the publication of several minor hadith works by Sufis who flourished in the late third/ninth and first half of the fourth/tenth centuries. Analysis of the data in these works and a computational examination of prosopographical evidence suggests that these influential early Sufis developed durable strategies for cooperating with contemporary élite hadith scholars.

This argument proceeds in three parts. The first section identifies important points of contact during the third–fourth/ninth–tenth centuries between the hadith specialists and Sufis, a category of actor that Ahmet Karamustafa has aptly termed the 'traditionist Sufi'.[10] These early traditionist Sufis are typified by their reputation as prominent local Sufis and for their varying levels of renown as scholars of hadith. The second section identifies instances in the split–reconciliation hypothesis wherein evidence of early traditionist

Sufis' activity has been misconstrued or unduly marginalised. Finally, the statistical analysis of a network comprising both early élite hadith specialists (*ḥuffāẓ*; sg. *ḥāfiẓ*) and traditionist Sufis suggests that: (1) the hadith-transmission network suffered a significant disruption in its stratum of maximum activity, that of the *ḥuffāẓ*, in the first half of the fourth / tenth century, when the early traditionist Sufis studied here were active; and (2) during this period, early traditionist Sufis were able to construct a distinctive niche for their activities in the hadith-transmission network, despite never influencing the development of hadith transmission in the same measure as the *ḥuffāẓ*.

Early Traditionist Sufis

The focus of this study rests on the interstitial role of five early traditionist Sufis: Abū al-ᶜAbbās Aḥmad ibn Muḥammad *ibn Masrūq* al-Ṭūsī (d. 298 or 299 / 911–13); Abū Saᶜīd Aḥmad ibn Muhammad ibn Ziyād *ibn al-Aᶜrābī* (d. 340 / 952); Abū Muḥammad Jaᶜfar ibn Muḥammad ibn Nuṣayr *al-Khuldī* (d. 348 / 959); Abū ᶜAmr Ismāᶜīl *ibn Nujayd* (d. 366 / 976–7?); and Abū ᶜAbd Allāh Aḥmad ibn ᶜAṭāᵓ *al-Rūdhbārī* (d. 369 / 980).[11] This section briefly introduces these figures' Sufi and *ahl al-ḥadīth* credentials, specifically highlighting their composition of minor hadith works.

Ibn Masrūq was born around 215 / 830–1, according to the reckoning of al-Khaṭīb al-Baghdādī (d. 463 / 1071).[12] After moving to Baghdad, probably in his teenage years, he made the acquaintance of influential Sufis and their affiliates, such as al-Ḥārith ibn Asad al-Muḥāsibī (d. 243 / 857–8), al-Sarī al-Saqaṭī (d. 253 / 867), and Abū al-Qāsim al-Junayd (d. 297 / 910–11), as both al-Sulamī in his *Ṭabaqāt* and Abū Nuᶜaym in *Ḥilyat al-awliyāᵓ* report.[13] An account in the latter source illustrates the esteem Ibn Masrūq was accorded by his Sufi contemporaries. When al-Junayd in a dream asks a group of 'surrogates' (*qawman min al-abdāl*), 'Is there any in Baghdad who is one of the saints (*awliyāᵓ*)?' they identify Ibn Masrūq.[14] Prior to his establishment of Sufi contacts, Ibn Masrūq studied with some of the most prominent hadith specialists in Baghdad, including ᶜAlī ibn al-Madīnī (d. 234 / 849) and Aḥmad ibn Ḥanbal (d. 241 / 855); he would go on to teach the Shāfiᶜī jurist and *ḥāfiẓ*, Abū Bakr Muḥammad ibn ᶜAbd Allāh al-Ṣayrafī (d. 330 / 942). In spite of this association with such prestigious figures, Ibn Masrūq was not admired by later hadith experts: ᶜAlī al-Dāraquṭnī (d. 385 / 995) declared him to be 'not strong, transmitting problematic reports (*muᶜḍilāt*)'; Ibn Ḥajar al-ᶜAsqalānī (d. 852 / 1449) repeats the charge in *Lisān* al-Mīzān.[15] Ibn Masrūq is credited with expertise on *rubāᶜīyāt*, a contemporary genre of profane love poetry: his notice in *Tārīkh Baghdād* highlights his discourses on the subject of love.[16] A single work of his, titled *al-Qanāᶜah* ('Equanimity'), appears to have circulated amongst hadith specialists through the time of Aḥmad al-Dhahabī (d. 748 / 1348).[17] Because this work is not known to be extant, one can only speculate as to its contents, although nine lines from a love poem allegedly quoted from it appear in Ṣalāḥ al-Dīn al-ᶜAlāᵓī's (d. 761 / 1359–60) *Ithārat al-fawāᵓid al-majmūᶜah*.[18]

Ibn al-Aʿrābī was a native of Basra who taught in Damascus and eventually moved to the Ḥijāz, where he became, in al-Dhahabī's view, the 'chief scholar of Mecca' (*shaykh al-ḥaram*).[19] As a Sufi, he is most celebrated for compiling a now-lost prosopographical work, *Ṭabaqāt al-nussāk*, as Alexander Knysh notes in a recent encyclopaedia entry.[20] Regrettably, Knysh's bibliography fails to include references to a substantial body of primary and secondary literature concerning his subject. Ibn al-Aʿrābī's most significant influence on the course of Sufism is a legacy of Andalusian students who transmitted several works that appear to be lost, as can be gathered from Ibn Khayr al-Ishbīlī's (d. 575/1179) *Fahrasah* and other bibliographic works.[21] As a student of hadith, Ibn al-Aʿrābī cultivated a close relationship with Abū Dāwūd al-Sijistānī (d. 275/889) and transmitted recensions of the latter's *Sunan* and *Kitāb al-zuhd*.[22] Among his most famous students was the *ḥāfiẓ* Ibn Mandah (d. 395/1005).[23] Ibn al-Aʿrābī's younger contemporary Abū al-Qāsim al-Ṭabarānī (d. 360/971) rated him 'trustworthy' (*thiqah*), with the proviso that he was prone to 'harmless mistakes' (*awhām lā taḍurru*).[24] Uniquely among the figures studied here, al-Dhahabī included Ibn al-Aʿrābī in his *Tadhkirat al-ḥuffāẓ*.[25] A number of Ibn al-Aʿrābī's works are extant and have been published, including a voluminous accounting of his instructors in the sciences of hadith, variously titled *Kitāb al-Muʿjam* or *Muʿjam Ibn al-Aʿrābī*.[26] In addition to his transmission of a Companion-centric recension of Abū Dāwūd's *Kitāb al-Zuhd*,[27] he compiled his own work on the topic. This has been published twice in Egypt, first by Majdī Fatḥī al-Sayyid, and later by Khadīja Muḥammad Kāmil.[28]

Al-Khuldī was a native of Baghdad who is recorded as having performed the *ḥajj* fifty-six times.[29] As a Sufi, al-Khuldī's fame rests on two prominent contributions to the historiography of the group. Like Ibn al-Aʿrābī, he is also credited with having written a prosopographical work on Sufis, now lost; a possible reference to the contents of this book is preserved in the *Fihrist* of Ibn al-Nadīm (d. 380/990?), who reports that he had an autograph copy of a work by al-Khuldī.[30] Relatedly, al-Khuldī's transmission of a significant number of the sayings of his teacher al-Junayd substantially affected the latter's reputation for mystical 'sobriety' (*ṣaḥw*); he was also a close follower of Ibn Masrūq.[31] In addition to these literary interests, al-Khuldī was an active participant in hadith transmission. In *Tadhkirat al-ḥuffāẓ*, al-Dhahabī classes him as 'one of the great teachers of the world' (*min mashāyikh al-dunyā*) in a recounting of Abū Nuʿaym al-Iṣfahānī's early tutors.[32] Al-Khuldī also transmitted to al-Dāraquṭnī,[33] who, along with al-Ḥākim al-Nīsabūrī (d. 405/1014) and al-Khaṭīb al-Baghdādī, rated him *thiqah*.[34] Al-Khuldī's extant works supply additional details about his career. For instance, he taught at the royal Friday mosque (*jāmiʿ al-Manṣūr*) in Baghdad: Nabīl Saʿd al-Dīn Jarrār has published records of four of these sessions dated to 337/948–9.[35] Another lecture, titled *al-Fawāʾid wa-al-zuhd wa-al-raqāʾiq wa-al-marāthī*, contains hadith as well as other narrative material and was also edited by Majdī Fatḥī al-Sayyid Ibrāhīm.[36] This work circulated in Baghdad and Damascus;

in the latter, the *ḥāfiẓ* Jamāl al-Dīn al-Mizzī (d. 742/1342) transmitted it to al-Dhahabī, who appears to confirm this in a remark that he possessed a copy of al-Khuldī's dictations (*majālis amālīh*).[37]

Ibn Nujayd was a Nishapuri scholar and mystic. His reputation for piety and scholarship was such that Ibn al-Jawzī (d. 597/1201) would indelibly memorialise him as 'the lordly traditionist' (*al-muḥaddith al-rabbānī*).[38] His main contribution to the history of Sufism is the bequest to his grandson al-Sulamī of a sizable library.[39] This material may have been acquired during Ibn Nujayd's early travels, which took him to Rayy and Baghdad; in the latter, he studied hadith with ᶜAbd Allāh ibn Aḥmad ibn Ḥanbal (d. 290/903).[40] His student al-Ḥākim rated him *thiqah*.[41] As an author, Ibn Nujayd compiled a fascicle (*juz*ᵓ) which, like al-Khuldī's *al-Fawā*ᵓ*id*, reached al-Dhahabī; the latter judged this to have been amongst the highest quality hadith works in his possession.[42] The text has been published twice, first as part of a collection edited by Khallāf Maḥmūd ᶜAbd al-Samīᶜ and again by Bilal Orfali and Gerhard Böwering.[43]

Less is known about al-Rūdhbārī, who travelled widely and died in Manwāth (modern Lebanon).[44] Al-Sulamī identifies him as 'the *shaykh* of the Levant' and as the nephew of another prominent Baghdadi Sufi, Abū ᶜAlī al-Rūdhbārī (d. 322/935–6).[45] Otherwise, neither al-Sulamī nor Abū Nuᶜaym associates him by name with other Sufis, although he was a prominent informant for Abū Naṣr al-Ṭūsī, author of a famous theoretical work on Sufism, *Kitāb al-Lumaᶜ fī al-taṣawwuf*.[46] As for al-Rūdhbārī's reputation in hadith circles, al-Khaṭīb al-Baghdādī judged him harshly for transmitting hadiths in a severely incorrect manner (*rawá aḥādīth ghalaṭan fāḥishan*); Ibn Ḥajar repeats al-Khaṭīb's charge and gives the correct death date, but mistakenly refers to al-Rūdhbārī by his uncle's teknonym (*kunyah*).[47] Despite this judgement, al-Rūdhbārī was well-known to at least two prominent *ḥuffāẓ*, having studied under al-Qāḍī Ismāᶜīl ibn al-Ḥusayn al-Maḥāmilī (d. 330/942) and teaching Abū ᶜAbd Allāh Muḥammad al-Ṣūrī (d. 441/1049). Like al-Khuldī, the younger al-Rūdhbārī lectured on hadith at a *jāmi*ᶜ, though in Ṣūr; Bernd Radtke has published a record of three such lectures in a recent volume.[48]

To better understand the importance of these individuals as exponents of both the Sufi and hadith-specialist communities, an examination of why they have not figured prominently in previous studies proves instructive.[49] The next section relates how evidence of early traditionist Sufis' status and activity in hadith transmission has been misapprehended or downplayed in order to highlight discrete aspects of the split–reconciliation hypothesis of interaction between these two groups.

The 'Split–Reconciliation Hypothesis' Revisited

As a paradigm for understanding hadith-specialist and Sufi relations, the split–reconciliation hypothesis posits two essential stages: an initial, sharp rift between the two parties, followed by an eventual rapprochement. Under scrutiny, it becomes evident that this model operates according to three key assumptions: non-overlapping membership, especially at the élite level; non-overlapping methodologies or epistemologies; and the importance of a single individual who effectively closed the rift between the two sides. However, much scholarship develops a specific thesis concerning only one of these elements independently from the others; therefore, it will be useful to pull together the arguments for this model to evaluate their merits.

Although several scholars have contributed to the split–reconciliation model, Melchert's studies are remarkable for their detailed presentation of an initial cleavage, based primarily on prosopographical evidence. In one study, based on a comparison of Sufi prosopography and hadith-centric *rijāl* literature, he finds negative evidence of substantial overlap of the groups' memberships. That is, 'outstanding hadith transmitters from the tenth century onward were seldom outstanding Sufis, and likewise outstanding Sufis were seldom outstanding experts in hadith'.[50] In some cases, Melchert claims to have found evidence that early Sufis, 'oppose[d] outright the collection and transmission of hadith'.[51] Additionally, Melchert contends that a significant split took place between the early Sufis and Aḥmad ibn Ḥanbal and his early successors, the *Ḥanābilah*, some of whom were leading hadith specialists.[52] Recep Şentürk elaborates Melchert's prosopographical explorations through the conceptual lens of 'interdomain brokerage' among *ḥuffāẓ*, identifying instances where an individual *ḥāfiẓ* was also recognised as an expert in another field (for example: grammar or poetry).[53] In the resulting analysis, Şentürk finds that only a single *ḥāfiẓ*, apparently Ibn al-Aᶜrābī, exhibited inter-domain brokerage between the Sufi and hadith-specialist networks before the year 349/960. This finding does not appear to be confined to Sufis, as only about 14 per cent (178/1226) of all *ḥuffāẓ* exhibited excellence in more than one domain.[54]

Given the low rate of inter-domain brokerage between Sufis and hadith specialists, several scholars have concentrated on describing the factors that drove the apparent split. Brown, for one, identifies an interest in the technicalities of hadith as a crucial boundary marker between the two groups. In agreement with Louis Masignon and Hamid Algar concerning the type of hadith favoured by Sufis and other mystics like al-Ḥusayn ibn Manṣūr al-Ḥallāj (ex. 309/922), Brown further argues that even when Sufis did concern themselves with genres of hadith, their preference for reports that were dubiously 'divine' in provenance (hadith *qudsī*) or 'loose' (*mursal*) defied the rigorous standards of validity set by the hadith specialists.[55] Lahcen Daäif extends this argument by acknowledging the hadith-specialist credentials of al-Sulamī and Abū Nuᶜaym, while simultaneously accusing them of circumventing the criteria for *al-jarḥ wa-al-taᶜdīl* ('transmitter criticism') in order to rehabilitate feeble scholars or blatant forgers.[56] Additionally, Brown maintains that Sufis' intellectual interest in living *isnād*s linking the individual with the Prophet concerned not the transmission of the example of the Prophet and Companions, but of a *khirqah*, a distinctive initiatory garment.[57] He supports this contention through a reference to Ibn al-Nadīm's account in the *Fihrist*, portraying al-Khuldī's employment of an *isnād* not as a means for authenticating hadith, but rather for demonstrating the unbroken lineage of prominent Sufis 'from the Prophet'.[58]

Finally, with respect to the reconciliation stage of this model, numerous scholars have attempted to locate a single individual who brought the ongoing rift to a close. A century of scholarship has continually pushed the date of this rapprochement earlier. Duncan MacDonald first proposed Abū Ḥāmid al-Ghazālī (d. 505/1111) as the synthesiser of Sufi experience and 'orthodox' sensibilities.[59] Soon thereafter, Ignaz Goldziher found a forerunner to al-Ghazālī's example in Abū al-Qāsim al-Qushayrī (d. 465/1072), a finding later scrutinised by A. J. Arberry.[60] Rkia Cornell argues that al-Sulamī almost single-handedly wedded the mystical worldview of Sufism to the hadith-philic epistemology of the Shāfiʿī school of law, a process she terms the '*uṣūl*-ization' of Sufism.[61] A fully tenth-century reconciliation is proposed by Florian Sobieroj, who details the exploits of Abū ʿAbd Allāh Muḥammad *ibn Khafīf* al-Shīrāzī (d. 371/982), who attempted to ease the agitation between Shirazi hadith specialists and Sufis.[62] In Ibn Khafīf, Karamustafa finds his first instance of a 'traditionist Sufi' and extends the sobriquet to Abū al-Ḥasan ʿAlī ibn Jahḍam al-Hamadhānī (d. 414/1023–4).[63] Most recently, Melchert has tentatively cast Ibn al-Aʿrābī as a key harmonising figure because of his roles as transmitter of Abū Dāwūd's *Sunan* and as a prominent student of al-Junayd.[64]

The data that underpin these arguments clearly suggest increasing specialisation and coherence amongst and between these two movements during the third–fourth/ninth–tenth centuries, as Melchert notes.[65] This being the case, these studies that portray resolutely distant relations between early Sufis and their hadith-specialist counterparts until a relatively late date consequentially misstate or over-state key evidence for their claims. The following points illustrate this contention through the example of the traditionist Sufis or their close contemporaries, as well as data related to the former group's minor hadith works.

On the issue of the low rate of inter-domain brokerage between hadith specialists and Sufis, it must be admitted that the negative evidence that is gleaned from a comparison of the respective prosopographical literature is compelling. Nevertheless, a simple error sometimes weakens the portrayal of certain aspects of a 'split'. One example of this relates to Melchert's observation that many Sufis rejected hadith transmission outright. In support of this contention, he relates an anecdote involving al-Khuldī, who is alleged to have 'reminisced that he had not gone to hear ʿAbbās al-Dūrī [a noted student of Aḥmad ibn Ḥanbal; d. 271/884] in his youth because a Sufi had discouraged him'.[66] For this report, Melchert cites *Tārīkh Baghdād*; but in fact the text reads: 'I went to ʿAbbās al-Dūrī while I was young, and I wrote down one lesson on his authority', after which a scuffle occurs between al-Khuldī and an anonymous hadith-hostile Sufi.[67] While the point stands that, in the person of the unnamed foil, some Sufis may have openly discouraged engagement with hadith specialists, other historical figures like al-Khuldī proved willing to risk any resulting opprobrium to learn from their contemporaries.

Reliance on prosopographical data as indicative of a lack of overlapping networks implicates other issues related to the argument from silence; what appears to be firm evidence may equally indicate a 'mismatch' of salient data.[68] One example of this comes in the presentation of the intersection of *Ḥanābilah* and Sufi networks. Here, Melchert restricts his attention almost exclusively to figures from the first generation (*ṭabaqah*), of a total of five, in al-Sulamī's *Ṭabaqāt*, the only exception being al-Junayd, whose notice appears in the second generation. This limited scope precludes the consideration of other figures largely contemporary with al-Junayd, who are reliably tied both to Sufis and the *Ḥanābilah*, like Abū al-ᶜAbbās ibn ᶜAṭāʾ al-Ādamī (ex. 309/922), from the third generation.[69] At other times, results obtained through an argument from silence seem overly restrictive. In the discussion of 'leading' Sufis with established relationships with the *Ḥanābilah*, Melchert does not consider Ibn Masrūq and his teachers, Muḥammad ibn al-Ḥusayn al-Burjulānī (d. 238/852–3)[70] and Muḥammad ibn Manṣūr al-Ṭūsī (d. Baghdad, 254/867),[71] because of their alleged failure to meet the following criteria: association with al-Junayd or his teachers; a record of 'mystical' rather than 'ascetical' sayings; and a legacy of 'important' Sufi disciples.[72] As noted above, Ibn Masrūq's bona fide relationship with al-Junayd, his status as one of the *awliyāʾ* with an interest in mystical love theory, and his formative teaching relationship with another important Sufi – al-Khuldī – build a strong case for considering his role in maintaining cooperative links with an influential cadre of hadith specialists.[73]

The discussion of discursive differences between Sufis and hadith specialists also suffers from intermittent imprecisions. For instance, and contrary to Brown's claim that al-Khuldī's *khirqah*-specific *isnād* reached back 'to the Prophet', the account given in the *Fihrist* contains neither a reference to a *khirqah* nor a direct invocation of Muḥammad's legacy. Instead, al-Khuldī's *isnād* ends with Anas ibn Mālik (d. *c.* 91–3/709–12), one of the most highly-respected Companions in the eyes of later authorities of hadith.[74] Similarly, the contention that early mystics and Sufis were unconcerned with the sophisticated discourse of hadith scholarship is belied by several records of such activity. The earliest of these is the *Nawādir al-uṣūl fī maᶜrifat aḥādīth al-rasūl* by the important early mystic al-Ḥakīm al-Tirmidhī (d. 318/936 or 320/938?).[75] Similarly, al-Sulamī's extensive correspondence with al-Dāraquṭnī concerning his opinions on transmitters also sheds light on the appeal of scrutinising the technicalities of *isnād*s to at least one important Sufi who was active in the fourth/tenth century.[76] Despite a seeming lack of evidence that the early traditionist Sufis discussed above engaged with technical issues on this level, the surviving minor hadith works by Ibn al-Aᶜrābī, al-Khuldī, Ibn Nujayd and al-Rūdhbārī, described above, demonstrate a concern with transmitting authenticated material (see, Table 4.1). Including repetitions, these works contain a total of 362 accounts; approximately 53 per cent of these (180) constitute reports about the Prophet or Companions, the quality of which hews closely to the criteria espoused by hadith specialists.[77] When judged by the coincidence of reports from the so-called 'Six Books' accepted by Sunni hadith scholars, or later 'adjustments' to the 'proto-canon' by Ibn Khuzaymah (d. 311/924), al-Ṭabarānī and al-Dāraquṭnī,[78] the contents of these minor Sufi works certainly must not be dismissed as spurious. In fact, almost 80 per cent (107/134) of the Prophetic material in these works accords with material in the hadith-specialist corpus. In this regard, it is unsurprising that later eminent hadith specialists like al-Mizzī and al-Dhahabī found otherwise marginal works like al-Khuldī's and Ibn Nujayd's to be worthy of preservation and transmission.

Finally, these data strongly support the analytical utility of Karamustafa's category of 'traditionist Sufis', who were both prominent Sufis and, at the least, reliably connected to respected hadith specialists. In fact, rather than a single figure effecting the closure of an existing rift, the traditionist Sufis expanded upon the initial model of cooperation provided by Ibn Masrūq, who was active in élite hadith transmission circles as early as the first half of the third/ninth century. However, one should not push these conclusions too far. The scarcity of early traditionist Sufis and the lone example of Ibn al-Aᶜrābī as a *ḥāfiẓ* confirms Melchert and Şentürk's conclusion that outstanding hadith transmitters were seldom outstanding Sufis, and vice versa. Furthermore, although figures like al-Khuldī devoted themselves to both the circle of al-Junayd, and learning and teaching hadith, it is certainly possible that some contemporary Sufis or hadith transmitters were discouraged from pursuing both specialisations. Nevertheless, the contention that by the mid-fourth/tenth century the major factions of the hadith-specialist and Sufi movements 'had been separated for more than a century', gains a useful measure of qualification, insofar as this small contingent of traditionist Sufis replicated successful relations with both sides during this period.

If I have characterised the interpretive strategies of the split–reconciliation hypothesis correctly, then it should be clear that persuasive evidence of either an all-encompassing rift between the hadith specialists and Sufis, or a momentous reunion between them, is lacking. Rather, and in spite of the tensions which may have contributed to the differentiation of Baghdadi Sufism and hadith specialists, the example of these early traditionist Sufis suggests that there existed persistent and ultimately successful efforts to engage in both pursuits. Thus, there is a clear need to account for the nature of the traditionist Sufis' cohort with greater specificity than has heretofore been achieved. The next section proposes network analysis as one method that can realise this ambition.

The Dynamics of Hadith Transmission: A Network Analysis

By studying the statistical properties of networks, researchers in numerous fields have gained significant insights into the structure and strategies of cooperative or competitive behaviour.[79] In the field of Islamic studies, the methodological and analytical insights of network analysis remain mostly unrealised, apart from a small group of social historians.[80] In relation to the study of hadith, the invocation a 'network' as a matrix of sustained relationships functions mostly as an abstraction, and does not engage more technical literature on the subject.[81] Here, the discussion will be limited to describing in formal terms the dynamics of the hadith-transmission network of the third–fourth / ninth–tenth centuries, and to observing evidence of traditionist Sufis' development of their own hierarchical niche therein.[82]

Before elaborating the specifics of the historical hadith-transmission network, an explanation of some key concepts in the field of network studies will demonstrate their utility. Every network is composed of nodes and edges. In this case, the nodes are figures who transmitted hadith, the edges a record of the association of two figures in a teacher–student relationship. Because it is known in the case of hadith transmitters that influence is transmitted through an edge – from a teacher (source) to a student (target) – it is possible to employ concepts that have been developed through the observation of 'directional' networks. Two interdependent measures that have proven useful in studying the properties of these networks are 'prominence' and 'centrality'.[83] Generally speaking, 'prominence' refers to the number of connections that obtain for a given node, which is often referred to as its 'degree'. 'Centrality' can be defined in terms of a given node's local or global density of connections to other nodes; for instance, a given node can be 'central' in relation to other nodes in its immediate vicinity (that is, other nodes with which it is directly connected by an edge), a situation expressed by the metric 'harmonic closeness'. Separate metrics are used to deduce the influence a given node exerts over the structure of an entire network; these include 'eigenvector' and 'betweenness' centrality. Nodes that exhibit high levels of eigenvector or betweenness centrality thus strongly influence the development of a directed network.[84] In the present study, these metrics will serve to illuminate the niche that traditionist Sufis occupied vis-à-vis contemporary *ḥuffāẓ*.

To date, Şentürk's *Narrative Social Structure* represents the most extensive application of network theory to hadith transmission. The work is an attempt to use abstract models of social evolution with the aim of supplementing narrative accounts of large-scale historical networks.[85] Unfortunately, Şentürk at times contributes to the discussion through negative example, as in his treatment of the earliest periods of hadith transmission.[86] However, his analyses of other aspects of the network properties of *ḥuffāẓ* prove highly prescient of results obtained through more traditional modes of scholarship. This can be seen in his treatment of the concept of 'geodesic distance', a metric that correlates strongly with 'betweenness', discussed above. In studying this network property, he aims to show that hadith specialists actively sought to minimise the geodesic distance between themselves and the Prophet Muḥammad by connecting themselves to highly prominent hadith transmitters of earlier generations.[87] With respect to this property, Şentürk has solidly quantified the existence of two distinct temporal phases of hadith transmission amongst *ḥuffāẓ*. In the first phase (*c.* 100–360/718–970), edge formation between a given *ḥāfiẓ* and his teachers and students occurred at a distance of two geodesic units (that is, teachers were, on average, from two 'generations' earlier, students from two later). The stability of this pattern eroded sharply beginning around 361/971, whereafter the geodesic distance of teacher and student interactions spanned only one generation.[88] Şentürk infers that this apparent sea change in the pattern of the cooperative association of *ḥuffāẓ* is attributable to the canonisation of the *Ṣaḥīḥayn* and other Sunni hadith works. This conclusion, derived only from the analysis of documented edges between nodes in the hadith-transmission network of *ḥuffāẓ*, prefigures with extraordinary precision Brown's timeline of the 'intensive process of canonization' to which these works were subjected.[89]

If Şentürk's data concerning the macro-evolution of the élite stratum of the hadith-transmission network between the third/ninth and the fifth/eleventh century can be accepted as largely correct,[90] then these data can be used as a basis for investigating the processes of hierarchical differentiation within this network, as well. This task involves selecting a cadre of *ḥuffāẓ* that represent the maximum level of activity in the hadith-transmission network, as well as identifying the patterns of association for other actors, such as traditionist Sufis. In order to delimit the number of *ḥuffāẓ* under consideration, the three most 'central' *ḥuffāẓ* of a given generation, as determined by Şentürk, are used to develop the network 'skeleton'. Duncan J. Watts has demonstrated the utility of assigning a 'substrate' to this initial structure in order to establish a lower boundary for the analysis of patterns of association.[91] In the present study, this substrate comprises the three leading *ḥuffāẓ* from the earliest stratum with which Ibn Masrūq did not establish a relationship as a student; the upper boundary of the network includes the students of the 'second wave' of traditionist Sufis, the generation of al-Sulamī and Abū Nuᶜaym (Table 4.2).

From this nodal skeleton, additional nodes are added by compiling the node and edge lists of these figures' 'significant' teachers and students as they are preserved in two works: al-Dhahabī's *Siyar aᶜlām al-nubalāʾ* and al-Khaṭīb's *Tārīkh Baghdād*.[92] Here, 'significant' indicates that a given node has at least two edges, with at least one other node. A node can thus be significant given the following minimum conditions: (1) node (*x*) is connected by an edge with at least two other nodes (*y*) and (*z*); or, (2) *Siyar* and *Tārīkh Baghdād* both record that node (*x*) was connected to node (*y*).[93] The choice of *Siyar* and *Tārīkh Baghdād* to provide this data can be defended on the basis of two considerations. First, the more catholic scope of al-Dhahabī's *Siyar*, compared with *Tadhkirat al-ḥuffāẓ*, offers a wider pool of data to describe the traditionist Sufis. Whereas only Ibn al-Aᶜrābī merits a biographical notice in *Tadhkirat al-ḥuffāẓ*, all of the traditionist Sufis appear in *Siyar*. As for *Tārīkh Baghdād*, it serves, in some cases, as one of the first prosopographical works to preserve extensive records of traditionist Sufis' contacts with hadith specialists. However, unlike in the *Siyar*, neither Ibn al-Aᶜrābī nor Ibn Nujayd has a biographical notice in *Tārīkh Baghdād*. This mismatch of data introduces a bias in the resulting analysis towards Ibn Masrūq, al-Khuldī and al-Rūdhbārī, although this can be justified: if the Sufis tied strongly to Baghdad played as important a role in the development of the movement as is commonly accepted, then capturing the clearest possible picture of the associations that traditionist Sufis formed in Baghdad should be prioritised.

There are 439 significant nodes in this model of the hadith-transmission network (*c*. 165–442/780–1050), and 1,336 directed edges between them.[94] Using the network analysis software *Gephi*, we compute the metrics of degree, and eigenvector, harmonic closeness, and betweenness centralities in order to provide a working basis to describe macro-trends of edge formation within this network (Table 4.3). The distributions for degree and eigenvector centrality are normal, meaning that they conform roughly to the 'bell-shaped curve'. However, the distributions for harmonic closeness and betweenness centralities exhibit a pronounced right-tailed skew, indicating that these metrics identify only a small number of nodes with significant scores. For the model of the hadith-transmission network under consideration, a mere thirty-two nodes (7.3 per cent of total) exhibit non-trivial harmonic centrality, and twenty-nine nodes (6.6 per cent of total) exhibit non-trivial betweenness centrality.[95] Because the properties of harmonic closeness and betweenness exclude large parts of this representation of the hadith-transmission network, it can be said that this network exhibits a pronounced hierarchy. We turn now to an examination of the contributions of the hadith specialists and traditionist Sufis to this process of hierarchisation.

For every metric related to the *ḥuffāẓ* there is a clear and steep drop-off from the third/ninth to the fourth/tenth century, although an analysis of distinctive subsets of *ṭabaqah* (X) shows that a high degree of variability in network metrics was possible even at the highest reaches of the hadith-transmission network (Table 4.4). The average degree roughly halves between *ṭabaqah* (IX) and the final *ṭabaqah* (XIV), members of which died in the fifth/eleventh century. The density of significant connections craters both in terms of local (harmonic) and global (eigenvector) centrality: the latter metric decreases by nearly 92 per cent from a zenith in the mid-third-/ninth-century *ṭabaqah* (IX) to the mid-fourth-/tenth-century *ṭabaqah* (XIII); the former metric drops by approximately one-third (~ 34 per cent) from *ṭabaqah*s (IX)–(XIII). Likewise, the drop in betweenness (~ 59 per cent) during this same stretch suggests that *ḥuffāẓ* who died in the second half of the fourth/tenth century were less effective catalysts for the influence of their teachers' generations. The evidence of a significant shake-up of the the stratum of *ḥuffāẓ* in the hadith transmission network is unmistakable. This feature of the *ḥuffāẓ* network may, in part, help to contextualise the decrease in geodesic distance throughout the network that Şentürk has identified.

As for traditionist Sufis, the metrics for their activities can be characterised in relation to the *ḥuffāẓ* as both inferior and relatively stable with respect to the *ḥuffāẓ*. From the time of Ibn Masrūq to al-Rūdhbārī, there is either slight convergence in the metrics of degree or centrality relative to contemporary hadith specialists or none at all, with the obvious exception of Ibn al-Aᶜrābī (Tables 4.5, 4.6). This finding suggests a further instance of hierarchisation between most of the traditionist Sufis and their hadith-specialist contemporaries. A similarly stable aspect of the traditions Sufi stratum of activity involves their role as teachers, particularly their ability to attract students who became *ḥuffāẓ*. According to previously outlined data, every traditions Sufi examined here proved to be a productive teacher who taught at least one *ḥāfiẓ*, and sometimes multiple *ḥuffāẓ*. This finding of consistent interactions between the traditionist Sufi and *ḥuffāẓ* strata in the hadith transmission network suggests that the 'second wave' of early traditionist Sufis represented by Ibn al-Aᶜrābī, al-Khuldī, Ibn Nujayd, and al-Rūdhbārī reflect the dynamics of a particularly crucial phase of cooperation between hadith specialists and Sufis. A fuller treatment of the available data would determine the criteria by which to distinguish Ibn al-Aᶜrābī from his fellow traditionist Sufis, but the success of al-Khuldī, Ibn Nujayd and al-Rūdhbārī in influencing the topmost stratum of hadith scholarship, without becoming themselves *ḥuffāẓ*, suggests the existence of distinctive hierarchical niche for these actors within the hadith-transmission network. The example of later traditionist Sufis like Ibn Khafīf, al-Sulamī and al-Qushayrī, underscores the resilience of this niche with the passage of time.

Conclusion

Despite precarious numbers, an early cohort of traditionist Sufis exhibited positive loyalties to both the hadith-specialist and Sufi communities during the latter half of the third / ninth and the entirety of the fourth / tenth centuries. As a Sufi, each was remembered as among the most impactful and well-respected figures of his era and locale by later Sufi historians. As participants in hadith transmission, traditionist Sufis enjoyed relationships with élite hadith specialists; this latter group at times praised the merits of the Sufis' hadith scholarship and also played a key role in the transmission of their minor hadith works. Network analysis of records of the patterns of association between *ḥuffāẓ* and traditionist Sufis confirms that most early traditionist Sufis can be distinguished hierarchically from contemporary *ḥuffāẓ*. Nevertheless, close analysis of these records also indicates traditionist Sufis effectively directed cooperation between the two movements. The success of traditionist Sufis in constructing a niche within the hadith-transmission network thereby provided a model that endured for centuries within the wider Sunni community.

Table 4.1 Concurrence between traditionist Sufi and proto-canonical hadith works*

Author	Prophetic Reports			Companion Reports		Other
	'Six Books'	'Adjustment'	None	Six Books	Adjustment	
Ibn al-Aʿrābī**	17	2	9	4	3	80
Al-Khuldī (a)	3	2	1	3	1	40
Al-Khuldī (b)	33	13	4	9	8	10
Ibn Nujayd	33	2	8	10	3	7
Al-Rūdhbārī	15	1	9	9	1	18
Totals	101	20	31	35	20	155

* The works considered here are Ibn al-Aʿrābī, *Kitāb al-Zuhd* (ed. al-Sayyid); al-Khuldī (a), *Fawāʾid*, and (b), *Majālis*; Ibn Nujayd, *Juzʾ* (ed. Orfali and Böwering); Rūdhbārī, *Majālis*. These counts are taken from the editors' notes and *takhrīj*. Note that Radtke erroneously describes four reports as missing in the proto-canon (Radtke, *Materialien*, D, XII [found in Ibn Khuzayma, *Ṣaḥīḥ*]), or six books (Radtke, *Materialien*, D, XXXII, XXIII, XXXVI [found in Ibn Mājah, *Sunan*]).
** Note that there are twenty-two repetitions of reports in *Kitāb al-Zuhd*.

Table 4.2 Most 'central' *ḥuffāẓ* by *ṭabaqah*,* arranged chronologically

Generation	'Central' Figures
VII	ʿAbd Allāh ibn al-Mubārak (d. 181/797); Yaḥyá ibn Saʿīd al-Qaṭṭān (d. 198/813); Sufyān ibn ʿUyaynah (d. 198/814)
VIII	Abū Dāwūd al-Ṭayālisī (d. 204/819?); Abū Nuʿaym al-Faḍl ibn Dukayn (d. 219/834); Abū Zakariyāʾ al-Naysābūrī (d. 226/840)
IX	Yaḥyá ibn Maʿīn (d. 233/848); Isḥāq ibn Rāhawayh (d. 238/853); Aḥmad ibn Ḥanbal (d. 241/855)
X**	(a) Muḥammad ibn Ismāʿīl al-Bukhārī (d. 256/870); Muslim ibn al-Ḥajjāj (d. 261/875); Abū Zurʿah al-Rāzī (d. 264/880) (b) Abū ʿAbd Allāh Muḥammad ibn Yaḥyá al-Dhuhlī (d. 258/872); Abū Ḥātim al-Rāzī (d. 277/890); Abū Dāwūd al-Sijistānī (d. 275/889)
XI	Muḥammad Ibn Mājah (d. 273/887); Aḥmad ibn Shuʿayb al-Nasāʾī (d. 303/915); Abū Bakr Muḥammad ibn Isḥāq ibn Khuzaymah (d. 311/924)
XII	Abū Ḥāmid Ibn al-Sharqī (d. 325/937); Abū Bakr Muḥammad ibn ʿAbd Allāh al-Ṣayrafī al-Shāfiʿī (d. 330/942); al-Qāḍī al-Maḥāmilī (d. 330/942)
XIII	Abū ʿAlī al-Naysābūrī (d. 349/960); Abū al-Qāsim Sulaymān al-Ṭabarānī (d. 360/971); ʿAlī al-Dāraquṭnī (d. 385/995)
XIV	Abū ʿAbd Allāh Muḥammad Ibn Mandah (d. 395/1005); al-Ḥākim al-Naysābūrī (d. 405/1014); Abū Nuʿaym al-Iṣfahānī (d. 430/1038)

* Şentürk, *Narrative Social Structure*, 222–3.
** Figures from (a) are taken from Şentürk's list. The first two figures from (b) are taken from Brown's discussion (*Canonization*, 86–90) of the pushback against the *Ṣaḥīḥayn*; additionally, Abū Dāwūd is included as a control for a *ḥāfiẓ* strongly connected to a traditionist Sufi (Ibn al-Aʿrābī).

Table 4.3 Mean metrics of prominence and centrality among *ḥuffāẓ*

Generation	Death Date Range	Degree	Eigenvector Centrality	Harmonic Closeness Centrality	Betweenness Centrality*
VII	181–98/797–814	161.6	0.289	0.409	N/A**
VIII	204–26/819–40	143.3	0.116†	0.421	0.00072
IX	223–41/847–55	198.3	0.474	0.519	0.00780
X (*a*)	256–64/870–7	165.6	0406	0.498	0.00645
X (*b*)	258–75/871–89	120	0.335	0.437	0.00281
XI	273–311/887–924‡	79.6	0.160	0.417	0.00428
XII	328–54/940–64	82	0.124	0.378	0.00401
XIII	349–85/960–95	56.3	0.039	0.342	0.00325
XIV	405–430/1005–38	95.3	0.032	0.400	N/A

* The range for recorded degrees of betweenness centrality is 0.359 (al-Rūdhbārī) to 285.777 (Aḥmad ibn Ḥanbal).
** In the case of both (VII) and (XIV), the betweenness centrality measure is incomplete, as it does not account for the connections, respectively, to teachers and students, and markedly skews the impression of the importance of these generations. Eigenvector and harmonic closeness centrality measures, are, however, useful for context, as will be argued.
† The relatively low degree of betweenness in *ṭabaqah* (VIII) can be attributed to the fact that figures in this *ṭabaqah* were sometimes taught by those who preceded even *ṭabaqah* (VII); therefore, this latter group is not well-represented in the dataset, and many of the nodes did not form 'significant' connections, as described above.
‡ Neither the eigenvector nor betweenness centrality metrics for XI includes Ibn Mājah because he evinces the lowest possible score of 0 based on the data compiled here. This is because all his teachers were connected only to him, and therefore considered not 'significant' by the criteria given above. The inverse principle holds for his score in the metric of harmonic centrality, in which he evinces the highest possible score of 1. The measure of his degree and eigenvector centrality is therefore also based uniquely on connections to his students.

Table 4.4 Variability in prominence and centrality in *ṭabaqah* (X)

Generation	Figures	Degree	Harmonic Closeness Centrality	Eigenvector Centrality	Betweenness Centrality
X (*a*)	al-Bukhārī	158	0.508	0.453	0.01034
	Muslim	258	0.532	0.414	0.00795
	Abū Zurᶜah al-Rāzī	81	0.455	0.351	0.00106
X (*b*)	Abū ᶜAbd Allāh al-Dhuhlī	95	0.404	0.304	0.00129
	Abū Ḥātim al-Rāzī	116	0.445	0.369	0.00288
	Abū Dāwūd al-Sijistānī	149	0.460	0.333	0.00426

Table 4.5 Comparison of traditionist Sufis with contemporary *ḥuffāẓ* (*fl.* third / ninth century)

Figures	Metrics with Normal Distribution*		Metrics with Right-skewed Distribution**	
	Degree	Eigenvector Centrality	Harmonic Closeness Centrality	Betweenness Centrality
X–XI	117.2 (± 21.7)	0.282 (± 0.048)	72%	89.6%
Ibn Masrūq	32 (–4.1)	0.095 (–3.9)	53.1% (–19.9%)	75.9% (–13.7%)

* Measures for *ḥuffāẓ ṭabaqahs* are given as 'mean (standard error of the mean)'. Raw values for traditionist Sufis are followed by the 'z-score' in parentheses. The latter describes the distance from the raw score from units of standard error of the mean. A score of –1 thus indicates the figure is one standard error below average, –2 indicates two standard errors below average, and so on.

** Given the low number of nodes which evince non-trivial measures of these metrics (29, and 32, respectively), scores for both *ḥuffāẓ* and traditionist Sufis given as percentile, calculated according to the normal cumulative distribution function, given that no attempt was made here to fit the data to a model; the disparity between the traditionist Sufis percentile and that of the mean of the contemporary *ṭabaqah* is given in parentheses. A measure of 90% is a value above which 10% of the observations may be found.

Table 4.6 Comparison of traditionist Sufis with contemporary *ḥuffāẓ* (*fl.* fourth / tenth century)

Figures	Metrics with Normal Distribution		Metrics with Right-skewed Distribution	
	Degree	Eigenvector Centrality	Harmonic Closeness Centrality	Betweenness Centrality
XII–XIII	70.9 (± 11.1)	0.076 (± 0.018)	28.1%	65.6%
Ibn al-Aᶜrābī	42 (–2.5)	0.061 (–0.8)	96.9% (+68.8%)	41.4% (–24.2%)
Al-Khuldī	59 (–1.6)	0.019 (–3.1)	21.9% (–6.2%)	48.3% (–17.3%)
Ibn Nujayd	30 (–3.6)	0.002 (–4.1)	3.1% (–25.0%)	0.0% (N/A)
al-Rūdhbārī	23 (–4.2)	0.023 (–2.9)	12.5% (–15.6%)	13.8% (–51.8%)

Notes

1. Roy P. Mottahedeh, *Loyalty and Leadership in an Early Islamic Society*, 2nd edn (Princeton, NJ: Princeton University Press, 2001). Compare with Hugh Kennedy, 'The Late ᶜAbbāsid Pattern', in Chase F. Robinson (ed.), *The New Cambridge History of Islam, vol. 1: The Formation of the Islamic World, Sixth to Eleventh Centuries* (Cambridge: Cambridge University Press, 2010), 360–93; Maaiike van Berkel, Nadia El-Cheikh, Hugh Kennedy and Letizia Osti (eds), *Crisis and Continuity*

at the Abbasid Court: Formal and Informal Politics in the Caliphate of Muqtadir (295–320/908–32), Islamic History and Civilization, Studies and Texts, 102 (Leiden: Brill, 2013); and esp. Jonathan A. C. Brown, '[Revised] A Man for All Seasons: Ibn ᶜUqdah and Crossing Sectarian Boundaries in the 4th/10th Century', *Al-ᶜUṣūr al-Wusṭā* 24 ([2008] 2016): 139–44.

2. Mottahedeh, *Loyalty and Leadership*, 4. The nature of 'positive loyalties', as expressed in oaths and vows, is discussed at ibid., 40–1.
3. Marshall G. S. Hodgson, *The Venture of Islam*, 3 vols (Chicago: University of Chicago Press, 1974), 1:408. Hodgson relies extensively on the first editions of two works by Louis Massignon, *Passion d'al-Hosayn-Ibn-Mansûr al-Hallâj: martyr mystique de l'Islam, exécuté à Bagdad le 26 Mars 922. Étude d'histoire religieuse*, 4 vols, 2nd edn (Paris: Paul Geuthner, [1922] 1975), translated as *The Passion of al-Ḥallāj: Mystic and Martyr of Islam*, trans. Herbert Mason, 4 vols (Princeton, NJ: Princeton University Press, 1982), 1 (subsequently cited as *Passion*, according to the [1975] / [1982] editions); and Louis Massignon, *Essai sur les origines du lexique technique de la mystique musulamane*, 2nd edn (Paris: J. Vrin, [1922] 1954), 300–1, translated as *Essay on the Origins of the Technical Language of Islamic Mysticism*, trans. Benjamin Clark (Notre Dame, IN: Notre Dame University Press, 1997), 203–4 (subsequently cited as *Essay*, according to the [1954] / [1997] editions). Compare with J. Spenser Trimingham, *The Sufi Orders in Islam* (Oxford: Oxford University Press, 1971); Eric S. Ohlander, *Sufism in an Age of Transition: ᶜUmar al-Suhrawardī and the Rise of the Islamic Mystical Brotherhoods*, Islamic History and Civilization, Studies and Texts, 71 (Leiden: Brill, 2006).
4. For the development of the hadith specialisation across the third/ninth and fourth/tenth centuries, see G. H. A. Juynboll, *Muslim Tradition* (Cambridge: Cambridge University Press, 1981), 161–217; Eerik Dickinson, *The Development of Early Sunnite* Ḥadīth *Criticism. The* Taqdima *of Ibn Abī Ḥātim al-Rāzī (240–854/327–938)*, Islamic History and Civilization, Studies and Texts, 38 (Leiden: Brill, 2001); Christopher Melchert, 'The Piety of the Hadith Folk', *International Journal of Middle East Studies* 34 (2002): 425–39; Scott C. Lucas, *Constructive Critics,* Ḥadīth *Literature, and the Articulation of Sunnī Islam: the Legacy of the Generation of Ibn Saᶜd, Ibn Maᶜīn, and Ibn Ḥanbal*, Islamic History and Civilization, Studies and Texts, 51 (Leiden: Brill, 2004); Jonathan A. C. Brown, *The Canonization of al-Bukhārī and Muslim: the Formation and Function of the Sunnī* Ḥadīth *Canon*, Islam (*sic*) History and Civilization, Studies and Texts, 69 (Leiden: Brill, 2007), 47–208. For Sufism during this period, see, in addition to n. 3 above, ᶜUmar al-Farrūkh, *al-Taṣawwuf fī al-Islām* (Beirut: Maktabat al-Munayminah, 1366/1948), 56–71; Paul Nwyia, *Éxegèse coranique et langage mystique: Nouvel essai sur le lexique technique des mystiques musulmanes*, Série 1: Pensée Arabe et Musulmane 49 (Beirut: Dar El-Machreq, 1970); Christopher Melchert, 'The Transition from Asceticism to Mysticism at the Middle of the Ninth Century C.E.', *Studia Islamica* 83 (1996): 51–70; Bernd Radtke, '*Taṣawwuf*: Early Development in the Arabic and Persian Lands', in *Encyclopaedia of Islam*, 2nd edn, eds Peri Bearman, Thierry Bianquis, C. E. Bosworth and Wolfhart P. Heinrichs (Brill Online; subsequently cited as *EI*²); Gerhard Böwering, 'Early

Sufism Between Persecution and Heresy', in Frederik de Jong and Bernd Radtke (eds), *Islamic Mysticism Contested: Thirteen Centuries of Controversies and Polemics*, Islamic History and Civilization, Studies and Texts, 29 (Leiden: Brill, 1999), 1–21; Josef van Ess, 'Sufism and Its Opponents: Reflections on *topoi*, Tribulations and Transformations', in Frederik de Jong and Bernd Radtke (eds), *Islamic Mysticism Contested* (Leiden: Brill, 1999), 22–44; Alexander Knysh, *Islamic Mysticism: A Short History*, 2nd edn (Leiden: Brill, 2010), 43–67; Christopher Melchert 'Baṣran Origins of Classical Sufism', *Der Islam* 83 (2005): 21–40; Ahmet T. Karamustafa, *Sufism: the Formative Period*, New Edinburgh Islamic Surveys (Edinburgh: Edinburgh University Press, 2007), 1–37. Laury Silvers, *A Soaring Minaret: Abu Bakr al-Wasiti and the Rise of Baghdadi Sufism* (Albany, NY: State University of New York Press, 2012, 17–34, 45–60, argues for continuity between hadith specialists and Sufis without directly addressing previous scholarship. Some scholarship connects third-/ninth-century currents directly to developments in the second/eighth century; e.g., Annemarie Schimmel, *Mystical Dimensions of Islam* (Chapel Hill, NC: University of North Carolina Press, 1975), 42–80; Richard Gramlich, *Alte Vorbilder des Sufitums*, Akademie der Wissenschaften und der Literature Mainz Veröffentlichungen der Orientalischen Kommission 42, 1–2 (Wiesbaden: Harrassowitz, 1995–6).

5. Melchert, 'Piety of the Hadith Folk', 412–13.
6. Melchert, 'Piety of the Hadith Folk', 411.
7. Melchert, 'Piety of the Hadith Folk', 411–12.
8. Melchert, 'Transition', 53; Melchert, 'Early Renunciants', 408.
9. Brown, *Canonization*, 99–135.
10. Karamustafa, *Sufism*, 59–60.
11. For manuscript and biographical references, see Fuat Sezgin, *Geschichte des arabischen Schrifttums*, 10 vols + indices (Leiden: Brill, 1967–2007), (a) 1:660, No. 29 (Ibn al-Aᶜrābī); (b) 1:661, No. 30 (al-Khuldī); (c) 1:662, No. 34 (Ibn Nujayd); (d) 1:663, No. 36 (al-Rūdhbārī; Sezgin incorrectly gives his *kunyah* as 'Abū ᶜAlī'). Ibn Masrūq does not appear in this work.
12. Al-Khaṭīb al-Baghāddī, *Tārīkh madīnat al-salām* (= *Tārīkh Baghdād*), ed. Bashshār ᶜAwwād Maᶜrūf, 17 vols (Beirut: Dār al-Gharb al-Islāmī, 1422/2002), 6:279–84, No. 2772 (subsequently cited as *TB*). Al-Dhahabī also records the variant dates given: Aḥmad al-Dhahabī, *Siyar aᶜlām al-nubalāʾ*, ed. Shuᶜayb al-Arnaʾūṭ et al., 25 vols (Beirut: Muʾassasat al-Risālah, 1401–9/1981–8), 13:494–5 (subsequently cited as *SAN*); compare with al-Dhahabī, *Taʾrīkh al-islām wa-wafayāt al-mashāhīr wa-l-aᶜlām*, ed. Bashshār ᶜAwwād Maᶜrūf, 19 vols (Beirut: Dār al-Gharb al-Islāmī, 1408/1988), 6:896, No. 69, *sub annos* AH 291–300 (subsequently cited as *TI*), where he also records both dates. Further prosopographical treatment appears in Bernd Radtke (ed.), *Materialien zur alten islamischen Frömmigkeit*, Basic Texts of Islamic Mysticism, 2 (Leiden: Brill, 2009), xv–vi.
13. Abū ᶜAbd al-Raḥmān al-Sulamī, *Ṭabaqāt al-ṣūfiyah*, ed. Nūr al-Dīn Shuraybah (Cairo: Jāmiᶜat al-Azhar, 1953, rep. 1407/1987), 237–41 = *Kitab ṭabaqāt al-ṣūfiyah*, ed. Johannes Pedersen (Leiden: Brill, 1960), 448–52; subsequently cited as *ṬṢ*, according to the [1953]/[1960] editions. Abū Nuᶜaym Iṣfahānī, *Ḥilyat al-awliyāʾ*

wa-ṭabaqāt al-aṣfiyāʾ, 10 vols (Cairo: Maṭbaᶜat al-Saᶜādah,, 1352–7 / 1932–8, repr. Beirut: Dār al-Fikr, 1400 / 1980), 10:213–16, No. 548; subsequently cited as *ḤA*, all citations referring to the tenth volume.

14. *ḤA*, 214.1–3; *TB* 6:282. Modern scholarship portrays *abdāl* as a subclass of the *awliyāʾ*. For studies of the various usage of these terms, see Hussein La-Shayʾ and Farzin Negahban, 'Abdāl', in *Encyclopaedia Islamica*, eds Farhad Daftary and Wilferd Madelung (Brill Online); Jacqueline Chabbi, 'Abdāl', in *Encyclopedia Iranica*, ed Ehsan Yarshater (1985), 1 / 2:173–4 (henceforth cited as *EIr*); Rebecca Masterton 'A Comparative Exploration of the Spiritual Authority of the *Awliyāʾ* in the Shiᶜi and Sufi Traditions', *American Journal of Islamic Social Sciences* 32(1) (2015): 49–74; and Rana Mikati, 'On the Identity of the Syrian *abdāl*', *Bulletin of the School of Oriental and African Studies (BSOAS)* 80 / 1 (2017): 21–43. I am indebted to Christopher Melchert for alerting me to this last reference.
15. Ḥamzah ibn Yūsuf al-Sahmī, *Suʾālāt Ḥamzah ibn Yūsuf al-Sahmī lil-Dāraquṭnī wa-ghayrihi min al-mashāyikh fī al-jarḥ wa-al-taᶜdīl*, ed. Muwaffaq ibn ᶜAbd Allāh ibn ᶜAbd al-Qādir (Riyadh: Maktabat al-ᶜĀrif, 1404 / 1984), 158, No. 165; *TB* 6:283; Ibn Ḥajar al-ᶜAsqalānī, *Lisān* al-Mīzān, 7 vols (Hyderabad: Majlis Dāʾirat al-Maᶜārif, 1329–31; repr. Dār al-Maᶜārif al-Niẓāmīyah, 1390 / 1971), 1:292, No. 866 = ed. ᶜAbd al-Fattāḥ Abū Ghuddah, 9 vols + index (Beirut: Maktabat al-Maṭbūᶜāt al-Islāmīyah, 1423 / 2003), 1:646, No. 803 (subsequently cited as *LM*, according to the [1971] / [2002] editions).
16. In *TB* (6:279), the first quotation for Ibn Masrūq, through al-Khuldī, is a love poem. Al-Sulamī quotes Ibn Masrūq as approving the practice of *samāᶜ al-rubāᶜīyāt* (*ṬṢ* 239 / 234–5), which fits Melchert's conception of a 'mystic' in 'Baṣran Origins', 248. Compare with Tilman Seidensticker, 'An Arabic Origin of the Persian Rubāᶜī?' *Middle Eastern Literatures* 14(2) (2011): 155–69, here 162; and Willem Stoetzer, 'Rubāᶜī', *EI*[2]. On love poetry in the third / ninth and fourth / tenth centuries, generally, see Thomas Bauer, *Liebe und Liebesdichtung in der Arabischen Welt des 9. und 10. Jahrhunderst: eine literatur- und mentalitätgeschichtliche Studie des arabischen Ġazal*, Diskurse der Arabistik, 2 (Wiesbaden: Harrassowitz, 1998).
17. Al-Dhahabī notes the title in *SAN* (*'samiᶜnā* al-Qanāᶜah *min taʾlīfih'*) and *TI* 53:244, *sub anno* 722, where he records that Ibn Rawāḥah (d. 722 / 1322) received the work through a licence (*ijāzah*). The title was also known to Abū ᶜUbayd Allāh al-Rūdānī (d. 1094 / 1682–3) as in his *Ṣilat al-khalaf bi-mawṣūl al-salaf*, ed. Muḥammad Ḥajjī (Beirut: Dār al-Gharb al-Islāmī, 1408 / 1988), 336, and Muḥammad ibn Jaᶜfar al-Kattānī (ex. 1345 / 1927), *al-Risālah al-mustaṭrafah li-bayān mashhūr kutub al-sunnah al-musharrafah* (Cairo: Maktabat al-Kulliyāt al-Azharīyah and Beirut: M. A. Kharmā, 1913), 67. Compare with Stefan Weninger, Qanāᶜa *(Genügsamkeit) in der arabischen Literatur: anhand des* Kitāb al-Qanāᶜa wa-t-taᶜaffuf *von Ibn Abī d-Dunyā*, Islamkundliche Untersuchungen 154 (Berlin: Klaus Schwarz, 1992), 200–1; *apud* Radtke, *Materialien*, xvi.
18. Ṣalāḥ al-Dīn al-ᶜAlāʾī, *Ithārat al-fawāʾid al-majmūᶜah fī al-ishārah ilá al-farāʾid al-mawsūᶜah*, ed. Muḥammad ibn Ḥayyās Āl Marzūq al-Zahrānī (Medina: Maktabat al-ᶜUlūm wa-al-Ḥikam), 1425 / 2004), 307–8.

19. *ṬṢ*, 428–30/443–8; *ḤA*, 375–6, No. 655; *SAN* 15:407–11; *TI* 25:184–6, *sub anno* AH 340; *LM* 1:308–9, No. 927/1:670–1, No. 758. For his time in Damascus, see Ibn ᶜAsākir, *Tārīkh Dimashq*, ed. ᶜUmar ibn Gharāmah al-ᶜAmrawī, 80 vols (Beirut: Dār al-Fikr, 1415/1995), 5:553–7, No. 144. Al-Dhahabī confers the honorific '*shaykh al-ḥaram*' on several other notable hadith specialists, including Ibn al-Mundhir al-Naysābūrī (d. 318/930), as discussed in Gavin N. Picken, 'A Scholar of the Holy Precincts: the Life, Works, and Methodology of Ibn al-Mundhir al-Nīsābūrī', *Oriens* 38 (2010): 185–215, here 191, n. 27; and Rāḍī al-Dīn Ibrāhīm ibn Muḥammad ibn Ibrāhīm ibn Abī Bakr al-Ṭabarī al-Shāfiᶜī (d. 722/1322), as discussed in *Sufi Inquiries and Interpretations of Abū ᶜAbd al-Raḥmān al-Sulamī (d. 412/1021) and a Treatise of Traditions by Ismāᶜīl b. Nujayd al-Naysābūrī (d. 366/976-7)*, ed. Bilal Orfali and Gerhard Böwering (Beirut: Dar El-Machreq, 2010), 21 (Introduction). Picken translates the phrase as 'the scholar of the Holy Precincts'; Orfali and Böwering do not translate it.
20. Alexander Knysh, 'Abū Saᶜīd Ibn al-Aᶜrābī', in *Encyclopaedia of Islam*, 3rd edn, eds Kate Fleet, Gudrun Krämer, Denis Matrinage, John Nawas and Everett Rowson (Brill Online; subsequently cited as *EI*³). Compare with his comments in *Islamic Mysticism*, 95–7.
21. Ibn Khayr al-Ishbīlī, *Fahrasat Ibn Khayr al-Ishbīlī*, ed. Muḥammad Fuʾād Manṣūr (Beirut: Dār al-Kutub al-ᶜIlmīyah, 1998), 251, Nos 627–34 = ed. Bashshār ᶜAwwād Maᶜrūf and Muḥammad Bashshār ᶜAwwād (Tunis: Dār al-Gharb al-Islāmī, 2009), 454, Nos 644–51. See also the references in Manuela Marin, 'Abû Saᶜîd Ibn al-Aᶜrâbî et le développement du soufisme en al-Andalus', *Revue du monde musulman et de la Méditerranée* 63/4 (1992): 28–38; Nada Saab, 'Ṣūfī Theory and Language in the Writings of Abū Saᶜīd Aḥmad ibn ᶜĪsā al-Kharrāz (d. 286/899)', PhD dissertation, Yale University, 2004, 72–5.
22. For Ibn al-Aᶜrābī's role in the transmission of Abū Dāwūd's works, see James Robson, 'The Transmission of Abū Dāwūd's "*Sunan*"', *BSOAS* 14/3 (1952): 579–88, esp. 582–3; and Christopher Melchert, 'The Life and Works of Abū Dāwūd al-Sijistānī', *al-Qanṭara* 29/1 (2008): 9–44, esp. 22–34 (*al-Sunan*) and 18, n. 52, 36–8 (*al-Zuhd*).
23. *SAN* 15:407.
24. Al-Daraquṭnī, who transmits the judgement, apparently concurred: see Nāyif ibn Ṣalāḥ ibn ᶜAlī al-Manṣūrī, *al-Dalīl al-mughnī li-shuyūkh al-imām Abī al-Ḥasan al-Dāraquṭnī*, with assistance from Abū al-Ḥasan Muṣṭafá ibn Ismāᶜīl al-Sulaymānī, Saᶜd ibn ᶜAbd Allāh al-Ḥamīd and Ḥasan Maqbūlī al-Ahdal (Riyadh: Dār al-Kiyān, 1428/2007), 124, No. 88.
25. Al-Dhahabī, *Tadhkirat al-ḥuffāẓ*, reprint (Beirut: Dār al-Kutub al-ᶜIlmīyah, [1375/1953] 2002), 3:47–8 [852], No. 830.
26. Ibn al-Aᶜrābī, *Muᶜjam Ibn al-Aᶜrābī*, ed. ᶜAbd al-Muḥsin ibn Ibrāhīm ibn Aḥmad al-Ḥusaynī, 3 vols in 1 (Riyadh: Dār Ibn al-Jawzī, 1418/1997) = *Kitāb al-Muᶜjam*, ed. Muḥammad Ḥasan Maḥmūd Ḥasan Ismāᶜīl and Misᶜar ᶜAbd al-Ḥamīd al-Saᶜdanī (Beirut: Dār al-Kutub al-ᶜIlmīyah, 1424/2003). Another work contains traditions of affectionate touching: Ibn al-Aᶜrābī, *al-Qubal wa-al-muᶜānaqah wa-al-muṣāfaḥah*, ed. Majdī Fatḥī al-Sayyid (Cairo: Maktabat al-Qurʾān, 1407/1987) =

ed. ᶜAmr ᶜAbd al-Munᶜim Sulaym (Cairo: Maktabat Ibn Taymīyah and Jeddah: Maktabat al-ᶜIlm, 1416/1996).

27. For the manuscript, see Sezgin, as cited above, n. 11(a). Melchert ('Life and Works', 36) notes, following Robson, that other, longer, versions were known to Ibn Khayr al-Ishbīlī and Ibn Ḥajar; furthermore, he observes that, 'there is no account of [the manuscript's] transmission from Abū Dāwūd through Ibn al-Aᶜrābī'. One edition of *Kitāb al-Zuhd* suggests several possible transmission pathways from Abū Dāwūd through Ibn al-Aᶜrābī. These are based on a small number of citations of accounts found in both Abū Dāwūd's *Kitāb al-Zuhd* and the works of Abū Sulaymān al-Khaṭṭābī (d. 388/998), Aḥmad ibn al-Ḥusayn al-Bayhaqī (d. 458/1066), and al-Dhahabī: Abū Dāwūd al-Sijistānī, *Kitāb al-Zuhd riwāyat Ibn al-Aᶜrābī ᶜanhu*, ed. Abū Tamīm Yāsir ibn ibn Muḥammad and Abū Bilāl Ghunaym ibn ᶜAbbās ibn Ghunaym (Ḥulwān: Dār al-Mishkāh, 1414/1993), 20–1.
28. This title is likewise published in two editions: Ibn al-Aᶜrābī, *al-Zuhd wa-ṣifat al-zāhidīn*, ed. Majdī Fatḥī al-Sayyid Ibrāhīm (Ṭanṭā: Dār al-Ṣaḥābah lil-Turāth, 1408/1988) = *Kitāb fīhi maᶜnā al-zuhd wa-al-maqālāt wa-ṣifat al-zāhidīn*, ed. Khadīja Muḥammad Kāmil and ᶜĀmir al-Najjār (Cairo: Maṭbaᶜat Dār al- Kutub al-Miṣrīyah, 1998).
29. *ṬṢ*, 434–9/454–61; *ḤA*, 381–2, No. 663; *TB* 8:145–52, No. 3668 (for the *ḥajj* account); *SAN* 15:558–60; *TI* 25:396–7, *sub anno* AH 348.
30. Ibn al-Nadīm, *al-Fihrist lil-Nadīm*, ed. Ayman Fuʾād Sayyid, 2 vols + Index, 2nd edn (London: Al-Furqan Islamic Heritage Foundation, 1430/2009), 1:655–66 (*maqālah* 5, *fann* 5). Jawid Mojaddedi, *The Biographical Tradition in Sufism: the* ṭabaqāt *Genre from al-Sulamī to Jāmī* (Richmond: RoutledgeCurzon, 2001), 54–7, contends that Abū Nuᶜaym's references to al-Khuldī's *kitāb* do not indicate a 'book', but does not refer to *al-Fihrist*. Compare with the counter-arguments of Rkia L. Cornell in al-Sulamī, *Early Sufi Women: Dhikr al-niswah al-ṣūfiyāt al-mutaᶜabbidāt*, ed. and trans. Rkia L. Cornell (Louisville: Fons Vitae, 1999), 53, n. 133, and Devin J. Stewart, 'The Structure of the *Fihrist*: Ibn al-Nadīm as a Historian of Islamic Law and Theology', *International Journal of Middle East Studies* 39 (2007): 369–87, here 380–2. I hope to settle the issue definitively in a separate study.
31. *ṬṢ*, 434/454. For the relationship with al-Junayd, see the brief comments in Massignon, *Essay*, 304, n. 2/206, n. 351; Knysh, *Islamic Mysticism*, 25. For his association with Ibn Masrūq, see below, n. 73.
32. Al-Dhahabī, *Tadhkirat al-ḥuffāẓ* 3:297 [1092], No. 933.
33. ᶜAlī al-Dāraquṭnī, *Sunan al-Dāraquṭnī wa-yalīhi al-Taᶜlīq al-mughnī ᶜalá al-Dāraqṭunī*, ed. Shuᶜayb Arnaʾūṭ, ᶜAbd al-Munᶜim al-Shalabī and Muḥammad Shams al-Ḥaqq ᶜAẓīmābādī, 6 vols (Beirut: Muʾassasat al-Risālah, 1425/2004), 5:379, No. 4486. Compare with Muqbal ibn Hādī al-Wādiᶜī, *Tarājim rijāl al-Dāraquṭnī fī Sunanihi alladhīna lam yutarjam lahum fī* al-Taqrīb *wa-lā fī* Rijāl *al-Ḥākim* (Ṣanᶜāʾ: Dār al-Āthār, 1420/1999), 172, No. 398.
34. For al-Dāraquṭnī, see above, n. 33, and Manṣūrī, *Dalīl*, 162, No. 142. For al-Ḥākim, see Nāyif ibn Ṣalāḥ ibn ᶜAlī al-Manṣūrī, *al-Rawḍ al-bāsim fī tarājim shuyūkh al-Ḥākim*, with assistance from Abū al-Ḥasan Muṣṭafá ibn Ismāᶜīl al-Sulaymānī,

Sa^c^d ibn ^c^Abd Allāh al-Ḥamīd and Ḥasan Maqbūlī al-Ahdal, 2 vols (Riyadh: Dār al-^c^Āṣimah, 1432/2011), 1:387, No. 259. For al-Baghdādī, see *TB* 8:145, repeated in *SAN* 15:559.

35. Nabīl Sa^c^d al-Dīn Jarrār (ed.), *Majmū^c^ fīhi ^c^asharat ajzā^ɔ^ ḥadīthīyah* (Beirut: Dār al-Bashā^ɔ^ir al-Islāmīyah, 2001), 203–12, 213–21, 274–81, 294–301. Note that the Index (ibid., 524) indicates only the first two sessions.
36. Al-Khuldī, *al-Fawā^ɔ^id wa-al-zuhd wa-al-raqā^ɔ^iq wa-al-marāthī*, ed. Majdī Fatḥī al-Sayyid (Ṭanṭā: Dār al-Ṣaḥābah lil-Turāth, 1989), 52.
37. *SAN* 15:559.
38. Ibn al-Jawzī, *al-Muntaẓam fī tārīkh al-rusul wa-al-umam*, 12 vols (Hyderabad: Dār al-Ma^c^ārif al-^c^Uthmānīyah, 1358/1939), 7:84.
39. *ṬṢ* 454–8/476–80; *SAN* 16:146–8; *TI* 26:335–6 *sub anno* AH 366. The most comprehensive study of al-Sulamī is now Jean-Jacques Thibon, *L'Œuvre d'Abū ^c^Abd al-Raḥmān al-Sulamī 325/937–412/1021 et la formation du soufisme* (Beirut and Damascus: Presses d'IFPO, 2009). For relations between al-Sulamī and Ibn Nujayd, see Thibon, *L'Œuvre*, 609 (Index), s.v., 'Ismā^c^īl b. Nuğayd'.
40. For further discussion of these contacts, see Najib Mayel Heravi and Daryoush Mohammed Poor, 'Abū ^c^Amr Ibn Nujayd', *Encyclopedia Islamica* (Brill Online).
41. Al-Manṣūrī, *Rawḍ* 1:372, No. 248.
42. *SAN* 16:146; *apud* Ibn Nujayd, *Sufi Inquiries*, 22 n. 53 (Introduction).
43. Ibn Nujayd, *Juz^ɔ^ fīhi min aḥādīth Abī ^c^Amr Ismā^c^īl ibn Nujayd ibn Aḥmad ibn Yūsuf al-Sulamī*, in *al-Fawā^ɔ^id ta^ɔ^līf ^c^Abd al-Wahhāb ibn Muḥammad ibn Isḥāq ibn Yaḥyá ibn Mandah al-^c^Abdī al-Iṣfahānī*, ed. Khalaf Maḥmūd ^c^Abd al-Samī^c^, 2 vols (Beirut: Dār al-Kutub al-^c^Ilmīyah, 1423/2002), 319–39 = Bilal Orfali and Gerhard Böwering (eds), *Sufi Inquiries* (Beirut: Dar El-Machreq, 2010), 83–92.
44. *ṬṢ*, 497–500/527–32; *TB* 6:552, No. 2431; *SAN* 16:227–8; *TI* 26:410–11, *sub anno* AH 369. Nicholson erroneously contends he died at Ṣūr in Abū Naṣr al-Sarrāj al-Ṭūsī, *The Kitáb al-Luma^c^ fi ^ɔ^l-taṣawwuf*, ed. R. A. Nicholson, E. J. W. Gibb Memorial series, 22 (Leiden and London: Brill and Luzac, 1914), xviii; compare the treatment, based on late evidence, in Daphna Ephrat, *Spiritual Wayfarers, Leaders in Piety*, Harvard Middle Eastern Monographs, 40 (Cambridge, MA: Harvard University Press, 2008), 221 (Index), s.v., 'al-Rūdhbārī, Aḥmad b. ^c^Aṭā^ɔ^'.
45. For the quotation, see *ṬṢ*, 497/527. On Abū ^c^Alī, see *ṬṢ*, 354–60/362–9; *ḤA*, 356–7, No. 638. Elsewhere (*Early Sufi Women*, 241), al-Sulamī quotes al-Rūdhbārī's maternal aunt, Abū ^c^Alī's sister, saying that her nephew was not a real Sufi while her brother was; *apud* Arin Shawkat Salamah-Qudsi, 'A Lightning Trigger or a Stumbling Block: Mother Images and Roles in Classical Sufism', *Oriens* 39/2 (2011): 199–226, here 203.
46. Al-Sarrāj, *Kitāb al-Luma^c^*. Al-Rūdhbārī also appears in numerous reports in al-Sulamī's *Ṭabaqāt* (cited throughout as 'Aḥmad ibn ^c^Aṭā^ɔ^'), through al-Sarrāj.
47. *TB* 5:552, repeated in *SAN* 17:627; *LM* 1:222, No. 689/1:537–8, No. 635.
48. Radtke, *Materialien*, 217–59 (part D).
49. For instance, none of these figures receives individual treatment in Gramlich, *Alte Vorbilder*.
50. Melchert, 'Early Renunciants', 414–15. Compare with Michael Cooperson,

Classical Arabic Biography: The Heirs of the Prophets in the Age of al-Maʾmūn, Cambridge Studies in Islamic Civilization (Cambridge: Cambridge University Press, 2000), 154–87, elaborating on Massignon's description of the famous ascetic Bishr al-Ḥāfī (d. 227/841).

51. Melchert, 'Piety of the Hadith Folk', 413.
52. Melchert, 'The Ḥanābila and Early Sufis', and Melchert, 'al-Barbahārī', *EI*[3]. Compare with the studies of later figures in George Makdisi, 'The Hanbali School and Sufism', in *Actas IV. Congresso de Estudios Arabes e Islámicos: Coimbra-Lisboa 1 a 8 de setembro de 1968* (Leiden: Brill, 1971), 71–84; reprinted in *Religion, Law and Learning in Classical Islam*, Variorum Collected Studies series, 347 (Burlington, VT: Variorum, 1991). Melchert ('Transition', 65–6) correctly recognises that not all opponents of the Sufis were necessarily hadith specialists or *Ḥanābilah*; compare with Maher Jarrar, 'Ghulām Khalīl', *EI*[3].
53. Recep Şentürk, *Narrative Social Structure: Anatomy of the Hadith Transmission Network 610–1505* (Palo Alto: Stanford University Press, 2005), 203–4, fig. 7.1.
54. Şentürk, *Narrative Social Structure*, 203. Note that Şentürk examines al-Dhahabī's *Tadhkirat al-ḥuffāẓ*, Jalāl al-Dīn al-Suyūṭī's (d. 911/1505) *Ṭabaqāt al-ḥuffāẓ*, and Ibn Ḥibbān al-Bustī's (d. 354/965) *Mashāhīr ʿulamāʾ al-amṣār*.
55. Jonathan A. C. Brown, *Hadith: Muhammad's Legacy in the Medieval and Modern World* (Oxford: Oneworld, 2009), 193–5. Compare with Massignon, *Essay*, 120–2/83–4; thereafter (ibid., 184–91/127–34) reference to hadith *mursal* refers to late second-/eighth-century usage. Elsewhere (*Passion* 3:344–52/3:327–54), Massignon discusses al-Ḥallāj's use of the *isnād* to relate visionary experiences, and his interpolation of celestial objects and phenomenological events in place of human tradents. Compare with S. M. Zwemer, 'The So-Called Hadith Qudsi', *Moslem World* 12/3 (1922): 263–75; William Graham, *Divine Word and Prophetic Word in Early Islam: a Reconsideration of the Sources, with Special Reference to the Divine Saying or* ḥadîth qudsî, Religion and Society, 7 (The Hague: Mouton, 1977); and Hamid Algar, 'Hadith iv. in Sufism', in *Encyclopædia Iranica* 11/5, 451–3.
56. Lahcen Daaïf, 'Dévots et renonçants: L'autre catégorie de forgeurs de hadiths', *Arabica* 57 (2010): 201–50, here 217–18.
57. Brown, *Hadith*, 184–91.
58. Brown, *Hadith*, 189.
59. Duncan B. Macdonald, 'The Life of al-Ghazzālī, with Especial Reference to His Religious Experiences and Opinions', *Journal of the American Oriental Society* 20 (1899): 71–132, here 123–7.
60. Ignaz Goldziher, *Introduction to Islamic Theology and Law*, trans. Andras and Ruth Hamori, Modern Classics in Near Eastern Studies (Princeton, NJ: Princeton University Press, 1981), 157–60; A. J. Arberry, 'Qushayri as Traditionist', in Johannes Pedersen (ed.), *Studia Orientalia, Ioanni Pedersen septuagenario* (Hauniea: E. Munksgaard, 1953), 12–20. On al-Qushayrī, generally, see now Martin Nguyen, *Sufi Master and Qurʾan Scholar: Abū 'l-Qāsim al-Qushayrī and the* Laṭāʾif al-ishārāt, Qurʾanic Studies series, 8 (Oxford: Oxford University Press, with the assistance of Institute of Ismaili Studies, 2012).
61. Cornell, *Early Sufi Women*, 43–7.

62. Florian Sobieroj, *Ibn Ḫafīf aš-Šīrāzī und seine Schrift zur Novizenerziehung (Kitāb al-Iqtiṣād). Biographische Studien, Edition und Übersetzung*, Beiruter Texte und Studien 57 (Beirut: Franz Steiner, 1998), 425 (Index), s.v., 'Ḥadīṯfälschen', 'Ḥadīṯgelehrte' and 'Ḥadīṯstudium'.
63. Karamustafa, *Sufism*, 57–8; Sobieroj, *Ibn Ḫafīf*, 133–4. Ibn Jahḍam's reputation suffered in hadith-specialist circles. According to al-Dhahabī (*SAN* 17:275–6), he lied (*yakdhib*), and transmitted 'catastrophically bad' reports (*maṣāʾib*).
64. Christopher Melchert, 'Abū Nuʿaym's Sources for *Ḥilyat al-awliyāʾ*: Sufi and Traditionist', in Geneviève Gobillot and Jean-Jacques Thibon (eds), *Les maîtres soufis et leurs disciples IIIe–Ve siècles de l'hégire (IXe–XIe s.). Enseignement, formation et transmission* (Beirut and Damascus: Presses de l'IFPO, 2012), 102–13, here 108.
65. Melchert, 'Abū Nuʿaym's Sources', 107. However, this contradicts his earlier assertion ('The Piety of the Hadith Folk', 410) that, 'the lines dividing *hadith* transmission . . . and Sufis may have been clear [later ...], but the *Ḥilya* is evidence that they were less so in Abū Nuʿaym's'.
66. Melchert, 'Piety of Hadith Folk', 413.
67. The Arabic text (*TB* 8:145) reads: '*maḍaytu ilá ʿAbbās al-Dūrī wa-anā ḥadathun wa-katabtu ʿanhu majlisan wāḥidan*'; repeated, citing al-Baghdādī, in *SAN* 15:559. The anecdote seems to have been first reported in al-Muḥassin al-Tanūkhī, *Nishwār al-muḥāḍarah wa-akhbār al-mudhākarah*, ed. ʿAbbūd al-Shālijī al-Maḥāmī, 7 vols (Beirut: Dār Ṣādir: 1995), 3:117; *apud* Florian Sobieroj, 'The Muʿtazila and Sufism', Frederik de Jong and Bernd Radtke (eds), *Islamic Mysticism Contested* (Leiden: Brill, 1999), 68–92, at 87 n. 95.
68. For the quotation, see Timothy McGrew, 'The Argument from Silence', *Acta Analytica* 29 (2014): 215–28, here 226. Melchert ('Abū Nuʿaym's Sources', 102–6) has observed this phenomenon in a comparison of Abū Nuʿaym's *ḤA* and dedicated hadith works.
69. For Ibn ʿAṭāʾ, see Paul Nwyia, *Trois oeuvres inédites de mystiques musulmanes*, Nouvelle série: Langue arabe et pensée islamique, 7 (Beirut: Dar El-Machreq, 1973), 25–32; Richard Gramlich, *Abu 'l-ʿAbbās Ibn ʿAṭāʾ: Sufi und Koranausleger*, Abhandlungen für die Kunde des Morgenlandes 51, 2 (Stuttgart: Deutsche Morgenländische Gesellschaft, 1995); Martin Nguyen, 'Ibn ʿAṭāʾ al-Ādamī', *EI*³.
70. Sezgin, *GAS* 1:638, No. 8; Radtke, *Materialien*, xiii–v.
71. *SAN* 12:212–14. Melchert has not consulted this notice in which al-Dhahabī, following Abū Saʿīd al-Naqqāsh (d. 412/1021–2), identifies al-Ṭūsī as a teacher (*ustādh*) to the famous Sufi Abū Saʿīd al-Kharrāz (d. 277/888–9), the author of a highly regarded mystical treatise titled *Kitāb al-Ṣidq*. On their relationship, see Saab, 'Ṣūfī Theory', 25–7. On al-Naqqāsh, see the editors' Introductions in al-Naqqāsh, *Fawāʾid al-ʿIraqīyīn*, ed. Majdī Fathī al-Sayyid (Cairo: Maktabat al-Qurʾān, 1410/1990) = ed. ʿAmr ʿAbd al-Munʿim Sālim (Cairo: Dār al-Ḍiyāʾ, 2006). In the same notice al-Dhahabī transmits the testimony of Abū Bakr al-Marrūdhī (d. 275/888), who is quoted as asking Aḥmad ibn Ḥanbal about al-Ṭūsī, with the latter responding, 'I only know good things about him – a prayerful man (*ṣāḥib al-ṣalāh*).'
72. Melchert, 'Ḥanābilah', 357–8.

73. Joseph Norment Bell, 'Al-Sarrāj's *Maṣāri^c al-^cushshāq*: a Ḥanbalite Work?', *JAOS* 99(2) (1979): 235–48, here 242–4. Al-Khuldī relies on Ibn Masrūq for more than half (28/52) of the transmissions in *al-Fawā^ʾid*.
74. G. H. A. Juynboll, *Encyclopedia of Canonical Ḥadīth* (Leiden: Brill, 2007), 131–4, and 'Anas b. Mālik', *EI*³.
75. Abū ^cAbd Allāh Muḥammad ibn ^cAlī, *Nawādir al-uṣūl fi ma^crifat aḥādīth al-rasūl wa-yalīhi* Mirqāt al-wuṣūl *ḥawāshī* Nawādir al-uṣūl, ed. Muṣṭafá ibn Ismā^cīl al-Dimashqī (Beirut: Dār Ṣādir, 1972; first published Istanbul, 1294/1877). For an appraisal of the manuscript tradition and concordance of hadith from the Sunni tradition, see Abdurrahman Aliy, *'Nawādir al-Uṣūl' des al-Ḥakīm al-Tirmidhī: Ein Beitrag zur mystischen Ḥadīth-Kommentierung* (Inaugural-Dissertation: Ruhr Universität Bochum, 2003). Bernd Radtke argues that the work 'offers a wealth of statements and thoughts about classical mysticism', in *Drei Schriften des Theosophen von Tirmiḏ*, Bibliotheca Islamica, 35b (Stuttgart: Franz Steiner, 1996), 2. More generally, Yahya Maquet ('al-Ḥakīm al-Tirmiḏhī', *EI*²) argues that, '[Al-Tirmidhī was] a traditionalist, he adopted numerous themes characteristic of the *Ahl al-ḥadīṯh*, refused to accept discussion of the Ḳurʾān and of the Sunna, repudiated *kalām* and controversies, rejected reason and personal opinion (*raʾy*), and showed clear sympathy for the Ḥanbalīs, and also for the Umayyads rather than the ^cAbbāsids'.
76. Abū ^cAbd al-Raḥmān al-Sulamī, *Suʾālāt Abī ^cAbd al-Raḥmān al-Sulamī lil-imām al-Dāraquṭnī fi al-jarḥ wa-al-ta^cdīl wa-^cilal al-ḥadīth*, ed. Abū ^cUmar Muḥammad ibn ^cAlī al-Azharī, Silsalat al-suʾālāt al-ḥadīthīyah, 3 (Cairo: al-Fārūq al-Ḥadīthah, 1427/2006). Al-Dāraquṭnī also appears as an immediate informant in *ṬṢ*, 15/23.
77. The remaining accounts concern significant Followers like al-Ḥasan al-Baṣrī (d. 110/728), Baghdadi Sufis like al-Junayd, or poetry.
78. In using these terms, I am indebted to the formulation of Jonathan A. C. Brown, 'Criticism of the Proto-Hadith Canon: Al-Dāraquṭnī's Adjustment of the *Ṣaḥīḥayn*', *Journal of Islamic Studies* 15/1 (2004): 1–37. The works include al-Ṭabarānī's *al-Mu^cjam al-kabīr, al-Mu^cjam al-awsaṭ* and *al-Mu^cjam al-ṣaghīr*; al-Dāraquṭnī's *Mustakhraj*; and Ibn Khuzaymah's *Ṣaḥīḥ*.
79. The literature is voluminous. An approachable volume concerning structured cooperation and competition is Matthew O. Jackson, *Social and Economic Networks* (Princeton, NJ: Princeton University Press, 2008). A standard reference of network measures is Mark E. Newman, *Networks: An Introduction* (Oxford: Oxford University Press, 2008). I thank Paul Hooper for introducing me to these works.
80. For example: Richard Bulliet, *Patricians of Nishapur: a Study in Medieval Islamic Social History* (Cambridge, MA: Harvard University Press, 1972); Carl Petry, *The Civilian Elite of Cairo in the Later Middle Ages* (Princeton, NJ: Princeton University Press, 1981); Monique Bernards, 'Grammarians' Circles of Learning: a Social Network Analysis', in *^cAbbāsid Studies II: Occasional Papers of the School of ^cAbbāsid Studies, Leuven 28 June–1 July 2004*, Orientalia Lovaniensia analecta, 177 (Leuven: Peeters, 2010), 143–64.

81. For one instance of this usage, juxtaposed to the otherwise excellent theoretical examination of a 'canon', see Brown, *Canonization*, app. 1.
82. On the ubiquity of the concept of hierarchies during this period, see Louise Marlow, *Hierarchy and Egalitarianism in Islamic Literature* (Cambridge: Cambridge University Press, 1997). Compare with the formal investigation of Aaron Clauset, Chris Moore and Mark E. Newman, 'Hierarchical Structure and the Prediction of Missing Links in Networks', *Nature* 453 (2008): 90–101. On 'niches', see Manfred Laubichler and Jürgen Renn, 'Extended Evolution: a Conceptual Framework for Integrating Regulatory Networks and Niche Construction', *Journal of Experimental Zoology* (Mol. Dev. Evol.) 3248 (2015): 565–77; and Jürgen Renn and Manfred Laubichler, 'Extended Evolution and the History of Knowledge', in Friedrich Stadler (ed.), *Integrated History and Philosophy of Science: Problems, Perspectives and Case Studies* (Berlin: Springer, 2017), 109–25. I thank Nayely Velez-Cruz for bringing these last two works to my attention.
83. On these and other metrics of centrality, see Newman, *Networks*, 168–92.
84. Mark E. Newman, 'Finding Community Structure in Networks Using the Eigenvectors of Matrices', *Physical Review E* 74036104 (2006): 1–19; Philip Bonacich, 'Some Unique Properties of Eigenvector Centrality', *Social Networks* 25/4 (2007): 555–64.
85. See esp. Maxim Romanov, 'Toward Abstract Models of Islamic History,' in Elias Muhanna (ed.), *Digital Humanities and Islamic and Middle East Studies* (Berlin: Walter de Gruyter, 2015), 117–50.
86. The point is raised in the following reviews: Behnam Sadeki, 'Review: *Narrative Social Structure* . . . by Recep Şentürk', *Journal of Interdisciplinary History* 38(2) (2007): 328–9; Christopher Melchert, 'Review: *Narrative Social Structure* . . . by Recep Senturk', *Journal of Islamic Studies* 19/1 (2008): 115–17.
87. Şentürk, *Narrative Social Structure*, 38–41.
88. Şentürk, *Narrative Social Structure*, 137, fig. 5.1.
89. Şentürk, *Narrative Social Structure*, 31, 41–3. Brown states, 'the canonical culture surrounding the *Ṣaḥīḥayn* seems to have emerged in Baghdad in . . . al-Dāraquṭnī's career in the mid- to late fourth / tenth century' (*Canonization*, 264).
90. It is possible that either al-Dhahabī's or al-Suyūṭī's peculiar conception of the contours of the earlier generations within the *ḥuffāẓ* network was influenced by the hard boundaries of group specialisation that obtained in Mamlūk Syria and Egypt.
91. Duncan J. Watts, *Small Worlds: the Dynamics of Networks between Order and Randomness*, Princeton Studies in Complexity (Princeton, NJ: Princeton University Press, 1999), 23–5.
92. Melchert, 'Review', advises the collection of this type of data.
93. See the comments on the distortional effects of singly-connected nodes in Newman, *Networks*, 188.
94. Mathieu Bastian, Sebastian Heymann and Mathieu Jacomy, '*Gephi*: An Open Source Software for Exploring and Manipulating Networks', in *Proceedings of the Third International ICWSM Conference: International AAAI Conference on Weblogs*

and Social Media (2009): 361–2. The total of unweighted edges is 1,666, meaning *TB* and *SNA* mutually confirm 330 edges (~ 19.8 per cent of the total).

95. 'Non-trivial' means there is at least one non-zero figure computed for five places past the decimal.

CHAPTER

5

THE COMMON LINK AND ITS RELATION TO HADITH TERMINOLOGY

Ali Aghaei*

Introduction

The 'common link' is not a newly coined term. Its history goes back to the middle of the twentieth century when Joseph Schacht first used it. Schacht, who was mainly concerned with the dating of hadiths,[1] discovered a peculiar phenomenon in their *isnāds*: the 'common transmitters'. If different *isnāds* of a given hadith are gathered and put together, almost all of them meet at a certain point at a common transmitter, whom he named the 'common link', and then through a single strand reach back to an authority such as a Companion or the Prophet himself.[2] According to Schacht, 'the existence of a significant common link (N.N.) in all or most *isnāds* of a given tradition would be a strong indication in favour of its having originated in the time of N.N.'.[3] In other words, he believed that drawing on information obtained through the common link one can identify the origin of that particular hadith in terms of time and place.[4] From his time onwards, 'the common link' has played a prominent role in modern hadith studies and has been used by those scholars who would date hadiths based on *isnād* analysis.[5]

But was this phenomenon recognised by Muslim hadith scholars and traditionists (*muḥaddithūn*), and can one find some traces of this recognition in the Islamic hadith literature as well? Hadith scholars have coined a plethora of technical terms (*muṣṭalaḥāt al-ḥadīth*) to define the various features of hadiths and the qualifications of their transmitters. Is it possible to find amongst them some terms that, in one way or another, correspond to the common link or be considered as its equivalent?

In his prominent study, Schacht notices that Muslim hadith scholars already recognised this phenomenon:

> It was observed, though of course not recognised in its implications, by the Muhammadan scholars themselves, for instance by al-Tirmidhī in the

> concluding chapter of his collection of traditions. He calls traditions with N.N. as a common link in their *isnād*s 'the traditions of N.N.', and they form a great part of the traditions which he calls *gharīb*, that is transmitted by a single transmitter at any stage of the *isnād*.[6]

With this clarification, Schacht related the common link to the 'single transmitter' (*munfarid/mutafarrid*) in *gharīb* (literally 'strange') hadith. He was also aware that along with the *isnād*s with a common link, there are sometimes other *isnād*s that sidestep the common link.[7] At first glance, it seems that in such a case, 'the common link is not alone and his hadith is not *gharīb*'.[8] But Schacht regards these strands as 'additional' and possibly 'introduced later'. He means that they originated 'by the creation of improvements [i.e., the backward growth of *isnād*s] which would take their place beside the original chain of transmitters, or by the process which [Schacht] described as spread of *isnād*s'.[9]

G. H. A. Juynboll, like Schacht, held that the common link was known to Muslim hadith scholars. However, 'they never took the issue any further but for hints at it in the case of auspicious hadith forgers or allusions to certain key figures', and therefore they did not develop or expand upon its concept and function as much as it deserved.[10] Juynboll elaborated on the common-link phenomenon in several articles.[11] He pointed, here and there, to the connection between 'single transmitter' in *gharīb* traditions and the common link.[12] He also suggested that the term *madār* (literally 'pivot', 'turning point') could be considered the equivalent of the common link.[13] Finally, in an article devoted to technical terms in classical hadith literature, he showed that the terms *madār* and *tafarrud/infirād* (isolated transmission) and their cognate verbal forms, namely, *dāra, yadūru* ᶜ*alā* and *tafarrada/infarada bi-*, have a firm connection to the common link. Therefore, one may certainly use the term *madār* as an equivalent for the common link.[14]

Juynboll also noticed that in hadith works, sometimes beside the *isnād*s of a hadith that branch out from one and the same transmitter, other transmission lines (*ṭuruq*; sing. *ṭarīq*) are also observable which do not pass through him. According to the traditional perspective, the existence of such transmission lines entails that the transmitter in question could not be the *madār* and that his transmission line was not a single strand (*munfarid*).[15] Juynboll, however, considered these additional *isnād* strands, which have usually been called *mutābi*ᶜ*āt* (sing. *mutābi*ᶜ; literally 'following') or *shawāhid* (sing. *shāhid*; literally 'witness') in hadith literature, as fabrications of a somewhat later time and called them 'diving' strands.[16] Thus, from amongst the Islamic hadith terms, Juynboll picked out some – apparently apt and appropriate – equivalents for both the common link and diving strands.

Halit Özkan, in his article 'The Common Link and its Relation to the *Madār*', both examined the use of the term *madār* in the Islamic hadith literature and sought to disprove Juynboll's claim. According to him, because of 'significant differences between the understanding and use of *madār* by both classical and contemporary Muslim scholars, on the one hand, and Juynboll's notion of the *common link*, on the other', these two terms cannot be considered equivalents.[17] To highlight the conceptual and functional differences between the two terms, the *madār* and the common link, Özkan cites some examples in which transmitters from the generation of the Companions or the old Successors (*kibār al-tābiʿīn*) were regarded as the *madār*s of hadiths.[18] According to him, this usage of the term *madār* is evidently in contrast to the concept of the common link according to Juynboll, who holds that 'no Companions served as a common link (or *madārs*)' and 'the first *madār*, Abū al-ʿĀliya Rufayʿ b. Mihrān al-Riyāḥī, was a Successor'.[19] Thus, 'if, like Juynboll, we treat the terms *common link* and *madār* as equivalent', he argues, '*pace* Juynboll, the dissemination of a hadith would have taken place in the generation of the Companions, not in that of the Successors'.[20]

In his second objection, Özkan points to the existence of several of *madārs* in the *isnād*s of a hadith, which contradicts Juynboll's idea. According to Juynboll, 'there can be only one common link in an *isnād*' and 'after the common link, there may be one or more partial common links', whereas Özkan cites examples in which Muslim scholars designate more than one person as the *madār* of a single hadith, sometimes in the same generation.[21] He then asserts that, if one considers the *madār*s in these examples as the equivalent of common links one faces even more problems. First, if we ascribe the wording of a particular hadith to the *madār*, as Juynboll does for the common link, then which of the two or three *madār*s formulated the wording of the hadith? Secondly, how can we explain Muslim scholars' recognition of the existence of transmitters other than the *madār* on the same level as the *madār* without identifying them as such?[22]

Özkan's third objection is about the relation between the *madār* and *tafarrud*. He claims that, 'Most Muslim scholars do not treat these two terms as synonyms.'[23] To prove his claim, he refers to the cases in which the term *madār* is concurrently used with expressions like 'he is not the only transmitter' or 'his hadith has a *mutābiʿ* or *shāhid*'. He thinks that 'If *madār* and *tafarrud* were synonyms, this usage would be meaningless.'[24]

In this chapter, through an analytical study of the meaning and application of the terms mentioned above in the works of early, late and contemporary Muslim scholars, I will verify Schacht and Juynboll's suggested equivalent terms from Islamic tradition for the common link.[25] Henceforth, I will compare different interpretations of Western scholars of this phenomenon with those of early Muslim scholars. I will also show that the points on which Özkan has based his arguments are not sufficient to justify his criticism of Juynboll's suggested equivalents for the term common link.

The Use of the Term *gharīb* by al-Tirmidhī

Al-Tirmidhī (d. 279/892) in his book *Kitāb al-ʿIlal* – which appears at the end of his famous hadith collection – divides the *gharīb* hadiths into four categories, of which the first two completely and the fourth one may partially correspond to the term common link:

1. A hadith transmitted through a single strand (*lā yurwá illā min wajh wāḥid*); for instance, about a hadith that Ḥammād ibn Salamah (d. 167/784) narrates from Abū al-ʿUsharāʾ, the unknown (*majhūl*) transmitter, from his father from the Prophet, he states: 'This hadith is transmitted only (*tafarrada bihī*) by Ḥammād ibn Salamah from Abū al-ʿUsharāʾ, and no other hadith narrated from Abū al-ʿUsharāʾ from his father is known.' Since this hadith is disseminated only on the authority of Ḥammād, al-Tirmidhī has called it 'the hadith of Ḥammād ibn Salamah'.[26]
2. A hadith known only on the authority of one of the transmitters (*lā yuʿrafu illā min ḥadīthih*), but would become well-known through being prolifically narrated from him; for instance, the hadith of the 'prohibition of selling or donating the patronage' (*al-nahy ʿan bayʿ al-walāʾ wa-hibatih*) is known only through ʿAbd Allāh ibn Dīnār (d. 127/744–5), and hence al-Tirmidhī has regarded it as the hadith of ʿAbd Allāh ibn Dīnār. For al-Tirmidhī, other *isnād*s that do not go through ʿAbd Allāh are errors (*wahm*),[27] as had already been alleged by Muslim ibn al-Ḥajjāj (d. 261/875).[28]
3. A hadith with an addition (*ziyādah*) in the *matn* (text). In al-Tirmidhī's view, 'This addition may be acceptable provided that it is transmitted by the one who has reliable retentiveness (*ḥifẓ*).'[29] He cites as an example for this case a hadith by Mālik ibn Anas (d. 179/795) from Nāfiʿ from Ibn ʿUmar about *zakāt al-fiṭr*, in whose text the expression '*min al-muslimīn*' is an addition. Whereas many others had transmitted this very hadith by Nāfiʿ without this addition, some like al-Shāfiʿī (d. 204/820) and Ibn Ḥanbal (d. 241/855) argued and decided on the basis of Mālik's addition.[30]
4. A hadith regarded as *gharīb* due to the *isnād* through which it is transmitted, whose *matn* is transmitted through several other *isnād*s. In other words, there is a problem in one of the *isnād*s which leads to its being considered *gharīb*. For example, the hadith by the Prophet that reads, 'The believer eats only (what fills) one intestine, while the unbeliever eats (what fills) seven intestines' (*al-muʾminu yaʾkulu fī miʿan wāḥidin wa-l-kāfiru yaʾkulu fī sabʿati amʿāʾ*), is transmitted through Abū Kurayb Muḥammad ibn al-ʿAlāʾ (d. 248/862) < Abū Usāmah Ḥammād ibn Usāmah (d. 201/816–17) < Burayd ibn ʿAbd Allāh ibn Abī Burdah < his grandfather Abū Burdah < Abū Mūsá al-Ashʿarī. Al-Tirmidhī confirmed that this hadith was transmitted from the Prophet through different authorities,[31] but the *isnād* of the already mentioned version is *gharīb*. Then he quotes al-Bukhārī (d. 256/870): 'This is the hadith of Abū Kurayb from Abū Usāmah, being known only through this very *isnād*.'[32]

The first two categories are not much different[33] because in both a hadith by one shaykh (the hadith master) is transmitted through a single strand (*tafarrada bih*) and at times because of several transmission lines from that shaykh, it has become well-known (*yashtahiru 'l-ḥadīthu li-kathrati man rawá ᶜanhu*).[34] As for the third and fourth categories, the case is a bit different. In these two, the *matn* of the hadith is supposed to have been transmitted through various strands, but one of the transmitters presents yet a different version of that hadith containing information additional to the already known version (the third category), or gives a single strand not mentioned before him (the fourth category). However, in the two latter categories, the *tafarrud* of the transmitter is the key element in the *gharābah* of the hadith. Therefore, the *gharīb* hadith may be divided into two general categories: (1) a hadith transmitted only through one strand, while its *matn* is not known through any other strand – whether it would become well-known later as a result of the multiplicity of the transmission through a single transmitter (*munfarid*) or not; and (2) a hadith of which a version is transmitted isolated (*mutafarrid*) through a single strand, but whose *matn* is known through various strands – whether there would be additions in its *matn* or not.[35]

It is evident that the major element in *gharābah* of both the categories is *tafarrud*. Through studying the hadiths which al-Tirmidhī in his hadith collection considered *gharīb*, this very fact would be confirmed. Beside many cases in which al-Tirmidhī implicitly refers to the *tafarrud* of the transmission through expressions such as 'it is not known but only through his transmission' (*lā yuᶜrafu illā min ḥadīthih*) or 'it is not narrated save through a single strand' (*lā yurwá illā min wajh wāḥid*), there are also several cases where he takes the *tafarrud* of the transmitter as an indicator to the *gharābah* of hadiths.[36]

The Term *gharīb* in the Terminology of the Hadith Critics

One can find examples of the relation between the two terms *gharīb* and *tafarrud* in the works of the early hadith critics. Some examples will be mentioned here:

- Ibn Maᶜīn (d. 233/847) regarded a hadith by Nūḥ ibn Darrāj as *gharīb*, for – as he would claim – 'No one besides him transmits this tradition' (*laysa yarwīhi aḥadun ghayruh*).[37]
- Ibn Ḥanbal (d. 241/855) regarded a hadith by Hushaym ibn Bashīr (d. 183/799) from Yaḥyá ibn Saᶜīd ibn Qays al-Ansạrī (d. 144/761–2) as *gharīb*, for beside him no one transmitted it from Yaḥyá ibn Saᶜīd.[38]
- Ibn ᶜAdī (d. 365/976) regarded *gharīb* a hadith that Abū al-Miqdām ᶜAmr ibn Thābit al-Kūfī (d. 172/788–9) transmitted from Ismāᶜīl ibn Khālid al-Aḥmasī and affirmed that 'Apart from ᶜAmr ibn Thābit, no one else has transmitted it.'[39]
- Al-Dāraquṭnī (d. 385/995) used some expressions indicating *tafarrud* along with the word *gharīb*. For instance, he considered *gharīb* a hadith

> transmitted from Sulaymān ibn Mihrān al-Aᶜmash (d. 148/765) by Jarīr ibn ᶜAbd al-Ḥamīd (d. 188/804) because nobody else has transmitted it from al-Aᶜmash.[40]

As indicated so far, the major feature of the *gharīb* is that it has been transmitted by only one transmitter through a single strand. Hence, Ibn al-Ṣalāḥ (d. 643/1245), in defining the *gharīb*, writes, 'The hadith which one of the transmitters is alone in transmitting is called *gharīb*.'[41] This is so obvious that later hadith scholars did not even distinguish between the *gharīb* and the *fard* (isolated hadith). Ibn Ḥajar al-ᶜAsqalānī (d. 852/1449) defines the *gharīb* as such: 'The hadith that only a single person transmitted; this *tafarrud* can occur in any part of the *isnād*.'[42] To clarify, he then adds that it is possible that this *tafarrud* would happen either: (1) in 'the base (*aṣl*) of the *isnād*' – that is, that part of the *isnād* which all the complete *isnād*s have in common, even if after this various strands would branch out from a single transmitter;[43] or (2) in the middle of the *isnād*, where several transmitters relate a hadith from a Companion, while a single transmitter is alone (*munfarid*) in relating it from one of those transmitters. In the latter case, the hadith can be one of those called well-known (*mashhūr*) per se, yet considering the single transmitter, the hadith would be called *fard* or *gharīb*. According to Ibn Ḥajar, the former would be called *al-fard al-muṭlaq* ('absolutely isolated') and the latter *al-fard al-nisbī* ('relatively isolated').[44]

Dividing the *fard* into 'absolute' and 'relative' is compatible with the above-mentioned twofold classification of the *gharīb*. Because the attributes 'absolute' and 'relative' refer to the nature of the *infirād*/*tafarrud* of the hadith, if the hadith is transmitted through a single strand and no other *isnād* can be found for it, the *fard* will be considered 'absolute'. On the contrary, if the hadith is transmitted through several *isnād*s, but one transmitter is alone in providing his special *isnād* strand, his hadith will be called *fard* due to that certain *isnād*, even if the hadith is well-known.[45]

The classification of the *fard* as 'absolute' and 'relative' goes back to Ibn al-Ṣalāḥ. After him, hadith scholars followed it.[46] Before Ibn al-Ṣalāḥ, al-Ḥākim al-Naysābūrī mentions several categories of the *fard* – including the *tafarrud* of the people of a certain city, that of a certain transmitter from one of the hadith authorities, and that of the people of a certain city from the people of another city – together with some examples for each category.[47] Indeed, it seems that al-Ḥākim did not intend to give a perfect definition of the term *fard* but only presented examples for various *fard*s. Therefore, one can put each one of his examples into either the absolute category or the relative one. For instance, some of the examples he has given for the *tafarrud* of the people of a certain city are absolute *fard* while others are relative. Nevertheless, by adding sub-categories to the twofold classification of the *fard*, some later hadith scholars tried to harmonise Ibn al-Ṣalāḥ's definition with that of al-Ḥākim.[48]

The *mutābi**ʿāt*, the *shawāhid* and the Process of *iʿtibār al-ḥadīth*

Yet how can one distinguish *al-fard al-muṭlaq* from *al-fard al-nisbī*? It becomes clear through the early hadith critics' statements that, to study and criticise each hadith, they collected its different *isnād*s and thence, by comparing them with one another, alongside other evidence, decided on the authenticity of the hadith. According to Ibn Ḥanbal, 'one cannot understand a hadith if its transmission lines are not gathered'.[49] Ibn al-Madīnī (d. 234/849) concedes that 'the errors of a hadith will remain unrecognised if its transmission lines are not collected'.[50] Even to estimate the qualification of a transmitter, they would compile and investigate his hadiths.[51] Ibn Ḥibbān al-Bustī (d. 354/965) in his *Ṣaḥīḥ* explains the procedure of authentication (*iʿtibār*) of hadiths by means of an example:

> Suppose that Ḥammād ibn Salamah [(d. 167/784)] transmitted a hadith from Ayyūb [al-Sakhtiyānī (d. 131/749?)] from [Muḥammad] Ibn Sīrīn [(d. 110/729)] from Abū Hurayrah from the Prophet and we do not find this hadith with any other student of Ayyūb ...: we first examine this hadith to see whether several of Ḥammād's students transmitted it from him or only one. If it is found that several of his students transmitted it [from him], then it is known that Ḥammād indeed transmitted it. If it is found to be the transmission of a weak [transmitter] from him [i.e., Ḥammād], then it is ascribed to that transmitter, not to him. When it is established that he [i.e., Ḥammād] did transmit from Ayyūb something that no one else did . . . it should be examined to see whether any reliable transmitter other than Ayyūb transmitted this hadith from Ibn Sīrīn. If that is found, then it is known that the hadith has an original version (*aṣl*) to which it goes back. If what is described is not found, it should then be examined to see whether any reliable transmitter other than Ibn Sīrīn transmitted this hadith from Abū Hurayrah. If that is found, then it is known that the hadith has an original version. If what is said is not found, then it should be examined to see whether anyone transmitted this hadith from the Prophet other than Abū Hurayrah. If that is found, it is established that the hadith has an original version. If it is not found . . . then it is known that the report is undoubtedly a forgery and that the transmitter who alone transmitted it (*tafarrada bihī*) is the one who forged it.[52]

Through this detailed clarification, it becomes evident that in early times *iʿtibār al-ḥadīth* includes the comprehensive study of the transmission lines of the hadith.[53]

The usage of the term *iʿtibār*, however, becomes looser with later hadith scholars. In their terminology, *iʿtibār* simply means to study a certain hadith that is transmitted isolated to find out whether the hadith is also narrated by other transmitters or not. This analysis begins with the original transmitter's shaykh and goes on to the last part of the *isnād*; that is, the Companion. In other words, one should investigate to see whether the hadith is transmitted by other transmitters from the shaykh of the original transmitter or not; if not, from the shaykh of that shaykh, and so on. This process will be repeated until it reaches the Companion. The hadith that is found on one of these stages (*ṭabaqāt*) is called *mutābiᶜ* (pl. *mutābiᶜāt*), and this process of investigation is named *mutābaᶜah*. If the *mutābiᶜ* is found in none of these *isnād* stages, then it is investigated whether a hadith with a similar meaning is also transmitted or not. Such a hadith is called *shāhid* (pl. *shawāhid*), and the process is named *istishhād*. A hadith lacking *mutābiᶜāt* and *shawāhid* is called *al-fard al-muṭlaq*.[54]

It should be noted that, compared with the original version (*aṣl*) of the hadith, the *mutābiᶜāt* and the *shawāhid* are less authoritative. They are to be transmitted merely to strengthen the *aṣl*; in other words, one would trust the *aṣl* but neither the *mutābiᶜāt* nor the *shawāhid*.[55] Therefore, Ibn al-Ṣalāḥ mentions that al-Bukhārī and Muslim would at times use, as their *mutābiᶜāt* and *shawāhid*, the narrations of those whose hadiths alone could not be used as proof (*lā yuḥtajju bi-ḥadīthihī waḥdah*) and would sometimes even be considered 'weak' transmitters (*ḍaᶜīf*; pl. *ḍuᶜafāᵓ*).[56] As al-Qāḍī ᶜIyāḍ (d. 544/1149) explains, the selection and categorisation of hadiths in Muslim's *Ṣaḥīḥ* are based on this very principle. The hadiths of his *Ṣaḥīḥ* are of three groups: the first group are the hadiths of those whose 'retentiveness' (*ḥifẓ*) and 'accuracy' (*itqān*) are agreed upon; the second group are the hadiths of those who are considered to have lesser retentiveness and accuracy; and, finally come the hadiths of the third group, whose 'reliability' (*thiqah*) is disputed. In each chapter of his book, Muslim has ordered the hadiths according to the afore-mentioned categories: the hadiths belonging to the first category come first as *aṣl* and are followed by the hadiths of the second and third categories as *mutābiᶜ* or *shāhid*.[57] Another example for this claim can be found in the terminology employed in assessing transmitters' reliability (*al-jarḥ wa-l-taᶜdīl*). Ibn Abī Ḥātim al-Rāzī (d. 327/938) presents an eight-level classification for transmitter competence in a descending order. On the highest level are placed *thiqah* (reliable) and *mutqin* (accurate) transmitters, whose hadiths could be used as proof (*yuḥtajju bihī*), and on the lowest level *matrūk al-ḥadīth* (abandoned in hadith) and *kadhdhāb* (liar) transmitters. From amongst all of them, the hadiths of those who belong to the lowest level of reliable transmitters, that is, *ṣāliḥ al-ḥadīth* (good in hadith), and the first three levels of unreliable transmitters that are disparaged, that is, *layyin al-ḥadīth* (soft in hadith), *laysa bi-qawī* (not strong) and *ḍaᶜīf al-ḥadīth* (weak in hadith), are used in *iᶜtibār al-ḥadīth*.[58]

Tafarrud and its Relation to the Terms *shādhdh* and *munkar*

Early hadith scholars held a strict position regarding *tafarrud* of transmitters. In the process of *iᶜtibār al-ḥadīth*, if they failed to find a *mutābiᶜ* or a *shāhid*, they would simply label that particular hadith *shādhdh* (anomalous) or *munkar* (unfamiliar) and set it aside. Al-Khaṭīb al-Baghdādī (d. 463/1071) dedicates a whole chapter of his book *al-Kifāyah* to the negative statements of some early hadith critics, namely, Shuᶜbah ibn al-Ḥajjāj (d. 160/776–7), ᶜAbd al-Raḥmān ibn al-Mahdī (d. 198/814) and Ibn Ḥanbal, about the *shādhdh*, *munkar* and *gharīb*.[59] According to Ibn Rajab al-Ḥanbalī (d. 795/1393), if a hadith was transmitted by a single transmitter and lacked a *mutābi*ᶜ, the early hadith scholars 'would consider it a defect (ᶜ*illah*) in that hadith . . . and *fard* hadiths even from the reliable authorities would not be accepted'.[60] Quoting Abū Bakr Aḥmad ibn Hārūn al-Bardījī (d. 301/914), who defines *munkar* as 'a hadith that a person would transmit from the Companions or the Successors whose *matn* could not be recognised otherwise than through him', Ibn Rajab regards the terms *fard* and *munkar* as equivalents.[61] In order to affirm this claim, he cites various examples regarding which critics such as Ibn Ḥanbal, al-Bardījī and Abū Ḥātim al-Rāzī (d. 277/890) considered some hadiths transmitted by reliable transmitters to be *munkar*.[62] The definitions suggested for the term *shādhdh* by al-Ḥākim al-Naysābūrī (d. 405/1014) and Abū Yaᶜlá al-Khalīlī (d. 446/1054) are also based on *tafarrud*: a hadith that 'is transmitted isolated and has no *mutābi*ᶜ' – even though al-Ḥākim considers the 'reliability of the transmitter' a necessary condition for the given hadith in order to be regarded as *shādhdh*,[63] while al-Khalīlī does not make it dependent on any condition.[64] As Ibn al-Ṣalāḥ rightly conceived, the definitions of al-Ḥākim and al-Khalīlī entail the equivalence of *fard* and *shādhdh*, and as a result lead to the rejection of hadiths regarded as *fard*.[65]

The position of the Muslim jurists and later hadith scholars, however, was gradually adjusted over time. Revising the early hadith scholars' terminology, they tried to provide a ground for accepting those *fard*s which were transmitted by reliable transmitters (*thiqāt*). Ibn Ḥazm al-Andalusī (d. 456/1064) was the first to state that, 'One should accept a hadith that the reliable transmitter related from the Prophet through a reliable transmitter . . . whether that hadith is transmitted through other transmission lines or transmitted only through that single strand.'[66] This idea implies the categorical acceptance of the isolated transmission of the reliable transmitter (*tafarrud al-thiqah*), and it was followed by other hadith scholars and jurists after Ibn Ḥazm, such as Ibn al-Qaṭṭān al-Fāsī (d. 628/1231), who believed that *infirād* (equivalent to *tafarrud*) 'would cause no defect in a hadith, so long as its transmitter was reliable'.[67]

Accordingly, using a statement ascribed to al-Shāfiᶜī, Ibn al-Ṣalāḥ presents yet a new definition for the term *shādhdh* (and also *munkar*).[68] According to him:

> when a transmitter is alone in transmitting a hadith, it should be examined. If the hadith he transmitted conflicts with what was transmitted by someone superior to him in retentiveness and accuracy, the hadith that he is alone in transmitting is *shādhdh* and *munkar*. If in his narration there is no conflict with what someone else transmitted – and it is something only he (and no one else) transmitted – then the transmitter who is alone in transmitting it is examined. If he is upright (ᶜ*adl*) and retentive (*ḥāfiẓ*) and his exactitude and accuracy may be trusted, then the hadith that he is alone in transmitting is accepted, and his being alone in transmitting the hadith does not impugn it . . . If he is one of those whose

> retentiveness and accuracy in transmission may not be trusted for the hadith that he is alone in transmitting, then his *tafarrud* pierces it and tears it from the domain of sound (*ṣaḥīḥ*) *hadith*.[69]

Finally, Ibn al-Ṣalāḥ divides the rejected *shādhdh* into two groups: (1) the *fard* that conflicts with that of the reliable transmitter; and (2) the *fard* whose transmitter does not possess sufficient reliability and precision to counteract the unfamiliarity and weakness that isolation and anomaly engender.[70] He then takes the *munkar* to be synonymous with the rejected *shādhdh* and repeats this very twofold classification for that as well.[71] The hadith scholars after Ibn al-Ṣalāḥ also repeated the same pattern and hence prevented many *fards* from being considered *munkar* or *shādhdh*.[72]

The *madār* of the Hadith

Although the term *madār* is not defined as a technical term in the manuals of hadith terminology (*muṣṭalaḥ al-ḥadīth*), studying its prevalent and diverse use in the hadith literature, one can identify its technical meaning. To distinguish the usage of this word as a technical term in hadith terminology from its other applications, one should consider the context in which the term *madār* is used.

In those cases in which the word *madār* is used to signify one single transmitter – the most frequent application of this word in the hadith literature – one can regard it as a technical term. This term mostly follows formulas such as 'The *madār* of this hadith is upon so-and-so (transmitter)' (*madāru 'l-ḥadīthi ᶜalá fulān*).[73] Sometimes it is used in a verbal form like 'This hadith revolves around so-and-so (transmitter)' (*yadūru 'l-ḥadīth ᶜalá fulān*).[74] At times, synonymous nouns and verbs are also used to indicate the same; for instance, *rajaᶜa, yarjiᶜu* instead of *dāra, yadūru,* following the pattern 'This hadith goes back to so-and-so (transmitter)' (*yarjiᶜu 'l-ḥadīthu ilá fulān*). Corroborating this interpretation is the concurrent use of these words; for example, 'This report has no *madār* to which it could go back' (*laysa l-il-khabari madārun yarjiᶜu ilayh*);[75] 'Their *madār* and their return (*rujūᶜ*) are to so-and-so (transmitter)' (*madāruhum wa-rujūᶜuhum ilá fulān*);[76] 'The *madār* of this hadith goes back to so-and-so (transmitter)' (*madāru 'l-ḥadīthi yarjiᶜu ilá fulān*).[77] Other expressions are also applied indicating a *madār* in the *isnāds* of a hadith; for instance, 'This hadith is known through so-and-so (transmitter)' (*hādhā 'l-ḥadīthu maᶜrūfun bi-fulān*,[78] *hādhā 'l-ḥadīthu yuᶜrafu bi-fulān* or *lā yuᶜrafu hādhā 'l-ḥadīthu illā bi-fulān*[79]), or 'this hadith belongs to so-and-so (transmitter)' (*al-ḥadīthu li-fulān*).[80] These expressions are comparable to what al-Tirmidhī uses for *gharīb* hadiths.[81]

Hadith scholars have used the term *madār* for certain hadiths with a unique feature: those hadiths, although transmitted with various *isnāds*, that all have a common transmitter, with the rest of the *isnād*[82] remaining the same from that common transmitter to the Prophet. This transmitter, who is the converging point where all the different *isnāds* of a hadith meet and who transmits the hadith through a single strand from the Prophet, is called *madār*. This feature fits very well the aforementioned definition of the common link.[83] As we have already seen, this phenomenon is called *al-fard al-muṭlaq* or *gharīb* in hadith terminology.[84] The typical example of this phenomenon is the famous hadith of intention: 'Deeds are to be appraised only by their intentions' (*innamā l-aᶜmālu bi-n-nīyāt*). This hadith is found in the hadith collections with various *isnāds* that all go back to Yaḥyá ibn Saᶜīd ibn Qays al-Anṣārī (d. 144/761–2?). Thenceforth, Yaḥyá transmits it through a single strand, Muḥammad ibn Ibrāhīm al-Taymī (d. 120/737–8) < ᶜAlqamah ibn Waqqāṣ al-Laythī < ᶜUmar ibn al-Khaṭṭāb < the Prophet.[85] This reveals why al-Khalīlī regarded Yaḥyá as the *madār* of this hadith.[86]

The Usage of the Term *madār*

In early hadith literature, the term *madār* does not appear frequently. Its earliest usage is apparently in a saying by the well-known hadith scholar ᶜAbd al-Raḥmān ibn al-Mahdī, describing a *mursal* ('loose') hadith by Abū al-ᶜĀliyah Rufayᶜ ibn Mihrān al-Riyāḥī (d. 93/711–12) about laughter during prayer (*al-ḍaḥik fī al-ṣalāh*). Abū al-ᶜĀliyah is regarded as the *madār*, since different transmission lines of this hadith go back to him. When ᶜAlī ibn al-Madīnī, the famous hadith scholar and critic, asked ᶜAbd al-Raḥmān about other transmission lines of this hadith, in which Abū al-ᶜĀliyah is not included, he replied: *laysa yadūru hādhā 'l-ḥadīthu illā ᶜalá Abī 'l-ᶜĀliyah* ('this hadith revolves only around Abū al-ᶜĀliyah').[87]

Another early use of the term *madār* – and, of course, in a yet different context – can be found in ᶜAlī ibn al-Madīnī's *ᶜIlal*. By studying the *isnāds* of the hadiths and classifying them in four different centres, namely, Mecca, Medina, Basra and Kufa, Ibn al-Madīnī identifies six persons as the bases of *isnāds*: Ibn Shihāb al-Zuhrī (d. 124/742) in Medina, ᶜAmr ibn Dīnār (d. 126/743–4) in Mecca, Qatādah ibn Diᶜāmah al-Sadūsī (d. 118/736) and Yaḥyá ibn Abī Kathīr (d. 132/749–50) in Basra, and Abū Isḥāq ᶜAmr ibn ᶜAbd Allāh al-Sabīᶜī (d. 127/744–5) and Sulaymān ibn Mihrān al-Aᶜmash (d. 148/765) in Kufa.[88] They are, in fact, certain famous transmitters from different hadith centres who alone transmitted various hadiths and these very hadiths were spread only through them. Al-Ḥākim concedes that 'each of these hadith authorities alone transmitted from some shaykhs so that beside him no one else transmitted from them.'[89] In a chapter titled 'Those from whom no one has related except for a single transmitter', al-Ḥākim cites the names of some of these hadith authorities,[90] including al-Zuhrī, who was alone in transmitting from more than twenty Successors,[91] ᶜAmr ibn Dīnār, Yaḥyá ibn Saᶜīd al-Anṣārī, Abū Isḥāq al-Sabīᶜī, and Hishām ibn ᶜUrwah (d. 146/763–4), each of whom was alone in transmitting from a group of Successors. It is the case also for Mālik ibn Anas (who was alone in transmitting from almost ten of the shaykhs of Medina), Sufyān al-Thawrī (who was alone in transmitting from more than ten shaykhs) and Shuʿbah ibn al-Ḥajjāj (who was alone in transmitting from around thirty shaykhs).[92] Al-Ḥākim, in the last part of his book, gives a detailed list of the well-known transmitters from the generation of the Successors and the Successors of the Successors from different regions of the Muslim world, whose isolated transmissions were regarded as acceptable (*maqbūl*).[93]

Although the word *madār* was not frequently used as a technical term during the first Islamic centuries, in the fourth and fifth centuries it became very common among hadith scholars and critics. An outstanding application of this term can be seen in *ʿilal* books such as Ibn ʿAdī's *al-Kāmil fī ḍuʿafāʾ al-rijāl* and al-Dāraquṭnī's *al-ʿIlal al-wāridah fī al-aḥādīth al-nabawīyah*. Ibn ʿAdī and al-Dāraquṭnī use this term in two different contexts.

1. Sometimes, they call a transmitter the *madār* of a prophetic hadith; that is, the person to whom the various lines of transmission go back. For instance:
   - Saʿd ibn Saʿīd ibn Qays al-Anṣārī (d. 141/758–9) is regarded as the *madār* of two prophetic hadiths.[94] The first one is transmitted from ʿUmar ibn Thābit al-Anṣārī from Abū Ayyūb al-Anṣārī,[95] the second from ʿAmrah (or ʿUrwah ibn al-Zubayr?) from ʿĀʾishah.[96]
   - ʿUthmān ibn ʿAṭāʾ al-Khurāsānī (d. 151/768–9) is considered the *madār* of the hadith ascribed to Dhū al-Aṣābiʿ al-Juhanī, a Companion of the Prophet, regarding Jerusalem.[97]
2. In criticising some *isnād*s of a prophetic hadith that do not have a *madār*, they sometimes compare those *isnād*s with others that do have a *madār* and hence mention their defects. In other words, relying on the reputation of the hadith through the *madār*'s narration, they criticise other lines of transmission. For example:
   - Ḥasan ibn Yazīd al-Kūfī transmits a prophetic hadith with the following *isnād*: al-Suddī < Aws ibn Ḍamʿaj al-Ḥaḍramī < Ibn Masʿūd. Ibn ʿAdī assumes that this transmission line is not reliable because the *madār* of this hadith is Ismāʿīl ibn Rajāʾ al-Zabīdī, who related it from al-Ḥaḍramī from Ibn Masʿūd.[98]
   - Regarding the different *isnād*s that are mentioned for the hadith of laughter during the prayer, Ibn ʿAdī says, 'They [i.e., al-Ḥasan al-Baṣrī, Qatādah, Ibrāhīm al-Nakhaʿī, and al-Zuhrī] have transmitted this hadith, either as *mursal* or *muttaṣil* (uninterrupted), while their *madār* and their reference all go back to Abū al-ʿĀliyah.' He then analyses the mentioned *isnād*s in detail and thence concludes, 'This is his hadith [i.e., Abū al-ʿĀliyah's], known through him.'[99]
   - Al-Dāraquṭnī regards Bakr ibn ʿAbd Allāh al-Muzanī as the *madār* of a hadith transmitted from al-Mughīrah ibn Shuʿbah from the Prophet. He considers erroneous other *isnād*s of this hadith, in which instead of Bakr other transmitters like Abū

ᶜUthmān al-Nahdī, Anas, and Ḥumayd al-Ṭawīl narrated from al-Mughīrah, and states that the *madār* of this hadith is Bakr.[100]

Another example of the use of the term *madār* is found in al-Ḥākim's *al-Mustadrak ᶜalá* al-Ṣaḥīḥayn. In this book, he compiles the hadiths that, based on the principles of al-Bukhārī and Muslim, should be considered sound (*ṣaḥīḥ*), although they are not included by the *shaykhayn*, meaning al-Bukhārī and Muslim, in their hadith collections. In explaining the absence of these hadiths in their collections, he makes use of the term *madār*. As an example, he brings up a prophetic hadith on the recitation of the Qurᵓān narrated by ᶜAlī ibn Abī Ṭālib and labels its *isnād* as *ṣaḥīḥ*. He then states, 'Neither of the *shaykhayn* relied on ᶜAbd Allāh ibn Salamah as a proof, whereas he is not disparaged, and the *madār* of this hadith is upon him.'[101]

In later hadith works, the term *madār* is used in the context of hadith classification. Since the term *madār* per se indicates neither the discrediting (*al-jarḥ*) nor the accrediting of transmitters (*al-taᶜdīl*), it is used in combination with other technical terms, often regarding the discrediting – and in some limited cases, regarding the accrediting – of transmitters, so that the qualification of the transmitter, and as a result the status of the hadith, can be determined. Therefore, as Özkan correctly recognised, the term *madār*, in the context of hadith criticism, is considered 'a crucial point' of the *isnād*; that is, a transmitter in the *isnād* on whose qualification the soundness or weakness of the hadith relies.[102] This use of the term is especially evident in *al-Sunan* of al-Bayhaqī (d. 458 / 1066) and *al-Istidhkār* and *al-Tamhīd* of Ibn ᶜAbd al-Barr (d. 463 / 1071); of each some examples are mentioned:

- Abān ibn Abī ᶜAyyāsh is regarded as the *madār* of a hadith on '*qunūt al-witr qabla al-rukūᶜ*' (special invocation of the *witr* prayer before the bowing) and it is said that Abān is *matrūk* (abandoned).[103]
- The *madār*s of a hadith about intentional murder with a sword are Jābir ibn Yazīd al-Juᶜfī and al-Qays ibn Rabīᶜ, whose hadiths are not relied on as proof (*lā yuḥtajju bihimā*).[104]
- Abū Qudāmah Ḥārith ibn ᶜUbayd al-Iyādī is regarded as the *madār* of a hadith about *sujūd al-mufaṣṣalāt* (prostrations called for in connection with late chapters of the Qurᵓān), who was discredited by Yaḥyá ibn Maᶜīn (*ḍaᶜᶜafahū*).[105]
- It is stated that the hadith about warranting the debt of a dead man by ᶜAlī ibn Abī Ṭālib that ᶜAṭīyah ibn Saᶜd al-ᶜAwfī transmitted from Abū Saᶜīd al-Khudrī revolves around ᶜUbayd Allāh ibn Walīd al-Waṣṣāfī, who is very weak (*ḍaᶜīf jiddan*).[106]
- The hadith of killing believers as punishment for killing unbelievers is regarded as weak because it revolves around Ibrāhīm ibn Abī Yaḥyá, who is not reliable (*laysa lahū wajh*).[107]
- The hadith *lā nadhra fī maᶜṣiyatin wa-kaffāratuhū kaffāratu yamīn* ('there is no vow to commit a sin and its atonement is that of an

oath') is transmitted by ᶜImrān ibn Ḥuṣayn as well as ᶜĀʾishah (or Abū Hurayrah?); the *madār* of the first narration is considered to be Muḥammad ibn al-Zubayr al-Ḥanẓalī[108] and that of the second one is Sulaymān ibn Arqam.[109] Both transmitters are weak and therefore the hadith scholars regard Muḥammad's hadiths as *munkar* and Sulaymān's as *matrūk*.
- ᶜĀṣim ibn ᶜUmar ibn Qatādah, who is seen as the *madār* of a hadith narrated by Rāfiᶜ ibn Khadīj from the Prophet, is weak (*laysa bi-qawī*).[110]

By investigating different uses of the term *madār*, one may clarify its relation to the terms *tafarrud*/*infirād* becomes apparent as well. These two terms are sometimes used together. For example, Zayd ibn al-Ḥawārī al-ᶜAmmī is considered the *madār* of a hadith on the virtue of repeating one's ablutions and it is said that he is alone in transmitting this hadith.[111] It is often the case that the *tafarrud*/*infirād* of a *madār* in the transmission of a hadith is mentioned implicitly. For example, ᶜAbd al-Karīm ibn Abī al-Mukhāriq is cited as the *madār* of a hadith about 'the meat of animals' and it is underlined that aside from him no one else transmitted this hadith (*laysa yarwīhi ghayruhū*).[112] One can also add, to the already mentioned examples, many cases in which the transmitter is described as being alone (*munfarid*/*mutafarrid*) in transmitting the hadith, without being labelled *madār*.[113]

In later times, the diverse and widespread use of the term *madār* is seen in hadith commentaries by well-known scholars like al-Nawawī (d. 676 / 1277),[114] Ibn al-Turkumānī (d. 750 / 1349),[115] al-Zaylaᶜī (d. 762 / 1360),[116] Ibn al-Mulaqqin (d. 804 / 1401),[117] al-Haythamī (d. 807 / 1405),[118] al-Būṣīrī (d. 840 / 1436),[119] Ibn Ḥajar al-ᶜAsqalānī (d. 852 / 1449)[120] and al-ᶜAynī (d. 855 / 1451).[121] Furthermore, during this time there was an attempt to moderate the critical approach of the early hadith scholars and critics about the *madār*s and their hadiths. While in the early hadith literature the term *madār* had a mainly negative connotation in regard to the transmitter and to the hadith transmitted by him, the later hadith commentators, by collecting different versions of the hadith, tried to disassociate the *madār* from *tafarrud* and hence to promote the quality of his hadith. Therefore, although a transmitter who was considered weak by the early hadith scholars would be regarded as 'the *madār* of the hadith', it is also stated that he is not the only one who transmitted the hadith; that it was also transmitted by others, who are regarded as reliable. In other words, later commentators sought to find one or more *mutābiᶜ*s or *shāhid*s for any *fard* hadith. Consider the following instances:

- Ibn al-Turkumānī regarded al-Aᶜmash's version of the hadith on *qunūt al-witr qabla al-rukūᶜ* as a *mutābiᶜ* for Abān ibn Abī ᶜAyyāsh's one, stating that the transmitters of this version are all reliable.[122] By contrast, al-Bayhaqī had already considered Abān the *madār* of the hadith and hence al-Aᶜmash's one was invalid.[123]

- Al-Būṣīrī regarded the *madār* of a hadith by ᶜAbd Allāh ibn Masᶜūd from Ibrāhīm ibn Muslim al-Hajarī as weak, yet he mentions that it was not only Ibrāhīm who transmitted this hadith, for it had a *mutābiᶜ*; besides, a *shāhid* can also be found in Muslim's collection.[124]
- Al-Būṣīrī regarded ᶜAbd al-Raḥmān ibn Ziyād al-Ifrīqī as the *madār* of the hadith of Abū Ayyūb on 'the claim of a Muslim on a Muslim',[125] who was regarded as weak by early hadith scholars and stringent critics like Ibn Ḥanbal, Ibn Maᶜīn, al-Tirmidhī and al-Nasāʾī. Nevertheless, al-Būṣīrī stresses that he was not alone in transmitting this hadith and that a *shāhid* for this hadith was transmitted by Muslim from Abū Hurayrah.[126]
- Ibn Ḥajar al-ᶜAsqalānī transmitted a hadith from Ibn ᶜAbbās about 'three things that the Prophet made obligatory upon himself and recommended for others'. The *madār* of this hadith is Abū Janāb al-Kalbī, who used to tamper with *isnād*s (*mudallis*) and was also a weak transmitter, whose hadiths were regarded as weak by early hadith scholars. Ibn Ḥajar added, 'It is not just Abū Janāb who transmitted it: this hadith has two *mutābiᶜ*s, though whose transmitters are weak.'[127]
- Ibn ᶜAbd al-Barr regarded ᶜAbd al-Raḥmān ibn Isḥāq al-Wāsiṭī as the *madār* of the hadith on the issue that the sacred months are always thirty days and considered him weak.[128] By contrast, al-ᶜAynī did not accept his being a *madār* because this hadith has a *mutābiᶜ* whose transmitters in the *isnād* are all reliable.[129]
- Al-Bayhaqī regarded al-Haramī ibn ᶜAbd Allāh as the *madār* of Khuzaymah ibn Thābit al-Anṣārī's hadith from the Prophet on 'anal intercourse with women' and hence considered erroneous ᶜUmāra ibn Khuzaymah's narration from his father, which is transmitted only through Ibn ᶜUyaynah.[130] Ibn al-Turkumānī objects to the idea of considering al-Haramī as *madār* and refers as proof to other versions that other transmitters related from Khuzaymah, although some of them had been already mentioned by al-Bayhaqī himself.[131]

Sometimes, the later hadith commentators would not find it sufficient to cite only the *mutābiᶜ* or *shāhid*, but would also find another *madār* for the hadith. An example is the hadith of *man ṣāma Ramaḍān wa-sittan min Shawwāl* ('whoever fasts Ramadan and six days of Shawwāl').[132] Ibn ᶜAdī identified Saᶜd ibn Saᶜīd ibn Qays al-Anṣārī as the *madār* of this hadith, which was narrated by Abū Ayyūb al-Anṣārī. To the contrary, by mentioning a similar *hadith* by Jābir ibn ᶜAbd Allāh al-Anṣārī, al-Būṣīrī indicated ᶜAmr ibn Jābir al-Ḥaḍramī as the *madār* of this hadith and cited Abū Ayyūb's hadith as its *shāhid*.[133] Al-Būṣīrī, indeed, provided for Saᶜd's hadith not just one hadith as *shāhid* but a collection of *shawāhid* which themselves have an independent *madār*; that is, Abū Ayyūb.

The *madārs*' Generation and the Validity of their Isolated Hadiths

By reviewing the names of the transmitters who, in the hadith literature, are listed under titles such as 'the authorities around whom *isnāds* revolve' or 'the *madārs* of the hadiths', it becomes clear that the major part of these transmitters belongs to the young Successors' generation (*ṣighār al-tābiᶜīn*) or the generation after the Successors (*atbāᶜ al-tābiᶜīn*).[134] To explain this, one needs to take into consideration the origin and development of the *isnād* system in the first two centuries. The *isnād* 'as an institution' and 'as a compulsory authentication device' and its spread amongst the transmitters originated in the late seventies of the first century AH/second half of the seventh century CE, and then the various centres of learning adopted the *isnād* at varying rates. That means that the people became accustomed to giving authorities for their reports at the earliest by the end of the first/seventh century or at the beginning of the second/eighth century, when the Successors flourished.[135] It is only after this period, that is, around the second half of the second/eighth century, that hadith transmission became widespread and the *isnād* investigation grew common. Thereafter, the attempt to compile the hadiths and their transmission lines became popular amongst the traditionists to the extent that one would even travel to other lands, near and far afield, in order to hear hadiths and acquire elevated *isnāds* (*al-isnād al-ᶜālī*).[136] It is obvious that during this time, hadiths would be transmitted isolated (*mutafarrid*) and the later hadith scholars would see no defect in them. It is also asserted that the *tafarrud* of the transmitters in this period is admissible, because they were the immediate conveyers of the prophetic tradition (*al-sunnah al-nabawīyah*).[137] After the formation of the circles of learning hadiths and the prevalence of hadith teaching and learning in the public assemblies, transmission lines of hadiths also increased in number, and the hadith scholars' attempt was then to compile the different transmission lines. From this time on, the hadith scholars decided to detect *fards* and *gharībs* and to compensate for their *taffarud* and *gharābah* through finding *mutābiᶜāt* and *shawāhid*. Al-Dhahabī's statement in this regard is insightful. According to him, accepting a *fard* depends on the level to which the transmitter belongs:

> If one of the Successors were alone in transmitting, his hadith would be regarded as *ṣaḥīḥ*. If the transmitter belonged to the generation after the Successors, his hadith would be labelled *ṣaḥīḥ gharīb*. And if he were to be one of the students of the Successors of the Successors, his hadith would be called *gharīb* and *fard*. However, the *tafarrud* of the last group is very rare.[138]

He, of course, adds that some would be more cautious in accepting the *tafarrud* of the generation of the Successors of the Successors and would also occasionally avoid calling them *ṣaḥīḥ* and *gharīb* simultaneously. Rather, some scholars regarded their *fards* – like those of Hushaym ibn Bashīr and Ḥafṣ ibn Ghiyāth (d. 194/809–10) – as *munkar*.[139] Al-Dhahabī also confirms that *tafarrud* seems implausible by the transmitters of the generation after the Successors of the Successors and, in his opinion, there is almost a consensus that the last group's *fard*s are considered *munkar*.[140]

This strict attitude towards the transmitters of the generation after the Successors is also found in the words of the early hadith scholars. In response to the question, 'Whose transmission is not acceptable?' Shuʿbah ibn al-Ḥajjāj maintained, 'The one who transmitted from well-known people what others did not know.'[141] Muslim highlights this principle in the introduction to his *Ṣaḥīḥ* as well as in his *Kitāb al-Tamyīz*. According to him, if a transmitter related a hadith from well-known people like al-Zuhrī and Hishām ibn ʿUrwah, whose hadiths are famous amongst the traditionists on account of the high number of their students and the people who transmit from them, that was nevertheless unknown to their students (*lā yaʿrifuhū aḥadun min aṣḥābihimā*), then the hadith of this person cannot be accepted.[142] Perhaps the statement by Abū Dāwūd al-Sijistānī (d. 275/889) could also be put in the same context, when he states, 'The *gharīb* cannot be taken as a proof, even if someone like Mālik ibn Anas or Yaḥyá ibn Saʿīd al-Anṣārī has transmitted it and the great authorities and reliable transmitters related.'[143] The cases that al-Ḥākim includes in the second category of the *fard* are also of this kind: 'The hadith that some person alone transmitted from the hadith authorities.'[144] He cites some examples of this category and at the end emphasises that examples of it are many. The instances given by him match exactly the already mentioned definition of *al-fard al-muṭlaq*.[145] This category also accords with the definition provided by Ibn Mandah for the *gharīb*. According to him, 'The *gharīb* is an isolated hadith transmitted isolated from the authorities, such as al-Zuhrī and Qatādah, whose hadiths would be compiled.'[146]

The common ground in these statements is that when an isolated hadith is transmitted from the hadith authorities, considering the high number of their students and popularity of their hadiths, one should doubt the authenticity and validity of such a transmission. This implies that from the transmitters who were not of that high status and popularity or did not have large teaching circles to disseminate their hadiths so widely one can expect isolated hadiths. It means that the *tafarrud* of the common links – who belong to the generation of the young Successors or a generation after that – in transmitting the hadiths does not seem implausible. However, for later generations, it is expected that their hadiths would be transmitted through several transmission lines, since the students of the common links, that is, the partial common links, would not encounter the restrictions of the former generations and were living at a time when the hadith transmission system was well organised. This idea fits well with Juynboll's view: *tafarrud* at the level of the 'common links' and several transmission lines at the later levels of the 'partial common links'. It also confirms Juynboll's condition for the historicity of a common link, while he requires at least three (or two, in his later works) partial common links to substantiate the historicity of an *isnād* bundle. On the contrary, various single strands from the transmitters of a particular time when hadith teaching and learning had sufficiently grown and the *isnād* system had been stabilised might only make an unhistorical 'spider'.[147]

The Relation between the Terms *madār* and Common Link

The relationship between the terms *gharīb, tafarrud/infirād* and *madār* has become apparent. It has also been clarified that there is a firm association between what the Western scholars regard as the common link and these terms, especially the *madār*. Perhaps the most significant similarity between the terms *common link* and *madār* is found in the definition given for them, which is confirmed by the given examples. By gathering various *isnād*s found in the hadith collections in support of one particular hadith and putting them together – especially when they are incorporated in a visual diagram, one renders the common link or *madār* visible. As Juynboll observes, 'from the bottom up one finds first a single row or strand of mostly three, four or more names beginning with the Prophet or another ancient authority. Where the names start fanning out in branches, we find the common link',[148] '. . . who hears something from (seldom more than) one authority and passes it on to a number of pupils, most of whom pass it on in their turn to two or more of their pupils.'[149]

Despite this principle commonality, the Muslim hadith scholars' understanding of the common link phenomenon fundamentally differs from that of the Western scholars, something which goes back to differences between the Western and Islamic approaches. The Muslim scholars' primary concern has always been the issue of authority (*ḥujjīyah*), because hadith has always been regarded as one of the main religious sources, be it for *fiqh* (law), *kalām* (theology) or *tafsīr* (Qurʾānic exegesis). Western scholars study hadith from a different perspective. In their view, the authenticity (*aṣālah*) of hadith, not its authority, is of greater significance.[150] Hence, it is possible to find a hadith that is regarded as weak or fictitious by Muslim scholars, whereas for Western scholars it would contain valuable information regarding the particular historical time and age when the hadith was forged. Conversely, a hadith that Muslim scholars would take as proof for a legal decision or as support for a theological viewpoint or exegetical interpretation would not necessarily be regarded by Western scholars as historically reliable and authentic. Whereas Western scholars, especially Schacht and Juynboll, take the *tafarrud* of the *madār* / the common link as noticeable historical evidence to establish the historical origin and development of a hadith, early Muslim hadith scholars and critics did not take the *tafarrud* of the transmitter necessarily but as an indicator of the weakness of the hadith, rather as a sign signalling a defect in its transmission and would, therefore, examine the accuracy of its transmission. Considering the evidence of reliability and the generation to which the *madār* and his transmitter(s) belong, as well as the fame (*shuhrah*) of the *matn* of the hadith transmitted by the *madār* and its agreement or disagreement with other well-known hadiths, they would decide on the soundness or weakness and finally on the authority of the hadith.

Referring to this very fact, Özkan concludes that the terms common link and *madār* are not equivalent:

> The common link and *madār* may resemble one another in some respects, and there may be a vague structural similarity between them, but both have different contexts, occurrences, and usages, as well as different interpretations, implications and consequences . . . Each term emerged in different circumstances (time and place) and belongs to a different terminological structure.[151]

There is no doubt that these two terms come from different scientific and cultural contexts. One should consider, however, that both terms are addressing one and the same phenomenon. *Pace* Özkan, to relate these two different contexts to each other and to provide evidence from both paradigms to gain a better understanding of the very phenomenon is not only correct but also highly desirable.

Özkan's arguments regarding his criticism of the equivalence of the terms *madār* and common link are far from convincing. On the strength of the information presented in the earlier parts of the present chapter, I argue briefly against his points of objection. Concerning his first objection, that finding some *madār*s among the generation of the Companions or the old Successors contradicts the concept of the common link, one should distinguish between the existence of such cases in the hadith literature and the question of how to interpret the evidence. Juynboll does not claim that by gathering the *isnād*s of hadiths, common links can never be found in those generations. He rather holds that such common links are not real, and he labels them 'seeming common links'.[152] Of course, as Özkan himself mentions,[153] not all scholars who use the common-link phenomenon for dating hadiths agree with Juynboll's interpretation.[154] However, they also do not agree among themselves regarding the issue of how one could explain the appearance of a common link on the level of the Companions in a way that would be compatible with the historical facts of the first century.[155]

The argument just mentioned holds true as well for Özkan's second objection; that is, the problem of the plurality of the *madār*s in one and the same hadith. We should once again differentiate between the phenomenon itself and the interpretation thereof. According to Juynboll's interpretation, if a *real* common link had to exist, there would not be more than one, and that too could be identified through differentiating between the *isnād*s containing the 'partial common links' and the 'single strands'. According to another interpretation of the common link, the existence of two or more common links in one and the same generation implies the existence of a common source, from whom they all received the hadith. The accuracy of this claim can be verified by comparing the *mutūn* of the different versions of the hadiths transmitted from each of these common links and examining the correlation between these *mutūn* and their *isnāds*.[156]

Finally, concerning the claim that the *madār* is not an equivalent of *tafarrud*, it should be pointed out that, apart from the inconsistencies in Özkan's examples,[157] he fails to consider the discrepancies in the application of the term *madār* by early and late hadith scholars. As shown in the preceding sections, early hadith scholars' usage of the term *madār* implicitly (or sometimes explicitly) indicates the *tafarrud* of the transmitter in relating the hadith as well. Many attempts, however, were made by later hadith scholars to modify the rigorous approach of early hadith scholars and critics to the *madārs* and the hadiths transmitted by them. While in the early literature, the term *madār* was mainly used with a negative connotation about the transmitter and his hadith, later hadith commentators, through collecting different versions of the hadith and finding *mutābiʿāt* or *shawāhid* for his *fard,* tried to prevent the *madār* from being discredited because of his *tafarrud* and to improve the quality of his hadith.[158]

Apart from these shortcomings, the most serious problem in Özkan's study is that he confines the interpretation of the common link to Schacht and Juynboll's,[159] whereas there are other explanations for this phenomenon. Schacht, and following him Juynboll, regarded the common link (or a person who used his name) as the one who put into circulation the hadith text and the single strand from the common link to the Prophet as 'fictitious', and thus, the time of the common link as the *terminus post quem* for the emergence of the hadith.[160] Others have considered the common link as the outcome of forgeries and fabrications devised in the following generations in *isnāds* of hadiths and hence questioned its validity for the purposes of dating hadiths.[161] There is yet a third group of scholars who regard the two previous interpretations as the result of hasty generalisations and consider the common link to be the 'early systematic collectors' of the hadiths, who sought to compile the knowledge of preceding generations and to disseminate them to their students. Through this interpretation, one could then better explain the existence of a single strand before and several branches after the common link.[162] This interpretation could also find support among the works of the early traditionists and hadith critics. As already mentioned, the famous transmitters of different hadith centres, who lived at the end of the first / seventh century and the beginning of the second / eighth century, are called *madārs* because they are considered to be responsible for the dissemination of hadiths – which they were mostly alone in transmitting – in their locales whose *isnāds* go back to them. Upon this very consideration, their isolated transmission seems not a defect to their hadiths and therefore was accepted by hadith scholars in the third and fourth / ninth and tenth centuries. Considering this interpretation of the common-link phenomenon can lead to a better understanding of the relation between the common link and the Muslims' hadith terminology, especially its use by early hadith scholars.

Notes

* Special thanks go to my colleagues Andreas Ismail Mohr, Pavel Pavlovich and Andreas Görke for their critical reading and feedback on the final version of this study. I am grateful to Devin Stewart for proofreading the text and for his kind help with polishing my English.

1. Joseph Schacht, *The Origins of Muhammadan Jurisprudence* (Oxford: Clarendon Press, 1950), 163–79.
2. Schacht, *Origins of Muhammadan Jurisprudence*, 171.
3. Schacht, *Origins of Muhammadan Jurisprudence*, 172.
4. See Schacht, *Origins of Muhammadan Jurisprudence*, 175–6.
5. For a general review of the issue, see Harald Motzki, 'Dating Muslim Traditions: a Survey', *Arabica* 52(2) (2005): 204–53, at 219–42.
6. Schacht, *Origins of Muhammadan Jurisprudence*, 172.
7. For example, Schacht, *Origins of Muhammadan Jurisprudence*, 173, 181–2.
8. Halit Ozkan (*sic*, hereafter referred to as Özkan), 'The Common Link and its Relation to the *Madār*', *Islamic Law and Society* 11(1) (2004): 42–77, at 44, n. 14.
9. Schacht, *Origins of Muhammadan Jurisprudence*, 171.
10. G. H. A. Juynboll, *Muslim Tradition: Studies in Chronology, Provenance and Authorship of Early Ḥadīth* (Cambridge: Cambridge University Press, 1983), 216.
11. See G. H. A. Juynboll, *Studies on the Origins and Uses of Islamic Ḥadīth* (Aldershot: Variorum, 1996).
12. For example, see G. H. A. Juynboll, 'The Role of Non-Arabs, the *Mawālī*, in the Early Development of Muslim *Ḥadīth*', *Le Muséon* 118 (2005): 355–86, at 164.
13. See G. H. A. Juynboll, 'Some *Isnād*-Analytical Methods Illustrated on the Basis of Several Woman-Demeaning Sayings from *Ḥadīth* Literature', *Al-Qanṭara* 10 (1989): 343–83, at 214–15; G. H. A. Juynboll, 'Nāfi[c], the *Mawlā* of Ibn [c]Umar, and His Position in Muslim *Ḥadīth* Literature', *Der Islam* 70 (1993): 207–44, at 214–15.
14. G. H. A. Juynboll, '(Re)appraisal of Some Technical Terms in *Ḥadīth* Science', *Islamic Law and Society* 8 (2001): 303–49, at 307, 311.
15. For instance, see Juynboll, '(Re)appraisal of Some Technical Terms', 311–12.
16. Juynboll, '(Re)appraisal of Some Technical Terms, 315–19.
17. Özkan, 'Common Link and its Relation to the *Madār*', 42.
18. Özkan, 'Common Link and its Relation to the *Madār*', 52–4.
19. Özkan, 'Common Link and its Relation to the *Madār*', 51, citing G. H. A. Juynboll, 'Some Notes on Islam's First *fuqahā*'', *Arabica* 39 (1992): 287–314, at 295–6.
20. Özkan, 'Common Link and its Relation to the *Madār*', 52.
21. Özkan, 'Common Link and its Relation to the *Madār*', 55–60.
22. Özkan, 'Common Link and its Relation to the *Madār*', 60.
23. Özkan, 'Common Link and its Relation to the *Madār*', 64. 'In the *ḥadīth* literature,' he himself concedes, 'we find cases in which the two terms appear to have the same meaning', but he considers this true 'only on occasion, as in some examples found in Ibn Ḥajar', which he interestingly uses in his argument against Juynboll; see ibid., 55–7.

24. Özkan, 'Common Link and its Relation to the *Madār*', 64.
25. Regarding this issue, two theses have been published: one on the term *madār* and its application in hadith works; the other on the notion of *tafarrud* and the circumstances of its being accepted or refused by Muslim hadith scholars. While in these two books a plethora of materials has been gathered from hadith literature, both authors fail to present consistent and intelligible pictures of the phenomena. I have to acknowledge, however, that I have much benefited from their works, particularly in preparing the raw material for the present study. See Muḥammad Mujīr al-Khaṭīb al-Ḥasanī, *Maᶜrifat madār al-isnād wa-bayān makānatihī fī ᶜilm ᶜilal al-ḥadīth*, 2 vols (Riyadh: Dār al-Maymān, 1428/2007), and ᶜAbd al-Jawād al-Ḥamām, *al-Tafarrud fī riwāyat al-ḥadīth wa-manhaj al-muḥaddithīn fī qabūlihī wa-raddih*, Mashrūᶜ miʾat risālah jāmiᶜīyah sūrīyah, 13 (Damascus: Dār al-Nawādir, 1429/2008).
26. Muḥammad ibn ᶜĪsá al-Tirmidhī, *al-Jāmiᶜ al-kabīr*, ed. Bashshār ᶜAwwād Maᶜrūf, 6 vols (Beirut: Dār al-Gharb al-Islāmī, 1996), 6:251–2, also 3:147–8, *al-aṭᶜimah* 13, *bāb mā jāʾa fī al-dhakāh fī al-ḥalq wa-l-labbah*, No. 1481; see also Yūsuf ibn ᶜAbd al-Raḥmān al-Mizzī, *Tuḥfat al-ashrāf bi-maᶜrifat al-aṭrāf*, ed. ᶜAbd al-Ṣamad Sharaf al-Dīn, 14 vols (Bhiwandi: al-Dār al-Qayyimah, 1384–1403/1965–82), 11:222–3, No. 15694; see also G. H. A. Juynboll, *Encyclopedia of Canonical Ḥadīth* (Leiden: Brill, 2007; hereafter *ECḤ*), 164.
27. Al-Tirmidhī, *Jāmiᶜ*, 6:252; see also 2:517–18, *al-buyūᶜ* 20, *bāb mā jāʾa fī karāhiyat bayᶜ al-walāʾ wa-hibatih*, No. 1236, and 4:5–6, *al-walāʾ wa-l-hibah* 2, *bāb mā jāʾa fī al-nahy ᶜan bayᶜ al-walāʾ wa-ᶜan hibatih*, No. 2126, where he considers the hadith to be *ḥasan ṣaḥīḥ*; see also al-Mizzī, 5:447, No. 7132, 5:449–50, No. 7150, 5:453, No. 7171, 5:454, No. 7186, 5:455, No. 7189, 5:456, No. 7199, 5:460, No. 7223, 5:464, No. 7250; see also Juynboll, *ECḤ*, 5.
28. Muslim ibn al-Ḥajjāj al-Qushayrī, *al-Jāmiᶜ al-ṣaḥīḥ*, 8 vols ([Istanbul]: al-Maṭbaᶜah al-ᶜĀmirah, 1330–4), 4:216, *al-ᶜitq* 4, *bāb al-nahy ᶜan bayᶜ al-walāʾ*, No. 1506: *'al-nās kulluhum ᶜiyāl ᶜalá ᶜAbd Allāh ibn Dīnār fī hādhā al-ḥadīth'*. For a detailed discussion of this hadith, see Schacht, *Origins of Muhammadan Jurisprudence*, 173–4; M. Mustafa Al-Azami, *On Schacht's Origins of Muhammadan Jurisprudence* (Riyadh: King Saud University, 1985; repr. Oxford: Oxford Centre for Islamic Studies, 1996), 200–5.
29. Al-Tirmidhī, *Jāmiᶜ*, 6:252–3. For a comprehensive study of addition (*ziyādah*) in hadith and analysis of Muslim hadith scholars and critics' approach towards this phenomenon, see Jonathan A. C. Brown, 'Critical Rigor vs. Juridical Pragmatism: How Legal Theorists and *Ḥadīth* Scholars Approached the Backgrowth of *Isnāds* in the Genre of *ᶜIlal al-Ḥadīth*', *Islamic Law and Society* 14(1) (2007): 1–41.
30. Al-Tirmidhī, *Jāmiᶜ*, 2:54–5, *al-zakāh* 35, *bāb mā jāʾa fī ṣadaqat al-fiṭr*, No. 676, 6:253. Bashshār ᶜAwwād Maᶜrūf, the editor of al-Tirmidhī's collection, adds in a note that Mālik is not the only one who narrated this addition but that this version of the hadith has several *mutābiᶜ*s. For a detailed analysis of this tradition transmitted through Mālik < Nāfiᶜ < Ibn ᶜUmar and its relation to the common-link phenomenon, see Juynboll, 'Nāfiᶜ, the *Mawlā* of Ibn ᶜUmar', 207–44. For a critique of Juynboll's article, see Harald Motzki, 'Quo vadis *Ḥadīṯ*-Forschung?

Eine kritische Untersuchung G. H. A. Juynboll: "Nāfi^c^, the *Mawlā* of Ibn ^c^Umar, and His Position in Muslim *Ḥadīth* Literature"', *Der Islam* 73(1) (1996): 40–80, and 73(2) (1996): 193–231; English version 'Whither *Ḥadīth* Studies?', trans. Frank Griffel, in Harold Motzki with Nicolet Boekhoff-van der Voort and Sean Anthony, *Analysing Muslim Traditions: Studies in Legal, Exegetical and* Maghāzī Ḥadīth, Islamic History and Civilization, Studies and Texts, 78 (Leiden: Brill, 2010), 47–124.

31. For other versions of the hadith, see al-Mizzī, *Tuḥfah* 2:305, No. 2753: Jābir ibn ^c^Abd Allāh al-Anṣārī, 6:19, No. 7357, 6:45, No. 7445, 6:79, No. 7576, 6:131, No. 7864, 6:147, No. 7950, 6:159, No. 8046, 6:176, No. 8156, 6:221, No. 8391, 6:249–50, No. 8517: ^c^Abd Allāh ibn ^c^Umar, 9:416, No. 12739, 10:85–6, No. 13412, 10:196, No. 13847: Abū Hurayrah. See also Juynboll, *ECḤ*, 553–4.
32. Al-Tirmidhī, *Jāmi^c^*, 6:253–4; cf. al-Mizzī, 6:440–1, No. 9050 (Abū Mūsá's version). For more examples, see al-Tirmidhī, *Jāmi^c^*, 6:254–7.
33. Nūr al-Dīn ^c^Itr, *Manhaj al-naqd fī ^c^ulūm al-ḥadīth* (Damascus: Dār al-Fikr, 1399/1979), 398. What al-Ḥākim al-Naysābūrī mentions in his categorisation of *gharīb* hadiths is compatible with the two first categories presented by al-Tirmidhī. See Muḥammad ibn ^c^Abd Allāh al-Ḥākim al-Naysābūrī, *Kitāb Ma^c^rifat ^c^ulūm al-ḥadīth*, ed. Mu^c^aẓẓam Ḥusayn (Cairo: Dār al-Kutub al-Miṣrīyah, 1356/1937), 94–6.
34. In the same sense, other expressions have been used such as '*mashhūr ^c^inda ahli 'l-^c^ilm*' and '*rawá ^c^anhu ghayru wāḥidin mina 'l-a^ɔ^immah/ahli l-^c^ilm*'.
35. Here, I have adopted ^c^Itr's general categorisation of the *gharīb*: (1) *al-gharīb matnan wa-isnādan*, which is a hadith transmitted only through one strand; and (2) *al-gharīb isnādan wa-lā matnan*, which is a hadith whose *matn* is well-known for its transmission through various strands from one transmitter, while a version thereof is transmitted via a single strand from another one (aside from the well-known transmission line). According to him, other categories, such as '*al-gharīb matnan lā isnādan*', '*al-gharīb ba^c^ḍ al-matn*' and '*al-gharīb ba^c^ḍ al-sanad*', all may be referred to the first two categories (^c^Itr, *Manhaj*, 397–9).
36. See, for example, al-Tirmidhī, *Jāmi^c^*, 1:436, *al-ṣalāh* 187, *bāb mā jā^ɔ^a fī al-ṣalāh ^c^alá al-dābbah*, No. 411; 1:556, *al-ṣalāh* 278, *bāb mā jā^ɔ^a fī ṣalāt al-istisqā^ɔ^*, No. 556; 3:365, *al-libās* 28, *bāb mā jā^ɔ^a fī al-qumuṣ*, No. 1762; 3:427, *al-aṭ^c^imah* 41, *bāb mā jā^ɔ^a fī al-tasmiyah*, No. 1848; 3:517, *al-birr wa-l-ṣilah* 46, *bāb mā jā^ɔ^a fī al-ṣidq wa-l-kadhib*, No. 1972; 4:372, *al-īmān* 13, *bāb mā jā^ɔ^a anna al-islām bada^ɔ^a gharīban*, No. 2629; 5:49, *al-qirā^ɔ^āt* 1, *bāb fī fātiḥat al-kitāb*, No. 2929; 5:174, *tafsīr al-Qur^ɔ^ān* 10, *bāb wa-min sūrat al-tawbah*, No. 3096; 5:355, *tafsīr al-Qur^ɔ^ān* 70, *bāb wa-min sūrat al-muddaththir*, No. 3327; 5:395, *al-da^c^awāt* 11, *bāb mā jā^ɔ^a fī raf^c^ al-aydī*, No. 2126.
37. Yaḥyá ibn Ma^c^īn, *Tārīkh Yaḥyá ibn Ma^c^īn: riwāyat al-^c^Abbās ibn Muḥammad al-Dūrī*, ed. ^c^Abd Allāh Aḥmad Ḥasan, 2 vols (Beirut: Dār al-Qalam, n.d.), 2:25. For another example, see ibid., 2:231, '*hādhā gharīb laysa yuḥaddithu bihī illā …*'
38. Aḥmad ibn Muḥammad ibn Ḥanbal, *Kitāb al-^c^Ilal wa-ma^c^rifat al-rijāl*, ed. Waṣī Allāh ibn Muḥammad ^c^Abbās (Beirut: al-Maktab al-Islāmī, 1408/1988), 2:277, '*lam nasma^c^hu min ghayri Hushaym ^c^an Yaḥyá ibn Sa^c^īd*.' See, for another example, ibid., 3:91.

39. Abū Aḥmad ᶜAbd Allāh Ibn ᶜAdī, *al-Kāmil fī ḍuᶜafāʾ al-rijāl*, ed. Suhayl Zakkār and Yaḥyá Mukhtār Ghazzāwī, 7 vols (Beirut: Dār al-Fikr, 1405/1988), 1:26, *'lā aᶜlamu yarwīhi ghayru ᶜAmr ibn Thābit'*. For other examples, see ibid., 1:30, 40, 355, 416 and passim. See also, for other expressions he used, 1:233, *'mā aᶜlamu lahū ṭarīqan ghayra hādhā'*, 1:312, *'lā yurwá illā min hādhā 'l-wajh'*.
40. ᶜAlī ibn ᶜUmar al-Dāraquṭnī, *al-ᶜIlal al-wāridah fī al-aḥādīth al-nabawīyah*, ed. Maḥfūẓ al-Raḥmān al-Salafī, 11 vols (Riyadh: Dār Ṭaybah, 1405–16/1985–96), 4:176, *'huwa gharībun ᶜani 'l-Aᶜmashi lā aᶜlamu ḥaddatha bihī ᶜani 'l-Aᶜmashi hākadhā ghayru Jarīr'*. For other examples, see ibid., 5:248, *'huwa gharībun ᶜanhu tafarrada bihī Muḥammadu 'bnu Jaᶜfarini bni Abī Kathīrin ᶜanhu'*; 11:295, *'gharībun ᶜani 'l-Thawrīyi tafarrada bihī ᶜanh'*.
41. *'Al-ḥadīthu 'lladhī yanfaridu bihī baᶜḍu 'l-ruwāti yūṣafu bi-'l-gharīb'*; ᶜUthmān ibn ᶜAbd al-Raḥmān ibn al-Ṣalāḥ, *Muqaddimat Ibn al-Ṣalāḥ*, ed. ᶜĀʾishah ᶜAbd al-Raḥmān Bint al-Shāṭiʾ (Cairo: Dār al-Maᶜārif, [1990]), 456. See also Muḥyī al-Dīn Abū Zakarīyāʾ Yaḥyá ibn Sharaf al-Nawawī, *al-Taqrīb wa-al-taysīr li-maᶜrifat sunan al-bashīr al-nadhīr*, ed. Muḥammad ᶜUthmān al-Khisht (Beirut: Dār al-Kitāb al-ᶜArabī, 1405/1985), 86; Badr al-Dīn Muḥammad ibn Ibrāhīm ibn Jamāᶜah, *al-Manhal al-rawī fī mukhtaṣar ᶜulūm al-ḥadīth al-nabawī*, ed. Muḥyī al-Dīn ᶜAbd al-Raḥmān Ramaḍān (Damascus: Dār al-Fikr, 1406/1986), 55.
42. *'Al-gharīb: wa-huwa mā yatafarradu bi-riwāyatihī shakhṣun wāḥidun fī ayyi mawḍiᶜin waqaᶜa 'l-tafarrudu bihī mina 'l-sanad'*; Shihāb al-Dīn Abu al-Faḍl Aḥmad b. ᶜAlī Ibn Ḥajar al-ᶜAsqalānī, *Nuzhat al-naẓar fī tawḍīḥ* Nukhbat al-fikar fī muṣṭalaḥ ahl al-athar, ed. ᶜAbd Allāh ibn Ḍayf Allāh al-Ruḥaylī (Riyadh: [n.p.], 1422/2001), 54. Since Ibn Ḥajar, hadith scholars have adopted the same definition; for instance, see ᶜItr, *Manhaj*, 396, *'huwa 'l-ḥadīthu 'lladhī tafarrada bihī rāwīhi sawāʾun tafarrada bihī ᶜan imāmin yujmaᶜu ḥadīthuhū aw ᶜan rāwin ghayri imām'*.
43. On the notion of 'root (*aṣl*) of the *isnād*', see below.
44. Ibn Ḥajar, *Nuzhat al-naẓar*, 64–5.
45. Ibn al-Ṣalāḥ, *Muqaddimah*, 257–8.
46. For example, see al-Nawawī, *Taqrīb*, 43; Ibn Jamāᶜah, *Manhal*, 51.
47. Al-Ḥākim al-Naysābūrī, *ᶜUlūm al-ḥadīth*, 96–102.
48. For example, see Ibn Ḥajar, *al-Nukat ᶜalá Kitāb Ibn al-Ṣalāḥ*, ed. Masᶜūd ᶜAbd al-Ḥamīd al-Saᶜdanī and Muḥammad Fāris (Beirut: Dār al-Kutub al-ᶜIlmīyah, 1414/1994), 291.
49. *'Al-ḥadīthu idhā lam tajmaᶜ ṭuruqahū lam tafhamhu'*; see Aḥmad ibn ᶜAlī al-Khaṭīb al-Baghdādī, *al-Jāmiᶜ li-akhlāq al-rāwī wa-ādāb al-sāmiᶜ*, ed. Muḥammad ᶜAjjāj al-Khaṭīb, 2 vols (Beirut: Muʾassasat al-Risālah, 1416/1996), 2:315.
50. *'Al-bābu idhā lam tujmaᶜ ṭuruquhū lam yatabayyan khaṭaʾuhū'*; al-Khaṭīb, *Jāmiᶜ*, 2:316. For a similar expression from Yaḥyá ibn Maᶜīn, see Ibn Maᶜīn, *Tārīkh* 2:211, *'law lam naktubi 'l-ḥadītha min thalāthīna wajhan mā ᶜaqalnāh'*.
51. In reference to this kind of investigation, the hadith critics used the cognate verbal form of the term *iᶜtibār* (*iᶜtabara, yaᶜtabiru*); see, for example, Abū Jaᶜfar Muḥammad ibn ᶜAmr al-ᶜUqaylī, *Kitāb al-Ḍuᶜafāʾ al-kabīr*, ed. ᶜAbd al-Muᶜṭī Amīn Qalᶜajī, 4 vols (Beirut: Dār al-Kutub al-ᶜIlmīyah, 1404/1998), 1:144; ᶜAbd al-Raḥmān ibn Abī Ḥātim Muḥammad al-Rāzī, *Kitāb al-Jarḥ wa-l-taᶜdīl*, 9 vols (Hyderabad: Majlis

Dā'irat al-Maᶜārif al-ᶜUthmānīyah, 1360–72), 2:378; Muḥammad ibn Aḥmad Ibn Ḥibbān al-Bustī, *Kitāb al-Thiqāt*, ed. Muḥammad ᶜAbd al-Muᶜīd Khān, 9 vols (Hyderabad: Majlis Dār'irat al-Maᶜārif al-ᶜUthmānīyah, 1393–1403/1973–83), 4:336, 6:132, 7:343, 8:293, 492; Ibn ᶜAdī, *Kāmil*, 2:63, 3:36, 4:82.

52. Ibn Ḥibbān, *Ṣaḥīḥ Ibn Ḥibbān bi-tartīb al-Amīr ᶜAlā' al-Dīn ᶜAlī al-Fārisī* (d. 739/1338–9), ed. Shuᶜayb al-Arna'ūṭ, 18 vols (Beirut: Mu'assasat al-Risālah, 1414/1993), 1:155. The English translation with some modification is adapted from Eerik Dickinson, *The Development of Early Sunnite Ḥadīth Criticism: the Taqdima of Ibn Abī Ḥātim al-Rāzī (240/854–327/938)*, Islamic History and Civilization, Studies and Texts, 38 (Leiden: Brill, 2001), 89.
53. For a detailed discussion on the methods used by early Sunnite hadith scholars for examination and authentication of hadiths, see Dickinson, *Development of Early Sunnite Ḥadīth Criticism*, 80–126.
54. Ibn al-Ṣalāḥ, *Muqaddimah*, 247–8. For a detailed definition, see Abū al-Faḍl ᶜAbd al-Raḥīm ibn Ḥusayn al-ᶜIrāqī, *Sharḥ al-tabṣirah wa-al-tadhkirah*, ed. ᶜAbd al-Laṭīf Hamīm and Māhir Yāsīn Faḥl (Beirut: Dār al-Kutub al-ᶜIlmīyah, 1423/2002), 1:258. In the hadith collections one can find some cases in which the expression *lā yutābaᶜu ᶜalayhi* appears to indicate the isolation of a hadith; e.g., see Abū ᶜAbd Allāh Muḥammad ibn Ismāᶜīl al-Bukhārī, *Ṣaḥīḥ al-Bukhārī*, 9 vols (Beirut: Dār Ṭawq al-Najāh, 1422/[2001]; repr. of Bulaq: al-Maṭbaᶜah al-Kubrá al-Amīrīyah, 1311–12), 3:16, *jazā' al-ṣayd* 17, *bāb lubs al-silāḥ l-il-muḥrim*, No. 1844; 7:11, *al-nikāḥ* 25, *bāb mā yaḥillu min al-nisā' wa-mā yaḥrumu*, No. 5105; 7:46, *al-ṭalāq* 12, *bāb al-khulᶜ wa-kayfa al-ṭalāq fīhi*, No. 5273; Abū Dāwūd Sulaymān ibn Ashᶜath al-Sijistānī, *Sunan Abī Dāwūd*, ed. Muḥammad Muḥyī al-Dīn ᶜAbd al-Ḥamīd, 4 vols (Beirut: al-Maktabat al-ᶜAṣrīyah, n.d.; repr. of Cairo: al-Maktabah al-Tijārīyah al-Kubrá, [1354/1935]), 1:90, *al-ṭahārah* 123, *bāb al-tayammum fī al-ḥaḍar*, No. 330; 2:275, *al-ṭalāq* 27, *bāb fī al-liᶜān*, No. 2251; 2:332, *al-ṣawm* 79, *bāb al-muᶜtakif yadkhulu al-bayt li-ḥājatihī*, No. 2468; al-Tirmidhī, *Jāmiᶜ*, 3:40, *al-aḥkām* 28, *bāb mā jā'a fī-man malaka dhā raḥim maḥram*, No. 1365; 4:11, *al-qadar* 1, *bāb mā jā'a fī al-tashdīd fī al-khawḍ fī al-qadar*, No. 2133; 4:114, *al-fitan* 78, No. 2266; 4:305, *ṣifat al-jannah* 11, *bāb mā jā'a fī ṣifat al-khayl*, No. 2544; 5:40, *faḍā'il al-Qur'ān* 20, No. 2918; 5:171, *tafsīr al-Qur'ān* 10, *bāb wa-min sūrat al-tawbah*, No. 3092; 5:492, *al-daᶜawāt* 85, No. 3516; 5:498, *al-daᶜawāt* 91, No. 3525.
55. ᶜItr, *Manhaj*, 420–1.
56. Ibn al-Ṣalāḥ, *Muqaddimah*, 248. See also Abū al-Fidā' Ismāᶜīl ibn ᶜUmar Ibn Kathīr, *al-Bāᶜith al-ḥathīth sharḥ Ikhtiṣār ᶜulūm al-ḥadīth*, ed. Aḥmad Muḥammad Shākir (Beirut: Dār al-Kutub al-ᶜIlmīyah, n.d.), 56: '*yughtafaru fī bābi 'l-shawāhidi wa-'l-mutābiᶜāti mina 'l-riwāyati ᶜan ḍaᶜīfi 'l-qarībi ḍaᶜfi mā lā yughtafaru fī 'l-uṣūl*', which implies the lower ranking of the *mutābiᶜ* and *shāhid* than the *aṣl*.
57. Abū al-Faḍl ᶜIyāḍ ibn Mūsá al-Qāḍī, *Sharḥ Ṣaḥīḥ Muslim lil-Qāḍī ᶜIyāḍ al-musammá bi-Ikmāl al-muᶜlim bi-fawā'id Muslim*, ed. Yaḥyá Ismāᶜīl, 9 vols (Manṣūrah: Dār al-Wafā', 1426/2005), 1:86–7; also see the introduction of Muslim, *Jāmiᶜ*, 1:88–106, and its translation, G. H. A. Juynboll, 'Muslim's Introduction to His *Ṣaḥīḥ*', *Jerusalem Studies in Arabic and Islam* 5 (1984): 263–311, esp. 267.

58. Ibn Abī Ḥātim al-Rāzī, *Jarḥ*, 2:37; see also Ibn Ṣalāḥ, *Muqaddimah*, 248. However, the permissive approach of the later hadith scholars towards *mutāba*ᶜ*ah* and *istishhād* by referring to weak transmitters' hadiths runs counter to the rigorous method of early hadith critics, and hence is subjected to some criticism; see Dickinson, *Development of Early Sunnite Ḥadīth Criticism*, 95–6. For a detailed discussion with various examples of the futile usage of *mutāba*ᶜ*ah* and *istishhād*, see Ṭāriq ibn ᶜIwaḍ Allāh, *al-Irshādāt fī taqwiyat al-aḥādīth bi-l-shawāhid wa-l mutābi*ᶜ*āt* (Cairo: Maktabat Ibn Taymīyah, 1417 / 1998).
59. Al-Khaṭīb al-Baghdādī, *Kitāb al-Kifāyah fī* ᶜ*ilm al-riwāyah*, ed. Aḥmad ᶜUmar Hāshim (Beirut: Dār al-Kitāb al-ᶜArabī, 1405 / 1985), 171–3; see also ibid., 469–72.
60. Zayn al-Dīn ᶜAbd al-Raḥmān Ibn Rajab al-Ḥanbalī, *Sharḥ* ᶜIlal *al-Tirmidhī*, ed. Nūr al-Dīn ᶜItr, 2 vols ([n.p.]: Dār al-Mallāḥ, 1398/ 1978), 1:352. See also Ibn al-Ṣalāḥ, *Muqaddimah*, 244, who expresses that many of the hadith scholars considered the isolated hadith to be *mardūd* ('rejected'), *munkar* ('unfamiliar') or *shādhdh* ('anomalous') (*iṭlāq al-hukm* ᶜ*alá al-tafarrud bi-l-radd aw al-nakirah aw al-shudhūdh*).
61. Ibn Rajab, *Sharḥ*, 1:450. However, al-Bardījī asserts that 'if a *matn* is known, even though it is transmitted through a single strand, it is not then considered *munkar* or *ma*ᶜ*lūl*'; see ibid., 1:452.
62. Ibn Rajab, *Sharḥ*, 1:451–6. In one case, Ibn Ḥanbal quotes Yaḥyá ibn Saᶜīd al-Qaṭṭān as saying, 'The hadith is *munkar* so far as it is known from no more than a single strand.'
63. Al-Ḥākim, ᶜ*Ulūm al-ḥadīth*, 119.
64. Abū Yaᶜlá Khalīl ibn ᶜAbd Allāh al-Khalīlī al-Qazwīnī, *al-Irshād fī ma*ᶜ*rifat* ᶜ*ulamā*ᵓ *al-ḥadīth*, ed. Muḥammad Saᶜīd ᶜUmar Idrīs, 3 vols (Riyadh: Maktabat al-Rushd, 1409), 1:176–7.
65. Ibn al-Ṣalāḥ, *Muqaddimah*, 237.
66. Abū Muḥammad ᶜAlī ibn Aḥmad Ibn Ḥazm al-Andalusī, *al-Iḥkām fī uṣūl al-aḥkām*, ed. Aḥmad Shākir, 8 vols (Cairo: Maṭbaᶜat al-ᶜĀṣimah, n.d.), 1:125–6; see also ibid., 2:208–10.
67. Abū al-Ḥusayn ᶜAlī ibn Muḥammad Ibn al-Qaṭṭān al-Fāsī, *Bayān al-wahm wa-l-īhām al-wāqi*ᶜ*ayn fī* Kitāb al-Iḥkām, ed. Ḥusayn Āyt Saᶜīd, 6 vols (Riyadh: Dār al-Ṭaybah, 1418 / 1997), 5:461.
68. Ibn al-Ṣalāḥ, *Muqaddimah*, 237: 'The *shādhdh* is not a hadith that only a single reliable transmitter (and no one else) relates. Rather, the *shādhdh* is the one a reliable transmitter relates that conflicts with what other people have related' (*laysa 'l-shādhdhu min an yarwiya 'l-thiqatu mā lā yarwīhi ghayruhū, innamā 'l-shādhdhu an yarwiya 'l-thiqatu ḥadīthan yukhālifu mā rawá 'l-nās*). See also al-Ḥākim, ᶜ*Ulūm al-ḥadīth*, 119; al-Khaṭīb, *Kifāyah*, 171; Ibn Rajab, *Sharḥ* 1:352. Thus, al-Shāfiᶜī apparently, as ascribed to him, makes it conditional not only on the transmission of 'a reliable transmitter', but also on its 'not conflicting with others' transmission'.
69. Ibn al-Ṣalāḥ, *Muqaddimah*, 243.
70. Ibid.
71. Ibn al-Ṣalāḥ, *Muqaddimah*, 244–6.

72. For a detailed discussion, see Ibrāhīm al-Lāḥim, '*Tafarrud al-thiqah bi-l-ḥadīth*', *al-Ḥikmah* 240 (2004): 117–56, at 140–56. For a similar approach to the issue of *ziyādat al-thiqah*, i.e., the addition made by the reliable transmitter, see Jonathan A. C. Brown, 'Criticism of the Proto-*Hadith* Canon: al-Dāraquṭnī's Adjustment of the *Ṣaḥīḥayn*', *Journal of Islamic Studies* 15(1) (2004): 1–37, at 8–11; Brown, 'Critical Rigor'; Ali Aghaei, '*Mowājehe-ye moḥaddethān-e mosalmān bā padīde-ye "roshd-e wārūne-ye sanadhā"*' ('Backward Growth of *isnād*s from the Viewpoint of Muslim Hadith Scholars'), *Ṣaḥīfe-ye mobīn* 48 (2011): 175–205.
73. For example, Ibn ᶜAdī, *Kāmil* 1:211, 431, 2:298, 326, 3:119–20, 201, 253, 352, 353, 7:292; al-Dāraquṭnī, *ᶜIlal*, 5:131, 7:139. Similar formulas such as '*madāru 'l-isnādi ᶜalá fulān*' and '*madāru 'ṭ-uruqi ᶜalá fulān*' are also used.
74. For example, Ibn ᶜAdī, *Kāmil* 3:170, 4:205, 7:170; Abū Bakr Aḥmad ibn al-Ḥusayn al-Bayhaqī, *Kitāb al-Sunan al-kubrá wa-fī dhaylihī al-Jawhar al-naqī li-ᶜAlāʾ al-Dīn ibn ᶜAlī ᶜUthmān al-Mārdīnī al-Shahīr bi-Ibn al-Turkumānī*, 10 vols (Hyderabad: Majlis Dāʾirat al-Maᶜārif al-Niẓāmīyah, 1344–55), 1:147, 2:313, 380, 6:73, 8:31, 9:274.
75. For example, Ibn Ḥibbān, *Kitāb al-Majrūḥīn min al-muḥaddithīn wa-al-ḍuᶜafāʾ wa-al-matrūkīn*, ed. Maḥmūd Ibrāhīm Zāyid, 3 vols (Aleppo: Dār al-Waᶜy, 1395–6/1975–6), 1:240.
76. For example, Ibn ᶜAdī, *Kāmil* 4:105.
77. For example, al-Dāraquṭnī, *ᶜIlal* 7:204–5.
78. For example, Ibn ᶜAdī, *Kāmil* 1:233, 390, 2:27, 147, 155, 197, 259, 265, 302, 3:106, 364, 6:200, 5:39, 277, 378, 7:18.
79. For example, Ibn ᶜAdī, *Kāmil* 1:166, 173, 177, 188, 190, 198, 244, 257, 327, 363 and passim.
80. For example, Ibn ᶜAdī, *Kāmil* 1:8, 185, 3:170.
81. See above.
82. This part of the *isnād* is called *aṣl al-sanad* ('the root of the *isnād*'). See Ibn Ḥajar, *Nuzhat al-naẓar*, 64: '*aṣlu 'l-sanadi ayi 'l-mawḍiᶜu 'lladhī yadūru 'l-isnādu ᶜalayhi wa-yarjiᶜu wa-law taᶜaddati 'ṭuruqu ilayhi wa-huwa ṭarafuhu ʾlladhī fīhi 'ṣ-aḥābī*'; see also Muḥammad ibn al-Murtaḍá al-Zabīdī, *Bulghat al-arīb fī muṣṭalaḥ āthār al-ḥabīb*, ed. ᶜAbd al-Fattāḥ Abū Ghuddah (Aleppo: Maktabat al-Maṭbūᶜāt al-Islāmīyah, 1408), 178, who uses the terms *aṣl al-sanad* and *madār* concurrently.
83. See above.
84. See above.
85. See al-Mizzī, *Tuḥfah* 8:91–3, No. 10612. Al-Dhahabī provides a long list of persons who transmitted this hadith from Yaḥyá ibn Saᶜīd al-Anṣārī. See Shams al-Dīn Muḥammad ibn Aḥmad al-Dhahabī, *Siyar aᶜlām al-nubalāʾ*, ed. Shuᶜayb Arnaʾūṭ et al., 25 vols (Beirut: Muʾassasat al-Risālah, 1401–9/1981–8), 5:476–81. See also Juynboll, *ECḤ*, xx–xxi, 676–7. While in the later collections attempts are made to provide *mutābiᶜāt* and *shawāhid* for this hadith, none of them are accepted by the hadith critics. For an overview of the issue, see Muḥammad ibn Jaᶜfar al-Kattānī, *Naẓm al-mutanāthir fī al-ḥadīth al-mutawātir* (Cairo: Dār al-Kutub al-Salafīyah, n.d.), 24–8.
86. Al-Khalīlī, *Irshād*, 1:167; see also Ibn Ḥajar, *Talkhīṣ al-ḥabīr fī takhrīj aḥādīth al-Rāfiᶜī*

al-kabīr, ed. ᶜĀdil Aḥmad ᶜAbd al-Mawjūd and ᶜAlī Muḥammad Muᶜawwaḍ, 4 vols (Beirut: Dār al-Kutub al-ᶜIlmīyah, 1419/1989), 1:215–16.

87. See Yaᶜqūb ibn Sufyān al-Fasawī, *Kitāb al-Maᶜrifah wa-l-tārīkh*, ed. Akram Ḍiyāʾ al-ᶜUmarī, 3rd edn, 4 vols (Medina: Maktabat al-Dār, 1410/1989), 2:153; Ibn ᶜAdī, *Kāmil* 3:170, '*ḥadīth al-ḍaḥik fī al-ṣalāh . . . kulluhū yadūru ᶜalá Abī 'l-ᶜĀliyah*'; cf. al-Mizzī, *Tuḥfah* 13:193, No. 18642. For other early usages of *madār*, see, e.g., al-Bukhārī, *al-Tārīkh al-ṣaghīr*, ed. Maḥmūd Ibrāhīm Zāyid, 2 vols (Aleppo and Cairo: Dār al-Waᶜy and Dār al-Turāth, 1396/1977), 2:35; al-Bukhārī, *Kitāb al-Tārīkh al-kabīr*, 8 vols (Hyderabad: Maṭbaᶜat Jamᶜīyat Dāʾirat al-Maᶜārif al-ᶜUthmānīyah, 1360–84), 5:233, 6:461; al-Fasawī, *Maᶜrifah* 2:154, 3:33.

88. '*Al-isnād yadūru ᶜalá sittah*': ᶜAlī ibn ᶜAbd Allāh Ibn al-Madīnī, *al-ᶜIlal*, ed. Muḥammad Muṣṭafá al-Aᶜẓamī, 2nd edn (Beirut: al-Maktab al-Islāmī, 1392/1972, repr. 1400/1980), 36–7. He states that the knowledge of these six scholars is then transferred to later hadith collectors, such as Ibn Jurayj (d. 150/767–8?), Muḥammad ibn Isḥāq (d. 151/768), Maᶜmar ibn Rāshid (d. 154/770–1), Saᶜīd ibn Abī ᶜArūbah (d. 156/773), ᶜAbd al-Raḥmān ibn ᶜAmr al-Awzāᶜī (d. 157/774), Shuᶜbah ibn al-Ḥajjāj, Sufyān al-Thawrī, Ḥammād ibn Salamah, Abū ᶜAwānah al-Waḍḍāḥ ibn ᶜAbd Allāh (d. 176/792–3), Mālik ibn Anas, Hushaym ibn Bashīr and Sufyān ibn ᶜUyaynah (d. 198/814); see ibid., 37–9. See also al-Khaṭīb, *Jāmiᶜ*, 2:448–9, where under the title *maᶜrifat al-shuyūkh alladhīna tadūru al-asānīd ᶜalayhim*, before quoting from Ibn al-Madīni, he quotes a similar statement from Abū Dāwūd al-Ṭayālisī (d. 203–4/818–19): 'Knowledge could be found with four persons: al-Zuhrī, Qatādah, Abū Isḥāq, and al-Aᶜmash.'

89. '*Kullu imāmin min aʾimmati 'l-ḥadīthi qad tafarrada bi-riwāyatin ᶜan shuyūkhin lam yarwi ᶜanhum ghayruh*': al-Ḥākim, *ᶜUlūm al-ḥadīth*, 161.

90. In hadith terminology, they are called *wuḥdān* (singular *wāḥid*); see ᶜItr, *Manhaj*, 136–7.

91. Muslim says, 'About ninety hadiths from the Prophet are transmitted by al-Zuhrī of which none is transmitted by others': *Jāmiᶜ*, 5:82, *al-aymān* 2, *bāb man ḥalafa bi-'l-Lāt wa-l-ᶜUzzá*, No. 1647.

92. Al-Ḥākim, *ᶜUlūm al-ḥadīth*, 159–61; see also Ibn Ṣalāḥ, *Muqaddimah*, 557–8. Muslim provides a long list of those transmitters who are alone in relating hadiths in addition to the names of more than 240 transmitters who alone related from them: see Muslim, *al-Munfaridāt wa-l-wuḥdān*, ed. ᶜAbd al-Ghaffār Sulaymān al-Bundārī and Muḥammad al-Saᶜīd ibn Basyūnī Zaghlūl (Beirut: Dār al-Kutub al-ᶜIlmīyah, 1410/1988).

93. '*Al-aʾimmah al-thiqāt al-mashhūrīna min al-tābiᶜīna wa-atbāᶜihim mimman yujmaᶜu ḥadīthuhum*': al-Ḥākim, *ᶜUlūm al-ḥadīth*, 240–9. See also Abū ᶜAbd Allāh Muḥammad ibn Isḥāq ibn Mandah, *Shurūṭ al-aʾimmah: risālah fī bayān faḍl al-akhbār wa-sharḥ madhāhib ahl al-āthār wa-ḥaqīqat al-sunan wa-taṣḥīḥ al-riwāyāt*, ed. ᶜAbd al-Raḥmān ᶜAbd al-Jabbār al-Farīwāʾī (Riyadh: Dār al-Muslim, 1416/1995), 32, '*hum aʾimmatu d-dīni wa-ḥuffāẓuhū . . . ilayhim intahá ᶜilmu 'l-asānīd . . . yuqbalu infirāduhum*'. For similar lists, see ibid., 44–67; al-Khaṭīb, *Jāmiᶜ*, 2:457–8.

94. Ibn ᶜAdī, *Kāmil*, 3:352–3.

95. *'Man ṣāma Ramaḍāna wa-atbaᶜahū bi-sittin min Shawwālin fa-huwa ṣāʾimu 'l-dahr'*: al-Mizzī, *Tuḥfah*, 3:100–1, No. 3482.
96. *'Kasru ᶜaẓmi 'l-mayyiti ka-kasrihī ḥayyan'*; see al-Mizzī, *Tuḥfah*, 12:407, No. 17893.
97. *'ᶜAlayka bi-Bayt al-Maqdis …'*; Ibn ᶜAdī, *Kāmil*, 3:119–20. For a similar example, see al-Dāraquṭnī, *ᶜIlal*, 11:323, Abū Sufyān Ṭarīf ibn Shihāb al-Saᶜdī as *madār*; cf. al-Mizzī, *Tuḥfah*, 3:465, No. 4357.
98. Ibn ᶜAdī, *ᶜIlal*, 2:326; cf. al-Mizzī, *Tuḥfah*, 7:325–6, No. 9976, *'yaʾummu 'l-qawma aqraʾuhum li-kitābi 'Llāh'*. For another example, see Ibn ᶜAdī, *Kāmil*, 2:326, where he considers Abū Isḥāq al-Sabīᶜī the *madār* of the hadith narrated through Nājiyah ibn Kaᶜb al-ᶜAnazī from ᶜAlī ibn Abī Ṭālib and hence discredits the transmission of Ḥasan ibn Yazīd from al-Suddī. See also al-Dāraquṭnī, *ᶜIlal*, 4:144; cf. al-Mizzī, *Tuḥfah*, 7:449–50, No. 10287.
99. Ibn ᶜAdī, *Kāmil*, 3:166–70; cf. Juynboll, *ECḤ*, 42.
100. Al-Dāraquṭnī, *ᶜIlal*, 7:137–9; cf. al-Mizzī, *Tuḥfah*, 8:470, No. 11489. For other examples, see al-Dāraquṭnī, *ᶜIlal*, 5:130–1, 7:204–5.
101. Al-Ḥākim, *al-Mustadrak ᶜalá* al-Ṣaḥīḥayn, ed. Yūsuf ᶜAbd al-Raḥmān al-Marᶜashlī, 4 vols (Beirut: Dār al-Maᶜrifah, n.d.), 1:152.
102. Özkan, 'Common Link and its Relation to the *Madār*', 61.
103. Al-Bayhaqī, *Sunan*, 3:41.
104. Al-Bayhaqī, *Sunan*, 8:42.
105. Al-Bayhaqī, *Sunan*, 2:313.
106. Al-Bayhaqī, *Sunan*, 6:73
107. Al-Bayhaqī, *Sunan*, 8:30–1; cf. al-Fasawī, *Maᶜrifah*, 3:33, quoting ᶜAlī ibn al-Madīnī.
108. Abū ᶜUmar Yūsuf ibn ᶜAbd Allāh Ibn ᶜAbd al-Barr, *al-Istidhkār al-jāmiᶜ li-madhāhib fuqahāʾ al-amṣār*, ed. Sālim Muḥammad ᶜAṭāʾ and Muḥammad ᶜAlī Muᶜawwaḍ, 8 vols (Beirut: Dār al-Kutub al-ᶜIlmīyah, 1421/2000), 5:185; Ibn ᶜAbd al-Barr, *al-Tamhīd li-mā fī al-Muwaṭṭaʾ min al-maᶜānī wa-l-asānīd*, ed. Muṣṭafá ibn Aḥmad al-ᶜAlawī and Muḥammad ᶜAbd al-Kabīr al-Bakrī, 24 vols (Morocco: Wizārat ᶜUmūm al-Awqāf wa-l-Shuʾūn al-Islāmīyah, 1387/1967), 2:64, 6:96; cf. al-Mizzī, *Tuḥfah*, 8:177, 179–80, 205, Nos 10808, 10822 and 10891, respectively.
109. Ibn ᶜAbd al-Barr, *Istidhkār*, 5:185; Ibn ᶜAbd al-Barr, *Tamhīd*, 2:64, 6:96; see also Ibn ᶜAdī, *Kāmil*, 3:253; cf. al-Mizzī, *Tuḥfah*, 12:367, 372, Nos 17770 and 17782, respectively.
110. Ibn ᶜAbd al-Barr, *Tamhīd*, 4:328, 23:386; cf. al-Mizzī, *Tuḥfah*, 3:157, No. 3582, 11:204, No. 15670. For other instances, see Ibn ᶜAbd al-Barr, *Istidhkār*, 1:68, 2:310, 3:243; Ibn ᶜAbd al-Barr, *Tamhīd*, 1:162, 2:22, 46, 119, 4:102, 5:258, 6:39, 8:115; Abū al-Faraj ᶜAbd al-Raḥmān ibn ᶜAlī ibn al-Jawzī, *Kitāb al-Mawḍūᶜāt*, ed. ᶜAbd al-Raḥmān Muḥammad ᶜUthmān, 3 vols (Medina: al-Maktabah al-Salafīyah, 1386–8/1966–8), 1:316, 331, 3:111, 217, 247, 262; al-Jawzī, *al-ᶜIlal al-mutanāhiyah fī al-aḥādīth al-wāhiyah*, ed. Khalīl Mays, 2 vols (Beirut: Dār al-Kutub al-ᶜIlmīyah, 1403/1983), 1:145–6, 149, 334, 367, 2:644, 811, 884, 915.
111. Ibn ᶜAbd al-Barr, *Istidhkār*, 1:193; Ibn ᶜAbd al-Barr, *Tamhīd*, 20:259; cf. al-Mizzī, *Tuḥfah*, 6:51, No. 7460.
112. Ibn ᶜAbd al-Barr, *Tamhīd*, 1:161. For other examples, see Ibn ᶜAbd al-Barr, *Istidhkār*,

1:526, 'lā mimman yuḥtajju bihī fī-mā khūlifa fīh'; Ibn ʿAbd al-Barr, Tamhīd, 2:163, 'laysa ʿindahum mimman yuḥtajju bihī fī-mā khūlifa fīhi awi 'nfarada bih', 21:59, 'laysa mimman yuḥtajju bi-mā 'nfarada bihī', 24:18, 'laysa bi-ḥujjatin fī-mā 'nfarada bihī'.

113. See above.
114. Al-Nawawī, Khulāṣat al-aḥkām fī muhimmāt al-sunan wa-qawāʿid al-Islām, ed. Ḥusayn Ismāʿīl al-Jamal, 2 vols (Beirut: Muʾassasat al-Risālah, 1418/1997), 1:87, 207, 369, 452, 499, 538, 2:769, 791, 1013, 1017.
115. ʿAlāʾ al-Dīn ʿAlī ibn ʿUthmān Ibn al-Turkumānī, al-Jawhar al-naqī fī al-radd ʿalá al-Bayhaqī, under al-Bayhaqī, Sunan, 1:67, 146, 148, 2:77, 180, 390, 396, 3:42, 286, 295, 4:166, 5:32, 108, 323, 7:112, 124, 126, 197, 455, 477, 9:190.
116. Jamāl al-Dīn ʿAbd Allāh ibn Yūsuf al-Zaylaʿī, Naṣb al-rāyah fī takhrīj aḥādīth al-Hidāyah, ed. Muḥammad ʿAwwāmah, 5 vols (Jeddah: Dār al-Qiblah l-il-Thaqāfah al-Islāmīyah, 1418/1997), 1:52–3, 138–9, 196, 209, 332, 353, 395, 405, 2:198, 252, 300, 3:232, 4:40–2, 202, 333.
117. Sirāj al-Dīn Abū Ḥafṣ ʿUmar ibn ʿAlī Ibn al-Mulaqqin, al-Badr al-munīr fī takhrīj al-aḥādīth wa-al-āthār al-wāqiʿah fī al-Sharḥ al-kabīr, ed. Muṣṭáfá Abū al-Ghayẓ et al., 10 vols (Riyadh: Dār al-Hijrah, 1425/2004), 1:383, 660, 2:168, 300, 554–5, 575, 3:101, 154, 4:8, 132, 186, 192, 223, 247–8, 326, 413, 5:55, 82, 182, 298, 305, 437, 6:62, 68, 222, 522, 674, 708, 712, 7:463, 504, 523, 601, 626, 632, 8:76, 118, 368, 745, 9:141, 247, 286, 293, 391, 460, 496, 538, 693.
118. Nūr al-Dīn ʿAlī ibn Abī Bakr al-Haythamī, Majmaʿ al-zawāʾid wa-manbaʿ al-fawāʾid, 10 vols (Beirut: Dār al-Kitāb al-ʿArabī, n.d.), 1:16, 64, 115, 137, 159, 219, 220, 240, 283, 2:54, 68, 142, 211, 229, 277, 4:65, 238, 328, 5:12, 122.
119. Aḥmad ibn Abī Bakr al-Būṣīrī, Miṣbāḥ al-zujājah fī zawāʾid Ibn Mājah, ed. Muḥammad al-Muntaqá al-Kashnāwī, 4 vols (Beirut, Dār al-ʿArabīyah, 1983–5), 1:154, 2:8, 55, 79, 99, 3:13, 85, 110, 182, 233, 4:113, 139; al-Būṣīrī, Itḥāf al-khiyarah al-maharah bi-zawāʾid al-masānīd al-ʿasharah, ed. Abū Tamīm Yāsir ibn Ibrāhīm, 8 vols (Riyadh: Dār al-Waṭan, 1420/1999), 1:91, 96, 105, 138, 142, 150, 167, 172, 182, 187, 200, 203, 225, 243, 251, 262, 275, 297, 305, 329, 338, 360, 367, 419, 446, 455 and passim (more than 200 instances).
120. Ibn Ḥajar, Talkhīṣ al-ḥabīr 1:119, 136, 215–16, 241, 266, 301, 302, 327, 336, 359, 381, 402, 408, 414, 676, 2:9, 45, 68, 169, 202, 237, 378, 391, 558, 3:19, 57, 162, 180, 321, 342–3, 454, 4:224, 234, 333, 355, 367, 428; Ibn Ḥajar, Fatḥ al-bārī fī sharḥ Ṣaḥīḥ al-Bukhārī, ed. Muḥibb al-Dīn al-Khaṭīb et al., 13 vols (n.p.: al-Maktabat al-Salafīyah, [1379/1960]), 1:411, 435, 573, 2:170, 288, 423, 501, 3:127, 4:13, 429, 5:58, 6:179, 8:28, 618, 681, 9:53, 205, 573, 580, 625, 10:26, 430, 11:368, 538, 579, 617, 12:354, 13:384, .
121. Badr al-Dīn Abū Muḥammad Maḥmūd ibn Aḥmad al-ʿAynī, ʿUmdat al-qārī sharḥ Ṣaḥīḥ al-Bukhārī, 25 vols (Beirut: Dār Iḥyāʾ al-Turāth al-ʿArabī, n.d.; repr. of Cairo: Idārat al-Ṭibāʿah al-Munīrīyah, 1348/1930), 1:19, 63, 3:97, 275, 279, 4:243, 5:107, 283, 287, 289, 6:188, 245, 307, 7:304, 8:39, 9:123, 10:285, 11:13, 77, 78, 13:55, 19:210, 268, 20:28, 21:160.
122. Ibn al-Turkumānī, Jawhar, 3:42–3. For more examples, see ibid., 5:108, 323–4, 7:112.
123. See above, n. 103.

124. Al-Būṣīrī, *Itḥāf al-khiyarah*, 3:41. For another example, see ibid., 7:321.
125. On his role as a *madār* in another *isnād*, see Ibn ᶜAbd al-Barr, *Istidhkār*, 2:309; Ibn ᶜAbd al-Barr, *Tamhīd*, 21:102.
126. Al-Būṣīrī, *Itḥāf al-khiyarah*, 5:514. For similar examples, see ibid., 1:150, 172, 200–1, 251, 275–6, 329, 419, 2:50, 192, 3:30, 78, 121, 176, 284, 302, 368–9, 390, 4:18, 62; al-Būṣīrī, *Miṣbāḥ al-zujājah*, 2:99, 3:13, 233, 4:139.
127. Ibn Ḥajar, *Talkhīṣ al-ḥabīr*, 2:45–6. For other examples, see ibn Ḥajar, *Fatḥ al-bārī*, 1:436, 2:501, 8:681.
128. Ibn ᶜAbd al-Barr, *Tamhīd*, 2:46. For his being disqualified, see Ibn ᶜAdī, *Kāmil*, 4:304.
129. Al-ᶜAynī, *ᶜUmdat al-qārī*, 10:285. For another example, see ibid., 11:78.
130. Al-Bayhaqī, *Sunan*, 7:197.
131. Ibn al-Turkumānī, *Jawhar*, 7:197; cf. al-Bayhaqī, *Sunan*, 7:196.
132. See above.
133. Al-Būṣīrī, *Itḥāf al-khiyarah*, 3:78.
134. Al-Khaṭīb al-Ḥasanī, *Maᶜrifat madār al-isnād*, 1:36, 55–77. It is the case also for the responsible transmitters of a major number of hadiths labelled *gharīb* in the *ᶜilal al-ḥadīth* literature (such as Ibn Abī Ḥātim's *ᶜIlal*, Ibn ᶜAdī's *Kāmil*, and al-Dāraquṭnī's *ᶜIlal*); see al-Ḥamām, *Tafarrud*, 292–3, 298.
135. Josef Horovitz, 'Alter und Ursprung des *Isnād*', *Der Islam* 8(1/2) (1917): 39–47, esp. at 43–4; James Robson, 'The *Isnād* in Muslim Tradition', *Transactions of the Glasgow University Oriental* Society 15 (1953): 15–26, esp. at 21–2; Juynboll, 'Some *Isnād*-Analytical Methods', 354; Juynboll, 'Nāfiᶜ, the *Mawlā* of Ibn ᶜUmar', 210; Juynboll, 'The Date of the Great *Fitna*', *Arabica* 20(2) (1973): 142–59; cf. also Motzki, 'Whither *Ḥadīth* Studies?', 50–1; for a more detailed discussion of the origin of the *isnād*; see Pavel Pavlovitch, 'The Origin of the *Isnād* and al-Mukhtār b. Abī ᶜUbayd's Revolt in Kūfa (66–7/685–7)', *al Qanṭara* 39(1) (2018): 17–48, esp. at 19–32, 41–4.
136. *Al-isnād al-ᶜālī* is one with a small number of transmitters, for the fewer transmitters mentioned in an *isnād*, the more 'elevated' it is considered; see Ibn al-Ṣalāḥ, *Muqaddimah*, 440.
137. Cf. Ibn Mandah, 32: '*hum aʾimmat al-dīn wa-ḥuffāẓuhū* . . . *ilayhim intahá ᶜilm al-asānīd wa-* . . . *yuqbalu infirāduhum*'.
138. Al-Dhahabī, *al-Mūqiẓah fī ᶜilm muṣṭalaḥ al-ḥadīth*, ed. ᶜAbd al-Fattāḥ Abū Ghuddah (Beirut: Dār al-Bashāʾir al-Islāmīyah, 1405/1985), 77.
139. Al-Dhahabī, *Mūqiẓah*, 77.
140. Al-Dhahabī, *Mūqiẓah*, 77–8.
141. '*Idhā ḥaddatha ᶜan al-maᶜrūfīn mā lā yaᶜrifuhū 'l-maᶜrūfūn*': Ibn ᶜAbī Ḥātim, *Jarḥ*, 2:32; Ibn ᶜAdī, *Kāmil*, 1:156. For a slightly different quotation, see Ibn Ḥibbān, *Majrūḥīn*, 1:74.
142. Muslim, *Jāmiᶜ*, 1:5–6; Muslim, *Kitāb al-Tamyīz*, ed. Muḥammad Muṣṭafá al-Aᶜẓamī (Riyadh: Maktabat al-Kawthar, 1410/1990), 172.
143. Abū Dāwūd, *Risālah ilá ahl Makka*, in *Thalāth rasāʾil fī ᶜilm muṣṭalaḥ al-ḥadīth*, ed. ᶜAbd al-Fattāḥ Abū Ghuddah (Beirut: Dār al-Bashāʾir al-Islāmīyah, 1426/2005), 47.

144. Al-Ḥākim, *ᶜUlūm al-ḥadīth*, 99: '*al-nawᶜ al-thānī min al-afrād aḥādīth yatafarradu bi-riwāyatihā rajul wāḥid ᶜan imām min al-aʾimmah*'.
145. Al-Ḥākim, *ᶜUlūm al-ḥadīth*, 99–100.
146. '*... al-aʾimmah mimman yujmaᶜu ḥadīthuhum*'; cf. Ibn Ṣalāḥ, *Muqaddimah*, 456.
147. For a discussion on other possibilities of appearance of single strands and isolated transmissions in hadith literature, see also Motzki, 'Whither *Ḥadīth* Studies?' 51–4; Motzki, 'Dating Muslim Tradition', 227–8, 238–40.
148. Juynboll, '(Re)appraisal of Some Technical Terms in *Ḥadīth* Science', 360.
149. Juynboll, 'Some *Isnād*-Analytical Methods', 351–2.
150. Michael Cook, *Early Muslim Dogma: a Source-Critical Study* (Cambridge: Cambridge University Press, 1981), 107–8.
151. Özkan, 'Common Link and its Relation to the *Madār*', 75.
152. In *ECḤ* (xxxviii), Juynboll points out that the oldest common link is the Successor Abū al-ᶜĀliyah Rufayᶜ ibn Mihrān al-Riyāḥī. For many examples he labelled transmitters 'seeming common links', not 'real common links': see also *ECḤ*, throughout the work.
153. Özkan, '(Re)appraisal', 52, n. 56.
154. For different conceptions of the common link, see Andreas Görke, 'Eschatology, History, and the Common Link: a Study in Methodology', in Herbert Berg (ed.), *Method and Theory in the Study of Islamic Origins*, Islamic History and Civilization, Studies and Texts, 49 (Leiden: Brill, 2003), 179–208, at 188–95.
155. See, for example, Motzki, 'Dating Muslim Traditions', 241–2.
156. For more detailed discussion, see Motzki, 'Dating Muslim Traditions', 251.
157. See above, n. 23.
158. As Özkan himself states, 'the commentators . . . typically search for the *mutābiᶜāt* or *shawāhid* of *isnād*s in which the *madār* is labelled as "weak"'; Özkan, 'Common Link and its Relation to the *Madār*', 65.
159. In his conclusion, he repeats the notion of the '"common link" in the Schachtian–Juynbollian sense': Özkan, 'Common Link and its Relation to the *Madār*', 77.
160. See Schacht, *Origins of Muhammadan Jurisprudence*, 163–75; Juynboll, *Muslim Tradition*, 206–17; Juynboll, 'Some *Isnād*-Analytical Methods', 353; Juynboll, *ECḤ*, xvi–xxviii.
161. See Cook, *Early Muslim Dogma*, 107–8; Michael Cook, 'Eschatology and the Dating of Traditions', *Princeton Papers in Near Eastern Studies* 1 (1992): 23–47; Patricia Crone, *Roman, Provincial and Islamic Law: the Origins of the Islamic Patronate* (Cambridge: Cambridge University Press, 1987), 29–30; Norman Calder, *Studies in Early Muslim Jurisprudence* (Oxford: Clarendon Press, 1993), 236–7.
162. Furthermore, one could also identify those transmitters who are responsible for the text variants and developments in different versions of the hadith through the application of the *isnād-cum-matn* analysis. See Motzki, 'Dating Muslim Traditions', 226–8, 238–41; Motzki, 'Whither *Ḥadīth* Studies?' 51–4. For a recent, comprehensive description and analysis of the *isnād-cum-matn* method, see Pavel Pavlovitch, *The Formation of the Islamic Understanding of Kalāla in the Second Century* AH *(718–816* CE*): Between Scripture and Canon*, Islamic History and Civilization, Studies and Texts, 126 (Leiden: Brill, 2016), esp. 22–49.

CHAPTER

6

HADITH CRITICISM BETWEEN TRADITIONISTS AND JURISPRUDENTS

Mutaz al-Khatib

Western scholarship on the methods developed by Muslim critics for evaluating the authenticity of hadith reports have focused predominantly on *isnād* criticism as opposed to *matn* criticism.[1] Through the mediating influence of Muslim modernists, the question of *matn* criticism in classical hadith scholarship and its sufficiency or lack thereof became a hotly debated topic in Muslim scholarship over the course of the twentieth century, and served as an important proxy for the broader question of the extent to which the Islamic tradition may or may not need far-reaching internal reform. Advocates of sweeping reform have pointed to the lack of *matn* criticism as an instance of the fideism and irrationality of the traditional *ᶜulamāᵓ*, while defenders of tradition have sought to prove that hadith critics did in fact apply *matn* criticism in their evaluation of hadith reports.[2] Efforts to substantiate the pedigree of *matn* criticism have often focused on the criteria for *matn* criticism (*ᶜalāmāt waḍᶜ al-ḥadīth*) found in post-formative manuals on *ᶜulūm al-ḥadīth* and on the different chapters related to *matn* in these manuals.[3] Other works have focused on the applications of *matn* criticism through a smattering of examples drawn from the generation of the Companions themselves[4] and on forged hadith literature, especially the works of Ibn al-Jawzī (d. 597/1201) and Ibn Qayyim al-Jawzīyah (d. 751/1350).[5]

Less attention has been given in Western scholarship to hadith criticism in the literature of jurisprudence (*uṣūl al-fiqh*). This chapter will present a comparative analysis of the theory and practice of *matn* criticism between traditionists (*muḥaddithūn*) and jurisprudents (*uṣūlīyūn*). When viewed from this comparative perspective, a number of new questions concerning *matn* criticism arise. What, precisely, was the nature of *matn* criticism among these two groups and to what extent, if at all, did their approaches overlap? In what ways did *matn* criticism differ across legal schools? In what ways was the approach to *matn* criticism among the adherents of some legal schools closer to that of hadith critics than it was among adherents of others? How was the practice of *matn* criticism shaped by the epistemological frameworks and overall aims of the separate disciplines of hadith and jurisprudence?

Hadith Critics' Criteria for *matn* Criticism

Hadith critics' use of *matn* criticism led them to identify several different categories of problematic hadiths. I have identified five categories here for the sake of convenience, and to a large extent they align with categories discussed in the mature genre of *ᶜulūm al-ḥadīth,* starting with the work of al-Ḥākim al-Naysābūrī (d. 405/1014) and al-Khaṭīb al-Baghdādī (d. 463/1071). First, was the criticism of anomalous reports (*al-taᶜlīl bi-al-tafarrud*). *Munkar, tafarrud, gharīb* and *shādhdh* were all used to denote hadiths that were anomalous in terms of their transmission, their contents or both.[6] The critics recognised that trustworthy narrators and even narrators of the highest calibre also narrated anomalous and objectionable reports. Determining whether the narration of anomalous reports detracted from the reputation of a given narrator or whether the narrator's reputation was sufficient to strengthen the quality of the anomalous report was an ultimately subjective judgement and there was no final agreement on this question among hadith critics.

The criticism of additions and interpolations (*al-taᶜlīl bi-al-ziyādah*) also had to do with anomalies. An addition (*ziyādah*) was defined as occurring when 'a group [of narrators] narrate a single hadith consisting of the same *matn* via the same *isnād* and one of the narrators includes an addition not mentioned by the other narrators'.[7] *Mudraj* refers to a subcategory of *ziyādah* in which the additional element is judged to be an interpolation that was not in fact part of the original *matn* or *isnād*. Early collectors like Muslim and al-Tirmidhī state that *ziyādah* can be accepted only from trustworthy narrators whose memories have proved to be especially reliable, but in practice this served more as a general guideline than an absolute criterion.[8]

A third approach employed by hadith critics was evaluating whether a hadith contradicted what they considered to be established information (*al-taᶜlīl bi-al-mukhālafah*). Such hadiths were said to suffer from a defect known as *shudhūdh* or *mukhālafah,* which consisted of an irreconcilable variance with more authentic hadiths, a well-established practice or even historical facts. Although these terms were originally used in an elastic, non-technical sense, *shudhūdh* came to refer to contradictions within the *matn* of a single hadith, such that one version contradicts other more established versions, while *mukhālafah* came to refer to the overall meaning of a hadith contradicting information established through other sources.[9]

Fourthly, hadith critics considered the extent of inconsistency found in the wording and meaning of various versions of a single report. A minor difference in wording, referred to as *ikhtilāf,* was usually tolerated if it could be reasonably harmonised or if preference could be established for one version over another. A subcategory of *ikhtilāf* known as *iḍṭirāb* referred to inconsistency in wording and meaning that was too extensive to be reconciled or to establish a preference for one version of the hadith over another.[10]

In addition to the foregoing, hadith critics identified several other kinds of miscellaneous errors that narrators made in their transmissions, which they classified under the generic category of error (*ghalaṭ*). Error included conflating two different hadiths and changing the wording of a hadith in a manner that corrupts its meaning through omission, misreading, misunderstanding and the like. Although such errors were most common among weak narrators, trustworthy narrators were not considered immune to them.

The Criteria of the Jurists

Hadith critics and jurists approached the hadith corpus with substantially different concerns. Whereas hadith critics were concerned predominantly with the authenticity of a given report in the sense of whether or not it was reliably attributed to the Prophet, jurists were concerned predominantly with its authority in the sense of whether or not it should be acted upon. Jurists and legal theorists debated the authority of hadiths within the genre of legal theory (*uṣūl al-fiqh*), whose structure and language were largely common to all four Sunni legal schools in spite of significant methodological differences between them. This genre built upon and standardised methods of legal reasoning that were already implicit among the foundational generations of the four schools. While all legal theorists used a common language, their senses of what sorts of *matn* criticism were acceptable differed substantially across the four schools. Even within a single school, a wide spectrum existed for the expression of 'rationalist' or 'traditionalist' tendencies. Figures like Abū Isḥāq al-Shīrāzī (d. 476/1083) and Ibn ʿAqīl (d. 513/1119) represented a rationalist tendency within the Shāfiʿī and Ḥanbalī schools, respectively, while figures like Ibn ʿAbd al-Barr (d. 463/1071) and al-Ṭaḥāwī (d. 321/933) represented a traditionalist tendency within the Mālikī and Ḥanafī schools. Furthermore, from roughly the fifth/eleventh century onwards, virtually all hadith scholars were affiliated with one of the four Sunni legal schools. Accordingly, there was a certain convergence between the theories of *matn* criticism operative among traditionists and jurists. However, in practice, approaches to *matn* criticism continued to be defined by the genre that a scholar wrote in as much as they were by affiliation with a particular legal school. Thus, although two figures like al-Zarkashī and Ibn Ḥajar both belonged to the Shāfiʿī school and wrote specialised works on hadith, the works of the former on legal theory and those of the latter on *ʿulūm al-ḥadīth* continued to frame *matn* criticism in markedly different ways.

The primary concerns of these two genres – authenticity and authority – obviously overlapped, but both hadith critics and jurists recognised that they were not identical. In theory, both parties recognised that it was possible to affirm that a given hadith was reliably attributed to the Prophet without affirming that it constituted a valid basis for action due to abrogation or some other consideration, and that the opposite was also true. Between these two affirmations, myriad possibilities existed for the four schools to debate how the authority of hadith reports should interact and be reconciled with the authority of other legal sources. The area of sharpest disagreement had to do with the authority of solitary reports (*akhbār al-āḥād*). The Shāfiʿīs and Ḥanbalīs were inclined to view these reports as trumping virtually all forms of legal evidence other than the Qurʾān and the *mutawātir sunnah,* whereas the Mālikīs and especially the Ḥanafīs frequently allowed other considerations to attenuate or override the authority of solitary reports. In the formative period, these different tendencies were already typified in the opposition of *ahl al-ḥadīth* and *ahl al-raʾy*. As the legal schools evolved and attempted to codify their interpretive principles, the inchoate disagreements that had divided their foundational generations were cemented and given more explicit theoretical grounding. In developed form, debates over the authority of solitary reports revolved around seven possible competing sources of authority.

1. Contradicting Reason

Jurists were virtually unanimous in holding that hadiths could be rejected if they were unreasonable. A classic formulation of this principle is that of the Shāfiʿī jurist Abū Isḥāq al-Shīrāzī:

> If a reliable narrator narrates a report it can be rejected on the basis of a number of considerations: one of them is that it should contradict what is known of necessity by reason (*mūjibāt al-ʿuqūl*). Its invalidity is thus known, for revelation conveys only that which is judged possible by reason.[11]

Although such expressions were ubiquitous in works on legal theory, Sunni jurists were also careful to circumscribe this principle with various conditions and caveats in an effort to ensure that it would not be employed too liberally. Among these was the stipulation that the contradiction be real (*ḥaqīqīyah*), meaning that all reasonable people would agree on it, and that it should occur within the purview of what is accessible to reason.[12] In addition, it would have to be impossible to find an interpretation for the report that accorded with reason.[13]

The parameters created by such stipulations could only take shape in practice and their general validity, though contested at the level of detail, obviously depended in large measure on a tacit agreement among legal theorists on the broadest outlines of the relationship of reason to metaphysics – an agreement shaped in large measure by the Sunni self-definition in opposition to the Muʿtazilīs and philosophers. Thus, the import of the reports cited to exemplify this principle were most often of a theological rather than a legal nature. On the side of affirming the probity of reason, legal theorists mentioned the notorious hadith in which the Prophet is made to say that God created himself from the sweat of a horse, which all people of sound reason judged impossible.[14] On the side of affirming the limits of human reason and the expansive possibilities of interpretation, jurists cited hadiths like the one in which the Prophet says that death will be brought in the form of a ram and slaughtered in front of the inhabitants of paradise and hell, which was conceivable not only because it would take place in the rationally inaccessible realm of the unseen (*al-ghayb*), but because the language of the report could be understood metaphorically.[15]

While the parties to the emergent Sunni consensus of the fifth/tenth century might have agreed that such clear cases were useful in covering the flanks vulnerable to attacks from more extreme traditionalist or rationalist parties, the broad parameters that they provided still left ample room to grind old axes. Thus, on the one hand, al-Khaṭīb al-Baghdādī accepted in principle the idea that irrational reports could be rejected and quotes Abū Isḥāq al-Shīrāzī verbatim in his *al-Faqīh wa-al-mutafaqqih*. On the other hand, in the same work he includes extensive polemics against those who would dismiss the Sunnah on the basis of *raʾy* and supposed contradictions that were highly redolent of longstanding traditionalist attacks against the Ḥanafīs.[16] Al-Khaṭīb's nod towards the principle that hadiths must accord with reason was characteristic of the emergent détente between rationalism and traditionalism in the realm of theology. However, the extent to which juristic understandings of *matn* criticism would be allowed to whittle down the body of acceptable solitary hadith reports remained a significant bone of contention in the realm of legal interpretation, with the Shāfiʿīs and Ḥanbalīs to one side of the spectrum arrayed against the Mālikīs and especially the Ḥanafīs on the other.

2. Contradicting the Qurʾān

The question of the nature of the relationship between the Qurʾān and hadith and how their relative authority should be defined was, of course, a major preoccupation of the discipline of legal theory and one of the most obvious points dividing the four *madhhab*s from one another. One of the implications of this question was whether a hadith could be rejected, or at least whether its legal implications could be ignored, because it contradicted the Qurʾān. Among Sunnis, the notion that a solitary hadith report could be rejected due to its contradicting the Qurʾān became virtually synonymous with the Ḥanafī school, with the Shāfiʿīs and Ḥanbalīs opposing them in granting greater authority to solitary reports and, for the most part, denying the possibility of contradiction to begin with. The Mālikīs fell somewhere in the middle, dismissing certain hadith reports that contradicted the Qurʾān in practice without laying claim to the notion as an indispensable feature of their school's methodology.

Dating the origins of this debate is beyond the scope of the present chapter.[17] The notion that hadith reports must be in agreement with the

Qurʾān in order to be accepted was enshrined explicitly in a *mursal* hadith attributed to Muḥammad al-Bāqir (d. *c.* 114/733) and in a *marfūʿ* hadith attributed to some Companions. Sunni hadith critics found these reports unacceptable.[18] In favour of the traditionalist point of view was a hadith in which the Prophet stated that he was 'given the Qurʾān and the likes of it along with it' and condemned a hypothetical individual who would lounge around on cushions declaring that the Qurʾān was all anyone needed.[19] Each side could cite several such reports in favour of their position.

The duelling conceptualisations of the appropriate relationship between the Qurʾān and Sunnah that found early expression in hadith reports were mirrored and extended in methodological debates among the founding generations of the legal schools. It comes as no surprise that one of the first written testimonies to endorse setting aside hadith reports that contradict the Qurʾān in favour of the Qurʾān comes from Abū Yūsuf (d. 182/798), the pupil of Abū Ḥanīfah (d. 150/767) and a qadi under the ʿAbbāsids:

> Narrations are increasing in abundance and from among them come things that are strange and unknown to the people of *fiqh*, not agreeing with the Book or the *sunnah*. So beware of anomalous hadiths and stick to what is attested by an abundance of hadiths, what the jurists (*fuqahāʾ*) know, and what is in agreement with the Book and the *sunnah*. Compare everything else with that, and [know that] whatever contradicts the Qurʾan is not from the Messenger of God, even if a narration has come down to that effect.[20]

Underpinning Abū Yūsuf's comments is a conception of the Sunnah that was defined by communal reception and broad attestation rather than any specifically-defined formal criteria for evaluating individual hadith reports. This conception of Sunnah, which was broadly shared among the so-called ancient schools, freely endorsed setting aside formally sound hadith reports that were not widely attested in favour of other forms of evidence, including the Qurʾān.[21]

The opposite pole in the debate was emphasised by al-Shāfiʿī, who cited Abū Yūsuf's discussion and responded to it as follows:

> As for the position that he adopted of negating hadith and subjecting it to comparison with the Qurʾan, even if this were the case, it would be a proof against his argument since hadith does not contradict the Qurʾan. Rather, the hadith of the Messenger of God clarifies the intent of God with respect to general and specific [language] and abrogating and abrogated [rulings]. Furthermore, the *sunnah* laid down by the Messenger of God is an obligation for people by God's command. So whoever accepts something from the Messenger of God has [ultimately] accepted it from God since God has clarified this in more than one place in his book.[22]

The argument in this passage formed one key element in al-Shāfiʿī's far-reaching reinterpretation of the Sunnah, which would vastly augment the authority of hadith in legal argumentation. Not only did an exclusively hadith-based conception of Sunnah supplant local traditions that functioned, in Abū Yūsuf's conception, as a cumulative repository in which Sunnah was distilled both from the unwieldy body of hadith reports and from the practice of the post-prophetic legal community; it also became effectively inconceivable that Sunnah could contradict the Qurʾān. Rather than ignoring the legal implications of hadith reports that sat in tension with local traditions or the legal sense of relevant Qurʾānic verses, in the framework laid out by al-Shāfiʿī one resolved such apparent tensions through any one of a number of harmonising tools.[23]

In the course of the third / ninth century, al-Shāfiʿī's theories rapidly reconfigured the terms on which debates concerning Islamic law took place. The force of his arguments within the legal community was attested both by extensions of his argument authored by traditionalists and by refutations authored by scholars unwilling to accept his comprehensive reformulation of the appropriate methods of legal reasoning. Among traditionalists, Aḥmad ibn Ḥanbal is reported to have written a treatise dedicated to arguing against the possibility of contradiction between sound hadith reports and the Qurʾān.[24] Among Ḥanafīs, the most influential defence against the arguments of al-Shāfiʿī was a work by the qadi ʿĪsá ibn Abān (d. 221 / 836), in which he refined and systematised the relatively informal approach to hadith among early Ḥanafīs in response to al-Shāfiʿī's polemics.[25] One of the key elements of al-Shāfiʿī's argument against his opponents was to point out their apparently arbitrary acceptance and rejection of formally sound hadith reports, since even the Ḥanafīs made use of certain solitary hadith reports that sat in apparent tension with the Qurʾān. ʿĪsá ibn Abān sought to provide the Ḥanafīs with a comprehensive criterion on the issue, arguing that a solitary hadith report could only particularise the general language of the Qurʾān if such an interpretation had already been accepted at a broad communal level by generations of scholars.[26] For ʿĪsá ibn Abān and the classical theorists of the Ḥanafī school, the issue ultimately revolved around the epistemological question of the degree of authority conferred upon hadith reports and other forms of legal evidence by their location along a spectrum of certainty. Their rejection of solitary hadith reports was based on the notion that the general meanings of the Qurʾān were certain at both the level of attribution (*thubūt*) and indication (*dalālah*) and could therefore not be particularised by a report that was merely probable at the level of attribution.[27]

In practice, the Ḥanafī stipulation of an absence of contradiction with the Qurʾān led to many substantive disagreements with the other three schools. For example, they rejected the hadith of Fāṭimah bint Qays indicating that an irrevocably divorced woman should not receive alimony due to the Qurʾānic verse stating, 'Let the women [in their waiting period] live in the same manner as you live yourselves, in accordance with your means. And do not harass them in order to make their lives miserable. And if they are with child, spend freely on them until they deliver ...' (Q. 65:6).[28] Similarly, they rejected the hadith allowing the testimony of a single just witness along with an oath from the plaintiff due to the stipulation for two witnesses in the Qurʾān (Q. 2:282).[29] The Mālikīs, although not known for restricting the authority of hadith on the basis of the Qurʾān to the same extent as the Ḥanafīs, also crafted their arguments on several issues in a similar fashion. They rejected a hadith prohibiting the consumption of birds of prey (lit. 'birds with talons') due to the general indication of the verse, 'Say: I do not find in what has been revealed to me anything forbidden for one who wishes to eat, other than carrion, flowing blood, the flesh of swine – it is loathsome – or a sinful offering over which any name other than God's has been invoked' (Q. 6:145).[30] They also rejected a hadith regarding the special procedure for washing vessels licked by dogs due to the verse that allowed the use of dogs in hunting (Q. 5:4), reasoning from this that their saliva must be pure.[31]

3. Contradicting the *mashhūr* Sunnah

In addition to their stipulation of non-contradiction of the Qurʾān, Ḥanafī legal theorists also specified that solitary hadith reports must not contradict the *sunnah mashhūrah* (or *maʿrūfah*) if they were to constitute valid legal evidence. *Mashhūr* hadiths were defined as reports that began as solitary reports with the first transmitter (the *ṣaḥābī*), but then became *mutawātir* among subsequent generations (the *tābiʿūn* onward).[32] Because such reports were considered tantamount to *mutawātir* reports, they were effectively certain in their attribution and thus enjoyed the same level of authority as other certain forms of evidence. In other words, *mashhūr* reports could particularise and abrogate the Qurʾān and *mutawātir* reports but could not be particularised or abrogated by solitary reports.[33]

On the basis of this stipulation the Ḥanafīs rejected a solitary hadith prohibiting the sale of ripe dates for dry ones because they considered it to contradict the *mashhūr* hadith concerning *ribā*, which allowed the equal and simultaneous exchange of dates in general, without any differentiation between ripe and dry ones.[34] They also included this reasoning in their rejection of the aforementioned hadith allowing the testimony of a single witness with an oath, since a *mashhūr* hadith specified that the plaintiff was required to present clear evidence (*bayyinah*) and that the accused could exonerate himself with an oath. Hence, allowing the plaintiff to confirm his claim with an oath would contradict the *mashhūr* hadith restricting the oath to the accused.[35]

4. Contradicting Consensus (*ijmāʿ*)

Ḥanafī jurists included several other stipulations for the acceptance of solitary reports that the majority of schools considered to be mere theoretical propositions without practical implications in legal interpretation. Among these stipulations was that the report should not contradict *ijmāʿ*. Although the concept of *ijmāᶜ* was eventually acknowledged by jurists of all schools, early hadith critics were wary of it insofar as it was often used to assert the primacy of local, inherited tradition against competing opinions. It was with such assertions in mind that al-Shāfiᶜī claimed that consensus could not occur in contradiction to the Sunnah.[36] Ibn Ḥanbal's expression of doubt concerning the occurrence of *ijmāᶜ* was likewise interpreted by Ibn Taymīyah as an expression of frustration with unfounded claims of *ijmāᶜ* asserted in the face of hadith reports that had not gained traction in a given local context.[37]

In spite of such pronouncements on the part of the earliest exponents of the traditionalist schools, by the fifth/eleventh century, Shāfiᶜī and Ḥanbalī legal theorists representative of the rationalist–traditionalist détente listed non-contradiction with *ijmāᶜ* as an explicit condition for the acceptance of solitary reports.[38] Even hadith critics like al-Khaṭīb al-Baghdādī followed suit.[39] It seems that for most theorists, however, this condition represented little more than a mental exercise that helped to clarify the interlocking hierarchy of legal evidence. Imām al-Ḥaramayn al-Juwaynī (d. 478/1085) even entertained the possibility of contradiction between consensus and a *mutawātir* hadith, stating that consensus would take precedence since the ruling indicated by the hadith could be subject to abrogation.[40] Imām al-Ḥaramayn quickly followed this statement by noting that the issue was merely hypothetical and that one should not allow oneself to get carried away with such propositions.[41]

The tenor of the discussion among the Ḥanafīs was considerably different. It is already clear that the Ḥanafīs were invested in defending the multi-layered and cumulative conception of Sunnah against the exclusive authority of hadith, and *ijmāᶜ* was one tool that could be used for this purpose. Al-Jaṣṣāṣ considered the precedence of *ijmāᶜ* over solitary reports to be the subject of consensus in itself, again with reference to the certain nature of consensus and the probabilistic nature of solitary reports. Due to its certain nature, *ijmāᶜ* could be grounds for dismissing solitary reports, but also for raising a ruling conveyed via a solitary report to the level of certainty.[42]

5. Solitary Hadiths Concerning Issues of General Concern

Another issue that divided the Ḥanafīs from the majority was whether a solitary hadith could be rejected because a single narrator transmitted something that ought to have been of general knowledge or concern. Once again, legal theorists of all schools discussed a category of reports that could be rejected on these grounds, but treated it more as an epistemological exercise than as a principle with any significant bearing on legal interpretation. Non-Ḥanafīs reasoned that major public events, such as civil strife or the dramatic death of a famous person in a large crowd, could not be reported by a single individual alone, and that if this were to occur, that individual would be proven a liar.[43]

The Ḥanafīs extended this reasoning to solitary hadith reports on legal and ritual matters under the rubric of what they referred to as *ᶜumūm al-balwá*.[44] The majority was willing to admit this standard with respect to the broadest rules, such as the obligation to pray five times a day, but did not believe that it applied to more detailed matters. Thus, a solitary report claiming that there are six daily prayers would be rejected, but not a solitary report pertaining to how the prayer should be performed.[45] The Ḥanafīs, however, believed that any ritual or legal teaching that all Muslims would need to know about could be rejected if it was conveyed only via a solitary report.

Application of this principle resulted in the Ḥanafīs rejecting several hadiths that were accepted by the other schools. They rejected a hadith narrated by a woman indicating that touching one's penis negated ablutions, reasoning that all men needed to know this ruling and that it could not truly go back to the Prophet if it was only narrated by a single woman.[46] On similar grounds they rejected hadiths concerning reciting the *basmala* out loud in prayer, raising the hands after *rukūᶜ*, the need to perform ablutions after consuming something touched by fire, and the need to perform ablutions after carrying a bier.[47]

6. Hadiths Contradicting *Qiyās*

Jurists of all schools discussed the notion of rejecting solitary reports that violated 'analogy' (*qiyās*) or 'analogy to principles' (*qiyās al-uṣūl*). This notion was the subject of both vigorous disagreement, even within schools, and considerable misunderstanding. The crux of the issue was what exactly was meant by *qiyās* or *qiyās al-uṣūl*, terms that were used interchangeably to a large extent. Although discussions of the issue in works of legal theory are extensive and diverse, as a general rule, it is fair to say that those who favoured this principle and those who opposed it were in fact referring to two different ideas.

Those opposed to rejecting hadiths on the basis of *qiyās* tended to think of *qiyās* as the familiar process of drawing an analogy between an issue for which there was no explicit textual indication and an issue for which there was an explicit textual indication, giving them the same ruling. On this basis, they argued that rejecting solitary reports on the basis of *qiyās* was obviously illegitimate, since it was in effect subordinating rulings established by the principal textual sources to rulings that were secondary to and derivative of those same sources. This understanding underpinned Shafiᶜī and Ḥanbalī polemics against the possibility of rejecting solitary reports on the basis of *qiyās*.[48]

A careful reading of the arguments of scholars who accepted the possibility of such rejection, chiefly Ḥanafīs and some Mālikīs, reveals that they used the terms *qiyās* and *qiyās al-uṣūl* in this context to refer to something other than the specific juristic tool of *qiyās* that extended a textual ruling to a new case through analogy. For these scholars, the term '*al-uṣūl*' seems to have referred to basic, non-negotiable principles of law, akin to what one finds in the genre of legal maxims (*qawāᶜid fiqhīyah*).[49] Solitary hadiths could be rejected if they clashed with such principles, which were considered to be widely and indisputably grounded in the principal textual sources of the law.[50] Thus, responding to the arguments of those who rejected the validity of *qiyās al-uṣūl*, al-Qarāfī (d. 684/1285) wrote, 'The texts on which the *qiyās* is based are not the same as the text over which the *qiyās* has been given precedence, so there is no contradiction.'[51] In other words, the proponents of this practice stressed the authority of principles that could be rooted in an array of texts over the authority of individual texts themselves.

Ultimately, this dispute brought into relief two differing conceptions of how hadith criticism was best carried out. Proponents of *qiyās al-uṣūl* highlighted the factors that gave rise to uncertainty in solitary reports, such as the widespread practice of narrating hadiths by paraphrase (*al-riwāyah bi-al-maᶜná*) and the differing levels of understanding (*fiqh*) possessed by different narrators. Because of such uncertainty, it was entirely reasonable to reject solitary reports that contradicted principles that were widely agreed on and rooted in more than a single text.[52] Specifying the exact point of disagreement, al-Sarakhsī wrote that 'If it is known for certain that [the report] was heard from the Messenger of God in a manner that contradicts *qiyās* and there are no grounds for suspicion concerning its transmission, then it is as if we had heard it from the Messenger of God and are required to leave aside any kind of *qiyās* in favour of [the report].'[53] Similarly, while the opponents of *qiyās al-uṣūl* agreed regarding the uncertain nature of solitary reports in theory, in practice they were reluctant to admit the suspicions raised by its proponents into their evaluation of hadith reports, which may account in part for their insistence on equating the practice with giving precedence to derivative forms of evidence over primary forms.

Aside from the overwhelming rejection of *qiyās al-uṣūl* among Shāfiᶜīs and Ḥanbalīs, there was no final agreement, even within schools, on exactly when this practice was legitimate. Some Ḥanafīs, such as al-Asmandī (d. 552/1157) and Ibn al-Humām (d. 861/1457), held that each case of contradiction should be treated individually on the basis of full consideration of the relevant evidence.[54] This was also the position of some Muᶜtazilī legal theorists, such as Abū al-Ḥusayn al-Baṣrī (d. 436/1044).[55] Perhaps the majority of Ḥanafīs, including figures such as ᶜĪsá ibn Abān, al-Bazdawī and al-Sarakhsī, stipulated that solitary reports be rejected on this basis whenever the narrator was not a jurist.[56] Some of the most influential figures of the Mālikī school, including al-Qarāfī and al-Shāṭibī (d. 790/1388), held that *qiyās al-uṣūl* always took precedence over solitary reports, but this was hardly the subject of agreement within the school.[57] Al-Bājī (d. 474/1081), Ibn al-Ḥājib (d. 646/1249) and al-Tilimsānī (d. 771/1369) all held that the correct position of the school was to prefer solitary reports over *qiyās* with some limited exceptions.[58]

Like the issues discussed above, the problem of *qiyās al-ūṣūl* is clarified further in its practical application. The Ḥanafīs and Mālikīs argued that this form of reasoning was already implicitly ratified in the time of the companions. They cited a report in which Ibn ᶜAbbās rejected a hadith stating that upon waking from sleep, one must wash one's hands before dipping them into a water container for ablutions, which was narrated by Abū Hurayrah. Ibn ᶜAbbās reasoned that many people's water containers were too heavy to tip over, and extracting water from them without dipping one's hands in them therefore clashed with the basic principle of removing unnecessary hardship.[59] Another hadith rejected by the Ḥanafīs was known as *ḥadīth al-muṣarrāh*, which referred to the under-handed practice of selling livestock after confining milk in their udders to make them seem more full. According to the hadith, also narrated by Abū Hurayrah, once the buyer realised that he had been duped after milking the animal, he was allowed to either keep the animal or return it along with a certain amount of dates to compensate for the milk. The Ḥanafīs held that this violated more basic legal principles, such as the principle that benefiting from any property entailed undertaking responsibility for it (*al-kharāj bi-al-ḍamān*) and the prohibition of the unequal exchange of staple foods under the category of *ribā*.[60]

7. Hadiths Contradicting Inherited Tradition

Similar to their consideration of the communal reception of hadiths, the Ḥanafīs and Mālikīs also took widespread practices handed down across generations as a standard against which to measure the authority of hadith reports. In general terms, the Ḥanafī sense of inherited tradition was more nebulous than that of the Mālikīs. We have already seen that early Ḥanafī jurists like Abū Yūsuf and ᶜĪsá ibn Abān took the communal reception of hadith reports into consideration in determining their applicability. One aspect of this was examining whether hadiths were acted upon by recognised authorities among early generations. Early Ḥanafīs such as ᶜĪsá ibn Abān reasoned that if the majority of such figures failed to act upon a given hadith, it must have been abrogated or incorrectly reported. Assuming otherwise would mean that these early authorities had deliberately contradicted the Prophet's teachings, which was absurd and would entail undermining the reliability of the majority of those who passed on the Prophet's teachings to begin with.[61] Later Ḥanafīs specified that this applied only to issues that would have been widely practised, as detailed above.[62] An example of how this standard was applied in practice is the report of al-Barāᵓ ibn ᶜĀzib (d. 72/691–2) concerning the *qunūt* supplication in the morning (*fajr*) and evening (*maghrib*) prayers.[63] The Ḥanafīs rejected the report because it was not widely practised.[64]

In principle, the Ḥanafī sense of inherited practice against which they measured hadith reports was not geographically restricted. They went so far as to specify that an inherited practice in any city in which a significant number of Companions and Followers (*tābiᶜīn*) settled was authoritative.[65] This stood in sharp contrast to the Mālikīs, who famously held that 'the praxis of the people of Medina' (*ᶜamal ahl al-madīnah*) were a more authoritative source than solitary hadith reports. The precise sense of *ᶜamal ahl al-madīnah* was implicit in the usage of the early generations of the Mālikī school.[66] By the time of al-Qāḍī ᶜAbd al-Wahhāb (d. 422/1031), al-Bājī and al-Qāḍī ᶜIyāḍ (d. 544/1149), the mature discourse of Mālikī legal theory divided *ᶜamal* into two types.[67] The first type is revelation-based issues transmitted and supported by actions that were passed down and practised by overwhelming numbers of people since the time of the Prophet (*mā ṭarīquhu al-naql wa-ittaṣal al-ᶜamal bihi*), so *al-madīnah* as a place itself is not meant. This type includes saying, doing and not doing widely practised issues such as the call to prayer (*adhān*), the *iqāmah, al-ṣāᶜ*, not taking *zakāh* from vegetables in spite of its effluent in Medina, and not reciting aloud '*bi-ism Allāh al-Raḥmān al-Raḥīm*'. The Mālikīs agreed that this category of *ᶜamal* was authoritative enough to override solitary reports. According to al-Qāḍī ᶜIyāḍ, it constituted:

> a proof whose authority must be accepted, and against which conflicting evidence such as solitary reports and analogy must be set aside, since this [type of] transmission is beyond doubt. It yields certain knowledge and therefore should not be set aside in favour of something that is merely likely.[68]

Even beyond the confines of the Mālikī school, some Shāfiᶜīs including Abū Bakr al-Ṣayrafī (d. 330/942) and some Ḥanbalīs, including Ibn Taymīyah and Ibn Qayyim al-Jawzīyah, considered this notion of *ᶜamal* to be authoritative within a limited scope that understands the concept of *ᶜamal* as something commonly narrated when it contradicts a single narration.[69] The second type of *ᶜamal* is the *ijtihād* of the Companions that was passed down to subsequent generations. The majority of Mālikīs did not give this type of *ᶜamal* precedence over solitary reports, although many North Africans and Andalusians did.[70] Perhaps the best known example of a hadith that the Mālikīs rejected based on *ᶜamal* is the hadith of Ibn ᶜUmar that states that the two parties to a sale may cancel it until they part from each another. The hadith was narrated by Mālik himself via an unassailable *isnād*, but he rejected its apparent implications because the people of Medina did not follow it in practice.[71]

Generally speaking, it is obvious that the Shāfiᶜīs were opposed to measuring hadith reports against inherited tradition. The notion of *ᶜamal* was far too nebulous for al-Shāfiᶜī, who addressed his erstwhile teacher Mālik saying, 'We still do not know what you mean by *ᶜamal* to this day, and I doubt that we ever shall.'[72] However, just as Ḥanafī and Mālikī jurists sharpened their respective notions of *ᶜamal* over time, later Shāfiᶜī jurists admitted that inherited tradition deserved consideration alongside hadith reports within a limited scope. Their aim was to harmonise the single hadith with the *ᶜamal* of Medina and the practice of Companions when they appeared to contradict each other. This is based on the assumption that the Companions cannot have intentionally violated the prophetic hadith without reason. Imām al-Ḥaramayn and al-Ghazālī argue that if it was established with certainty that authoritative figures among the Companions were aware of a hadith and did not act upon it and its meaning was decisive (*wa-kāna al-khabar naṣṣan lā yataṭarraqu ilayhi taʾwīl*), the hadith would have to be considered abrogated.[73] Although this position echoes that of the Ḥanafīs, the Shāfiʿī theorists were reluctant to concede too much ground to their opponents and were careful to couch concessions in reasoning that was acceptable to their tradition-based school. Imām al-Ḥaramayn wrote that 'what we mentioned here is not giving their [i.e., the Companions'] rulings precedence over the report. It is nothing more than holding fast to the *ijmāʿ* concerning interpreting their actions in a manner that renders them correct, so it is as if we have resorted to consensus in contradistinction to the hadith.'[74]

Summary and Conclusions

This investigation of *matn* criticism among hadith critics and jurists further weakens the claim that classical Muslim scholars ignored such criticism in their evaluation of hadith reports, revealing it to be an over-generalisation or a hasty judgement based on an incomplete survey of the various genres in which hadith criticism was debated and carried out. It is clear that even Ḥanbalīs and Shāfiʿīs could state unflinchingly that 'irrational' hadiths could not be accepted, even if the conception of reason brought to bear on the hadith corpus did not automatically exclude the material deemed ahistorical by the Orientalists. We have also seen that hadith critics were not averse to pointing out logical and chronological inconsistencies in formally authentic reports, even if this never constituted a central concern of their discipline.

In addition to substantiating the practice of *matn* criticism among classical hadith critics and jurists, this chapter highlights how the different disciplinary concerns of these two groups led to different approaches to *matn* criticism. Hadith critics were concerned primarily with concurrent investigations of the *isnād* and the *matn* that would allow them to draw detailed conclusions regarding several interrelated questions. On the one hand, they attempted to assess the reliability of individual hadiths or some of their components by applying the criteria set out above. At the same time, the sum total of their assessments of individual hadiths allowed them to draw conclusions concerning the reliability, memorisation and precision of particular narrators. *Isnād* and *matn* criticism, in other words, were deeply intertwined for hadith critics insofar as both ultimately rested on a broad, comparative survey of the hadith corpus that identified correlations between particular figures in the *isnād* and consistency or lack thereof in the contents of hadiths. The comparative methods employed by hadith scholars also enabled them to detect logical and chronological contradictions within the hadith corpus.

The jurists' approach to *matn* criticism was framed less in terms of authenticity as such, and more in terms of the issue of applicability. This broad conceptual difference was common to the genre of legal theory across all four Sunni schools, but the schools differed widely in terms of their practical approximation to the methods of hadith critics. The Shāfiʿīs and Ḥanbalīs added little to the approach of hadith critics by way of *matn* criticism and were largely content to allow formally authentic hadiths to stand as legal evidence. To the extent that they admitted criteria external to the methods of hadith critics, they considered them to be largely theoretical propositions without much practical impact on jurisprudential deliberations. Weighing formally sound hadith reports against most other forms of evidence was, for these jurists, tantamount to rejecting revelation in favour of faulty human reason.

The Mālikīs and Ḥanafīs, however, held that it was necessary to weigh formally sound solitary hadith reports against other forms of evidence *before* concluding that such reports should be considered reflective of revelation to begin with. In insisting on this process of verification through criteria external to the hadith corpus, the Mālikīs and Ḥanafīs were emphasising the mediated and fallible nature of hadith reports, which they believed were subject to human error as long as they were not transmitted on a massive scale. Underlying their concern with applicability, in other words, was a conception of authenticity that was informed by a greater degree of scepticism and more diverse criteria than those of both Shāfiʿī and Ḥanbalī jurists and hadith critics. As noted by Wael Hallaq, this emphasis on the mediated and fallible nature of formally sound *isnād*s is perhaps a point of limited correspondence between classical Muslim and modern Western approaches to analysing hadith.[75]

From the fifth/eleventh century onwards, certain shifts took place in the relationship between the methodologies of hadith critics and jurists. At the level of theory, later traditionists adopted certain conditions for accepting hadith reports from the discipline of legal theory, as shown by their inclusion of categories like contradiction of reason, the Qurʾān, *ijmāʿ* and *tawātur* in manuals of *ʿulūm al-ḥadīth*, called *ʿalāmāt al-waḍʿ*. These categories, however, seem to have had little effect on the actual practice of *matn* criticism among later hadith critics and the real application for this is to be found in the genre of forged hadith (*al-mawḍūʿāt*), narrations by weak narrators or contrivers, such as the books of al-Jūraqānī, Ibn al-Jawzī and Ibn Qayyim al-Jawzīyah.[76]

On the other side, the *uṣūlīs*, including Shāfiʿīs and Ḥanbalīs, have agreed that the hadith that contradicts axiomatic knowledge (*badahīyāt al-ʿuqūl*) or certain meaning (*al-ʿilm al-qaṭʿī*) should be disregarded. However, they disagree about how to apply this to single hadiths. Obviously, the Ḥanafī approach has left its effects on discussions. The Ḥanafī and Mālkī traditionist-jurisprudents, nonetheless, were more influenced by their profession than by their legal affiliation, especially when they wrote in two genres: *takhrīj* of the legal hadiths (*aḥādīth al-aḥkām*) of their legal schools, and the genre of sciences of hadith (*ulūm al-ḥadīth*). Writing in these genres was deeply influenced by the Shāfiʿī approach, especially the work of Ibn al-Ṣalāḥ and Ibn Ḥajar, who developed the most full-blown theory of hadith sciences. These developments, however, left no practical impact on the legal practice of other legal schools.[77] Thus, in spite of a certain kind of theoretical convergence between the notions of *matn* criticism operative among later hadith critics and jurists, the practice of *matn* criticism among the two groups remained distinctive because of the essential disagreements in the legal practice between the four *Sunni* schools.

Notes

1. For one critique, see Jonathan A. C. Brown, 'How We Know Early Ḥadīth Critics Did *Matn* Criticism and Why It's So Hard to Find', *Islamic Law and Society* 15 (2008): 143–84, at 146–8.
2. On debates over *matn* criticism in modern Muslim scholarship, see Daniel W. Brown, *Rethinking Tradition in Modern Islamic Thought* (Cambridge: Cambridge University Press, 1996), 95–100, 112–32 and passim; Jonathan A. C. Brown, 'The Rules of *Matn* Criticism: There Are No Rules', *Islamic Law and Society* 19 (2012): 356–96, at 384–94; Mutaz al-Khatib, *Radd al-ḥadīth min jihat al-matn: dirāsah fī manāhij al-muḥaddithīn wa-al-uṣūlīyīn* (Beirut: al-Shabakah al-ᶜArabīyah fī al-Abḥāth wa-al-Nashr, 2011), 17–25, 227–31.
3. The major works in this regard are Muṣṭafā al-Sibāᶜ ī, *al-Sunnah wa-makānatuhā fī al-tashrīᶜ*, PhD thesis, al-Azhar University, Cairo, 1949, and Nūr al-Dīn ᶜItr, *Manhaj al-naqd fī ᶜulūm al-ḥadīth* (Damascus: Dār al-Fikr, 1972). Al-Sibāᶜī focused on *ᶜalāmāt waḍᶜ al-ḥadīth;* ᶜItr reformulated *ᶜulūm al-ḥadīth* to show that the method of hadith criticism is comprehensive and covers both *isnād* and *matn*. It is also important to mention Ẓafar Aḥmad al-Tahānawī (d. 1394/1974), *Qawāᶜid fī ᶜulūm al-ḥadīth* (the first edition was in India in 1930), a manual focused on the Ḥanafī contribution to *matn* criticism.
4. The notion of collecting *Ṣaḥābah matn* criticism started with ᶜAbd al-Muḥsin ibn Ṭāhir al-Baghdādī (d. 489/1096), who collected a small number of reports. Badr al-Dīn al-Zarkashī (d. 794/1392) dedicated to it an important work published as *al-Ijābah li-īrād mā istadrakathu ᶜĀ᾽ishah ᶜalá al-ṣaḥābah*, ed. Saᶜīd al-Afghānī (Damascus: al-Maṭbaᶜah al-Hāshimīyah, 1939), later summarised by Jalāl al-Dīn al-Suyūṭī (d. 911/1505) in *ᶜAyn al-iṣābah*. For a critical analysis of these examples, see al-Khatib, *Radd al-ḥadīth*, 179–209.
5. The early works in this regard are Ṣalāḥ al-Dīn al-Idlibī, *Manhaj naqd al-matn ᶜinda ᶜulamā᾽ al-ḥadīth* (Beirut: Manshūrāt Dār al-Āfāq al-Jadīdah, 1983), Musfir al-Dumaynī, *Maqāyīs Ibn al-Jawzī fī naqd mutūn al-sunnah min khilāl kitābihi* al-Mawḍūᶜāt (Jeddah: Dār al-Madanī, 1984), and Ṣalāḥ al-Dīn al-Idlibī, *Maqāyīs naqd mutūn al-sunnah* (Riyadh: Maktabat al-ᶜUlūm wa-al-Ḥikam, 1995).
6. For more details, see al-Khatib, *Radd al-ḥadīth*, 237–71.
7. Ibn Rajab al-Ḥanbalī, *Sharḥ ᶜilal al-Tirmidhī*, 1:425.
8. Muslim, *Kitāb al-Tamyīz*, 189; Ibn Rajab al-Ḥanbalī, *Sharḥ ᶜilal al-Tirmidhī*, 418–19. For a detailed explanation of why the issue cannot be reduced to any particular standard, see al-Zaylaᶜī, *Naṣb al-rāyah fī takhrīj aḥādīth* al-Hidāyah, ed. Muḥammad ᶜAwwāmah, 5 vols (Jeddah: Dār al-Qiblah lil-Thaqāfah al-Islāmīyah, etc., n.d.), 1:336–7.

9. Al-Khatib, *Radd al-ḥadīth*, 116–17, 277–8. Ibn al-Ṣalāḥ, for example, did not differentiate between *munkar* and *shādhdh*. See Ibn al-Ṣalāḥ, *ᶜUlūm al-ḥadīth*, ed. Nūr al-Dīn ᶜItr (Damascus: Dār al-Fikr, 1986), 76; Ibn Ḥajar, *al-Nukat* 2:674.
10. On *muḍṭarib* and *mukhtalif* reports, see Ibn al-Ṣalāḥ, *Introduction*, 71–2 and 205–6, respectively.
11. Abū Isḥāq al-Shīrāzī, *al-Lumaᶜ fī uṣūl al-fiqh* (Beirut: Dār al-Kutub al-ᶜIlmīyah, 1985), 45; al-Khaṭib al-Baghdādī, *al-Faqīh wa-al-mutafaqqih*, ed. ᶜĀdil Yūsuf al-ᶜAzzāzī, 2 vols (Riyadh: Dār Ibn al-Jawzī, 2000), 1:354. See also al-Khaṭīb al-Baghdādī, *al-Kifāyah fī ᶜilm al-riwāyah*, ed. Aḥmad ᶜUmar Hāshim (Beirut: Dār al-Kitāb al-ᶜArabī, 1986), 33, 472; Ibn al-Jawzī, *Kitāb al-mawḍūᶜāt min al-aḥādīth al-marfūᶜāt*, ed. Nūr al-Dīn ibn Shukrī ibn ᶜAlī, 4 vols (Riyadh: Maktabat Aḍwāʾ al-Salaf, 1997), 1:151.
12. This can be understood through two indications: first, their expressions such as *mūjibāt al-ᶜuqūl, muqtaḍá al-ᶜaql, mā tadfaᶜu al-ᶜuqūl ṣiḥḥatahu bi-mawḍūᶜihā*; secondly, their examples for this type of hadith.
13. See, for example, al-Jaṣṣāṣ, *al-Fuṣūl fī al-uṣūl*, ed. ᶜUjayl Jāsim al-Nashmī, al-Turāth al-islāmī 14, 4 vols (Kuwait: Wizārat al-Awqāf wa-al-Shuʾūn al-Islāmīyah, 1994), 3:122.
14. Al-Kalwadhānī, *al-Tamhīd fī uṣūl al-fiqh*, ed. Mufīd Abū ᶜAmshah, 4 vols (Riyadh: Umm al-Qurā University 1985), 3:147–8; Muḥammad ibn ᶜAbd al-Ḥamīd al-Asmandī, *Badhl al-naẓar fī al-uṣūl*, ed. Muḥammad Zakī ᶜAbd al-Barr (Cairo: Maktabat Dār al-Turāth, 1992), 460–1.
15. Al-Qāḍī Abū Bakr ibn al-ᶜArabī defended the rational possibility of this hadith. See Ibn al-ᶜArabī, *al-ᶜAwāṣim min al-qawāṣim*, ed. ᶜAmmār Ṭālibī (Cairo: Maktabat Dār al-Turāth, 1997), 236–9, and Ibn Ḥajar al-ᶜAsqalānī, *Fatḥ al-Bārī*, 11:421. For the hadith, see among other places al-Bukhārī, *Ṣaḥīḥ, k. al-tafsīr* 19, No. 4730, and Muslim, *Ṣaḥīḥ, k. al-jannah, bāb al-nār yadkhuluhā al-jabbārūn*, No. 2850.
16. Al-Khaṭīb al-Baghdādī, *al-Faqīh wa-al-mutafaqqih* 1:374–96.
17. For this point, see Mutaz al-Khatib, 'ᶜArḍ al-hadith ᶜalá al-Qurʾān: al-nashʾah wa-al-masār wa-al-taḥawwulāt', in *al-Manāhij al-ḥadīthah fī al-dars al-Qurʾānī* (Beirut: Dār Madārik, 2011), 91–182.
18. In the *mursal* hadith the Prophet says, 'Hadiths from me will proliferate, so whatever you find attributed to me in agreement with the Qurʾan is indeed from me, and whatever you find attributed to me that contradicts the Qurʾan is not in fact from me.' In the *marfūᶜ* hadith, the Prophet says, 'Whenever you hear a narration attributed to me, you should consider and compare it with the Qurʾān. If it agrees with it, then it is from me; otherwise, it is not authentic.' See Abū Yūsuf, *al-Radd ᶜalá siyar al-Awzāᶜī*, ed. Abū al-Wafā al-Afghānī (Hyderabad: Lajnat Iḥyāʾ al-Maᶜārif al-Nuᶜmānīyah, n.d.), 25. For criticism of the two hadiths, see al-Shāfiᶜī, *al-Umm*, ed. Rifᶜat Fawzī ᶜAbd al-Muṭṭalib, 11 vols (Cairo: Dār al-Wafāʾ, 2001), 8:35; al-Shāfiᶜī, *al-Risālah*, ed. Aḥmad Shākir (Cairo: Maṭbaᶜat Muṣṭafā al-Bābī al-Ḥalabī 1940), 617–23; Abū ᶜUmar ibn ᶜAbd al-Barr, *Jāmiᶜ bayān al-ᶜilm wa-faḍlihi*, ed. Abū al-Ashbāl al-Zuhayrī, 2 vols (al-Dammam: Dār Ibn al-Jawzī, 1994), 2:1191; Ibn al-Jawzī, *Mawḍūᶜāt* 1:420. The notion of stipulating agreement with the Qurʾān is not only the opinion of Ibrāhīm al-Nakhaᶜī

(d. 96/714) and many Kufans, but is also attested in Ibāḍī and Shiᶜi sources. See Muḥammad Rawwās Qalᶜajī, *Mawsūᶜat fiqh Ibrāhīm al-Nakhaᶜī*, 2 vols (Egypt: Maṭābiᶜ al-Hayʾah al-Miṣrīyah al-ᶜĀmmah lil-Kitāb, 1979), 763–5, 772–4; al-Rabīᶜ ibn Ḥabīb, *al-Jāmiᶜ al-ṣaḥīḥ* (Oman: Wizārat al-Awqāf, 211), 15; Ibn Barakah, *Kitāb al-jāmiᶜ*, ed. ᶜĪsá Yaḥyá al-Bārūnī, 2 vols (Oman: Wizārat al-Turāth al-Qawmī wa-al-Thaqāfah, 1998), 1:279–80; Muḥammad ibn Yaᶜqūb al-Kulaynī, *Uṣūl al-kāfi*, 7 vols (Beirut: Manshūrāt al-Fajr, 2007), 1:40–1.

19. For the hadith, see among other places Abū Dāwūd, *Sunan, k. al-sunnah* 5, *bāb fi luzūm al-sunnah*, No. 4604, and Aḥmad ibn Ḥanbal, *Musnad* 4:131 *28:410–13*.
20. Abū Yūsuf, *al-Radd*, 31.
21. For the classical discussion of the conception of Sunnah operative among the 'ancient schools', see Joseph Schacht, *On the Origins of Muḥammadan Jurisprudence* (Oxford: Clarendon Press, 1967), 21–35 and passim; Wael B. Hallaq, *The Origins and Evolution of Islamic Law* (Cambridge: Cambridge University Press, 2005), 29–56, 102–21; ᶜAbd al-Fattāḥ Abū Ghuddah, *al-Sunnah al-nabawīyah wa-bayān madlūlihā al-sharᶜī* (Beirut: Dār al-Bashāʾir al-Islāmīyah, 1992).
22. Al-Shāfiᶜī, *al-Umm* 9:194.
23. Schacht points out that these harmonising tools were also used by al-Shāfiᶜī's predecessors, but much more sparingly. See Schacht, *Origins of Muḥammadan Jurisprudence*, 23.
24. For more information about this treatise, see Abū Yaᶜlá, *Ṭabaqāt al-ḥanābilah*, ed. Muḥammad Ḥāmid al-Fiqī, 2 vols (Cairo: Maṭbaᶜat al-Sunnah al-Muḥammadīyah, 1952), 2:64–5; Ibn Taymīyah, *Rafᶜ al-malām ᶜan al-aʾimmah al-aᶜlām*, ed. ᶜAbd Allāh Ibrāhīm al-Anṣārī (Sidon: al-Maktabah al-ᶜAṣrīyah, n.d.), 32. Ibn Qayyim al-Jawzīyah sometimes quotes this treatise; e.g., Ibn al-Qayyim, *Iᶜlām al-muwaqqiᶜīn ᶜan rabb al-ᶜālamīn*, ed. Ṭāhā ᶜAbd al-Raʾūf Saᶜd, 4 vols (Beirut: Dār al-Jīl, 1973), 2:367.
25. On ᶜĪsá ibn Abān and his refutation of al-Shāfiᶜī, see Murteza Bedir, 'An Early Response to Shāfiᶜī: ᶜĪsā b. Abān on the Prophetic Report (*khabar*)', *Islamic Law and Society* 9(3) (2002): 285–311; Ahmed El-Shamsy, *The Canonization of Islamic Law: a Social and Intellectual History* (New York: Cambridge University Press, 2013), 202–5; Muḥammad Zāhid al-Kawtharī, *Bulūgh al-amānī fi sīrat al-imām Muḥammad ibn al-Ḥasan al-Shaybānī* (Cairo: al-Maktabah al-Azharīyah lil-Turāth, 1998), 49–50. On 'Īsá's contribution to the Ḥanafī legal school, see Haytham ᶜAbd al-Ḥamīd Khaznah, *Taṭawwur al-fikr al-uṣūlī al-ḥanafi* (Beirut: Dār al-Kutub al-ᶜIlmīyah, 2015), 116–28. Al-Jaṣṣāṣ is the most important source for ᶜĪsá ibn Abān's opinions since his works are no longer extant, but al-Nadīm lists five books written by him, for which see al-Nadīm, *al-Fihrist*, ed. Ayman Fuʾād Sayyid, 4 vols (London: Muʾassasat al-Furqān, 2009), 2:24–5.
26. Al-Jaṣṣāṣ, *al-Fuṣūl fi ᶜilm al-uṣūl*, 1:174–5, 178, 183–4.
27. Al-Jaṣṣāṣ, *al-Fuṣūl fi ᶜilm al-uṣūl*, 1:158–9, 168.
28. For the hadith of Fāṭimah bint Qays, see Muslim, *Ṣaḥīḥ, k. al-ṭalāq* 6, *bāb al-muṭallaqah thalāthan lā nafaqah lahā*, No. 1480. It is interesting that al-Bukhārī does not include this hadith in his *Ṣaḥīḥ*, but does dedicate a specific chapter under the title *bāb qiṣṣat Fāṭimah bint Qays* and cites two Qurʾānic verses (65:1,

6) and narrates three hadith reports clarifying ᶜĀʾishah's critique of the report of Fatimah. For the Ḥanafī opinion, see al-Bazdawī, *Uṣūl al-Bazdawī* (Karachi: Maṭbaᶜat Jāwīd Press, n.d), 175; al-Jaṣṣāṣ, *al-Fuṣūl*, 1:108, 114; al-Sarakhsī, *Uṣūl al-Sarakhsī*, ed. Abū al-Wafā al-Afghānī, 2 vols (Hyderabad: Lajnat Iḥyāʾ al-Maᶜārif al-ᶜUthmānīyah, 1973), 1:365. Motzki concludes that 'there are definitely no sufficient grounds to dismiss the Fatima bint Qays story as the pure invention of this woman': Harald Motzki, *The Origins of Islamic Jurisprudence: Meccan Fiqh before the Classical Schools*, trans. Marion H. Katz, Islamic History and Civilization: Studies and Texts, 41 (Leiden: Brill, 2002), 158–67.

29. For the hadith, see Muslim, *Ṣaḥīḥ, k. al-aqḍiyah 2, bāb al-qaḍāʾ bi-al-yamīn wa-al-shāhid*, No. 1712. See al-Sarakhsī, *Uṣūl* 1:365-6; ᶜAlāʾ al-Dīn al-Bukhārī, *Kashf al-asrār ᶜan uṣūl Fakhr al-Islām al-Bazdawī*, ed. ᶜAbd Allāh Maḥmūd Muḥammad ᶜUmar, 4 vols (Beirut: Dār al-Kutub al-ᶜIlmīyah, 1997), 3:17–18.
30. Abū ᶜUmar Yūsuf Ibn ᶜAbd al-Barr, *al-Tamhīd li-mā fī* al-Muwaṭṭaʾ *min al-asānīd*, ed. Muṣṭafá al-ᶜAdawī and Muḥammad ᶜAbd al-Kabīr al-Bakrī, 20 vols (Morocco: Wizārat al-Awqāf wa-al-Shuʾūn al-Islāmīyah, 1967), 15:166. For the hadith, see Muslim, *Ṣaḥīḥ, k. al-ṣayd wa-al-dhabāʾiḥ 3, bāb taḥrīm akl kull dhī nāb min al-sibāᶜ wa-kull dhī mikhlab min al-ṭayr*, No. 1932.
31. Abū Isḥāq Ibrāhīm ibn Mūsá al-Shāṭibī, *al-Muwāfaqāt*, ed. ᶜAbd Allāh Darāz, 4 vols (Cairo: Dār al-Fikr al-ᶜArabī, n.d), 3:21; Muḥammad ibn Khalīfah al-Ubbī, *Ikmāl* Ikmāl a-muᶜlim fī sharḥ *Ṣaḥīḥ* Muslim, ed. Muḥammad Sālim Ḥāshim, 9 vols (Beirut: Dār al-Kutub al-ᶜIlmīyah, 1994), 2:58.
32. Al-Shāshī, *Uṣūl al-Shāshī* (Beirut: Dār al-Kitāb al-ᶜArabī, 1982), 272; al-Bazdawī, *Uṣūl*, 152.
33. Al-Bazdawī, *Uṣūl*, 59; al-Sarakhsī, *Uṣūl*, 1:133.
34. Al-Sarakshī, *Uṣūl* 1:367; al-Dabbūsī, *Taqwīm al-adillah fī uṣūl al-fiqh*, ed. Khalīl al-Mays (Beirut: Dār al-Kutub al-ᶜIlmīyah, 2001), 188–9. For the solitary report, see Abū Dāwūd, *Sunan, k. al-buyūᶜ* 18, *bāb al-thamar bi-al-tamr*, No. 3359; al-Tirmidhī, *Sunan, k. al-buyūᶜ* 14, *bāb mā jāʾa fī al-nahy ᶜan al-muḥāqalah wa-al-muzābanah*, No. 1225; al-Nasāʾī, *Mujtabá, k. al-buyūᶜ* 36, *bāb ishtirāʾ al-tamr bi-al-ruṭab*, Nos 4545–6. For the *mashhūr* report, see al-Bukhārī, *Ṣaḥīḥ, k. al-buyūᶜ* 74, *bāb bayᶜ al-tamr bi-al-tamr*, No. 2170; Muslim, *Ṣaḥīḥ, k. al-musāqāh* 15, *bāb al-ṣarf wa-bayᶜ al-dhahab bi-al-wariq naqdan*, Nos 1586–8.
35. Al-Dabbūsī, *Taqwīm*, 198; al-Sarakhsī, *Uṣūl* 1:367. For the *mashhūr* hadith accepted by the Ḥanafīs, see al-Bukhārī, *Ṣaḥīḥ, k. al-rahn* 16, *bāb idhā ikhtalafa al-rāhin wa-al-murtahin wa-naḥwahu fa-al-bayyinah ᶜalá al-muddaᶜī wa-al-yamīn ᶜalá al-muddaᶜá ᶜalayh*, No. 2514, and Muslim, *Ṣaḥīḥ, k. al-aqḍiyah* 1, *bāb al-yamīn ᶜalá al-muddaᶜā ᶜalayh*, No. 1711.
36. Al-Shāfiᶜī, *al-Risālah*, 322. See also the comments of Schacht, *Origins of Muḥammadan Jurisprudence*, 88–95.
37. For Ibn Ḥanbal's expression of doubt concerning the occurrence of *ijmāᶜ*, see Ibn Ḥazm, *al-Iḥkām fī uṣūl al-aḥkām*, 8 vols (Cairo: Dār al-Ḥadīth, 1984), 4:573. For Ibn Taymīyah's explanation of the statement, see Taqī al-Dīn Aḥmad Ibn Taymīyah, *al-Fatāwá al-kubrá*, ed. Muḥammad ᶜAbd al-Qādir ᶜAṭā and Muṣṭafá ᶜAbd al-Qādir ᶜAṭā, 6 vols (Beirut: Dār al-Kutub al-ᶜIlmīyah, 1987), 6:286–7.

38. Al-Shīrāzī, Lumaʿ, 45; al-Kalwadhānī, Tamhīd 3:150; al-Zarkashī, al-Baḥr al-muḥīṭ, ed. ʿAbd al-Qādir ʿAbd Allāh al-ʿĀnī, 6 vols (Kuwait: Wizārat al-Aqāf wa-al-Shuʾūn al-Islāmīyah, 1988), 4:342.
39. Al-Khaṭīb, Kifāyah, 472.
40. Imām al-Ḥaramayn, al-Burhān fī al-uṣūl, ed. ʿAbd al-ʿAẓīm al-Dīb (Doha: Qatar University, 1979), 1169.
41. Imām al-Ḥaramayn, al-Burhān, 1175.
42. Al-Jaṣṣāṣ, Fuṣūl 1:175–8.
43. Al-Kalwadhānī, Tamhīd 3:151; al-Shīrāzī, Lumaʿ, 45; Imām al-Ḥaramayn, al-Burhān, 587; al-Zarkashī, Baḥr 3:342; Ibn ʿAbd al-Shakūr al-Bahārī, Musallam al-thubūt, in ʿAbd al-ʿAlī Muḥammad, Fawātiḥ al-raḥamūt, ed. ʿAbd Allāh Maḥmūd Muḥammad ʿUmar, 2 vols (Beirut: Dār al-Kutub al-ʿIlmīyah, 2002), 2:155.
44. Al-Shashī, Uṣūl al-Shāshī, 1:284; al-Jaṣṣāṣ, al-Fuṣūl 2:293; al-Bukhārī, Kashf 3:16.
45. Imām al-Ḥaramayn, al-Burhān fī-l-uṣūl, 665–6; Muḥammad ibn ʿAlī ibn ʿUmar al-Māzarī, Īḍāḥ al-maḥṣūl min burhān al-uṣūl, ed. ʿAmmār al-Ṭālibī (Beirut: Dār al-Gharb al-Islāmī, 2001), 522–3.
46. Al-Sarakhsī, Uṣūl 1:367. Hadiths to this effect were also attributed to several male companions, but the Ḥanafīs considered the chains of narration to be defective. See al-Bukhārī, Kashf 3:18. For the hadith, see among other places Abū Dāwud, Sunan, k. al-ṭahārah 68, bāb al-wuḍūʾ min mass al-dhakar, No. 181.
47. Al-Sarakhsī, Uṣūl 1:369; al-Bukhārī, Kashf 3:18.
48. Al-Shīrāzī, Lumaʿ, 39; al-Samʿānī, Qawāṭiʿ al-adillah fī uṣūl al-fiqh, ed. ʿAbd Allāh al-Ḥakamī, 5 vols (Riyadh: Maktabat al-Tawbah, 1998) 2:377–8; Abū Yaʿlá Ibn al-Farrāʾ, al-ʿUddah fī uṣūl al-fiqh, ed. Aḥmad ibn ʿAlī al-Mubārakī, 5 vols (Riyadh: n.p., 1990), 3:894; Ibn ʿAqīl, al-Wāḍiḥ fī uṣūl al-fiqh, ed. ʿAbd Allāh ibn ʿAbd al-Muḥsin al-Turkī, 5 vols (Beirut: Muʾassasat al-Risālah, 1999), 3:403. For more details about this discussion, see al-Khatib, Radd al-ḥadīth, 409, 427.
49. On the qawāʿid as both a legal tool and a literary genre, see Intisar Rabb, Doubt in Islamic Law: a History of Legal Maxims, Interpretation and Islamic Criminal Law (Cambridge: Cambridge University Press, 2015); also a collective work, Maʿlamat Zāyid lil-qawāʿid al-fiqhīyah wa-al-uṣūlīyah, 41 vols (Abu Dhabi: Muʾassasat Zāyid, 2013).
50. See, for example, al-Sarakhsī, Uṣūl 2:144; al-Jaṣṣāṣ, Fuṣūl 2:300, 306, 311, 313, 331, 338. See also Ibn ʿAbd al-Barr's use of the term al-uṣūl al-mujtamaʿ ʿalayhā in this context in al-Istidhkār, ed. Sālim al-ʿAṭṭār and Muḥammad ʿAlī Muʿawwaḍ, 9 vols (Beirut: Dār al-Kutub al-ʿIlmīyah, 2000), 6:116, 278, 475, 485, 504, 535–6, 7:326, 8:548. See also the arguments of the present-day researcher al-Ḥājj Sālim, Mafhūm khilāf al-aṣl: dirāsah taḥlīlīyah fī ḍawʿ maqāṣid al-sharīʿah al-islāmīyah (Virginia: al-Maʿhad al-ʿĀlamī lil-Fikr al-Islāmī, 2008), 114–16, 153.
51. Al-Qarāfī, Sharḥ tanqīḥ al-fuṣūl fī ikhtiṣār al-maḥṣūl fī al-uṣūl (Beirut: Dār al-Fikr, 2004), 301.
52. See the arguments in al-Bazdawī, Uṣūl, 159, and al-Sarakhsī, Uṣūl 2:342.
53. Al-Sarakhsī, Uṣūl 2:342.
54. Al-Asmandī al-Ḥanafī, Badhl, 474; Ibn Amīr al-Ḥājj, al-Taqrīr wa-al-taḥbīr, 3 vols (Beirut: Dār al-Kutub al-ʿIlmīyah, 1983), 2:299.

55. Al-Baṣrī, *al-Muʿtamad fī uṣūl al-fiqh*, ed. Khalīl al-Mays, 2 vols (Beirut: Dār al-Kutub al-ʿIlmīyah, 1983), 2:166.
56. Al-Jaṣṣāṣ, *Fuṣūl* 3:127; al-Bazdawī, *Uṣūl*, 159; al-Sarakhsī, *Uṣūl* 2:342.
57. Shihāb al-Dīn al-Qarāfī, *Sharḥ*, 301; Shihāb al-Dīn al-Qarāfī, *Nafāʾis al-uṣūl fī sharḥ al-maḥṣūl*, ed. ʿĀdil ʿAbd al-Mawjūd and ʿAlī Muʿawwaḍ, 9 vols (Riyadh: Maktabat Nizār Muṣṭafā al-Bāz, 1995), 7:2984; al-Shāṭibī, *Muwāfaqāt* 3:21.
58. Al-Bājī, *al-Minhāj fī tartīb al-ḥijāj*, ed. ʿAbd al-Majīd Turkī (Beirut: Dār al-Gharb al-Islāmī, 1987), 124; Ibn al-Ḥājib, *Muntahá al-uṣūl wa-al-amal fī ʿilmay al-uṣūl wa-al-jadal* (Beirut: Dār al-Kutub al-ʿIlmīyah, 1985), 86–7; al-Tilimsānī, *Miftāḥ al-wuṣūl ilá bināʾ al-furūʿ ʿalá al-uṣūl*, ed. Muḥammad ʿAlī Farkūs (Beirut: Muʾassasat al-Rayyān, 1998), 322. See also the comments of Muḥammad al-Bashīr al-Ḥājj Sālim on Ibn al-Ḥājib in *Mafhūm khilāf al-aṣl*, 71–2.
59. Al-Jaṣṣāṣ, *al-Fuṣūl* 3:119–20; al-Asmandī, *Badhl*, 473; Amīr Bādishāh, *Taysīr al-Taḥrīr*, 4 vols in 2 (Cairo: Maṭbaʿat Muṣṭafá al-Bābī al-Ḥalabī, 1932), 3:118; al-Shāṭibī, *Muwāfaqāt* 3:20. For the hadith, see Muslim, *Ṣaḥīḥ*, k. al-ṭahārah 26, *bāb karāhat ghams al-mutawaḍḍiʾ wa-ghayrihi yadahu fī al-ināʾ*, No. 278; for criticism of this hadith, see Ibn Abī Shaybah, *Muṣannaf* 1:94; al-Bayhaqī, *al-Sunan al-kubrá* (Beirut: Dār al-Maʿrifah, 1992), 1:47.
60. Al-Bazdawī, *Uṣūl al-Bazdawī*, 159; al-Sarakhsī, *Uṣūl* 1:341; al-Shāshī, *Uṣūl* 276; al-Taftāzānī, *Sharḥ al-Talwīḥ ʿalá al-Tawḍīḥ*, 2 vols (Cairo: Maktabat Muḥammad ʿAlī Ṣubayḥ, n.d), 2:9; Amīr Bādishāh, *Taysīr* 3:52. For *ḥadīth al-muṣarrāh*, see among other places, al-Bukhārī, *Ṣaḥīḥ*, k. al-buyūʿ 64, *bāb al-nahy lil-bāʾiʿ an lā yuḥaffila al-ibil wa-al-baqar wa-al-ghanam wa-kull muḥaffalah*, No. 2148, and Muslim, *Ṣaḥīḥ*, k. al-buyūʿ 4, *bāb taḥrīm bayʿ al-rajul ʿalá bayʿ akhīh*, No. 1515. For *ḥadīth al-kharāj bi-al-ḍamān*, see among other places, Abū Dāwūd, *Sunan*, al-buyūʿ 73, *bāb fī man ishtará ʿabdan fa istaʿmalahu thumma wajada bihi ʿayban*, No. 3508, al-Tirmidhī, *Sunan*, k. al-buyūʿ 53, *bāb mā jāʾa fīman yashtarī al-ʿabd fa-yashtaghiluhu thumma yajidu bihi ʿayban*, No. 1285.
61. Al-Dabbūsī, *Taqwīm*, 203.
62. Amīr Bādishāh, *Taysīr* 3:74; al-Sarakhsī, *Uṣūl* 2:3–11.
63. Ibn Khuzaymah, *al-Ṣaḥīḥ*, ed. Muḥammad Muṣṭafá al-Aʿẓamī, 4 vols (n.p.: al-Maktab al-Islāmī, n.d.), 2:154.
64. Al-Jaṣṣāṣ, *Fuṣūl* 3:117.
65. Muḥammad Zāhid al-Kawtharī, *Taʾnīb al-Khaṭīb ʿalá mā sāqahu fī tarjamat Abī Ḥanīfah min al-akādhīb*, ed. Aḥmad Khayrī (Cairo: Maktabat al-Kullīyāt al-Azharīyah 1990), 300-1. See also al-Kawtharī, *Fiqh ahl al-ʿirāq wa-ḥadīthuhum*, ed. ʿAbd al-Fattāḥ Abū Ghuddah (Ḥalab: Maktab al-Maṭbūʿāt al-Islāmīyah, 1970), 35, 37.
66. For a detailed exposition of *ʿamal* in the usage of Mālik and later adherents of his school, see Umar F. Abd-Allah Wymann-Landgraf, *Mālik and Medina: Islamic Legal Reasoning in the Formative Period*, Islamic History and Civilization, 101 (Leiden: Brill, 2013), 219–506.
67. The opinion of al-Qāḍī ʿAbd al-Wahhāb was cited by al-Qarāfī, *Nafāʾis al-uṣūl fī sharḥ al-Maḥṣūl*, ed. ʿĀdil Aḥmad ʿAbd al-Mawjūd and ʿAlī Muḥammad Muʿawwaḍ, 9 vols (Mecca: Maktabat Nizār Muṣṭafá al-Bāz, 1997), 6:2710;

al-Bājī, *Iḥkām al-fuṣūl fī aḥkām al-uṣūl*, ed. ᶜAbd al-Majīd Turkī, 2 vols (Beirut: Dār al-Gharb al-Islāmī, 1995), 1:486–8; al-Qāḍī ᶜIyāḍ, *Tartīb al-madārik wa-taqrīb al-masālik li-maᶜrifat aᶜlām madhhab Mālik*, ed. Muḥammad ibn Tāwīt al-Ṭanjī, et al. (Rabat, etc.: various, 1966–83) 1:74. Wymann-Landgraf argues that Mālik's references to *ᶜamal* make a series of fine (if not always precise) distinctions between the original sources of a given practice (i.e., Prophetic and post-Prophetic) as well as the various levels of consensus that existed among the Medinese authorities on a given issue. He also argues that these distinctions were often implicit and at times were even lost on later adherents of Mālik's school. Important for our purposes is that he clarifies that the concern of ᶜIyāḍ and later jurists to differentiate between the various potential sources of *ᶜamal* was reflected in Mālik's own terminology, even if the neat distinctions that they made were not always easily distinguished in Mālik's own usage, which took an intergenerational, layered notion of legal authority for granted. See Wymann-Landgraf, *Mālik and Medina*, 232–8 and passim.

68. Al-Qāḍī ᶜIyāḍ, *Tartīb* 1:68–9. See also al-Bājī, *Iḥkām* 1:488; al-Shāṭibī, *Muwāfaqāt* 3:66–7.
69. Ibn Taymīyah, *Majmūᶜ* 20:308; Ibn Qayyim al-Jawzīyah, *Iᶜlām* 2:391–2; al-Zarkashī, *Baḥr* 6:253–4.
70. Al-Qāḍī ᶜIyāḍ, *Tartīb* 1:69–70; al-Qarāfī, *Nafāʾis* 6:2710.
71. Ibn Rushd, *Bidāyat al-mujtahid* (Beirut: Dār al-Maᶜrifah, 1982), 911; Ibn Rushd al-Jadd, *al-Muqaddimāt al-mumahhidāt li-bayān mā iqtaḍathu rusūm* al-Mudawwanah *min al-aḥkām al-sharᶜīyāt wa-al-taḥṣīlāt al-muḥkamāt li-ummahāt masāʾilihā al-mushkilāt*, ed. Muḥammad Ḥajjī and Saᶜīd Aḥmad Aᶜrāb, 3 vols (Beirut: Dar al-Gharb al-Islāmī, 1988), 2:95. Hadith Ibn ᶜUmar is in Mālik, *Muwaṭṭaʾ Mālik, k. al-buyūᶜ, bāb bayᶜ al-khiyār* 2:671.
72. Al-Shāfiᶜī, *Umm* 8:640.
73. Imām al-Ḥaramayn, *Burhān*, 1172; al-Ghazālī, *al-Mankhūl fī taᶜlīqāt al-uṣūl*, ed. Muḥammad Ḥasan Hītū (Damascus: Dār al-Fikr, 1980), 431.
74. Imām al-Ḥaramayn, *al-Burhān*, 1172–3
75. Wael B. Hallaq, 'The Authenticity of Prophetic Ḥadîth: a Pseudo-Problem', *Studia Islamica* 89 (1999): 75–90.
76. For more details, see al-Khatib, *Radd al-ḥadīth*, 99–106, 212–26.
77. See al-Khatib, *Radd al-ḥadīth*, 25–6; 157–65. The manner in which the Sunni legal schools' approaches to hadith evolved in response to al-Shāfiᶜī's thesis and the influence of the hadith movement over the centuries is a subject of perennial debate in Western scholarship and cannot be pursued in detail here. See, for example, Behnam Sadeghi, *The Logic of Law-Making in Islam: Women and Prayer in the Legal Tradition* (Cambridge: Cambridge University Press, 2013), 128–40; Christopher Melchert, 'Traditionist-Jurisprudents and the Framing of Islamic Law', *Islamic Law and Society* 8(3) (2001): 383–406; Abd-Allah, *Mālik and Medina*, 507–17. On the other side ᶜAbd al-Majīd Maḥmūd ᶜAbd al-Majīd has studied *fiqh ahl al-ḥadīth* in the third / ninth century. ᶜAbd al-Majīd, *al-Ittijāhāt al-fiqhīyah ᶜinda aṣḥāb al-ḥadīth fī al-qarn al-thālith al-hijrī* (Cairo: Maktabat al-Khānjī 1979).

CHAPTER

7

HADITH CRITICISM IN THE LEVANT IN THE TWENTIETH CENTURY: FROM *ẒĀHIR AL-ISNĀD* TO *ᶜILAL AL-ḤADĪTH*

Ahmad Snober*

The hadith criticism movement in the Levant in the twentieth century was arguably one of the most active hadith movements in the Islamic world. Therein, ample work was produced and many prominent names emerged, such as Nāṣir al-Dīn al-Albānī (1914–99), ᶜAbd al-Fattāḥ Abū Ghuddah (1917–97), Shuᶜayb al-Arnaᵓūṭ (1928–2016), Nūr al-Dīn ᶜItr (1934–) and Muḥammad ᶜAwwāmah (1940–). The hadith movement in the Levant developed significantly during the twentieth century and had a significant influence on other countries. It was characterised by clear ideological developments and doctrinal conflicts. The hadith movement in the Levant was also multi-faceted. Some scholars focused their attention on the written and oral transmission of hadith works, while others were concerned with the textual content of the hadith corpus and its exegesis. Certain specialists dedicated their efforts towards responding to Western criticisms and others towards hadith terminology. Nevertheless, hadith criticism received the most attention. In this chapter I analyse the major trends of hadith criticism in the Levant, focusing on the methods of authenticating hadiths. Understanding these trends in the Levant is instrumental in comprehending the development of hadith criticism in the Islamic world, since the Levant, with its intellectual and doctrinal diversity, has been an important centre of Islamic scholarship in general and the sciences of hadith in particular.

In this chapter, I argue that the common classification of hadith-criticism trends based on the doctrinal ideology of the scholar is uncritical and inaccurate.[1] The classification of hadith activity in the Levant should base its criteria solely on the methods of hadith criticism as this is the mechanism by which hadith criticism operates. Based on this, I demonstrate that there are two main trends. The first focuses on *ẓāhir al-isnād* (apparent dimension of the *isnād*) and adherence to the rules of the books of *uṣūl al-ḥadīth*. This approach is applied by al-Albānī, Abū Ghuddah and ᶜItr, despite their different ideological commitments. This trend dominated the religious and academic atmosphere in the Levant for almost a century. Although they opposed al-Albānī doctrinally, Abū Ghuddah and ᶜItr were generally consistent in applying his method of hadith criticism. The second trend I discuss here is that of criticism based on evidence and subtle flaws (*ᶜilal al-ḥadīth*), which appeared in Jordan in the 1980s through Hammām Saᶜīd (1944–) at the University of Jordan, and was subsequently developed and formulated by Ḥamzah al-Mallībārī (1952–), who taught in the same university from 1996 to 2000 and strongly propagated this trend. In the following pages, I first explore the history of hadith criticism in the Levant in the twentieth century and the emergence of al-Albānī's school of hadith criticism. I then analyse Abū Ghuddah and ᶜItr as models of hadith criticism in the Traditionalist school. Finally, I examine hadith criticism based on the subtle flaws and evidence represented by Ḥamzah al-Mallībārī.

Hadith Criticism based on *ẓāhir al-isnād* (Nāṣir al-Dīn al-Albānī)

Damascus was known for its school of hadith in the eighth/fourteenth century, which was hardly paralleled by any other school of hadith and hadith criticism.[2] However, the decline of this school began in the second half of the ninth/fifteenth century. Ibn-Nāṣir al-Dīn al-Dimashqī (d. 842/1438) in Damascus and Sibṭ Ibn al-ᶜAjamī (d. 841/1437) in Aleppo had no notable successors.[3] Ibn Zurayq (d. 900/1494),[4] who inherited their teaching, had only one notable student, Ibn Ṭūlūn (d. 953/1546), and both contributed little to the field of hadith criticism.[5] The decline increased in intensity during the Ottoman rule of the Levant through the beginnings of the Arab Renaissance (*al-nahḍah*). This decline can be observed in several ways. We hardly find notable Levantine scholars exercising hadith criticism. Even those who were named in biographical works as hadith scholars simply transmitted some prominent books of hadith with a moderate engagement in commentary.[6] Also, books of hadith terminology that appeared in this period are generally of the commentary genre with minimal engagement with topics of hadith criticism. A contributing factor to that decline may be the minimal interest in hadith criticism in educational institutions in that era. For example, Dār al-Ḥadīth al-Ashrafīyah, the prominent historical school of hadith, remained in a state of decline for decades during the Ottoman era.[7]

Indeed, the religious learning environment of the Ottoman era did very little to encourage the study of hadith criticism and generally focused on traditional Sunni jurisprudential and doctrinal beliefs. It may be observed that hadith criticism generally flourishes in environments of intellectual and doctrinal struggle, where there are competing parties for authenticity and authority, particularly when a certain group gives utmost authority to the text. In such an environment, the text's authenticity becomes prominent. This is usually not the case for groups that strictly adhere to traditional models of jurisprudence and theology. In the Ottoman era, we rarely find any group that passed over traditional schools of thought in order to deal with hadith sources directly. Rather, the scholarly norm was inclined towards doctrinal imitation. Often, hadith was narrated simply for blessing (*tabarruk*) and not for deducing rulings,[8] comparing evidence or critique of narrations even on a superficial level.[9]

Still, for many reasons, perhaps the most important of which was the intellectual cultural movement in Egypt and what Isaac Wiseman called the 'taste of modernity', preliminary efforts in hadith science began to emerge at the hands of reform movements by the end of the nineteenth century. Works such as Ṭāhir al-Jazāʾirī (d. 1338/1920), *Tawjīh al-naẓar ilá uṣūl al-athar*, and Jamal al-Dīn al-Qāsimī (d. 1332/1914), *Qawāʿid al-taḥdīth*,[10] may be characterised as signs of a revival of hadith science as they came in a new form that was in contrast to the text-commentary style of scholarly writing in the Ottoman era. They also advocate their view that reference to hadith and compliance with its teachings is mandatory, therefore inciting interest in the study of hadith. Nevertheless, neither scholar was a hadith critic in the true sense of the word.[11] Al-Qāsimī's main concern was to reform the religious learning environment from one of traditional purism to one of critique. However, as he was not versed in the field of transmitter criticism, the influence of hadith terminology was not clear in his line of thought. Therefore, his appraisals of certain hadith reports were generally dependent on contemporary hadith works such as al-Suyūṭī's *al-Jāmiʿ al-ṣaghīr* and *al-Jāmiʿ al-kabīr*.[12] The most notable student of al-Qāsimī was Muḥammad Bahjah al-Bīṭār (d. 1976), who shared his teacher's doctrinal orientation but did not write in the field of hadith sciences.

The attitude of al-Jazāʾirī and al-Qāsimī towards the predominant traditionalist environment was non-confrontational and their method of calling for reform did not engage directly with the scholarly or political state at the time. The situation shifted in the middle of the twentieth century with the emergence of al-Albānī as a hadith critic, directing his criticism towards the predominant traditionalist environment through the medium of hadith criticism, which was his most important tool that his counterparts lacked. The bold nature of al-Albānī's criticism can be attributed to several elements pertinent to the intellectual landscape of his time. First, the reform movement at the end of the nineteenth century paved the way for perspectives that contradicted the prevalent religious system in the Levant. Al-Albānī may have even attempted to align himself with this movement when he engaged in the evaluation and *takhrīj* (full referencing of hadiths with *isnād*s) of the hadith of some of its books, such as al-Qāsimī's book on the reform of mosques, which indicates an interest in al-Qāsimī's reformist project. Secondly, the relative intellectual freedom in the Levant in the early and middle twentieth century, especially in the face of the cultural developments witnessed in the region during that period, encouraged boldness. Intellectual discussions about nationalism, Arabism, Western civilisation, colonialism and secularism were always present in cultural gatherings.[13] Discussing these issues was a departure from the traditional religious form of education, thus weakening the authority of traditional scholars in such discussions and paving the path for many intellectuals and researchers from outside that circle. Thirdly, al-Albānī also possessed a bold personality from a young age, as he often related incidents in which he argued with his father on following schools of law, Sufism and other issues.[14] Fourthly, there seemed to be a weak influence of political power on the academic environment during the time of al-Albānī. Towards the middle of the twentieth century, Damascus witnessed unique political freedom, which made it easier for scholars to contradict mainstream schools of thought and present their ideas without fear of persecution. If we compare this with the incident of the *mujtahidūn* at the end of the Ottoman era, when al-Qāsimī and a group of scholars were taken to court because they held gatherings in which they were accused of claiming themselves capable of independent legal reasoning (*ijtihād*), the difference between the two periods becomes obvious.[15]

These conditions made it possible for al-Albānī to call so strongly against the prevailing traditionalist school, compared with al-Jazāʾirī and al-Qāsimī. However, al-Albānī may not be regarded as extending al-Jazāʾirī and al-Qāsimī's hadith methodology. Al-Albānī did not derive hadith knowledge from that class of scholars and did not study these sciences under someone else's tutelage.[16] Rather, his association with hadith science came from Egypt. Al-Albānī mentions that he greatly admired the works of Muḥammad Rashīd Riḍā (d. 1935) in hadith criticism, especially with the complete absence of this science in Damascus and its circles of learning.[17] Hence, he was influenced by Rashīd Riḍā's school and followed its methodology. Additionally, he was deeply interested in Aḥmad Shākir's (d. 1958) work and praised him in several of his own writings.[18]

Al-Albānī was very active in propagating his ideas and gathering a number of students in Syria. Among the causes for the spread of his message, the following stand out. He was committed to the project: he travelled frequently to spread his ideas and was resolute therein.[19] He also had strong ties with the Muslim Brotherhood at the beginning of his career as an active scholar. Under his influence, the Brotherhood of Damascus became closer to the Salafi school. Al-Albānī describes his relationship with the Brotherhood by saying that he was so connected that it was almost as if he had been one of them. Indeed, the majority of his students were from the Muslim Brotherhood not only in Damascus, but also in Lattakia, Aleppo and Idlib.[20] His relationship with Muṣṭafá al-Sibāʿī (d. 1964) is well known. Al-Sibāʿī respected al-Albānī and included him in private meetings of the Brotherhood. When *al-Muslimūn* magazine (supervised by Saʿīd Ramaḍān, the son-in-law of Ḥasan al-Bannā, and Muṣṭafá al-Sibāʿī) relocated to Syria in 1954, any question concerning hadith was referred to al-Albānī. He also wrote several articles for that magazine.[21] Al-Albānī then believed that the Brotherhood was the torchbearer of the Salafi message.[22] Later, differences arose between him and the movement.[23] A notable incident that reflects al-Albānī's relationship with the Brotherhood relates to one of the first articles he wrote in their bi-monthly magazine, *The Muslim Brotherhood*, in 1947. In the article, he commented on some of the hadiths mentioned by Sayyid Sābiq (d. 2000) in *Fiqh al-Sunnah*. The article was met with good reviews and even an encouraging letter from Ḥasan al-Bannā himself.[24] Al-Albānī's message was simple and touches upon the concerns of the public to whom his ideas were accessible. For example, he recalls that one of the issues that alienated him from the established scholarly community at that time was the issue of praying at graves. While he was still a young man, he discussed this with senior scholars of Damascus like Saʿīd al-Burhānī (d. 1967), to whom he wrote about it.[25] This letter became the basis of al-Albānī's treatise, *Tahdhīr al-sājid*. Al-Albānī aimed to show that the ruling on this issue could be easily inferred from several relevant hadiths and by judging the current practices of the masses.

Such an issue caused al-Albānī to turn to Wahhābī books on creed such as *Kitāb al-Tawḥīd* of Muḥammad ibn ʿAbd al-Wahhāb (d. 1792). He used such writings as textbooks in his teaching circles and as references in his works.[26] In 1954, when the Saudi traveller ʿAbd Allāh ibn Khamīs visited Damascus, he described al-Albānī's sessions teaching books of Wahhābī theology, surrounded by educated students, a clear sign of al-Albānī's departure from the traditional norms of religious education in the Levant.[27] It should be noted that al-Albānī began with issues that directly affected the community such as praying at graves, on which he published a book in 1958,[28] *Ādāb al-zifāf* (wedding etiquette) in 1952,[29] *Jilbāb al-muslimah* ('Muslim Women's Clothes') in 1951,[30] *Ṣifat ṣalāt al-nabī* ('Description of the Prophet's Prayer') in 1950, and *Aḥkām al-Janāʾiz* ('Rules of Funerals') in 1954.[31] He also wrote several articles for *al-Tamaddun al-islāmī* magazine, where he began writing in 1951. His first article therein was titled *Wujūb al-tafaqquh fī al-ḥadīth* ('The Obligation to Study Hadith'). Thereafter, beginning in 1953, he wrote a series of articles addressing the negative impact of unreliable and forged hadiths on the Muslim community. He later began another series focusing on authentic hadiths.[32]

It should be noted that al-Albānī commonly addressed controversial topics, and in doing so was able to facilitate the dissemination of his message and attract the attention of young sections of society. Al-Albānī also utilised various means of communication in order to connect with the educated élite and the general public, particularly published written material. In contrast, al-Albānī's opponents were generally not concerned with publishing; those who did publish focused primarily on interlinear commentaries and marginal glosses. While it is uncertain whether or not the Salafi movement of Saudi Arabia provided material support for al-Albānī during this time, their general support for spreading such ideas is well-known and is apparent in the written correspondence of al-Qāsimī and Maḥmūd Shukrī al-Ālūsī (d. 1924).[33]

In any case, the message of al-Albānī and his ideas spread widely in the Levant, especially since his Salafi thought called for holding on to the Qurʾān and the Sunnah and rejecting the adoption of traditional schools of law.

Hadith criticism was a very important component of this call. Al-Albānī engaged in the practice of *takhrīj* and determining the authenticity of hadiths on an unprecedented scale in his time. His articles on weak and authentic hadiths were the foundation for his massive hadith encyclopaedia published later. It is not an exaggeration to say that his writings dominated the field of hadith criticism in the Islamic world for decades. These writings remained a point of reference for scholars and researchers in the Arabophone world for many years.

Generally speaking, al-Albānī's method of hadith criticism was based on the method of *ẓāhir al-isnād* through an application of the principles detailed in the books of hadith terminology. The method of *ẓāhir al-isnād* depends mainly on the traits of the narrators to judge the authenticity of the hadiths, and takes the rules provided in the books of hadith terminology to be a consistent standard for evaluating hadiths even if doing so would involve contravening the actual rulings of earlier critics such as al-Bukhārī and his contemporaries. Hence, in situations where the two contradict each other, the principles of the books of hadith terminology are given precedence over the views of earlier hadith critics. His reliance on the *ẓāhir al-isnād* method may be observed through the following practices. First, al-Albānī adopted a near uniform application of the rules of the books of hadith terminology while neglecting additional evidence (*qarāʾin*), and refuting earlier scholars who used them. I argue here that this approach adopted by al-Albānī is quite unfeasible because the literal application of a given rule to a given hadith does not usually render consistent results. There are many examples of this phenomenon in his books. In a number of them, al-Albānī, according to the method of the school of *ẓāhir al-isnād*, focuses purely on a narrator's status *as a narrator* and uses that status to affirm the soundness of narrations that earlier scholars had considered to be unsound,[34] while rejecting the *qarāʾin* that earlier scholars considered in judging the authenticity of the hadith in question. Al-Albānī's position is that such factors are a type of speculation that should not be given priority over established rules.[35] This seems to stem from an assumption that such rules were applied uniformly throughout history.

It is useful to mention here an important point regarding the concept of *ziyādat al-thiqah* (additions by reliable transmitters) and its role in the disagreement between the two schools of hadith criticism discussed in this chapter. Al-Albānī accepts *ziyādat al-thiqah* and is inclined not to consider that a trustworthy narrator is mistaken. There is ample evidence for this inclination in his works and I provide here a handful of examples. Al-Albānī often asserts, '*Ziyādat al-thiqah* is acceptable.' He considers it a strong and steady principle and rejects, by means of this rule, any criticism of a hadith report by earlier critics. He also argues for *ziyādat al-thiqah* on the basis of the principle, 'He who memorised is a proof against him who did not.'[36] He often says, when he prefers to consider a hadith *marfūʿ* ('lifted'; that is, attributed to the Prophet) rather than *mawquf* ('stopped'; that is, the narration goes back only to the Companions), 'This narrator is trustworthy and his *marfūᶜ* hadith must be accepted', sometimes adding, 'as established in [the science of hadith] terminology'.[37]

Al-Albānī is generally reluctant to consider a trusted narrator to be mistaken. This is particularly true when it comes to additions (*ziyādah*), and his statements in this regard are numerous. For example, he says, 'Otherwise, a trusted narrator would be called deluded without evidence; rather, simply based on [a critic's] individual sense [or feeling]. Such methods have nothing to do with this science.'[38] Another is his saying, 'So-and-so is trustworthy and may not be considered deluded simply because someone disagrees with him. It is an acceptable addition (*ziyādah*).'[39]

Al-Albānī often criticises early scholars due to their rejection of *ziyādat al-thiqah*. He objects to Abū Dāwūd (d. 275/889), for example, in some of his rejections of *ziyādat al-thiqah*. He points out that, 'As far as we are concerned, this *iᶜlāl* (finding defects) means little because what we have is an addition by a trustworthy narrator and, [so], it is acceptable.'[40] Al-Albānī also objects to the opinion of al-Bayhaqī (d. 458/1066) about the same issue, saying, 'ᶜAbd al-ᶜAzīz is trustworthy and it is not permissible to consider him deluded just because Ayyūb disagrees with him.'[41] He also refutes al-Dāraquṭnī's (d. 385/995) discrediting of an addition in a report, saying, 'The truth is that this *isnād* is sound because Abū Kāmil is a trustworthy, accurate memoriser, and Muslim referred to him, so his addition is acceptable.'[42] Nevertheless, al-Albānī criticises Muslim (d. 261/875) and al-Dāraquṭnī's description of a hadith as being weak by saying:

> Muslim said that it had the defect of *irsāl* and al-Dāraquṭnī agreed with him saying, 'the known narration from Layth is *mursal*', as al-Khaṭīb narrates. However, the agreement of Qabīṣah and Ruwaym that it is *mawṣūl* through Layth does not leave me comfortable with [Muslim and al-Dāraquṭnī's] *iᶜlāl* as they both (Qabīṣah and Ruwaym) are trustworthy and the addition of a trustworthy narrator is acceptable.[43]

The situation is the same when both al-Bukhārī (d. 256/870) and al-Tirmidhī (d. 279/892) judge a particular chain of transmission to be flawed as *mursal*. Here, al-Albānī says:

> The first *mawṣūl* hadith report is narrated by trustworthy narrators who even appear in the narrations of Muslim, although al-Tirmidhī and al-Bukhārī consider it *mursal*. If it were not for Abū Muᶜāwiyah Muḥammad ibn Khāzim, who is known for some weakness in his memory, I would have said, 'He added a fully connected *isnād* and such an addition is acceptable from a trustworthy narrator.'[44]

This is generally al-Albānī's approach to criticism, of which there are myriad examples.

In a few cases, al-Albānī does not adhere to this rule and prefers the narrations of certain trusted narrators over others.[45] Still, this does not detract from the main contention that al-Albānī adheres to the school of *ẓāhir al-isnād* for several reasons. These examples are few in comparison with the numerous texts in which he expresses his position that *ziyādat al-thiqah*, as a rule, is reliable. When he dismisses this rule, he often points to the memory of some narrator who is known to err in his transmission. So this does not affect the consistency of his application of the principle of *ziyādat al-thiqah*, but rather is about criticising the accuracy of the narrator. As we have seen, if the narrator is reliable and accurate in the view of al-Albānī, or, in effect, the view of biographical works, this narrator's addition is acceptable, even if uncorroborated by other narrations.[46]

Al-Albānī also rarely examines *qarāʾin*. He clearly states that his practice is to refer to the principles of hadith criticism (*qawāʿid*) as set out by textbooks of hadith terminology (*muṣṭalaḥ*).[47] Even in circumstances where al-Albānī examines *qarāʾin*, he is clear that the final decision must be based on *qawāʿid*.[48] It is possible that the intellectual developments and re-examinations that took place in the Levant in the last few decades, and the prolonged debates surrounding the concept of *ʿilal* in hadith had influenced some of the later opinions of al-Albānī. It may be said that posthumous modifications were made to the later books of al-Albānī and therefore his method of criticism appeared to differ later on, as these examples were all in his late years. Volumes 9–15 of *Silsilat al-aḥādīth al-ḍaʿīfah* ('Compendium of Weak Hadiths') were all published after his death and the editor explains in the preface that it was not reviewed or edited by al-Albānī. Additionally, the editor makes clear that he occasionally modified some judgements of the hadiths based on his understanding of al-Albānī's method of hadith criticism.[49] These are all indications that there were posthumous modifications to al-Albānī's late works, and the extent of these modifications needs to be verified. It appears that al-Albānī's method does not depart from *ẓāhir al-isnād* tradition in hadith criticism.

The school of *ẓāhir al-isnād* is characterised by judging narrations based on the merits of the narrators. If the transmitter is trustworthy (*thiqah*) then the hadith is authentic (*ṣaḥīḥ*), if truthful (*ṣadūq*) then the hadith is good (*ḥasan*), and if weak then the hadith is weak (*ḍaʿīf*). This is most evident when a *ṣadūq* narrates a hadith that is narrated solely through him or her. The school of *ẓāhir al-isnād* usually acknowledges such a hadith as being *ḥasan* on the basis that the narrator is *ṣadūq*. However, this type of hadith would usually have been criticised by earlier scholars. This is evident in al-Albānī's work in many instances, both theoretical and practical. Theoretically, al-Albānī quotes and agrees with Aḥmad Shākir's position that the ruling (*ḥukm*) of a hadith is based on the *ḥukm* (classification) of its narrators. More specifically, after presenting the traditional twelve degrees of narrators mentioned by Ibn Ḥajar (d. 852/1449) in the introduction of *Taqrīb al-Tahdhīb*, Aḥmad Shākir says:

> He who belongs to the second or third degree, his hadith is considered *ṣaḥīḥ par excellence* . . . and he who belongs to the fourth rank (including *ṣadūq* and *lā baʾsa bihi*), his hadith is *ṣaḥīḥ* but of a lesser degree. This is the [level] considered *ḥasan* by al-Tirmidhī and left out by Abū Dāwūd . . .[50]

Al-Albānī also quotes al-Dhahabī (d. 748/1348) and Ibn Ḥajar on the degrees of narrators and comments: 'If the narrator belongs to the fourth degree, then his hadith is *ḥasan*, that being what Aḥmad Shākir states in *al-Bāʿith al-ḥathīth*.'[51] Al-Albānī considers many hadiths to be *ḥasan* according to this rule, and sometimes extends it to narrators of the fifth degree. Often, in consulting *Taqrīb al-Tahdhīb* of Ibn Ḥajar, if he finds that the author has described the narrator as being '*ṣadūq*, or *ṣadūq* who has errors', he considers his or her hadith *ḥasan*[52] and, by doing so, al-Albānī slightly differs from Aḥmad Shākir's approach in that the former is slightly more lenient.[53]

Additionally, al-Albānī often objects to some of the earlier scholars' appraisals of hadiths of this type as weak, arguing that these appraisals contradict the rules.[54] Al-Albānī's strict and literal adherence to the rules of *ẓāhir al-isnād* based on terminological textbooks is evident in his acceptance of several hadiths as *ḥasan* that other critics rejected because they were narrated by an individual *ṣadūq* who errs, whose uncorroborated reports are not considered acceptable.[55] The upshot is that al-Albānī adheres strictly to the approach of criticism by *ẓāhir al-isnād*. Even amongst Salafis, there are those who recognise al-Albānī's approach and those who disagree with him such as Muqbil ibn Hādī al-Wādiʿī (d. 2001) of Yemen and Muṣṭafá al-ʿAdawī (1954–) of Egypt.[56]

Al-Albānī's adherence to this approach can be attributed to several factors. As hadith criticism declined in the Levant and elsewhere in the nineteenth century, it was reasonable that re-engagement with hadith criticism would reach to the closest period of intellectual production, that of Ibn Ḥajar, a period that focused on terminology and transmitter criticism. Ibn Ḥajar authored significant textbooks such as *Nukhbat al-fikar* on hadith terminology, *al-Taqrīb* in multiple versions on reliable transmitters, and *Lisān al-Mīzān* on aspersed transmitters. The field today recognises that Ibn Ḥajar's works represent the summation and epitome of hadith science, indispensable to hadith specialists. Scholars of hadith in the period of Ibn Ḥajar and before him would often note the difference between technical hadith criticism and *takhrīj*, and would not usually reject appraisals by earlier scholars based on the books of terminology. There was a general acknowledgement that books of criticism were written as textbooks to train beginners and to document the judgements of earlier scholars, not as practical manuals in judging hadiths. A comparison between Ibn Ḥajar's *al-Nukat ʿalá Ibn al-Ṣalāḥ* and his *Nuzhat al-fikar*, not to mention his hadith criticism, would show clear manifestations of this distinction. This may in fact relate to the ordinary practice of hadith criticism in those times when a student was taught and trained directly by his teacher and was given the opportunity to excel under his teacher's guidance. Ibn Ḥajar learned this craft from his teachers, notably al-ᶜIrāqī (d. 806 / 1404), whom he accompanied for many years.[57] This process of hadith criticism as realised within a living tradition may have gone a long way towards limiting the excessive application of theoretical terminology to *isnāds*, unlike the method of al-Albānī, who significantly relied on these textbooks without formal training by way of a teacher–student relationship. Also, al-Albānī was influenced in this area by the works of Aḥmad Shākir, who himself adhered to the method of *ẓāhir al-isnād* in his criticism and may have been al-Albānī's only predecessor in that era. Al-Albānī once lamented that they had only met once.[58] This approach resulted in al-Albānī's overall production of a sheer volume of works in the area of hadith criticism and *takhrīj* that would have been impossible had he used the method of early scholars, examining each hadith in its own context and relying on the method of subtle defects.

Hadith Criticism in the Traditionalist School (Abū Ghuddah and ᶜItr)

When al-Albānī began his career in the middle of the twentieth century, there was little activity in the field of hadith criticism in the Levant and therefore al-Albānī received almost no serious challenge as scholars tended to warn against his method by criticising him personally as untrained by traditional scholars. Instead of addressing his method of hadith criticism, scholars tended to critique his ideas from the vantage point of traditional legal schools (*madhhabs*) and focused on how al-Albānī did not represent that tradition. It was not until the arrival of ᶜAbd Allāh al-Ḥabashī (1910–2008) in the Levant, who then wrote *al-Taᶜaqqub al-ḥathīth*, to which al-Albānī responded in two separate articles, that debates became hadith-focused and not based on adherence to traditional legal schools.[59] This trend continued with the writings of Nūr al-Dīn ᶜItr in the early 1970s.[60] Abū Ghuddah, however, did not discuss al-Albānī except in his work *Kalimāt fī kashf abāṭīl wa-iftirāʾāt*, and, even then, the majority of the book was more personal than academic in that it was a personal defence in the face of criticisms from al-Albānī. It is also notable that Abū Ghuddah dedicates the majority of the book to defending the reputation of Abū Ḥanīfah (d. 150 / 767) in hadith scholarship. I have only noted two occasions in which Abū Ghuddah addresses al-Albānī directly in matters of hadith scholarship.[61]

In the 1990s, Ḥasan al-Saqqāf (1961–) attempted to engage al-Albānī's work through a number of writings, notable amongst them *Tanāquḍāt al-Albānī al-wāḍiḥāt* ('Obvious Inconsistencies of al-Albānī'). However, al-Saqqāf's concerted efforts against al-Albānī were quite unsuccessful as his responses to al-Albānī did not, in fact, result from or represent a methodological difference in the study of hadith. Rather, their foundation was that of doctrinal and ideological differences between the Traditionalist Sunni school with the contemporary Salafi school. This divide, sometimes described as a *madhhabī* (legal school) vs non-*madhhabī* or a Sufi vs non-Sufi debate, formed the core of al-Saqqāf's critiques of al-Albānī. In reality, both camps adhered, in theory and practice, to the method of *ẓāhir al-isnād* and hadith terminology.

This is also the case with Nūr al-Dīn ᶜItr, who applies almost the exact method of al-Albānī and tends to apply the latter's stance on *ziyādat al-thiqah* (addition in content by reliable transmitters). To demonstrate the difference between the methodologies of criticism based on *ẓāhir al-isnād* and on circumstantial evidence, let us look at a hadith on wiping the socks during ablution (*al-masḥ ᶜalá al-jawrab*). Early hadith scholars tended to find fault with the narration that uses the word *jawrabayn* ('socks') as the narrator of that wording differed from the large number of narrators who narrated the hadith with the word *khuffayn* (leather socks) instead. While seemingly mundane in its topic, the hadith became a topic of discussion for early scholars.[62] ᶜItr considered the hadith with the '*jawrabayn*' wording acceptable and rejected the circumstantial evidence which early scholars used to question its validity. In this focus on the outlook of the *isnād* and rejection of circumstantial evidence, ᶜItr's method does not differ much from al-Albānī's, though their doctrinal differences remain stark.[63]

Similarly, ᶜItr rejects circumstantial evidence when discussing the hadith report of Ghaylān's conversion to Islam, which is narrated by one transmitter as *mursal* (loose) on one occasion and as *muttaṣil* (uninterrupted) on another occasion. This was enough reason for early scholars like Aḥmad ibn Ḥanbal (d. 241/855), al-Bukhārī, Muslim and Abū Zurᶜah al-Rāzī (d. 264/878) to dismiss the hadith as flawed. For ᶜItr, the addition of the *muttaṣil* narration is acceptable because it is an addition by a reliable transmitter.[64] Early scholars pointed out that Maᶜmar, while in Yemen, narrated the hadith as *mursal* whereas his narration in Basra, where his notes were not with him, was *muttaṣil*.[65]

As for Abū Ghuddah, as mentioned earlier, there is little evidence that he was seriously engaged in evaluating hadiths. When he occasionally examines reports, he shows a strong commitment to the method of *ẓāhir al-isnād* and a rejection of the use of circumstantial evidence that was so crucial to early scholars, such as in his study of the hadith of Ibn ᶜUmar on raising hands in prayer: 'He used to raise his hands only at the beginning of prayer and does not repeat [it].'[66] Abū Ghuddah accepts this addition 'and does not repeat [it]' as valid though he agrees that early scholars discredited it because the majority of transmitters did not include this addition in their narrations. This complete reliance on *ẓāhir al-isnād* also indicates a dogmatic commitment since the addition supports the Ḥanafī school, which Abū Ghuddah followed.

The Traditionalist school's adherence to a terminology- and rule-based method in evaluating hadith is also apparent in its stance on the issue of ruling on a hadith based on the rankings provided in biographical dictionaries, which is focused on transmitter criticism (*al-jarḥ wa-al-taᶜdīl*). Here, too, the practice of the Traditionalists is in agreement with that of al-Albānī. In this regard, Abū Ghuddah's comments on al-Dhahabī's rankings for narrators in his *Qawāᶜid ᶜulūm al-ḥadīth* ('The Rules of the Sciences of Hadith') are quite informative of his strict adherence to the classical school of *ẓāhir al-isnād*. Here he states:

> [Al-Dhahabī] ranked someone *ṣadūq* (truthful) at a lesser level than a *thiqah* (trustworthy) and higher than those who were described as *maḥalluhu al-ṣidq* (his place is truthfulness), *jayyid al-ḥadīth* (his hadith is somewhat good), *ṣāliḥ al-ḥadīth* (his hadith is all right), *ḥasan al-ḥadīth* (his hadith is fair) . . . Hadith scholars have ruled that the hadiths of narrators who are described with these terms are considered to be *ḥasan*. This practice is evident and widespread in books such as *Naṣb al-rāyah, Fatḥ al-bārī, Nayl al-awṭār* and others dealing with *takhrīj* and the classification of reports.[67]

Thereafter, he quotes Ibn Ḥajar's twelve ranks of hadith narrators. Ibn Ḥajar states, 'The fourth rank is he who is slightly below the third rank, and usually referred to as *ṣadūq* or *lā baʾsa bihi* (there is no issue with him).' Commenting on this, Abū Ghuddah says:

> By stating that the fourth rank is little below the third, al-Ḥāfiẓ Ibn Ḥajar points out that terms of this rank are indications of reliability but to a lesser level than the third rank. He also points out that narrations of fourth-rank narrators would be independently acceptable (*ḥasan li-dhātih*) and this goes back to their (classical hadith scholars') definition of *ḥasan* hadiths.

Further to the point, Abū Ghuddah then quotes Aḥmad Shākir as saying, 'The hadith of a fourth-rank narrator is authentic of the second degree, that which is called *ḥasan* by al-Tirmidhī.' Here, Abū Ghuddah indicates his approval of Shākir's analysis, saying, 'It is a very good clarification.'[68]

This agreement in theory and practice between the Traditionalist and contemporary Salafi schools most likely returns to the following. First, the circumstances and motives that prevented Salafi hadith critics from going further than Ibn Ḥajar in their historical reference and inspiration for hadith criticism are more acute amongst the Traditionalists. This is in large part due to Traditionalists' attempt to adhere, quite strictly, to 'tradition' in the sense of a scholarly inheritance, so that they usually tend not to bypass the authority of the major hadith commentaries, let alone authorities of the magnitude of Ibn Ḥajar. Hence, if a Salafi tradition that encourages reference to the early period of Islam as much as possible was unable to deal in frameworks from a period earlier than Ibn Ḥajar, the Traditionalists would be all the more hard-pressed to do so. Secondly, the Traditionalist school was not preoccupied with hadith criticism in general. In many ways, their entry into the field in the twentieth century was an act of defence rather than a serious engagement with the theories and practices of the field. Thirdly, the method of learning and teaching in the Traditionalist school does not encourage criticism in general and especially in the Levant, where scholars and their students seldom deviate from conventional modes of thinking.

The School of Circumstantial Evidence (*qarāʾin*) in the Levant

The school of *qarāʾin* may be defined as a school that does not consider hadith terminology to be applicable in judging hadith all or most of the time. Instead, what matters is the 'evidence' (*qarāʾin*) related to each individual hadith. It is from this perspective that the proponents of this method commonly say, 'To each hadith belongs its own form of critique.'[69] It also takes as a principle that the narrator is judged by what he or she narrates, not the opposite. Ḥamzah al-Mallībārī, a pioneer of this school, says of the relationship between the narrator and his or her narrations, 'Determining the narrator's characteristics and the level of his accuracy depends on the evaluation of his narrations; the former depends on the latter. Therefore, early scholars did not consider a narrator's rank the primary point of departure for judging a hadith.'[70] It is inaccurate to say that 'all the hadiths of a *ṣadūq* are *ḥasan*', for example, because he was lowered to that rank because of faults that appeared in his narrations. Hence, it is not possible to conclude that all his narrations are sound. Early scholars would look into circumstantial evidence for the narrator and the narration before judging an individual hadith and would not usually give a general ruling of reliability.

Among the most famous figures of this school are Ḥamzah al-Mallībārī, Ḥātim al-ᶜAwnī (1966–) and ᶜAbd Allāh al-Saᶜd (1962–). Most of these scholars are ideologically aligned to the Salafi school, but disagree strongly with al-Albānī's method of hadith criticism. This substantiates the main argument of this chapter that the classification of hadith trends in the twentieth century according to ideological and doctrinal alliances does not reflect the reality of these movements. Amongst these scholars, the most influential in the Levant has been al-Mallībārī, who moved to Jordan in 1996 and taught at the University of Jordan for four years. Still, in all likelihood, his success seems to have been secured through the groundwork previously provided by Hammām Saᶜīd, who paved the way for this school in the Jordanian hadith movement. These contributions can be seen in his important study on Ibn Rajab al-Ḥanbalī's *Sharḥ ᶜIlal al-Tirmidhī*. Saᶜīd's critical edition of the book begins with a substantial analysis of the subject, which may be seen as a ground-breaking work at a time when very few were even engaging with the topic. Also, Saᶜīd taught for years at the University of Jordan and introduced many of his post-graduate students to the field of *ᶜilal*. To name a few of his prominent students who have since had a significant impact on the field, ᶜAbd al-Karīm al-Wuraykāt (1964–), Asᶜad Tayyim and Sulṭān al-ᶜAkāylah (1953–) are all currently university professors and follow the approach of *ᶜilal al-ḥadīth*. It can be argued that Saᶜīd's work created fertile ground for the emergence of the school of circumstantial evidence in Jordan and thus paved the way for the spread of al-Mallībārī's ideas when he arrived in Jordan in 1996 and began teaching at the University of Jordan.

The writings of al-Mallībārī and his teaching methodology represented a strong criticism of the school of *ẓāhir al-isnād*. The most important of his books that spread in that era in Jordan were *al-Muwāzanah bayna al-mutaqaddimīn wa-al-muta᾽akhkhirīn* ('A Comparison between Scholars of the Early and Late Periods [in Methods of Hadith Criticism]') and *Naẓarāt jadīdah fī ᶜulūm al-ḥadīth* ('New Perspectives on Hadith Sciences').[71] These two books were well received in the Levant and generated significant discussions, to the extent that al-Albānī spoke out against al-Mallībārī in a recorded lecture titled *Bidaᶜ al-muḥdithīn ᶜalá al-muḥaddithīn* ('Innovations of Pseudo-Scholars of Hadith'). Al-Mallībārī himself did not shy away from criticising al-Albānī or others. Without explicitly mentioning him by name, al-Mallībārī frequently referred to al-Albānī's methods and offered an equally detailed critique in his *al-Muwāzanah* and *Naẓarāt*. In the second edition of *al-Muwāzanah*, he discusses Abū Ghuddah on the above-mentioned hadith on raising hands in prayer.

This movement, which began with Saᶜīd Hammām and Ḥamzah al-Mallībārī, is increasingly replacing the school of *ẓāhir al-isnād*, previously dominant in the Levant and throughout the Middle East. Nowadays, the predominant tendency among university professors in the Levant is to use the method of criticism based on the *ᶜilal* approach, which is becoming the main component of the hadith curriculum. There is also abundant research dedicated to the study of scholars and their methods of hadith criticism. For example, we note such methods in the works of al-Mallībārī's prominent students such as ᶜAbd al-Salām Abū Samḥah (1974–), who wrote a commendable analysis of *munkar* (objectionable) hadith reports, and Aḥmad ᶜAbd Allāh, whose analysis of al-Bukhārī's hadith criticism in his *al-Tārīkh al-kabīr* was met with significant criticism from Nūr al-Dīn ᶜItr, who dismisses the approach of *ᶜilal* altogether.

In the Levant, we note the increasing weakness of the *ẓāhir al-isnād* school's control over the academic landscape with an equal increase of influence from the school of *qarā᾽in*. This observation can be marked by the frequent rebuttals published by proponents of the *ẓāhir al-isnād* method, which in many ways indicate a sense of being under siege. We also note this predominance in the work of scholarly societies such as the 'Association of Hadith' in recent years. As of late, many of their academic conferences and seminars have focused on the differences between the two schools and the intellectual basis for both. This need to regularly compare the progress of both schools is a strong indication of the increased significance of the school of *qarā᾽in*.

In summing up the major points of this essay we note the following. The science of hadith criticism in the Levant remained almost stagnant from the middle of the ninth/fifteenth century until the beginning of the Arab Renaissance in the late Ottoman era, at which time two scholars, Ṭāhir al-Jazā᾽irī and Jamāl al-Dīn al-Qāsimī, began to focus their attention on the study of hadith. While both had little to offer by way of technical criticism, it was al-Albānī who revived hadith criticism in the Levant. A number of personal, social, political and intellectual factors contributed to al-Albānī's rise as a hadith critic and the widespread adoption of his ideas. His method of hadith criticism was, with rare exceptions, a strict application of the method of *ẓāhir al-isnād* in accordance with the terminology detailed in the classical textbooks of hadith terminology. Those who opposed al-Albānī from the Traditionalist school such ʿAbd al-Fattāḥ Abū Ghuddah and Nūr al-Dīn ʿItr also significantly relied in their hadith criticism on the method of *ẓāhir al-isnād*. The Jordanian hadith movement started by Hammām Saʿīd marked the beginnings of a form of hadith criticism different from that of *ẓāhir al-isnād*. This movement was further developed by Ḥamzah al-Mallībārī, whose work during the late 1990s provided a formal framework for the school of *qarāʾin*, allowing it to enjoy a wider area of approval amongst researchers.

The emergence of the *qarāʾin* school in recent decades is a natural and logical progress from the *ẓāhir al-isnād* school. The intellectual environment that prevailed during and immediately after the Ottoman era essentially neglected hadith criticism in its entirety. Hence, a leap from a state of no hadith criticism to one in which the familiar, if unused, terminology-based approach was not considered to be the final standard would have been too much to ask for. Rather, what was needed was a slow and somewhat natural progression. In reality, several historical events and intellectual trends were necessary for the school of *qarāʾin* to be able to form and mature. The rise of Salafism, the increased interest in hadith in general, and significant financial support for hadith projects all factored into creating an environment in which scholars were able to revisit hadith texts and historical criticism in a nuanced manner, eventually leading to an internal, method-based critique. Additionally, as researchers needed an academic setting in which they could challenge and explore previously held convictions without fear of backlash from the intellectual élite, Jordan, with its lack of traditional institutions of learning and plethora of opinions, was an ideal location. Indeed, it is difficult to think of a similar movement flourishing in neighbouring Syria as it would have quickly run up against strong opposition from its classical institutions and scholars.

To most appropriately classify hadith trends in the Levant and elsewhere, one must examine the forms of hadith criticism that manifest themselves in the region. It is inaccurate to speak of ideological or doctrinal schools of thought as the basis for assessing the trends of hadith criticism. As we have seen, one ideological school may exhibit various approaches to hadith criticism. Doctrinal differences do not necessarily relate to the theoretical or actualised practice of hadith criticism. Indeed, the common dependence on the method of *ẓāhir al-isnād* by Salafis and Traditionalists in the 1980s is a strong indication that even groups who are, in some ways, diametrically opposed in their creedal ideologies may not carry those differences over to their analysis of hadith.

Notes

* I would like to thank Omar Matadar, the director of Qasid Institute in Jordan, for his assistance in translating this chapter and Belal Abu-Alabbas for his valuable comments.

1. An example of this classification is Maḥmūd Saʿīd Mamdūḥ, *al-Ittijāhāt al-ḥadīthīyah fī al-qarn al-rābiʿ ʿashar al-hijrī*, 3rd edn (Cairo: Dār al-Baṣāʾir, 2009), 43–7. This chapter focuses on al-Albānī, Abū Ghuddah and ʿItr for the purpose of brevity and exploring the primary contenders. A study of scholars such as Shuʿayb al-Arnaʾūṭ and Muḥammad ʿAwwāmah would corroborate the findings of the present one.
2. Muḥammad ʿAzzūz, *Madrasat al-ḥadīth fī bilād al-Shām khilāl al-qarn al-thāmin al-hijrī* (Beirut: Dār al-Bashāʾir al-Islāmīyah, 2000).
3. Ibn Ḥajar says of Ibn Nāṣir al-Dīn, 'When the region lacked hadith scholars, he became the hadith scholar of the region.' Al-Sakhāwī then comments about Ibn Nāṣir al-Dīn that 'No one [of his excellence] succeeded him in the Levant. The gate was sealed there.' See al-Sakhāwī, *al-Ḍawʾ al-lāmiʿ li-ahl al-qarn al-tāsiʿ*, 12 vols (Cairo: Maktabat al-Quds, 1353–6, repr. Beirut: Dār Maktabat al-Ḥayāh, n.d.), 8:105–6. For a short biography of Sibṭ ibn al-ʿAjamī and an overview of his scholarly work, see Muḥammad ʿAwwāmah's study of al-Dhahabī's *al-Kāshif*, *al-Kāshif fī maʿrifat man lahu riwāyah fī al-kutub al-sittah*, ed. Muḥammad ʿAwwāmah and Aḥmad Muḥammad Namir al-Khaṭīb, 2 vols (Jeddah: Dār al-Qiblah lil-Thaqāfah al-Islāmīyah and Muʾassasat ʿUlūm al-Qurʾān, 1992), 1:212–80.
4. See Ibn Ṭūlūn, Shams al-Dīn Muḥammad, *al-Fulk al-mashḥūn fī aḥwāl Muḥammad ibn Ṭūlūn*, ed. Muḥammad Khayr Ramaḍān Yūsuf (Beirut: Dār Ibn Ḥazm, 1996), 35. Ibn Ṭūlūn states in his biography of Ibn Zurayq that none of his own teachers rivalled Ibn Zurayq in the sciences of hadith. However, al-Sakhāwī in his *al-Ḍawʾ al-lāmiʿ* and Ibn al-ʿImād in his *Shadharāt al-dhahab* note that Ibn Zurayq was not a leading scholar of hadith. See al-Sakhāwī, *Ḍawʾ* 7:169–70, and Ibn al-ʿImād, *Shadharāt al-dhahab fī akhbār man dhahab*, ed. Maḥmūd al-Arnaʾūt, 11 vols (Damascus: Dār Ibn Kathīr, 1986–95), 9:551.
5. Ibn Ṭūlūn was also a student of Yūsuf ibn ʿAbd al-Hādī, also known as Ibn al-Mibrad (d. 909/1503), but he does not note him as a leading scholar of hadith.
6. ʿAbd al-Razzāq al-Bīṭār mentions nineteen scholars who taught hadith science under the dome of al-Nisr, which was dedicated to Levantine scholars of the highest calibre in the Ottoman era, between 1050/1640 and the demise of the Ottoman Empire. See ʿAbd al-Razzāq al-Bīṭār, *Natījat al-fikr fī man darasa taḥta qubbat al-nisr*, ed. M. N. al-ʿAjamī (Beirut: Dār al-Bashāʾir al-Islāmīyah, 1998), 96. However, there is little hadith criticism in the works of these scholars, except for Ismāʿīl al-ʿAjlūnī (d. 1162/1748), the author of *Kashf al-khafāʾ*, a work dedicated to identifying weak hadiths that are well circulated among the masses, though the work itself shows little input from al-ʿAjlūnī himself. The teachers of al-ʿAjlūnī themselves do not exhibit significant hadith scholarship. One may say the same of the teachers of Aḥmad ibn Aḥmad ibn al-ʿAjmī al-Ḥalabī

(1086/1675), who composed an annotation to al-Suyūṭī's *Tadrīb al-rāwī*. See also ᶜUmar al-Nashūqātī's *Juhūd ᶜulamāʾ Dimashq fī riwāyat al-ḥadīth al-sharīf fī al-ᶜaṣr al-ᶜuthmānī* (Damascus: Dār al-Nawādir, 2012). Al-Nashūqātī notes that these efforts tended to focus on hadith narration rather than criticism, explaining the scarcity of works by Damascene scholars. Also, works related to hadith criticism included little input from these scholars, showing a lack of independent thought (see al-Nashūqātī, *Juhūd*, 16, 46).

7. Muḥammad Muṭīᶜ al-Ḥāfiẓ, *Dār al-ḥadīth al-ashrafiyah bi-Dimashq* (Damascus: Dār al-Fikr, 2001) 17–18, 23; al-Nashūqātī, *Juhūd*, 157.
8. ᶜAbd al-Razzāq al-Bīṭār, *Ḥilyat al-bashar fī tārīkh al-qarn al-thālith ᶜashar*, ed. Muḥammad Bahjah al-Bīṭār, 3 vols, 2nd edn (Beirut: Dār Ṣādir, 1993), 1:377. Al-Bīṭār observes that reading hadith merely for gaining blessings prevailed among students of hadith during the Ottoman era. See also al-Nashūqātī, *Juhūd*, 272–3.
9. Al-ᶜAjlūnī, *Kashf al-khafāʾ wa-muzīl al-ilbās ᶜammā ishtahara min al-aḥādīth ᶜalá alsinat al-nās*, 2 vols (Cairo: Maktabat al-Qudsī, 1351–2), 1:10, 2:262. Several scholars of the Levant, in personal records of what they had narrated from their teachers, listed chains of transmission that included spiritual unveilings. See Muḥammad Amīn ibn ᶜĀbdīn (d. 1252/1836), *ᶜUqūd al-laʾālī fī al-asānīd al-ᶜawālī*, ed. Muḥammad Ibrāhīm al-Ḥusayn (Beirut: Dār al-Bashāʾir al-Islāmīyah, 2010), 315, and al-Nashūqātī, *Juhūd*, 531–3.
10. I do not present Badr al-Dīn al-Ḥasanī (1850–1935) here because he specialised in narration and not in hadith criticism, as observable from the records of his writings and teaching sessions.
11. See Rashīd Riḍā's forward to Jamāl al-Dīn al-Qāsimī, *Qawāᶜid al-taḥdīth min funūn muṣṭalaḥ al-ḥadīth*, ed. Muḥammad Bahjah al-Bīṭār, 4th edn (Beirut: Dār al-Nafāʾis, 2006), 23. Al-Jazāʾirī wrote *ᶜUqūd al-laʾālī fī al-asānīd al-ᶜawālī*, printed in 1885, and another book titled *Mubtadaʾ al-khabar*, on hadith terminology, which is probably an abridgment of his *Tawjīh al-naẓar*. See Abū Ghuddah's introduction to *Tawjīh al-naẓar ilá uṣūl al-athar*, ed. Abū Ghuddah, 2 vols (Aleppo: Maktabat al-Maṭbūᶜāt al-Islāmīyah, 1995), 1:26.
12. Muḥammad Anas Sarmīnī, *al-Shaykh Muḥammad Jamāl al-Dīn al-Qāsimī wa-juhūduhu al-ḥadīthīyah: dirāsah taḥlīlīyah* (Beirut: Dār al-Bashāʾir al-Islāmīyah, 2010), 513.
13. Albert Hourani, *al-Fikr al-ᶜarabī fī ᶜaṣr al-nahḍah 1798–1939*, trans. Karīm ᶜAzqūl (Beirut: Dār al-Nahār, n.d.), 270–1, 311–12.
14. Al-Albānī thus describes the beginning of his confrontation with the predominant traditionalist religious environment: 'Then, God enabled me, without guidance from anyone, to study the rules and practice of hadith and Sunnah, after I was taught the basics of Ḥanafī jurisprudence and the so-called ancillary subjects such as grammar and rhetoric by my father and other scholars after graduating from al-Isᶜāf al-Khayrī Primary School. I then began to call on my brothers and companions to correct their creedal beliefs, to abandon the zealous following of traditional legal schools, to warn them of weak and fabricated hadiths, and to encourage them to revive the correct *sunan* that had been abandoned by even the scholars among them, such as the performance of Eid prayers in congregational areas, in Damascus.

This Sunnah then spread to Aleppo and other parts of Syria and continued its spreading until it reached Amman (Jordan) by some of our brothers. I warned people against building mosques over graves, and I wrote my book, *Taḥdhīr al-sājid min ittikhādh al-qubūr masājid* ('Warning the Prostrator against Taking Graveyards as Mosques'), at a time when some of my relatives used to go pray in the Umayyad mosque because it housed the tomb of Yaḥyá, as they claimed …' See al-Albānī, *Silsilat al-aḥādīth al-ṣaḥīḥah*, 9 vols in 7 (Riyadh: Maktabat al-Maʿārif, 1995–2002), 7:611, and Ibrāhīm al-ʿAlī, *Muḥammad Nāṣir al-Dīn al-Albānī, muḥaddith al-ʿaṣr wa-nāṣir al-sunnah* (Damascus: Dār al-Qalam, 2001), 22.

15. Muḥammad ibn Nāṣir al-ʿAjmī, *Imām al-Shām fi ʿaṣrih Jamāl al-Qāsimī: sīratuhu al-dhātīyah* (Beirut: Dār al-Bashāʾir al-Islāmīyah, 2009), 63–91.
16. Muḥammad ibn Ibrāhīm al-Shaybānī, *Ḥayāt al-Albānī wa-āthāruh wa-thanāʾ al-ʿulamāʾ ʿalayh* (Cairo: Maktabat al-Saddāwī, 1987), 45.
17. al-Shaybānī, *Ḥayāt al-Albānī*, 46.
18. Al-Albānī states, 'This does not prevent me from admitting that some recent scholars have made a great mark on this field of knowledge, and that we benefit from their scholarship, such as Aḥmad Shākir and other prominent scholars': *al-Silsilah al-ṣaḥīḥah* 4:15.
19. Nūr al-Dīn Ṭālib, *Maqālāt al-shaykh al-Albānī* (Riyadh: Dār Aṭlas, 2001), 179.
20. Al-Albānī, 'al-Albānī yarwī qiṣṣatahu maʿa al-ikhwān', *al-Mujtamaʿ*, 10 March 1981, (519), 29.
21. Ṭālib, *Maqālāt al-shaykh*, 164–72.
22. Al-Albānī, 'al-Albānī yataḥaddathu ʿan Sayyid Qutb wa-majallat *al-Mujtamaʿ*', *al-Mujtamaʿ*, 17 March 1981, (520), 24.
23. Al-Albānī, 'al-Albānī yarwī', 31. He attributes this split to organisational and factional issues in the Brotherhood.
24. Al-Albānī, 'al-Albānī yarwī', 29.
25. Al-Albānī, *al-Silsilah al-ṣaḥīḥah*, 7:611.
26. Al-ʿAlī, *al-Albānī*, 24.
27. Al-ʿAlī, *al-Albānī*, 24.
28. See the introduction to the second edition of al-Albānī's *Taḥdhīr al-sājid min ittikhādh al-qubūr masājid* (Beirut: al-Maktab al-Islāmī, 1392).
29. ʿAbd al-Raḥmān ibn Muḥammad al-ʿAyzarī, *Juhūd al-shaykh al-Albānī fi al-ḥadīth* (Riyadh: Maktabat al-Rushd, 2006), 50.
30. Al-ʿAyzarī, *Juhūd al-shaykh al-Albānī*, 56.
31. Al-ʿAyzarī, *Juhūd al-shaykh al-Albānī*, 50.
32. Ṭālib, *Maqālāt al-shaykh*, 18.
33. Muḥammad ibn Nāṣir al-ʿAjmī, *al-Rasāʾil al-mutabādalah bayna Jamāl al-Dīn al-Qāsimī wa-Maḥmūd Shukrī al-Alūsī* (Beirut: Dār al-Bashāʾir al-Islāmīyah, 2001), 12–13; also see 140, 149, 156–7, 164, 173–4.
34. For a serious study of al-Albānī's steadfast application of this *ẓāhir al-isnād* method, see Aḥmad Muḥammad al-Khalīl, *Mustadrak al-taʿlīl ʿalá Irwāʾ al-ghalīl: dirāsah ḥadīthīyah tuʿnā bi-bayān al-aḥādīth allatī ṣuḥḥiḥat fi al-Irwāʾ wa-aʿallahā al-aʾimmah al-mutaqaddimūn, maʿa sharḥ tilka al-ʿilal* (Dammam: Dār Ibn al-Jawzī, 2008).

35. Al-Albānī, *Irwāʾ al-ghalīl fī takhrīj aḥādīth Manār al-sabīl*, 9 vols (Beirut: al-Maktab al-Islāmī, 1979–87), 3:31, 4:50; al-Albānī, *al-Silsilah al-ṣaḥīḥah*, 5:227; al-Albānī, *Ṣaḥīḥ Sunan Abī Dāwūd*, 3 vols (Riyadh: Maktabat al-Maʿārif, 1998), 1:247.
36. Al-Albānī, *Irwāʾ* 4:157, 176, 5:326; al-Albānī, *al-Silsilah al-ṣaḥīḥah*, 5:153; al-Albānī, *Silsilat al-aḥādīth al-ḍaʿīfah*, 14 vols (Riyadh: Maktabat al-Maʿārif, 1412–25), 13:726.
37. See, for example, al-Albānī, *Aṣl ṣifat ṣalāt al-Nabī*, 3 vols (Riyadh: Maktabat al-Maʿārif, 2006), 1:409, 2:425,736, 3:969; al-Albānī, *Irwāʾ* 2:6, 338, 3:170; al-Albānī, *al-Silsilah al-ṣaḥīḥah*, 1:507, 812, 2:433, 681, 3:72, 180, 5:393, 610, 6:668, 8:1132; al-Albānī, *al-Silsilah al-ḍaʿīfah* 13:422; al-Albānī, *Ṣaḥīḥ Abī Dāwūd* 1:28, 109, 143, 2:326, 348.
38. Al-Albānī, *Ṣaḥīḥ Abī Dāwūd* 1:274.
39. Al-Albānī, *Irwāʾ* 2:77.
40. Al-Albānī, *Irwāʾ* 2:51.
41. Al-Albānī, *Irwāʾ* 2:77.
42. Al-Albānī, *al-Silsilah al-ṣaḥīḥah* 1:85.
43. Al-Albānī, *al-Silsilah al-ṣaḥīḥah* 2:293.
44. Al-Albānī, *al-Silsilah al-ṣaḥīḥah* 2:229.
45. Al-Albānī, *al-Silsilah al-ḍaʿīfah* 10:758, 12:89.
46. Muḥammad Ḥamdī Abū ʿAbduh, *Manhaj al-ʿallāmah al-muḥaddith al-Albānī fī taʿlīl al-ḥadīth* (Beirut: Dār al-Luʾluʾah, 2013), 185–6.
47. This approach has generally been dismissed as an unreliable representation of how early critics worked. See, for example, Leonard T. Librande, 'The Supposed Homogeneity of Technical Terms in Hadith Study', *Muslim World* 72 (1982): 34–50; Eerik Dickinson, *The Development of Early Sunnite Ḥadīth Criticism: the Taqdimah of Ibn Abī Ḥātim al-Rāzī*, Islamic History and Civilization, Studies and Texts, 38 (Leiden: Brill, 2001); and Belal Abu-Alabbas, 'The Principles of Hadith Criticism in the Writings of al-Shāfiʿī and Muslim', *Islamic Law and Society* 24 (2017): 311–35.
48. Al-Albānī, *al-Silsilah al-ḍaʿīfah* 10:758.
49. Al-Albānī, *al-Silsilah al-ḍaʿīfah* 9:4. Note that this volume was printed in 2001 after al-Albānī's demise.
50. Aḥmad Muḥammad Shākir, *al-Bāʿith al-ḥathīth sharḥ Ikhtiṣār ʿulūm al-ḥadīth* by Ibn Kathīr, comm'y by Nāṣir al-Dīn al-Albānī (Riyadh: Maktabat al-Maʿārif, 1996), 98.
51. Al-Albānī, *Ādāb al-zifāf fī al-sunnah* (Amman: al-Maktabah al-Islāmīyah, 1409), 227.
52. Al-Albānī, *Irwāʾ* 1:267, 3:408, 5:109, 332; al-Albānī, *Tamām al-minnah fī al-taʿlīq ʿalá fiqh al-sunnah*, 4th edn (Riyadh: Dār al-Rāyah, n.d.), 128; al-Albānī, *al-Silsilah al-ṣaḥīḥah* 1:516, 2:115.
53. Khālid Manṣūr al-Durays, *al-Ḥadīth al-ḥasan li-dhātihi wa-li-ghayrihi*, 5 vols (Riyadh: Dār Adwāʾ al-Salaf, 2005), 4:1856.
54. Al-Albānī, *Irwāʾ* 2:96; al-Albānī, *Tamām al-minnah*, 202.
55. Al-Durays, *Ḥadīth* 4:2014, 2017–19.
56. For more on this, see al-Khalīl, *Mustadrak al-taʿlīl*. He mentions about 149 hadith

reports in which al-Albānī disagrees with early scholars. See also Aḥmad al-Jābirī, *al-Dars al-ḥadīthī al-muᶜāṣir* (Beirut: Markaz Namāʾ, 2017), 72–7.

57. Ibn Ḥajar says about his teacher, al-ᶜIrāqī, 'We have not seen in this field anyone who was more knowledgeable than he was.' See Ibn Ḥajar, *Inbāʾ al-ghumr bi-abnāʾ al-ᶜumr*, Lajnat Iḥyā' al-Turāth al-Islāmī ser. 6, 3 vols (Cairo: al-Majlis al-Aᶜlā lil-Shuʾūn al-Islāmīyah, 1969–72), 2:276–7.
58. Al-Albānī, *al-Silsilah al-ḍaᶜīfah* 11:283.
59. Ṭālib, *Maqālāt al-shaykh*, 68–9.
60. Nūr al-Dīn ᶜItr, *Mādhā ᶜan al-marʾah*, 13th edn (Damascus: Dār al-Yamāmah, 2003), 232–47.
61. ᶜAbd al-Fattāh Abū Ghuddah, *Khuṭbat al-ḥājah laysat sunnah fī mustahall al-kutub wa-al-muʾallafāt* (Beirut: Dār al-Bashāʾir al-Islāmīyah, 1999).
62. Al-Bayhaqī, *al-Sunan al-kubrá*, ed. Muḥammad ᶜAbd al-Qādir ᶜAṭā, 3rd edn, 11 vols (Beirut: Dār al-Kutub al-ᶜIlmīyah, 2003), 1:284.
63. Nūr al-Dīn ᶜItr, *Iᶜlām al-anām sharḥ Bulūgh al-marām*, 7th edn, 4 vols (Damascus: Dār al-Farfūr, 1998), 1:186–7, and compare al-Albānī's *Irwāʾ* 1:137–8 and Māhir al-Faḥl, *al-Jāmiᶜ fī al-ᶜilal wa-al-fawāʾid*, 6 vols (Riyadh: Dār Ibn al-Jawzī, 2009), 2:189–201.
64. ᶜItr, *Iᶜlām al-anām* 3:344 – here, ᶜItr's judgement coincides with al-Albānī's in *Irwāʾ al-ghalīl* 6:292.
65. ᶜItr, *Iᶜlām al-anām* 3:344.
66. Muḥammad ᶜAbd al-Rashīd al-Nuᶜmānī, *al-Imām Ibn Mājah wa-kitābuh al-Sunan*, ed. ᶜAbd al-Fattāh Abū Ghuddah (Beirut: Dār al-Bashāʾir al-Islāmīyah, 1996?), 305.
67. See his edition of Ẓafar Aḥmad al-Tahānawī, *Qawāᶜid fī ᶜulūm al-ḥadīth*, ed. ᶜAbd al-Fattāh Abū Ghuddah, 3rd edn (Beirut, Dār al-Qalam, 1972), 245.
68. Al-Tahānawī, *Qawāᶜid fī ᶜulūm al-ḥadīth*.
69. Ḥamzah al-Mallībārī, *al-Muwāzanah bayna al-mutaqaddimīn wa-al-mutaʾakhkhirīn*, 2nd edn (Beirut: Dār Ibn Ḥazm, 2001), 12–16, 33–5.
70. Ḥamzah al-Mallībārī, *Naẓarāt jadīdah fī ᶜulūm al-ḥadīth* (Beirut: Dār Ibn Ḥazm, 2003), 86.
71. For more on the school of *qarāʾin*, see al-Mallībārī's two works mentioned in nn. 69 and 70.

CHAPTER

8

THE RECEPTION AND REPRESENTATION OF WESTERN HADITH STUDIES IN TURKISH ACADEME

Fatma Kızıl

Introduction

The question of how Western hadith studies have been perceived in Turkey cannot be discussed without reference to the Turkish Republic's broader efforts to rapidly Westernise virtually all spheres of Turkish culture. The newly-established state identified Western civilisation as the telos that guided and organised its multi-faceted reforms. The adoption of *Westernisation*[1] (*Garblılaşma*) as an explicit government policy, and especially the principles of laicism (1928–37) and language reform (1928), reshaped the very essence of the social fabric, with far-reaching effects on virtually all major institutions.[2] Higher religious education was no exception. The process of Westernisation began before the Republican era.

In many ways, the educational system could even be described as the primary conduit of Westernisation in the late Ottoman era. The moderate proposals for piecemeal adoption of Western technology and institutions advocated by the Ottomans gave way to more forceful demands for a comprehensive adoption of a secularising Western culture and worldview after the Second Constitutional Period (1908–18).[3] Şükrü Hanioğlu underlines the influence of foreign ideas on so-called *Garbcı* ('Westernising') intellectuals of this period, noting that their ideology consisted of a 'peculiar mixture of materialism, scientism, and Social Darwinism'.[4] Nearly all of the proposals voiced by *Garbcı* intellectuals of the Second Constitutional Period, like Kılıçzâde Hakkı[5] (d. 1960), were implemented in the Republican period. Policies such as the inclusion of women in the public sphere, the closure of Sufi lodges and madrasas, the abolition of *sharīʿah* courts, and the adoption of the Latin alphabet were all based on Kılıçzâde's proposals.[6]

It was also during the Second Constitutional Period that new educational institutions facilitated the spread of Western thought and culture among the Ottoman intellectual class. Halil İnalcık points out the importance of secondary (*idadi*) schools in this respect. The French language had already been the primary conduit for Western thought throughout the late Ottoman period, but the *idadi* schools greatly expanded French literacy among the intellectual class and consequently accelerated the pace of translation into Turkish as well. These schools were also secular, with Muslim and non-Muslim (*dhimmī*) students receiving their education together for the first time.[7]

Another institution that played an important role in the process of Westernising religious education in particular was the *Dârülfünûn*, the first institution of higher education besides the madrasas. The origins of this institution stretch back to 1845, but it was re-opened under the name of *Dârülfünûn-ı Şâhâne* in 1900, together with a four-year branch (faculty) of *Ulûm-i Âliyye-i Dîniyye* (Higher Religious Sciences). In 1914, the branch was abolished, and its students were transferred to the madrasas of *Dârü'l-Hilâfe*.[8]

In the Republican era, a three-year Faculty of Theology was opened at *Dârülfünûn* in 1924. This faculty had been planned as 'a kind of faculty of sociology',[9] which was conceived as a state apparatus that would bring the religious sphere into line with Republican reforms, but was closed in 1933 due to a dearth of students. Over the past half-century, new faculties[10] have been opened with an ideologically diverse academic staffing. As a result, these faculties drifted from the Republican goal of sustaining a single discourse in unison. Nonetheless, the founding principle of the first faculty continues to contribute to a negative assessment of today's faculties on the part of traditional and conservative elements of society.[11]

The unresolved issue these faculties face today is the question of how to engage in Islamic studies. To a significant extent, they are characterised by a hybridity that manifests itself on multiple levels. Since there are not two distinct majors such as theology and religious studies, the faculties undertake the mission of educating the clergy, so to speak, along with academics.[12] In addition, the curricula of the faculties consist of classes such as sociology of religion, psychology of religion and history of religions, which treat their subject as a social phenomenon, alongside the traditional subjects of *tafsīr*, *fiqh*, hadith, Islamic theology (*kalām*), Sufism and Arabic. Both academics with an inclination towards traditional scholarship and the preacher-led groups from outside the academy constantly compare the curricula of these faculties with the programmes of private foundations and informal madrasas that concentrate solely on classical Islamic texts and Arabic. The resulting perception is typically that these faculties and their graduates are not qualified to continue the legacy of classical Islamic scholarship.[13]

Hadith Scholars and Orientalism in Faculties of Theology before the 2000s

The methodological hybridity that has generally characterised the faculties of theology has also significantly affected the study of hadith. In the curriculum of the Faculty of Theology opened in 1924, one of the courses was 'hadīth and history of hadith'. Between 1925 and 1926, İzmirli İsmail Hakkı (d. 1946) taught the course and wrote a textbook for it titled *Târîkh-i ḥadîs* (1924), which he described as the first of its kind.[14] Traditionalists have claimed that İzmirli's book and the creation of a course on 'the history of hadith' were reflective of a trend towards treating the classical Islamic sciences as ineffective and irrelevant disciplines in general and reducing hadith to mere history in particular.[15] İzmirli's book, however, was largely a regular book of *muṣṭalaḥ al-ḥadīth* in terms of its content and the new course was not just on the 'history of hadith', but rather on 'hadith and history of hadith'.[16]

There is no indication that İzmirli's approach to the study of hadith was directly influenced by Western hadith studies, although he is generally regarded as one of the more progressive figures among the so-called 'Islamists' of the late Ottoman era.[17] He was, however, at least tangentially familiar with Islamic studies in the West. He was included in the commission established by the Ministry of Education to prepare a report on the Turkish translation of Reinhart Dozy's (d. 1883) *De Voornaamste Godsdienste: Het Islamisme* (1863) by Abdullah Cevdet (d. 1932).[18] He was also one of the authors of *İslâm-Türk Ansiklopedisi* ('Islamic–Turkish Encyclopedia'), a project conceived of as an indigenous Turkish response to the translation of Brill's *Encyclopaedia of Islam* (1913–36) in 1940.

Another important contributor to hadith studies in this period was Babanzade Ahmed Naim (d. 1934). The Directorate of Religious Affairs assigned him the task of translating al-Zabīdī's (d. 893/1488) *al-Tajrīd al-ṣarīḥ li-aḥādīth al-Jāmiʿi al-ṣaḥīḥ*. Although he ultimately completed only the first two of twelve volumes, Ahmed Naim also wrote a one-volume introduction to the work.[19] Under a section titled 'Hiç de Vechi Olmayan Bir Teşkîk' ('A Meaningless Doubt'), he criticised several assertions of Leone Caetani (d. 1935) concerning the early development of the hadith tradition, including the relatively late advent and foreign origins of the *isnād* and the inefficacy of oral transmission.[20]

Between the closure of the Faculty of Theology in 1933 and the opening of a new faculty in Ankara in 1949, the only significant academic work on hadith was a single article published by Zakir Kadiri Ugan (d. 1954). Although he was neither a faculty member nor a hadith scholar, Ugan was the author of the only article on hadith in the faculty journal *Dârülfünûn İlâhiyat Fakültesi Mecmuası*, which was published 1925–33. Ugan's article, 'Dinî ve Gayri Dinî Rivayetler' ('Religious and Non-Religious Narrations'), can be regarded as a significant precursor to the debates surrounding hadith that would unfold subsequently in Turkey. Unlike İzmirli and Arapkirli, Ugan is the first scholar who made favourable references to Western scholarship on hadith. Ugan argues that hadith scholars prioritised the *isnād* and neglected *matn* criticism in authenticating hadith.[21] In this, he echoed one of the well-known assertions of Western hadith scholars, especially Ignaz Goldziher (d. 1921), which was also shared by some Islamic modernists like Aḥmad Amīn (d. 1954) and Maḥmūd Abū Rayyah (d. 1970).[22] According to

Ugan, there were unreliable personalities amongst the Companions and the doctrine of the 'collective probity of the Companions' (*ta*ᶜ*dīl al-ṣaḥābah*) had led to the acceptance of many fabricated traditions. One of the Companions Ugan was particularly interested in was Abū Hurayrah.[23] On the basis of parallels between the narrations of Abū Hurayrah and Jewish sources, Ugan insisted that Abū Hurayrah must have borrowed from the latter. To support his negative assessment he enumerates several examples of Western scholars whose works contain criticism of this Companion: 'For example, we could mention Goldziher, one of the greatest hadith scholars, Sprenger, de Goeje, Dozy, Baron and Kremer [*sic*], and their followers among Russian scholars: Krackowsky and Krymskiy and so on.'[24]

The Faculty of Theology in Ankara

When the Faculty of Theology was reopened in Ankara in 1949, courses on core classical subjects such as *fiqh*, hadith, *tafsīr* and Islamic theology were not initially included in the curriculum. For this reason, Ahmet Hamdi Akseki (d. 1951), the Director of Religious Affairs of the period, maintained that the newly opened Faculty of Theology would not be able to train the much-needed clergy.[25] Since there were no Turkish scholars with doctoral degrees at the time, Muhammed Tayyib Okiç (d. 1977), a Bosnian scholar, was invited to establish the *tafsīr* and hadith departments of the faculty. Okiç would be the teacher of the first-generation hadith scholars of the Republican era.[26] He supervised Talât Koçyiğit (1927–2011) and M. Said Hatiboğlu's doctoral dissertations, the first Turkish dissertations on hadith, completed in 1957 and 1962, respectively. He was also one of the committee members who reviewed Fuad Sezgin's *Buhârî'nin Kaynakları Hakkında Araştırmalar* for his habilitation in 1954.

Having received his doctorate from the Faculty of Letters at the University of Paris (1931), Okiç had an extensive knowledge of Western studies not only on hadith but also on other Islamic disciplines as seen in one of his major works in Turkish, *Bazı Hadis Meseleleri Üzerine Tetkikler* ('Studies on Various Hadith Problems', 1956).[27] In this book, Okiç points out the diversity of the conclusions reached by Orientalists on the topic of hadith. In Okiç's opinion, even though they cannot be absolutely impartial, there are several moderate and unbiased Orientalists. For example, he contrasts the biases of figures like Henri Lammens (d. 1937) and Leone Caetani with the relative objectivity of a figure like Goldziher.[28] On the whole, it seems that Okiç did not engage in blanket dismissals of Orientalist scholarship, but evaluated its claims on a case-by-case basis. For example, while he objected to Josef Horovitz's (d. 1931) theory regarding the Jewish origin of the *isnād* system by arguing that Horovitz had identified the existence of only a remotely similar system, he also took sides with Horovitz against Caetani's chronology of the *isnād*.[29] Unlike Zakir Kadiri Ugan, Okiç seems not to have accepted the majority of Orientalists' critiques of the hadith tradition. He did, however, encourage his students Talât Koçyiğit and Mehmed Said Hatiboğlu to learn Western languages and study Orientalists' works.[30] While these two scholars both began work in this field, they would ultimately take Okiç's encouragement in different directions.

Talât Koçyiğit translated four articles by James Robson (d. 1981) into Turkish,[31] and also critiqued Goldziher's views in an article titled 'Analysis and Critique of Goldziher's Several Views on Hadith'.[32] Since he did not make any comments on Robson's views anywhere in the translations, Koçyiğit's evaluation of Western hadith studies must be gleaned primarily from his article responding to Goldziher.[33] While he was willing to admit that there were objective Orientalists who engaged in dispassionate research, Koçyiğit considered Goldziher to be among those who misrepresented their evidence in order to attack Islam, drawing several examples of this from Goldziher's *Muhammedanische Studien*.[34] In one such example, he criticises Goldziher's interpretation of the following report narrated by al-Ṭabarī, according to which Muᶜāwiyah said to Mughīrah ibn Shuᶜbah:

> Do not refrain from abusing ᶜAli and criticising him, nor from asking God's mercy upon ᶜUthman and His forgiveness for him. Continue to shame the companions of ᶜAli, keep them at a distance, and don't listen to them. Praise the faction of ᶜUthman, bring them near, and listen to them.[35]

Goldziher interprets these words as an official encouragement to promote and spread hadith reports against ᶜAlī and to suppress those in favour of him.[36] After pointing out that Muᶜāwiyah's instruction had nothing to do with hadith, Koçyiğit reaches the conclusion that 'Goldziher distorted the meaning of this report for the sake of a hidden intention'.[37]

Another objection of Koçyiğit against Goldziher concerned his allegations about the relationship of the prominent hadith scholar al-Zuhrī (d. 124/742) with the Umayyads. According to Koçyiğit, Goldziher wanted to show the existence of hadith scholars who had fabricated traditions in the service of the Umayyads and found al-Zuhrī to be a convenient target. As an example, Koçyiğit discusses Goldziher's argument that al-Zuhrī fabricated the tradition 'Do not travel to any mosques except three: al-Masjid al-Ḥarām, this mosque of mine, and al-Masjid al-Aqṣā',[38] in order to justify the religio-political policies of the Caliph ᶜAbd al-Malik (r. 65–86/685–705), who wished to substitute Qubbat al-Ṣakhrah for the Kaᶜbah as a pilgrimage site in order to prevent pilgrims from paying homage to the counter-Caliph ᶜAbd Allāh ibn al-Zubayr (d. 73/692) in Mecca. Koçyiğit argues that the notion that al-Zuhrī fabricated the hadith towards this end is not actually stated in Goldziher's source, al-Yaᶜqūbī's (d. after 292/905) *Tārīkh*, but is rather a speculative inference.[39] He also points out that the entire report may be little more than an anti-Umayyad polemic since al-Yaᶜqūbī was a Shiᶜi and the report is not corroborated in any other source.[40] Furthermore, Koçyiğit makes reference to a report in al-Dhahabī's (d. 748/1348) *Tadhkirat al-huffāẓ* stating that al-Zuhrī only met with ᶜAbd al-Malik in the year 80/699–700, several years after the Second Civil War (60–73/680–692) between ᶜAbd Allāh ibn al-Zubayr and the Umayyads.[41] Koçyiğit concludes his article by advocating an approach to Western hadith studies that would combine cautious awareness with a sense of distinct academic and confessional communities: 'Whatever the outcome of an Orientalist's studies about our own issues, we must receive it with caution. Of course, we will be aware of their studies, but we will not forget that we have to deal with our own issues by ourselves either.'[42]

The approach of Okiç's other student, Mehmed Said Hatiboğlu, to Western hadith studies is substantially different from that of Koçyiğit. Indeed, his dissertation, titled *İslami Tenkid Zihniyeti ve Hadis Tenkidinin Doğuşu* ('Critical Islamic Thought and the Birth of Hadith Criticism'),[43] follows the main arguments of Goldziher concerning the reflection of Islam's early political conflicts in the hadith tradition.[44] This was especially the case with respect to traditions in the genres of future tribulations (*fitan*) and Portents of the Last Hour (*ashrāṭ al-sāᶜah*), concerning which he wrote, 'It can be accepted that the atmosphere of terror created among Muslims by the events after the death of the Prophet gave rise to the majority of the material in this genre, especially that included under the topics of *fitan* and *ashrāṭ al- sāᶜah*.'[45]

In his dissertation, Hatiboğlu also refers to works of Sprenger, Caetani, Goldziher, Henri Lammens[46] and Duncan Black Macdonald (d. 1943), and quotes their views. He voices criticism against those scholars only in a limited number of instances.[47] However, in a later paper, Hatiboğlu also accused luminaries of Orientalist scholarship like Snouck Hurgronje (d. 1936) and Joseph Schacht (d. 1969) of engaging in arbitrary and far-fetched interpretations of their sources, arguing that it is necessary to check their original sources because of their biases. Nonetheless, these criticisms are on the whole eclipsed by his generally favourable approach towards Western scholars, especially Goldziher.[48]

The broad category of *fitan* traditions continued to be a subject of Hatiboğlu's studies. In his 1967 habilitation book *Hazreti Peygamber'in (s.a.v) Vefatından Emevilerin Sonuna Kadar Siyasi İçtimai Hadiselerle Hadis Münasebetleri* ('Relation of Hadith to Sociopolitical Events from the Death of the Prophet until the End of Umayyads') he argued again that the Prophet cannot be the source of *fitan* traditions.[49] In this work and others, we see that Hatiboğlu's rejection of the authenticity of these traditions is part of a larger theological project. Echoing a debate that has reverberated in modernist circles since the nineteenth century,[50] he takes the position that the Prophet did not receive any revelation outside of the Qurʾān and rejects the notion of 'non-recited revelation' (*waḥy ghayr matlūw*), which constituted the classical theological foundation for the authority of the Sunnah.[51]

'Critical Islamic thought', the main theme of Hatiboğlu's dissertation, would also become the driving force in his future studies and scholarship. He has continued to promote the critical revaluation of Islamic sources until today and has influenced a number of modernist scholars who would later gather around forums and institutions such as the journal *İslamiyat* (1998–2007) and two publishing houses known as Kitabiyat[52] (1997–2009) and Ankara Okulu Yayınları (1995–).[53] These scholars have focused on the critical re-valuation of classical Islamic scholarship as a whole and not just hadith studies, but nonetheless played a key role in the heated debates over hadith literature that became prominent during the 1990s when scholars from both the traditional and modernist camps came together in a series of symposiums.

Another important scholar connected to the Faculty of Theology in Ankara was Fuad Sezgin. Although Sezgin had worked under the supervision of Hellmut Ritter (d. 1971) until 1949 and spent most of his academic life in Istanbul, he worked at the Faculty of Theology in Ankara in 1951–3. In addition, as was mentioned above, Tayyib Okiç was among the committee members who accepted Sezgin's habilitation in 1954. In his habilitation, *Buhârî'nin Kaynakları*, Sezgin refuted the chronology given by Goldziher for the collection of traditions and emphasised the continuous written transmission of hadiths.[54] *Buhârî'nin Kaynakları* would become a respected but also neglected work over the subsequent years in Turkey.[55] In fact, after its first publication in 1956, the second edition was published only in 2001. One of the main reasons for this was that Sezgin left for Germany in 1961 after he was removed from his position at the university due to the military coup of 1960.

In the latter half of the twentieth century, the Faculty of Theology in Ankara trained a generation of scholars who followed developments in Western hadith studies. During this period, translations from Orientalists were published in the faculty journal *Ankara Üniversitesi İlâhiyat Fakültesi Dergisi*. In addition, books by scholars like Julius Wellhausen (d. 1918), Goldziher, Schacht and William Montgomery Watt (d. 2006) were translated into Turkish and published by the faculty press.[56]

Hadith Scholars and Orientalism in Faculties of Theology after the 2000s

Parallel to the continued engagement with Western scholarship in Ankara, the field of higher religious education diversified significantly with the opening of the so-called Higher Institutes of Islam (*Yüksek İslam Enstitüleri*) between 1959 and 1982. These institutes were opened specifically for the graduates of *imam-hatip* schools since the Faculty of Theology in Ankara accepted students only from regular high schools.[57] Unlike the faculty, these institutes followed a curriculum focusing mostly on classical Islamic texts and pedagogical formation. However, in 1982, the institutes were transformed into faculties of theology and started to follow a common curriculum similar to that of the Faculty of Theology in Ankara. After the transformation of the institutes into faculties of theology, the total number of faculties increased to eight, and fifteen new faculties were opened between 1988 and 2008. At the beginning of the fall semester, 2017, there were eighty-one faculties of theology that accepted students.[58]

This transformation in the overall landscape of higher Islamic education has had a significant and varied impact on the academic study of hadith. On the one hand, the increase in the number of programmes for higher education in Islamic Studies has gone hand in hand with significant growth in the number of academic studies of hadith and other topics within Islamic Studies. As for hadith studies, twelve theses were completed in the 1970s, sixty-seven theses in the 1980s, 304 in the 1990s and 505 in the first decade of the new millennium.[59] On the other hand, the opening of these new faculties also arguably led to a dilution in the presence and significance of Western studies on hadith in the broad sphere of the Turkish academy. The majority of the new theses completed since the 1970s focus either on the authority and authenticity of the Sunnah or on issues defined within the framework of classical hadith scholarship.[60] Thus, a recent review of theses on hadith completed through 2015 includes the relationship between Orientalism and hadith among the understudied subjects in the Turkish academy that require more attention.[61]

There has been, in fact, a small but perceptible increase in engagement with Western hadith studies in the faculties of theology in the past twenty years. This interest is reflected in part in the considerable increase in the number of translations from Western scholars, such as Josef Horovitz, Schacht, Alfred Guillaume (d. 1965), James Robson, Meir Jacob Kister (d. 2010), G. H. A. Juynboll (d. 2010), Harald Motzki (d. 2019) and Gregor Schoeler. It is also reflected in recent doctoral research. A number of dissertations have been written specifically on Western hadith studies, while many others are also shaped by current debates in Western scholarship in terms of their selection of subject matter. One of the most prominent examples of the dissertations responding to Western hadith studies is Bekir Kuzudişli's *Hadis Rivâyetinde Aile İsnadları* ('Family *Isnāds* in Hadith Transmission'), completed in 2005. Kuzudişli endeavoured to refute Schacht's claim that family *isnād*s were fabricated, arguing that such *isnād*s emerged because written documents were kept within the family as souvenirs and handed down to the following generation.[62] He also objected to Schacht's argument that family *isnād*s were not 'an indication of authenticity but only a device for securing its appearance'[63] by pointing out that hadith scholars did in fact criticise hadiths transmitted through family *isnād*s.[64]

Another dissertation about Western hadith studies is my own *Hukukî İçerikli Merfû Hadisler Bağlamında Müşterek Râvî Teorisi ve Tenkidi* ('Critique of Common-Link Theory Based on Legal *marfū*ᶜ *aḥādīth*'), completed in 2011.[65] In this dissertation, I compare Schacht and Juynboll's application of the common-link theory with Harald Motzki's interpretation while employing a case study to shed light on a variety of assertions connected with the common-link theory, such as the material growth of traditions, backward projection, gradual improvement of *isnād*s and the spread of *isnād*s. I apply the method of *isnād-cum-matn* analysis as developed by Motzki to a selected hadith cluster, but, unlike Motzki, while checking variants with each other,

I give the evaluation and judgements of hadith critics about transmitters' reliability a decisive role. In the end, I argue that *isnād-cum-matn* analysis, as applied in the dissertation, is an improved continuation of the *muᶜāraḍah* method discussed in classical hadith scholarship.[66]

The common-link theory and other methods of dating traditions is also the subject of Süleyman Doğanay's habilitation titled *Oryantalistlerin Hadisleri Tarihlendirmeye Yaklaşımları* ('Orientalists' Approach to Dating of Traditions', 2013).[67] The author is critical of Western scholars' methods of dating hadiths throughout the book and offers several case-by-case refutations of their claims. After the description of the methods, Doğanay reaches the conclusion that Orientalists' approaches are biased and overly sceptical.[68]

Despite this recent trend towards increased engagement with Western scholarship, the majority of dissertations still discuss only Turkish studies and primary and secondary Arabic sources in the compulsory section of the literature review. Goldziher continues to be the first name that comes to mind when one mentions Orientalism and the most well-known scholars after Goldziher are G. H. A. Juynboll and Harald Motzki.[69] The works engaging Western scholarship surveyed here serve only as representative examples of a larger body of literature that shares the tendency to emphasise the biases of Orientalist studies, their misuse of evidence and their overlooking of important information that does not support their arguments.[70] Academics who offer a more positive appraisal of Orientalist works are generally labelled by traditionalists as modernists, rendering Western hadith studies a powerful symbolic weapon in the debates over the authority and authenticity of hadith.

Scholarly Camps and Topics of Discussion

Debates over the authority and authenticity of hadith in Turkey have given rise to three main trends in scholarship: Istanbul-based traditionalists; Ankara-based modernists; and finally *Kur'ancılar* (*Ahl al-Qurʾān*).[71] The main issues at stake in the debates among these three trends can be summed up as the status of Sunnah in Islam, the authenticity of hadiths and, lastly, how to correctly understand the Sunnah in the modern world. While there are no hadith scholars among *Kur'ancılar*, the first two groups consist of academics specialising in hadith. Today, in different cities of Turkey, scholars from both camps work together at the same faculties. Even though the distinction between Istanbul and Ankara serves primarily as a synecdoche for the Faculty of Theology at Marmara (formerly Istanbul Higher Institute of Islam) and Ankara University, respectively, in the end, it denotes the approaches taken by individual scholars and not necessarily their geographical locations. The designation *Tarihselci* ('historicalists')[72] is often used by traditionalists as an umbrella label to describe their opponents. In particular, the term is used to refer to those scholars who argue that rulings and regulations in the Qurʾān and Sunnah are not universal but limited to the historical period and circumstances of the first Islamic community. It thus occurs mostly in the discussions of scholars of *tafsīr* and Islamic law. Fazlur Rahman and Naṣr Ḥāmid Abū Zayd (d. 2010) are the authorities appealed to most frequently by Turkish scholars on this issue. It seems that this fact, in addition to the translation and publication of Fazlur Rahman's (d. 1988) books by the Ankara Okulu publishing house, have played a role in the generalisation of the designation to include all progressive scholars in spite of the significant differences among them.

The *Kur'ancılar* (*ahl al-Qurʾān*) consist primarily of *tafsīr* scholars.[73] Technically speaking, this group does not reject the Sunnah completely.[74] Their criterion for accepting Sunnah is that it should be corroborated by the Qurʾān, which leads to the rejection of the great bulk of the Sunnah but not the rejection of Sunnah as such. Although this camp accepts the Sunnah of the Prophet as the best example in principle, they do not specify either its scope or how this example could be materialised in daily life.[75] Other trends have been more concerned with specifying the limits and scope of the Sunnah. For both traditionalists and modernists, the debate about the authority of the Sunnah has centred on parsing the different roles played by the Prophet and determining the normative implications of his actions in each of those roles. They discuss the extent to which it is possible to separate his Prophetic role from other, mundane roles; whether all of his actions should be considered to be based on non-recited revelation; and what these distinctions mean in terms of the binding nature and universal applicability of the Sunnah.

In the debates over hadith, the questions of authenticity and interpretation are intertwined partly because of perceptions of dissonance between the standards and expectations of the modern world and the Prophet's orders and practices. A case in point is how the three trends discuss the relationship between modern and Prophetic medicine. Scholars who adopt a critical perspective dismiss those hadiths that clash with principles of modern medicine because they reject the possibility of the Prophet's saying something that conflicts with reason or modern science. On the other hand, some modernists, mainly 'historicalists', regard such hadiths as authentic but understand them as the result of the Prophet's human and hence historical knowledge instead of universal and transcendental revelation. Rejecting both perspectives, most of the traditionalists, in turn, believe that the Prophetic medicine has miraculous attributes yet to be discovered by modern science. The views of classical scholars are treated as a repository of material that is drawn on selectively in order to challenge the opposing sides and accuse them of abandoning the Sunnah or the spirit of the Sunnah. While traditionalists argue that rejecting the hadiths regarded as authentic by previous generations will pave the way to abandoning Sunnah altogether, modernists accuse them of not understanding the Prophet or his mission, and hence accepting the hadiths reporting words or deeds that he could not have said or done. Therefore, debates around the authenticity and understanding of the traditions are inextricably bound up with the question of the authority of the Prophet and his Sunnah.

Critical scholars like Mehmet Emin Özafşar, Professor of Hadith at the Faculty of Theology in Ankara, emphasise that hadiths should not be viewed as the words, deeds and tacit approvals of the Prophet, but rather as words, deeds and tacit approvals that have been attributed to him.[76] According to Özafşar, the reflexive identification of transmitted reports with the Prophet leads to emotional reactions against critical attitudes towards hadith, and hence hinders rational argumentation.[77]

For critical scholars, the notion that content criticism is necessary goes hand in hand with the conviction that *isnād* criticism alone is insufficient to determine the authenticity of a hadith. These scholars have discussed the methods of content criticism extensively, which is referred to in Turkish by the term '*arz*', meaning comparison of the contents of a hadith with the Qurʾān, well-established Sunnah, reason, historical facts and the hard sciences. As a matter of fact, each of these types of *arz* was treated in distinct doctoral dissertations between 1997 and 2008.

The occurrence of a significant number of traditions in the *Ṣaḥīḥayn* criticised by the modernists on the basis of content criticism also gave rise to discussions about the reliability of these two canonical sources. A paper on the reliability of the *Ṣaḥīḥayn* by Yaşar Kandemir,[78] one of the leading scholars of the traditionalists, and its review by Mehmed Said Hatiboğlu can be described as the emblematic works in which the positions of the two opposing camps became crystallised.[79]

Lastly, Hayri Kırbaşoğlu merits mention as the most vocal and prolific author among critical scholars. His 1995 paper consists of a summary of the main arguments of critical scholars.[80] In this paper, Kırbaşoğlu defends the re-valuation of traditions, and prefers the designation 'progressive' instead of 'modernist'.[81] He states that viewing progressive scholarship as a direct result of Orientalists' influence leads to ignoring the problems originating from the hadith literature itself. Kırbaşoğlu also argues against the acceptance of the classical science of hadith criticism as the final method that cannot be criticised or changed.[82]

In 2002, Kırbaşoğlu published his *Alternatif Hadis Metodolojisi* ('Alternative Methodology of Hadith'), which drew on the results of the theses he had supervised over the years.[83] His main focus in the book was dogmatic traditions that he regarded as either later fabrications or distortions, mostly on the basis of the *argumentum e silentio*.[84] For example, he reached the conclusion that the so-called hadith of Jibrīl[85] was not known or not taken seriously by most of the hadith scholars in the first centuries or was regarded as fabricated based on its absence from sources such as Maᶜmar ibn Rāshid (d. 153/770?), *al-Jāmiᶜ*, Mālik (d. 179/795), *al-Muwattaʾ*, and ᶜAbd al-Razzāq (d. 211/827), *al-Muṣannaf*.[86] Having insisted on the importance of content criticism, Kırbaşoğlu argued that this method was used by the leading companions, the Muᶜtazilah, and also several *mujtahids*, including Abū Ḥanīfah.[87] But, according to him, this method was forgotten due to 'the hegemony of the classical science of hadith based on the *ahl al-ḥadīth*/Shāfiᶜī school'.[88] The work of Kırbaşoğlu, along with other scholars at the Faculty of Theology in Ankara, demonstrates the lasting influence of Mehmet Said Hatiboğlu within the school of Ankara (*Ankara Okulu*).[89]

Conclusion

The first Turkish translation from Western studies of Islam, Dozy's *De Voornaamste Godsdienste: Het Islamisme*, was published in the late Ottoman era. In the Republican era, another work, Caetani's *Annali dell'Islam* was translated into Turkish. While the intellectuals of the Ottoman and Republican eras accepted the necessity of Westernisation in varying degrees, they have taken a critical stance against Orientalists' works since the first translations. The first exception to this critical position was Zakir Kadiri Ugan, who voiced views similar to those of Orientalists about several important aspects of hadith literature. Although his scholarship was not as receptive as that of Ugan, Mehmed Said Hatiboğlu, one of the first-generation hadith scholars of the Republican era, was another exception. Hatiboğlu based his dissertation and habilitation on Goldziher's main thesis about the relation of hadiths to political events of the first two Islamic centuries. On the other hand, Talât Koçyiğit, Hatiboğlu's colleague at the Faculty of Theology in Ankara and the author of the first Turkish dissertation on hadith, remained critical of Western hadith scholarship, and it is still the prevalent attitude among Turkish scholars towards Orientalists' works.

Western hadith studies also have a role in the debates between traditionalist and progressive/modernist hadith scholars. Departure from the prevalent critical attitude against Orientalism is generally associated with Islamic modernism. Even though they might not be as fervent as in the 1990s, debates between traditionalist and modernist hadith scholars continue to be a driving force of academic debate in the field of Islamic Studies in Turkey, mostly because all parties consider defending their position is not just an academic but also a religious duty. The modernists devote nearly all of their attention to collecting problematic material that would justify revisiting the traditions accepted as authentic by scholars of previous generations. Traditionalists, in turn, not only dedicate most of their time to answering or explaining away the questions and criticisms voiced by the modernists, but also deny justified criticisms in order to avoid strengthening the position of their opponents. It seems that primary responsibility for breaking this vicious circle lies with the critical scholars. If they take a revisionist approach to the sources and compose their hadith collections using the new methods they propose in place of classical hadith criticism, it might lead to a more honest discussion between both parties. But it should be noted that sorting through the traditions would inevitably lead to a new *fiqh* and theology as well. Maybe this is why critical scholars in Turkey are unwilling to carry out their proposals.

As for Western influence on modern hadith debates in Turkey, this influence took the form of a major shift in the worldview especially due to Westernisation of the Second Constitutional Period in which Westernisation of the Republic of Turkey also had its origins. Turkish hadith scholars were inevitably affected by this transformation. On the other hand, it is difficult to determine any direct influence of Western hadith studies except for Zakir Kadiri Ugan and Mehmet Said Hatiboğlu's scholarship. Rather, it could be said that modern hadith discussions in Turkey have always been more of an extension of those in the Indian subcontinent and Egypt, turning progressive hadith scholarship of Turkish academics into a second-hand Islamic modernism.

Notes

1. On Atatürk's (d. 1938) policy of *Garblılaşma*, see Mustafa Kemal Atatürk, *Atatürk'ün Söylev ve Demeçleri*, 3 vols (Ankara: Atatürk Araştırma Merkezi Yayınları, 1997), 3:91.
2. Turkey's first step towards laicism was the exclusion of the sentence 'The religion of the state is Islam' from the Constitution in 1928. Afterwards, in 1937, the principle of laicism was added to the Constitution. The language reforms adopted consisted of purifying Turkish of loanwords and adopting the Latin alphabet instead of the Ottoman Turkish.
3. Şükrü Hanioğlu emphasises the difference between the *Garbcılık* of the Second Constitutional and Republican periods and a more general process of Westernisation, which started as early as the reign of Selim III (r. 1789–1807). See M. Şükrü Hanioğlu, 'II. Meşrutiyet Dönemi 'Garbcılığı'nın Kavramsallaştırılmasındaki Üç Temel Sorun Üzerine Not', *Doğu Batı Düşünce Dergisi* 31 (2005): 55–64, at 57.
4. M. Şükrü Hanioğlu, *A Brief History of the Late Ottoman Empire* (Princeton, NJ: Princeton University Press, 2008), 138.
5. Kılıçzâde was born in Niş (today's Niš in Serbia) and studied in *Mühendishâne-i Berrî-i Hümâyun*, an engineering school that educated engineer and artillery officers. In the Ottoman era, materialism and positivism were prevalent among students of *Mühendishaneler* (engineering schools) and *Tıbbiyeler* (medical schools). Almost all the prominent figures among the so-called *Garbcılar* (Westernisers) were graduates of these institutions. For Kılıçzâde's life and views, see Celal Pekdoğan, 'Kılıçzâde Hakkı', in *TDV İslâm Ansiklopedisi*, 44 vols (İstanbul: Türkiye Diyanet Vakfı, 1988–2013), 25: 415–16.
6. See Hanioğlu, *Brief History*, 185.
7. Halil İnalcık, 'II. Meşrutiyet', *Doğu Batı Düşünce Dergisi* 45 (2008): 11–16, at 13. Most of the intellectuals of the late Ottoman period spoke French as a foreign language. This continued in the Republican era; for example, Fuad Köprülü (1890–1966), who was among the graduates of *idadi*s during the Second Constitutional Period and later minister of foreign affairs in the Republican era, gave his speech in French at the twenty-second International Congress of Orientalists (R. N. Dandekar, 'The Twenty-Second International Congress of Orientalists, Istanbul,

15th–22nd September, 1951', *Annals of the Bhandarkar Oriental Research Institute* 32(1) (1951): i–xxiv, at vii). In one of his interviews, Atatürk also acknowledged French influence on the Ottoman intellectuals by saying 'We all had drunk from the spring of French culture.' See Atatürk, *Atatürk'ün Söylev* 3:89–90.

8. İbrahim Hatiboğlu argued that in the *Dârülfünûn* Muslims learned to look at Islamic issues as 'outsiders' (İbrahim Hatiboğlu, 'Transmission of Western Hadīth Critique to Turkey: On the Past and the Future of Academic Hadīth Studies', *Hadis Tetkikleri Dergisi* 4(2) (2006): 37–53, at 40). This is, however, a simplistic presentation of the issue. For example, the Branch and madrasas of *Dârü'l-Hilâfe* both followed a similar curriculum (Halis Ayhan, *Türkiye'de Din Eğitimi* (İstanbul: Marmara Üniversiteis İlahiyat Fakültesi Vafkı Yayınları, 1999), 39).
9. İsmail Hakkı Baltacıoğlu (d. 1978), the Chancellor of *Dârülfünûn*, described the faculty as 'some kind of faculty of sociology' (M. Ali Kirman, 'Türk Modernleşmesi ve Yüksek Din Eğitimi', in Tahsin Özcan et al. (eds), *Darülfünun İlahiyat Sempozyumu 18–19 Kasım 2009 Tebliğleri* (İstanbul: İstanbul Üniversitesi İlahiyat Fakültesi, 2010), 58).
10. In Turkey, 'Faculty of Divinity' and 'Faculty of Theology' are used interchangeably. I have used the latter exclusively, although some faculties prefer 'Faculty of Divinity' on their websites.
11. In his speech on re-opening of the Faculty of Theology in 1949, Baltacıoğlu admitted that mistakes had been made in 1924 for political reasons and emphasised the importance of religious formation for character-building (Ayhan, *Türkiye'de Din*, 21). Today, most vocal critics of faculties of theology are preachers and their followers outside the academy. Sometimes, these preachers publicly enter into polemics with various academics, mostly using social media.
12. While some of these faculty graduates continue their studies at the post-graduate level and become faculty members, most of the graduates work as teachers of religion (a compulsory course in the last year of elementary school, and throughout secondary and high school), imams (only male students) or preachers (both male and female students) under the Directorate of Religious Affairs.
13. Those who criticise the faculties of theology on the grounds that they are not the continuation of madrasas do not propose any viable alternative. Since they were officially closed in the Republican era, the madrasas continued their activities 'underground', especially in the eastern part of Turkey. Their relative lack of formal organisation prevents them from taking the necessary steps to improve their curricula.
14. İzmirli İsmail Hakkı, *Hadis Tarihi* (İstanbul: Darülhadis, 2002), 283. This course was also taught by Arapkirli Hüseyin Avni (d. 1954).
15. For example, see Mehmet Emin Özafşar, 'Hadisin Neliği Sorunu ve Akademik Hadisçilik', *İslâmîyât* 9(1–4) (2006): 147–66, at 158–9; Hatiboğlu, 'Transmission of Western Hadīth Critique to Turkey', 41ff.
16. See İzmirli, *Hadis Tarihi*, pp. 281–3. İzmirli, for his part, states at the end of his book that the subjects of hadith and history of hadith are the same and that the only difference between them is their classification of the same subject according to topics or periods, respectively.

17. Those who study the intellectual history of the late Ottoman Empire classify intellectuals of this era according to their political–religious positions as Ottomanists, Westernisers, Islamists and Turkists. See İsmail Kara, *Din ile Modernleşme Arasında Çağdaş Türk Düşüncesinin Meseleleri* (İstanbul: Dergah Yayınları, 2012), 39. The Islamists or Islamic revivalists believed that the way of saving the empire was through religious revival. They criticised the radical Westernisation and the materialist scientism of the likes of Bahâ Tevfik (d. 1914) and Abdullah Cevdet (d. 1932), but also argued for the necessity of modernisation in religious disciplines. On İzmirli's views in particular, see M. Sait Özervarlı, 'Alternative Approaches to Modernization in the Late Ottoman Period: İzmirli İsmail Hakkı's Religious Thought against Materialist Scientism', *International Journal of Middle East Studies* 39 (2007): 77–102.
18. Ali Birinci, 'İzmirli, İsmail Hakkı', in *TDV İslâm Ansiklopedisi* (İstanbul: Türkiye Diyanet Vakfı, 2001), 23:530–3, at 531. Because Dozy's *Het Islamisme* and Caetani's *Annali dell'Islam* were translated into Turkish in 1908 and 1924–7, respectively, Dozy and Caetani were among the most well-known Orientalists in that period, for which, see M. Şükrü Hanioğlu, 'Garbcılar: Their Attitudes toward Religion and Their Impact on the Official Ideology of Turkish Republic', *Studia Islamica* 86 (1997): 133–58, at 139.
19. Ahmed ez-Zebîdî, *Sahîh-i Buhârî Muhtasarı Tecrîd-i Sarîh Tercemesi ve Şerhi*, trans. Ahmed Naim and Kâmil Miras, 12 vols (Ankara: Diyanet İşleri Başkanlığı Yayınları, 1976). The first edition was published 1928–48. Kâmil Miras (d. 1957), the translator of the remaining volumes, revised the drafts of the third volume completed by Ahmed Naim after the latter's death.
20. ez-Zebîdî, *Sahîh-i Buhârî Muhtasarı* 1:74ff.
21. Zakir Kadiri Ugan, 'Dinî Rivâyetler', *İstanbul Üniversitesi İlahiyat Fakültesi Dergisi* 4 (2002): 207–57, at 221–2, 241. For an attenuation of this claim see Jonathan A. C. Brown, 'How We Know Early Ḥadīth Critics Did *Matn* Criticism and Why It's So Hard to Find', *Islamic Law and Society* 15 (2008): 143–84. Brown suggests that the term 'content criticism' more accurately captures the type of analysis intended by Western scholars than 'textual criticism'.
22. For Aḥmad Amīn and Abū Rayyah's views on *matn* criticism see Aḥmad Amīn, *Fajr al-Islām* (Beirut: Dār al-Kutub al-ᶜArabī, 1969), 217ff; Maḥmūd Abū Rayyah, *Adwāʾ ᶜalá al-sunnah al-muḥammadīyah* (Cairo: Dār al-Maᶜārif, n.d.), 258, 262–5. See also G. H. A. Juynboll, *The Authenticity of the Tradition Literature: Discussions in Modern Egypt* (Leiden: Brill, 1969), 43.
23. Ugan, 'Dinî Rivâyetler', 241, 243. For Abū Rayyah's criticisms of the doctrine of the collective probity of the Companions and of Abū Hurayrah, see *Adwāʾ*, 180–3, 312ff.
24. Ugan, 'Dinî Rivâyetler', 248.
25. Ahmed Hamdi Akseki, 'Dinî Müesseseler ve Din Eğitiminin Meselelerine Dair Rapor', in İsmail Kara (ed.), *Türkiye'de İslâmcılık Düşüncesi: Metinler Kişiler*, 3 vols (İstanbul: Kitabevi, 1997), 2:378. The fact that graduates of *imam-hatip* (high schools with extra courses on Islamic sciences) were not accepted to the Faculty shows that its primary purpose was not to train the clergy. For the

higher religious education of the graduates of *imam-hatip* schools, Yüksek İslam Enstitüleri (Higher Institutes of Islam) were established between 1959 and 1982. In 1982, all the institutes were transformed into faculties of theology.

26. İbrahim Hatiboğlu, 'Okiç, Muhammed Tayyib', in *TDV İslâm Ansiklopedisi*, 44 vols (İstanbul: Türkiye Diyanet Vakfı, 1988–2013), 33:336–8, at 337.
27. E.g., see Tayyib Okiç, *Bazı Hadis Meseleleri Üzerine Tetkikler* (İstanbul: Ankara Üniversitesi İlahiyat Fakültesi Yayınları, 1959), 5–6, 8–10, 28, 32–3.
28. Okiç, *Bazı Hadis*, 6.
29. Okiç, *Bazı Hadis*, 9.
30. İbrahim Hatiboğlu, 'M. Said Hatiboğlu ile M. Tayyib Okiç'in İlmi Kişiliği ve Tesirleri Üzerine', *Hadis Tetkikleri Dergisi* 5(2) (2007): 169–82, at 176.
31. In order of translation dates, these articles are 'The Transmission of Muslim's *Ṣaḥīh*', *Ankara Üniversitesi İlâhiyat Fakültesi Dergisi* 4(3/4) (1955): 8–20; 'The Transmission of Abū Dāwūd's *Sunan*', *Ankara Üniversitesi İlâhiyat Fakültesi Dergisi* 5(1–4) (1958): 173–82; 'Ibn Isḥāq's Use of the *Isnād*', *Ankara Üniversitesi İlâhiyat Fakültesi Dergisi* 10 (1962): 117–26; and 'Varieties of *Hasan* Tradition', *Ankara Üniversitesi İlâhiyat Fakültesi Dergisi* 11 (1963): 109–18.
32. Talât Koçyiğit, 'I. Goldziher'in Hadisle İlgili Bazı Görüşlerinin Tahlil ve Tenkidi', *Ankara Üniversitesi İlâhiyat Fakültesi Dergisi* 15 (1967): 43–55. Talât Koçyiğit's dissertation was *Hadislerin Toplanması ve Yazıyla Tespiti* ('Collection and Writing down of Traditions'). Koçyiğit, who worked in various positions at the faculty until his retirement, played a great role in the standardisation of hadith terminology in Turkish with his books on the history of hadith and hadith methodology. He maintained his traditionalist position in the Department of Hadith at the Faculty of Theology in Ankara, which is labelled as modernist by its traditionalist opponents.
33. In his article titled 'İslâm Hadisinde İsnad ve Hadis Râvilerinin Cerhi' ('*Isnād* in Islamic Tradition and Criticism of Hadith Transmitters'), Koçyiğit also objects to the chronology of *isnād*s given by Joseph Schacht and argues that the *fitnah* in Ibn Sīrīn's famous statement about the origins of the *isnād* is the Second Civil War (60–73/680–92). See Talât Koçyiğit, 'İslâm Hadisinde İsnad ve Hadis Râvilerinin Cerhi', *Ankara Üniversitesi İlâhiyat Fakültesi Dergisi* 9 (1961): 47–57, at 50.
34. Koçyiğit, 'I. Goldziher'in Hadisle', 43.
35. For this report, see Muḥammad ibn Jarīr al-Ṭabarī, *Tārīkh al-rusūl wa-al-mulūk*, ed. Muḥammad Abū al-Faḍl Ibrāhīm, Dhakhāʾir al-ʿArab 30, 11 vols (Cairo: Dār al-Maʿārif, 1960–77), 5:253–4, s.a. 51. For the translation, see *History of al-Ṭabarī, vol. 18: Between Civil Wars: The Caliphate of Muʿāwiyah* A.D. *661–680/*A.H. *40–60*, trans. Michael G. Morony, Bibliotheca Persica and SUNY Series in Near Eastern Studies (Albany, NY: State University of New York Press, 1987), 123.
36. Ignaz Goldziher, *Muslim Studies*, ed. S. M. Stern, trans. S. M. Stern and G. R. Barber, 2 vols (London: Allen & Unwin, 1971), 2:44.
37. Koçyiğit, 'I. Goldziher'in Hadisle', 46.
38. For the narrations coming from Zuhrī in the pre-canonical sources, see ʿAbd al-Razzāq b. Hammām al-Ṣanʿānī, *al-Muṣannaf*, ed. Ḥabīb al-Raḥmān al-ʿAzamī, 10 vols (Beirut: al-Majlis al-ʿIlmī, 1392/1972), 5:132, No. 9158; Abū Bakr ibn

ʿAbd Allāh ibn al-Zubayr al-Ḥumaydī, *al-Musnad*, ed. Ḥusayn Salīm Asad, 2 vols (Damascus: Dār al-Saqā, 1996), 2:181, No. 973; Abū Bakr ʿAbd Allāh ibn Muḥammad ibn Ibrāhīm Ibn Abī Shaybah, *al-Muṣannaf*, ed. Kamāl Yūsuf al-Ḥūt, 7 vols (Beirut: Dār al-Tāj, 1409/1989), 3:418–19; Aḥmad ibn Ḥanbal, *al-Musnad*, ed. Shuʿayb al-Arnaʾūṭ et al. (Beirut: Muʾassasat al-Risālah, 1416–21/1995–2001), 12:116, 191, also 13:165. For narrations in *al-kutub al-sittah*, see al-Bukhārī, *Ṣaḥīḥ*, *faḍl al-ṣalāh fī masjid Makkah wa-al-Madīnah* 1, *bāb faḍl al-ṣalāh fī masjid Makkah wa-al-Madīnahi*, No. 1189; Muslim, *Ṣaḥīḥ*, *al-ḥajj* 95, *bāb lā tushaddu al-riḥāl illā ilā thalāthat masājīd*, No. 511; Abū Dāwūd, *Sunan*, *al-manāsik* 94, *bāb ityān al-Madīna*, No. 2026; al-Nasāʾī, *Mujtabá*, *al-masājid* 10, *bāb mā tushaddu al-riḥāl ilayhi min al-masājid*, No. 700; Ibn Mājah, *Sunan*, *iqāmat al-ṣalāh* 196, *bāb mā jāʾa fī al-ṣalāh fī masjid Bayt al-Maqdīs*, No. 1409.

39. In the edition of *al-Tārīkh* (ed. M. T. Houtsma, 2 vols [Leiden: Brill, 1883], 2: 311) used by Goldziher, it is said that ʿAbd al-Malik had prevented the people of al-Shām from visiting Mecca because of ʿAbd Allāh ibn al-Zubayr. It is also reported that upon the people's protest, ʿAbd al-Malik said: 'Here! Ibn Shihāb transmits to you that the Prophet of God said, "Do not set out on a journey except for three mosques: al-Masjid al-Ḥarām, the *masjid* of mine, and Bayt al-Maqdis." Bayt al-Maqdis serves as the substitute to you for al-Masjid al-Ḥarām. And this rock which the Prophet is reported to have set his foot on while ascending to Heaven also substitutes for the Kaʿba.'
40. Koçyiğit, 'I. Goldziher'in Hadisle', 50. Koçyiğit's arguments parallel those of other Western scholars. S. M. Stern, the editor and co-translator of *Muhammedanische Studien*, describes this report as an 'anti-Umayyad invention': 'There is no doubt that in this extreme form, according to which ʿAbd al-Malik intended to substitute the pilgrimage to Jerusalem for the *ḥajj*, the tradition is an anti-Umayyad invention; yet it is not impossible that the Umayyads had a share in the propagation of traditions supporting the holiness of Jerusalem' (Goldziher, *Muslim Studies* 2:45). For Goitein's refutation of Goldziher's claim, see S. D. Goitein and O. Grabar, 'al-Ḳuds', in P. Bearman et al. (eds), *Encyclopaedia of Islam*, new edition (Leiden: Brill, 1960–2004), 5:325.
41. Al-Dhahabī, *Tadhkirat al-ḥuffāẓ*, 4 vols (Beirut: Dār al-Kutub al-ʿIlmīyah, n.d.), 1:109ff. Muṣṭafá al-Sibāʿī (d. 1964) refuted Goldziher's claims about al-Zuhrī using similar arguments. See Juynboll, *Authenticity of the Tradition Literature*, 109–12.
42. Koçyiğit, 'I. Goldziher'in Hadisle', 55.
43. The dissertation, completed in 1962, was published for the first time in 2015. See Mehmed Said Hatiboğlu, *İslami Tenkid Zihniyeti* (Ankara: Otto, 2016).
44. Hatiboğlu's translation of the second volume of *Muhammedanische Studien*, based on its French edition, has been published (Ankara: Otto, 2019).
45. Hatiboğlu, *İslami Tenkid Zihniyeti*, 60. He revised his view in his recent book as follows: 'The evidence we give from Qurʾān and *Sunna*, naturally, will lead us to the conclusion of regarding the reports about future events not mentioned in the Qurʾān as inauthentic' (Mehmed Said Hatiboğlu, *Hz. Peygamber ve Kur'an Dışı Vahiy* (Ankara: Otto, 2017), 157).

46. Hatiboğlu describes Lammens as a 'fierce enemy of Islam' (Hatiboğlu, *İslami*, 34).
47. He rejects Henri Lammens' claim that ᶜUmar (d. 23/644) ordered the murder of Saᶜd ibn ᶜUbādah (d. 14/635) (*İslami*, 35) and Goldziher's well-known argument that Muslims did not consider *mutūn* in their hadith criticism (*İslami*, 112, 134). He also states that *isnād* criticism started well before Goldziher assumed (ibid., 113). According to Hatiboğlu, *isnād* criticism must have started well before the time Ibn Sīrīn (d. 110/729) began to narrate hadiths since he said 'they' instead of 'we' in his well-known saying 'They did not ask about the *isnād*, but when *fitnah* arose they said, "Name for us your men."'
48. M. Said Hatiboğlu, 'Batı'da Hadis Çalışmaları Üzerine', in *Uluslararası Birinci İslam Araştırmaları Sempozyumu Tebliğler ve Müzakereler* (İzmir: Dokuz Eylül Üniversitesi, 1985), 81–94. Even Goldziher was not completely spared from criticism. For example, Hatiboğlu charges that Goldziher mistakenly believed the customary inclusion of the word '*al-ḥadīth*' at the end of a truncated transmission to be part of it.
49. Mehmed Said Hatiboğlu, *Hz. Peygamber'in Vefatından Emevilerin Sonuna Kadar Siyasi İçtimai Hâdiselerle Hadîs Münasebetleri* (Ankara: Otto, 2016), 19.
50. See Daniel Brown, *Rethinking Tradition in Modern Islamic Thought* (Cambridge: Cambridge University Press, 1996), 43, 51–9.
51. Hatiboğlu develops this view in a separate book published in 2009 titled *Hz. Peygamber ve Kur'an Dışı Vahiy* ('The Prophet and Revelation outside the Qurᵓān'). On *waḥy ghayr matlūw*, see al-Shāfiᶜī, *al-Umm*, ed. Rifᶜat Fawzī ᶜAbd al-Muṭṭalib, 11 vols (Mansoura: Dār al-Wafāᵓ, 2001), 3:11; Abū Bakr al-Sarakhsī, *Uṣūl al-Sarakhsī*, ed. Abū al-Wafā al-Afghānī, 2 vols (Beirut: Dār al-Kutub al-ᶜIlmīyah, 1414/1903), 2:90–1.
52. Since 2009, Otto, the publisher of Mehmed Said Hatiboğlu's works, has continued Kitabiyat's line.
53. Lütfi Sever, one of the founders of the Ankara Okulu Yayınları, previously worked with another publisher Fecr Yayınevi. The first book he published while working at Fecr Yayınevi was Muhammed Abduh's (d. 1905) *Kitāb al-Tawḥīd*.
54. M. Fuad Sezgin, *Buhârî'nin Kaynakları Hakkında Araştırmalar* (İstanbul: İbrahim Horoz, 1956; repr. Ankara: Kitabiyat, 2000), 23–6, 53, 59, 81–2, 88–9.
55. Studies on the sources of other hadith collections have started to be carried out recently. For a study on the sources of Muslim's (d. 261/875) *Ṣaḥīḥ*, see Dilek Tekin, 'Yazılı-Şifâhî Rivâyet Bağlamında Müslim'in Eser Sahibi Hocalarından Rivâyeti', unpublished PhD thesis, Marmara University, 2015.
56. Wellhausen's *Das arabische Reich und sein Sturz* in 1963, W. Montgomery Watt's *Islamic Theology and Philosophy* and *Muhammad at Mecca* in 1968 and 1986, respectively, Schacht's *An Introduction to Islamic Law* in 1977, Goldziher's *Die Zâhiriten* in 1982.
57. Ali Fuat Başgil (d. 1967), the politician and professor of law who proposed the opening of higher institutes of Islam, made a distinction between theologians educated at the Faculty of Theology and religious scholars to be educated at these institutions. According to Başgil, those who learn the philosophy of

religion and sociology of religion could become specialists or philosophers but not religious scholars. See Ayhan, *Türkiye'de Din Eğitimi*, 226.

58. A few of these faculties have programmes with courses held only in Arabic. For the experiences of these programmes, see Muhammet Beyler, '*Tajārib kullīyāt al-ilāhīyāt/al-ᶜulūm al-islāmīyah fī tadrīs al-ᶜulūm al-islāmīyah bi-al-lughat al-ᶜarabīyah fī jāmiᶜāt Turkīyah: Birnāmaj al-ḥadīth wa-ᶜulūmihi anmūdhajan*', *Hadis Tetkikleri Dergisi* 14(1) (2016): 51–73.
59. For the catalogue of the theses in Islamic studies between 1953 and 2015, see İsmail E. Erünsal et al., *İlâhiyat Fakültesi Tezler Kataloğu (1953–2015)* (İstanbul: Türkiye Diyanet Vakfı İslam Araştırmaları Merkezi, 2017). For an online catalogue, see at: http://ktp2.isam.org.tr/?blm=arailhtez&navdil=tr.
60. Salahattin Polat, 'Modern Dönemde Hadis İlminin Temel Meseleleri', in *Modern Dönemde Dinî İlimlerin Temel Meseleleri – İlmî Toplantı* (İstanbul: Türkiye Diyanet Vakfı İslam Araştırmaları Merkezi, 2007), 211–48, at 218–19; Halit Özkan, 'Cumhuriyet Dönemi Hadis Çalışmaları: Bir Hasıla', *Türkiye Araştırmaları Literatür Dergisi* 11(21) (2013): 9–39, at 30.
61. Özkan, 'Cumhuriyet Dönemi Hadis Çalışmaları: Bir Hasıla', 31.
62. Bekir Kuzudişli, *Hadis Rivâyetinde Aile İsnadları* (İstanbul: İşaret Yayınları, 2007), 129ff. Nabia Abbott also drew attention to the close relationship between the written documents and family *isnāds*. See Nabia Abbott, *Studies in Arabic Literary Papyri, vol. 2: Quranic Commentary and Tradition* (Chicago: University of Chicago Press, 1967), 1, 37.
63. Joseph Schacht, *The Origins of Muhammadan Jurisprudence* (Oxford: Clarendon Press, 1950, repr. 1975), 170.
64. Kuzudişli, *Hadis Rivâyetinde Aile İsnadları*, 498ff.
65. Fatma Kızıl, 'Hukukî İçerikli Merfû Hadisler Bağlamında Müşterek Râvî Teorisi ve Tenkidi', PhD thesis, Uludağ University, 2011. The dissertation was published in 2013 with the title *Müşterek Râvi Teorisi ve Tenkidi* (İstanbul: Türkiye Diyanet Vakfı İslam Araştırmaları Merkezi, 2013).
66. Other dissertations on Western hadith studies or that substantially cited Western scholars' works include the following: Sabri Kızılkaya, 'İsnad ve Metin Çözümlemeleri Bağlamında Geleneksel ve Yeni Yaklaşımlar' ('Traditional and New Approaches in the Context of *Isnād* and *Matn* Analyses'), PhD thesis, Ankara University, 2008; Kudrat Artikbaev, 'Rus Oryantalistlerin Hadis ve Siyer Çalışmaları' ('Studies of Russian Orientalists on Hadith and *Sīra*'), PhD thesis, Ankara University, 2010; and Sultanbek Aliyev, 'Rus Oryantalistlerin İslâmi İlimlerle İlgili Çalışmaları ve Hadis/Sünnete Yaklaşımları' ('Studies of Russian Orientalists on Islam and Their Approach to Hadith/Sunnah'), PhD thesis, Erciyes University, 2016. In addition, Rahile Yılmaz discusses Orientalists' dating of the *Muwattaʾ* and their arguments about *mursal isnāds* in her dissertation. See Rahile Yılmaz, 'Modern Hadis Tartışmaları Bağlamında Muvatta'daki Mürsel Rivâyetler' ('Mursal Hadīths in the *Muwattaʾ* in the Context of Modern Hadīth Discussions'), PhD thesis, Marmara University, 2014.
67. Süleyman Doğanay, *Oryantalistlerin Hadisleri Tarihlendirmeye Yaklaşımları* (İstanbul: Marmara Üniversitesi İlahiyat Fakültesi Yayınları, 2013).

68. Doğanay, *Oryantalistlerin Hadisleri Tarihlendirmeye Yaklaşımları*, 226. Besides the dissertations and habilitations, there are also an increasing number of articles about Western hadith studies after the 2000s. For example, see Halit Özkan, 'The *Common Link* and Its Relation to the *Madār*', *Islamic Law and Society* 11(1) (2004): 42–77. In this article, Özkan objects to Juynboll's assertion that the term *madār* in classical hadith terminology is the equivalent of the common link. Some of his main arguments are as follows: (a) the dates given for *madārs* go back to nearly forty years earlier than those of Juynboll's first common links; (b) unlike the common link, there could be more than one *madār* for a single hadith and more than one strand below the *madārs*.
69. See Hüseyin Akgün, *Goldziher ve Hadis* (Ankara: Araştırma Yayınları, 2014).
70. For a literature review of Turkish academics' work on Western hadith studies, see Fatma Kızıl, 'Türkiye'de Hadis Çalışmaları ve Oryantalizm', *Türkiye Araştırmaları Literatür Dergisi* 11(21) (2013): 303–31.
71. My use of these labels is based on the usage current among the three competing trends. Curiously, while the first group is described as 'traditionalist' both by the group itself and its opponents, the two other labels are used only by the opponents of the group in question. I have tried to use 'critical scholars' or 'progressive scholars' as much as possible instead of 'modernists', since no scholars referred to as modernist by their opponents accept this designation. As for the traditionalists in Turkey, even though the term 'late Sunnī traditionalists' coined by Jonathan Brown is more precise, I used 'traditionalists' in keeping with the usage of all parties to the debate. See Jonathan Brown, 'Scripture in the Modern World: the Quran and Hadith', in Jeffrey T. Kenney and Ebrahim Moosa (eds), *Islam in the Modern World* (London: Routledge, 2014), 13–33, at 29–30.
72. For the translation of *tarihselci*, I have followed Felix Körner's rendering. But also, as he points out, the 'English rendering (*sic*) do not capture the Turkish coinage precisely': Felix Körner, *Revisionist Koran Hermeneutics in Contemporary Turkish University Theology: Rethinking Islam* (Würzburg: Ergon, 2005), 68.
73. This trend was prominent in Turkey during the 1970s and 1980s in particular (Mustafa Öztürk, 'Dinî Hükümlerin Kaynağını Kur'an ile Sınırlandırma Eğiliminin Kaynakları ve Tutarlılığı', in Cengiz Kallek (ed.), *Dini Hükümlerin Kaynağı ve Dini Metinlerin Anlaşılması Konusundaki Çağdaş Yaklaşımlar Çalıştayı* (İstanbul: İSAM, 2010), 13–67, at 43). The most popular supporter of the discourse of 'Kur'an İslâmı' ('Islam derived only from the Qurʾān') was Yaşar Nuri Öztürk (d. 2016) during the latter half of the 1990s. As a kind of spokesperson of the reformed Islam supported by the secularists during the 1997 military memorandum, he was especially influential outside the academy by means of public television programmes. During that period, he was also the Dean of the Faculty of Theology at Istanbul University. One of the leading institutions promoting the views of the *Kur'ancılar* today is the Süleymaniye Vakfı, which was established by Abdülaziz Bayındır, Professor of Islamic Law at the Faculty of Theology at Istanbul University in 1998 (see the foundation's website at: https://www.suleymaniyevakfi.org).
74. In Turkey, those who completely reject the Sunnah of the Prophet are figures

outside the academy such as Edip Yüksel. Yüksel, currently residing in the United States, describes himself as 'one of the leading names of the Islamic reform movement', see at: http://19.org/tr/category/edipyuksel/0-edip-yuksel-kimdir, last accessed 22 January 2018. Another example is the anonymous group that authored the book *Uydurulan Din ve Kur'an'daki Din* ('Fabricated Religion vs Religion in the Qurʾān') (İstanbul: İstanbul Yayınevi, 2016), in which they describe legal regulations based on sources other than the Qurʾān as fabricated.

75. Öztürk, 'Dinî Hükümlerin Kaynağını Kur'an', 45.
76. Öztürk, 'Dinî Hükümlerin Kaynağını Kur'an', 152.
77. Özafşar, 'Hadisin Neliği ve Akademik Hadisçilik', 149.
78. M. Yaşar Kandemir, Professor of Hadith in the Faculty of Theology at Marmara University until his retirement in 1999, is currently working at the Centre for Islamic Studies (İSAM). He oversaw all the entries on hadith and wrote a great many of them in *TDV İslâm Ansiklopedisi* ('Turkey Religious Affairs Foundation Encyclopaedia of Islam') (1983–2016), consisting of forty-four volumes and two supplements. Betül Avcı, who studied its entries on Christianity, concludes that the encyclopaedia, despite certain shortcomings, tends to let the Christian tradition speak for itself rather than adopting an Occidentalist approach. See Betül Avcı, 'Contemporary Turkish Research on Christianity: a Critical Study of *TDV İslam Ansiklopedisi* Articles, and Dissertations Conducted between 1988 and 2010 at the Faculties of Theology at Marmara and Ankara Universities', PhD thesis, Pontifical Gregorian University, 2012, 72. For the online open-access version of the encyclopaedia, see at: https://islamansiklopedisi.org.tr.
79. M. Yaşar Kandemir, 'Sahîhayn'a Yöneltilen Tenkitlerin Değeri', in İsmail Lütfi Çakan (ed.), *Sünnetin Dindeki Yeri* (İstanbul: Ensar Neşriyat, 1998), 335–76; Hatiboğlu, Mehmed Said, 'Müslüman Âlimlerin Buhârî ve Müslim'e Yönelik Eleştirileri', *İslâmî Araştırmalar* 10(1–4) (1997): 1–14.
80. M. Hayri Kırbaşoğlu, 'Hadis İlminde Metodoloji Sorunu', *Sünnetin Dindeki Yeri* (İstanbul: Ensar Neşriyat, 1998), 427–97.
81. Kırbaşoğlu, 'Hadis İlminde Metodoloji Sorunu', 430.
82. Kırbaşoğlu, 'Hadis İlminde Metodoloji Sorunu', 432–3.
83. M. Hayri Kırbaşoğlu, 'Alternatif Hadis Metodolojisi', in İsmail Kurt and Seyit Ali Tüz (eds), *İslami İlimlerde Metodoloji/Usul Meselesi* (İstanbul: Ensar Neşriyat, 2005), 777–99, at 779.
84. M. Hayri Kırbaşoğlu, *Alternatif Hadis Metodolojisi* (Ankara: Kitabiyat, 2002), 149–50, 343, 354, 359.
85. Bukhārī, *Ṣaḥīḥ*, *īmān* 37, *bāb suʾāl Jibrīl ilá al-nabī ʿan al-īmān wa-al-islām wa-al-iḥsān wa-ʿilm al-sāʿah*, No. 50.
86. Kırbaşoğlu, *Alternatif Hadis Metodolojisi*, 354.
87. Kırbaşoğlu, *Alternatif Hadis Metodolojisi*, 173.
88. Kırbaşoğlu, *Alternatif Hadis Metodolojisi*, 173.
89. For example, Kırbaşoğlu holds similar views to those of Hatiboğlu about 'non-recited revelation' and hadiths about the future tribulations (*fitan*) and Portents of the Last Hour (*ashrāṭ al-sāʿah*). See *Alternatif Hadis Metodolojisi*, 198, 212–15.

CHAPTER

9

CAN DIFFERENT QUESTIONS YIELD THE SAME ANSWERS? ISLAMIC AND WESTERN SCHOLARSHIP ON SHIᶜI NARRATORS IN THE SUNNI TRADITION

Michael Dann

In the second/eighth and third/ninth centuries, roughly two hundred narrators labelled as Shiᶜis were active in the milieux that gave rise to the Sunni hadith tradition. Abū ᶜAbd al-Raḥmān al-Nasāʾī (d. 303/915), the compiler of the last of six hadith collections recognised as canonical by Sunnis, was himself associated with Shiᶜi sentiments and likely lost his life as a result.[1] These Shiᶜi narrators existed along a broad spectrum of theological and political orientations, but collectively embodied the high degree of sectarian ambiguity that characterised Islam's early centuries. Some of them played an important role in the development of nascent Shiᶜi sectarian identities, others were best known for their support of Shiᶜi-inspired rebellions against the Umayyad and ᶜAbbāsid dynasties, and yet others were at the forefront of the proto-Sunni milieu of the Iraqi garrison city of Kufa. What they shared in common was simply their participation in proto-Sunni traditionist circles and an association with some iteration of early Shiᶜism, a retrospectively ironic fact that has rendered them a perennial object of curiosity for subsequent generations of Sunni and Shiᶜi scholars.

In modern scholarship, these narrators have received the historiographical attention of historians working in the Western tradition of Islamic Studies, as well as that of Arab, Persian and Turkish scholars writing in a more or less confessional fashion. To date, the volume of work produced in non-Western languages significantly exceeds that of work produced in Western languages. This non-Western, or Islamic, scholarship can be further subdivided into works by Imāmī Shiᶜis, pro-ᶜAlid Sunnis and Sunnis working in confessional academic settings.

In what follows, I offer a summary of the Western scholarship and an analysis of the contemporary Islamic scholarship on this topic, focusing on the historiographical contributions made by the latter as seen from the standpoint of the former. In line with recent developments in the field of Qurʾānic studies, I argue that present-day Islamic scholarship undertaken by both Shiᶜis and Sunnis significantly advances our knowledge of the place of Shiᶜi narrators in the Sunni hadith tradition, even though it is often aimed at addressing normative questions of orthodoxy and sectarian boundaries foreign to the Western tradition of Islamic Studies.[2] I also examine how this scholarship is shaped and driven by commitments to particular sectarian narratives and an ahistorical, reified view of sectarian categories and boundaries. These commitments place limitations on the historiographical contributions of this scholarship, and it is largely for this reason that the work of Sunnis and Shiᶜis is best viewed in a complementary fashion. For the sake of clarity, my discussion is organised in the sections below under four broad categories, although there is substantial diversity within each: (1) Western Scholarship: State of the Field; (2) Imāmī Cataloguers; (3) Sunni Critics; and (4) Sunni Apologists-cum-Historians.

Western Scholarship: State of the Field

The vast majority of Western scholarship on Shiᶜi narrators in the Sunni tradition has not treated them as a distinct object of inquiry, but rather has incorporated them within studies of broader topics. These broader topics include chiefly studies of the Sunni and Shiᶜi hadith traditions, studies of ᶜAlid rebellions supported by traditionist scholars, and studies of the evolution of sectarian identities. Some of these studies focus on individual narrators and others focus more on how Shiᶜi narrators have been constituted and evaluated as a more general category.

Studies focused on the Sunni hadith tradition have taken the dominant Sunni framing of these narrators as a starting point for discussion. This framing consists in the question of whether and how one can narrate from 'innovators' (*mubtadiᶜah*), a category subsuming adherents of a variety of objectionable theological doctrines, including primarily Shiᶜis, Qadarīs (advocates of free will), Jabrīs (predestinarians), Khārijīs and individuals who believed that the Qurʾān was created. The most detailed study of this phenomenon to date is that of Christopher Melchert, who addressed the presence of 'innovators'/'sectaries' in the pre-canonical hadith milieu through a statistical survey of Ibn Ḥajar al-ᶜAsqalānī's (d. 852/1449) biographical dictionary of narrators, *Taqrīb al-Tahdhīb*. Melchert noted the relative prevalence of these trends in the period spanning roughly from the early second/eighth century to the mid-third/ninth century and identified a total of ninety Shiᶜis (seventy labelled as Shiᶜis and twenty with the more derogatory term Rāfiḍīs), making them the most prominent sectarian trend in the traditionist milieux of this period. He notes that the presence of Shiᶜis and other sectaries declined rapidly around the middle of the third/ninth century, and attributes this decline to the disappearance of some of these trends, their partial absorption within other schools (including Sunnism and Muᶜtazilism), and especially to the 'closing of ranks' among Sunni traditionalists in response to al-Maʾmūn's (r. 198–218/813–33) inquisition.[3]

Melchert's article offers preliminary answers concerning the prevalence of 'innovators'/'sectaries' in the proto-Sunni traditionist milieu that gave rise to the Six Books, but does not address the question of how these figures were evaluated by hadith critics. On this point, several studies on the development of Sunni hadith criticism concur that, as a rule, hadith critics did not reject narrators solely on the basis of their association with innovation or a sectarian trend.[4] This is hardly surprising given that the most authoritative voices in the genre of hadith sciences left little doubt that the early hadith compilers had narrated extensively from innovators. These same authorities, however, suggested that accepting the narrations of innovators should be subject to one of two conditions. Some argued that, although the narrations of innovators could be accepted in general, the narrations of proselytising (*du*ᶜ*āh*) innovators should be rejected. Others argued that the narrations of innovators could be accepted as long as they did not support the particular innovation that they espoused.[5]

To date, there has been no systematic study of how early hadith compilers approached this issue in practice, although two scholars have offered brief suggestive comments. Jonathan Brown has noted that even Muslim ibn al-Ḥajjāj (d. 261/875) narrated a hadith on the virtues of ᶜAlī from a well-known Shiᶜi, contravening the theoretical prohibition against narrating hadiths from innovators that support their doctrines.[6] Ghassan Abdul-Jabbar provides a different emphasis when he notes that if al-Bukhārī (d. 256/870) quotes a hadith from someone with unorthodox views, 'he does so with care' – a pregnant statement on which Abdul-Jabbar unfortunately does not elaborate any further.[7]

Aside from studying Shiᶜi narrators under the rubric of the problematic of narrating from innovators, it is also worth noting that Western scholarship on the Sunni hadith tradition has also adopted the taxonomies of early Shiᶜism provided by the tradition itself. Scholars like al-Dhahabī (d. 748/1348) and Ibn Ḥajar al-ᶜAsqalānī located Shiᶜi narrators on a terminological spectrum defined by terms like *tashayyu*ᶜ, *rafḍ* and *ghulūw* primarily on the basis of their attitudes towards the Companions, and Western scholars have cited their discussions for the purposes of providing a shorthand definition of the Shiᶜism of hadith narrators.[8]

Just as Western scholarship on the Sunni hadith tradition has framed Shiᶜi narrators largely according to the perspectives supplied by the Sunni hadith tradition itself, Western scholarship on Imāmī hadith literature also reflects the concerns of that tradition. The bio-bibliographical genre has long been a strength of Imāmī hadith scholarship, and has served as one basis for substantiating claims to the authenticity of narrations from the Imāms. Hossein Modarressi's seminal study of early Shiᶜi literature comes in this genre and provides biographical entries for a large number of narrators who were active in both Sunni and Shiᶜi milieux, along with references to narrations that presumably stem from their non-extant written collections in a wide array of later Imāmī, Zaydī and Sunni sources.[9] In two separate studies, Liyakat Takim analyses the evolution of the biographical profiles of prominent Imāmī narrators in both Sunni and Imāmī sources, revealing overlapping but distinctive perspectives on the doctrines they adhered to.[10]

Within studies of Zaydī Shiᶜism, a greater focus has naturally been accorded to the political and military activities of Shiᶜi traditionists. In a monograph on the emergence of the Zaydī Imāmate in Yemen, Cornelis van Arendonk compiled an extensive list of jurists and traditionists who supported early ᶜAlid rebellions, many of whom were Shiᶜis of one stripe or another.[11] The extent of, and reasons for, traditionist support of these rebellions has also been addressed by scholars such as Amikam Elad and Maher Jarrar.[12] One of the regrettable features of modern Islamic scholarship on Shiᶜi narrators in the Sunni tradition is the relative lack of Zaydī representation, which leads to significant blind spots as discussed in more detail in the Conclusion.

Perhaps the most penetrating Western scholarship on these narrators is found in studies that have sought to locate particular narrators along the spectrum of early Shiᶜi affiliations in the period in which intra-Shiᶜi boundaries were emerging but not yet completely drawn. This effort entails embedding these narrators within their socio-political contexts and adopting a more holistic perspective that draws on the literature of Imāmīs, Zaydīs and Sunnis alike. Maher Jarrar provides a comprehensive profile of Ibrāhīm ibn Abī Yaḥyá (d. 184/800–1?), a prominent but controversial Medinan scholar who straddled several nascent sectarian communities.[13] The works of Najam Haider and Josef van Ess stand out in this regard. Haider has argued that one of the primary lines demarcating different groups of Shiᶜis from one another, and determining the extent to which they were accepted among Sunnis in spite of pro-Shiᶜi theological and political inclinations, was adherence to characteristically proto-Sunni positions in matters of ritual law that became sectarian shibboleths.[14] In his monumental survey of theological trends in the early Muslim community, van Ess provides comprehensive profiles of several Shiᶜi narrators, drawing on heresiographical, biographical, historical and hadith literature. The narrators included in his survey are predominantly those mentioned in the heresiographical work of Pseudo-al-Nāshiʾ al-Akbar (d. 293/905–6), which provides the organising principle of van Ess's survey.[15] In keeping with his method in *Theologie und Gesellschaft*, he lets the profiles of these figures speak for themselves to a large extent, in the process providing a representative sample of the range of doctrines and political positions promoted by Shiᶜi narrators.[16]

Although collectively the Western scholarship surveyed here covers significant ground in the study of Shiᶜi narrators active in proto-Sunni milieux, it also raises many questions for further study. Answers to some of these questions can be found in, or at least suggested by, recent Islamic scholarship on the topic. I restrict myself here to advancing those questions that I believe this scholarship is most useful in answering: (1) what was the extent of Shiᶜi narrators' participation in proto-Sunni traditionist milieux?; (2) did the taxonomies of Shiᶜism created by medieval Sunni authors accurately reflect the spectrum of Shiᶜi doctrines and affiliations in these milieux?; and (3) to what extent did the theoretical positions on narrating from innovators adopted in the Sunni science of hadith accord with the practices of the compilers of hadith collections themselves?

Imāmī Cataloguers

The largest volume of modern Islamic scholarship on Shiᶜi narrators in the Sunni hadith tradition has been produced by Imāmī Shiᶜis. The contributions of Imāmī scholars have come primarily in the way of identifying Shiᶜi narrators and collating relevant biographical and bibliographical material on them. The interest of modern Imāmī scholars in Shiᶜi narrators stems largely from their utility in polemical debates on various points of perennial Sunni–Shiᶜi conflict. In the presentation of Imāmī authors, the widespread presence of Shiᶜi narrators in Sunni works can serve to refute Sunni charges against Shiᶜism, demonstrate systematic Sunni bias against Shiᶜis, and/or substantiate Shiᶜi doctrines on the basis of Sunni sources. Alternatively, in literature framed in a more ecumenical fashion, their presence may be construed as signifying an early social overlap between Sunnis and Shiᶜis, although this point is emphasised less frequently than the others.

The first modern Imāmī compilation of Shiᶜi narrators in the Sunni tradition was undertaken by the Lebanese scholar ᶜAbd al-Ḥusayn Sharaf al-Dīn al-Mūsawī (d. 1957), whose work has been paradigmatic for later authors writing on the subject. Al-Mūsawī's compilation occurs in the course of a highly contrived correspondence that purportedly took place between himself and the late Shaykh al-Azhar Salīm al-Bishrī (d. 1916) in 1911. According to al-Mūsawī, the original copies of their letters were destroyed. Al-Mūsawī's reconstruction of the exchange, which he states includes revisions and additions, was published in 1934, nearly two decades after al-Bishrī's death. In the published version of the correspondence, al-Mūsawī leads his curiously pliant interlocutor to the threshold of conversion to Imāmism step by step, providing him with the evidence for Imāmī claims from his own sources and leaving him to arrive at his own conclusions in an adulatory process of connect-the-dots.[17] Early in the exchange, al-Bishrī expresses a nebulous doubt regarding the historical reliability of Shiᶜi transmissions, which provides al-Mūsawī with the occasion to compile biographical entries on 100 Shiᶜi narrators from Sunni sources in an overwhelming display of the fact that Sunnis themselves relied on Shiᶜi narrators and transmissions.[18] The logical conclusion to be drawn from the impressive array of information is left for al-Bishrī to state in rhyming prose:

> There is nothing left to prevent the Sunnī from using [the narration of] his Shīᶜī brother as proof if he is reliable. Your opinion in this [matter] is the clear truth and the opinion of those who object is obstinacy and quarrelsomeness. Their

> statements regarding the invalidity of using [the narrations of] Shīʿīs as proof oppose their actions, and their actions on the occasion of presenting evidence contradict their statements . . . In such a short period you presented something fit to be dedicated for a monograph. I have named it for you – The Reliable Narrators among the Shīʿah in Sunnī Chains of Narration (*Asnād al-shīʿah fī isnād al-sunnah*) – and it will be the pinnacle in this subject, beyond which there is no path for a seeker, nor any route for an aspirant.[19]

Al-Mūsawī never compiled the suggested monograph, but the task was eventually undertaken more than half a century later by Muḥammad Jaʿfar al-Ṭabasī, a professor at the Qum *ḥawzah*, under the slightly modified title *Shīʿī Narrators in Sunnī Chains of Narration* (*Rijāl al-shīʿah fī asānīd al-sunnah*). In this work, al-Ṭabasī compiled more thorough biographical entries on 143 Shiʿi narrators, drawing on a wider range of Sunni sources. In addition to compiling basic biographical data on these narrators, documenting their association with Shiʿism in Sunni sources, and noting their presence in the Six Books, al-Ṭabasī also provides notations on any association these narrators may have had with the Twelve Imāms on the basis of Imāmī biographical sources.[20] The body of this work is not analytical, but it is framed by an introduction intended to guide the reader's interpretation of the data found throughout the compilation. On the one hand, al-Ṭabasī states that the compilation vitiates the Sunni charge that Shiʿis did not play a significant role in the narration and compilation of hadith. On the other hand, the compilation demonstrates a deeply entrenched Sunni bias against Shiʿi narrators:

> It is as if trustworthiness and Shīʿism were two things that cannot be conjoined in a Muslim narrator, or weakness and the absence of trustworthiness are two things inherent to every Shīʿī narrator! You will also see that the main condition for accepting a narration is that its narrator not be a Shīʿī ...[21]

The basic thesis of al-Ṭabasī is repeated in a more overtly polemical work on the evolution of hadith scholarship among Sunnis and Shiʿis by al-Sayyid Muḥammad ʿAlī al-Ḥilw, a scholar at the *ḥawzah* of Najaf. Drawing on established Imāmī interpretations of the events surrounding the succession to Muḥammad, al-Ḥilw presents Sunni hadith scholarship as a continuous conspiratorial effort, stretching from events at the end of Muḥammad's life through the Umayyad and ʿAbbāsid periods and beyond, to suppress the knowledge of Muḥammad's explicit designation of ʿAlī as his successor. He devotes a considerable portion of his discussion to cataloguing Shiʿi narrators, with special attention given to those who were rejected by Sunnis specifically because they narrated objectionable reports on ʿAlī's virtues.[22] Rejection on such grounds, for al-Ḥilw, serves as evidence that Sunni methods of narrator criticism were constructed around the aim of tendentiously justifying the events that marginalised ʿAlī during the early contestations over the succession to Muḥammad. He catalogues forty-seven such narrators as representative examples amid a fairly wide-ranging discussion. Although there is overlap between his list and those of al-Mūsawī and al-Ṭabasī, many of the narrators were not identified by either author.

The inclusion of such a compilation in a work otherwise dedicated to more standard items of Sunni–Shiʿi polemic is an indication of the salience that this topic has gained in contemporary Imāmī polemics and apologetics. A brief and seemingly random list of Shiʿi narrators in the Sunni tradition is found in one of the most widely read introductory works on Shiʿism, Muḥammad al-Ḥusayn Āl Kāshif al-Ghiṭāʾ's *Aṣl al-Shīʿah wa-uṣūluhā*.[23] Defending the authenticity of narrations from Shiʿis in Sunni works is also a major recurring theme in the works of Ayatollah ʿAlī al-Ḥusaynī al-Mīlānī.[24]

While al-Mūsawī's cataloguing project has typically been extended in polemical and apologetic directions, one group of Imāmī scholars has chosen to frame the phenomenon of Shiʿi narrators in the Sunni tradition in a relatively more ecumenical fashion. In 1995, the chief organisation for Sunni–Shiʿi ecumenism in Iran, the Global Assembly for Rapprochement between Islamic Schools, held a conference around the theme of narrators found in both Sunni and Shiʿi corpora of hadith, not all of whom were necessarily Shiʿis. The presentations at the conference were then compiled, edited and harmonised by a team of Iranian scholars into the form of a multi-volume compendium published in 2001. The work lists 1,092 narrators shared by Sunnis and Shiʿis and provides biographical entries on 274 of the most prominent figures.[25] The compilers shared at least one goal with al-Mūsawī, namely, proving that Shiʿis played a prominent role in preserving the Prophetic Sunnah, a phenomenon that they believe has received insufficient attention among Sunnis. Unlike al-Ṭabasī and al-Ḥilw, however, the authors do not construe the compilation as evidence of Sunni bias against Shiʿis.[26]

In assessing these works from the standpoint of Western scholarship, we can state that in terms of compilation, they constitute a valuable achievement. They exceed the most comprehensive Western survey of Shiʿi narrators by more than 50 per cent. The biographical material that they include from Imāmī sources, even if it is limited, is also a helpful initial step in providing a more well-rounded view of these figures. Although these Imāmī works stand in the genre of compendia and include very little analysis, the authors do frame their works with introductory remarks intended to guide the reader's interpretation of the compiled biographical data. These introductory remarks all engage in a significant conflation by using the vague, diffuse sentiment of *tashayyuʿ* identified by Sunni biographers to make implicit historical arguments about the much more specific phenomenon of Imāmism. Al-Ṭabasī does make a distinction between Imāmism and a more general form of Shiʿism, but the implications of this distinction are not applied analytically. The majority of early Shiʿis who contributed to transmitting Sunni hadith, and especially those who played a more prominent role, had only limited connections to the nascent Imāmī community in the second / eighth and third / ninth centuries.

The majority of Imāmīs, in turn, viewed the nature of many of these narrators' attachments to the Prophet's family as severely misguided. Friction between the nascent Imāmī and Zaydī communities of mid-second-/eighth-century Kufa was a defining feature of the city's Shiᶜi milieu. It is, perhaps, for this reason that most Imāmīs draw only sparingly on Imāmī biographical literature in the works surveyed above; a more detailed engagement with this literature would reveal that Imāmīs vigorously rejected many of the Shiᶜi narrators found in the Sunni tradition. It is only the work of the Global Assembly scholars that engages with Imāmī literature in a substantive fashion and includes anecdotes that portray non-Imāmī narrators in a negative light. These anecdotes, however, are frequently omitted from the Arabic translation of their work.[27] In spite of these shortcomings, this body of scholarship is successful in bringing to light a portion of the genealogy of Sunni tradition that, left to their own devices, Sunni scholars have tended to downplay or ignore.

Sunni Critics

An exception to this tendency within Sunni scholarship is found in the works of Muḥammad ibn ᶜAqīl al-ᶜAlawī (d. 1931) and Aḥmad ibn Ṣiddīq al-Ghumārī (d. 1961), two traditional Sunni scholars who were highly critical of the Sunni reception of Shiᶜi narrators. Ibn ᶜAqīl was a Ḥaḍramī *sayyid* who wore many hats, including those of an itinerant merchant, a founder of religious institutions and periodicals in southeast Asia, and a religious scholar with ties to the reformist circle of Rashīd Riḍā (d. 1935) and Shiᶜi scholars associated with the ecumenical *taqrīb* trend.[28] He was best known for controversial works in which he denounced Muᶜāwiyah and the Umayyads,[29] but also penned an entire monograph on Shiᶜi narrators in 1924, under the title *al-ᶜAtb al-jamīl ᶜalá ahl al-jarḥ wa-al-taᶜdīl* ('A Gentle Reproof of the People of Narrator Criticism'). Ibn ᶜAqīl argued that the collective weight of the Sunni hadith tradition displayed an entrenched bias against early Shiᶜis, ᶜAlī and *ahl al-bayt*, which he believed stood in marked contrast to the Sunni tradition's relatively favourable treatment of figures associated with anti-ᶜAlid trends, such as Khārijīs, Nāṣibīs and figures associated with the Umayyad dynasty.[30]

In general, Ibn ᶜAqīl treats the Sunni hadith tradition as an undifferentiated whole, but it is represented for him above all by the two towering figures of Mamlūk-era hadith scholarship, Ibn Ḥajar al-ᶜAsqalānī and Shams al-Dīn al-Dhahabī, in whose hands the Sunni hadith tradition is generally considered to have reached its apogee. The first target of his critique in this work is Ibn Ḥajar, who had also noticed an imbalance in the treatment of pro- and anti-ᶜAlid figures who fell afoul of later formulations of orthodoxy, but sought to justify and explain this imbalance rather than exploit it. Part of Ibn Ḥajar's effort was to offer precise definitions of the key terms used to designate early Shiᶜi narrators, including *tashayyuᶜ*, *shīᶜī*, *rafḍ* and *ghulūw*. These definitions exhibited a tendency to domesticate the phenomenon of Shiᶜism in the early hadith milieu within the framework of a Sunni historical outlook. In the introduction to his commentary on *Ṣaḥīḥ al-Bukhārī*, Ibn Ḥajar offered the following taxonomy of Shiᶜism:

> Shīᶜism is the love of ᶜAlī and preferring him over the Companions. Whoever gives him precedence over Abū Bakr and ᶜUmar is considered extreme in his Shīᶜism (*ghālin fi tashayyuᶜihi*) and is referred to as a *rāfiḍī*. Otherwise he is simply a Shīᶜī.[31]

Ibn ᶜAqīl argues that if this definition is accepted, many of the most prominent figures of Islam's first three generations must be considered *rāfiḍīs*, which would be a 'back-breaking' conclusion. He lists a large number of Companions whom he believes to have held this position, arguing that it would be absurd to consider them *rāfiḍīs*.[32]

In a work on weak narrators, Ibn Ḥajar offered another definition of extreme Shiᶜism that focused more on the question of denouncing ᶜAlī's opponents than on the issue of relative preference among the caliphs:

> The extreme Shīᶜī at the time of the predecessors (*salaf*) and in their customary usage [of the term] is one who speaks [ill] of ᶜUthmān, Ṭalḥah, al-Zubayr, and a group of those who fought against ᶜAlī, may God be pleased with him, and reviled him (*taᶜarraḍa li-sabbihi*). And the extreme one (*al-ghālī*) in our time and in our customary usage is the one who anathematises these great men and disavows the two Shaykhs [Abū Bakr and ᶜUmar] as well. Such [a person] is astray, a slanderer.[33]

Ibn ᶜAqīl notes that this definition is ambiguous, for many people fought against ᶜAlī. Does Ibn Ḥajar mean to imply that speaking ill of any of them renders one an extreme Shiᶜi, or only some of them? If Muᶜāwiyah is included here, then many prominent Companions, such as ᶜAlī's sons and ᶜAmmār ibn Yāsir, had, in fact, cursed him. Are they extreme Shiᶜis? Furthermore, the subject of the verb and the referent of the pronoun in the phrase '*taᶜarraḍa li-sabbihi*' are unclear. Does the phrase mean that speaking ill of those who fought against and reviled ᶜAlī renders one an extreme Shiᶜi? Or does it mean that speaking ill of one whom ᶜAlī himself reviled renders one an extreme Shiᶜi?[34]

These terminological questions set the stage for Ibn ᶜAqīl's historical argument. The first example that he gives of a Shiᶜi narrator is Miṣdaᶜ al-Muᶜarqab, who earned his epithet when an Umayyad governor cut his Achilles tendons because of his refusal to engage in the Umayyad ritual practice of reviling ᶜAlī. Refusing to curse ᶜAlī, for Ibn ᶜAqīl, is the sort of Shiᶜism that has long been condemned by the Sunni hadith tradition and has been used an excuse for dismissing pro-ᶜAlid and anti-Umayyad reports, all of which results in a profound distortion in the standard Sunni vision of early Islamic history.[35] The rest of the work consists of a refutation of Ibn Ḥajar's attempts to explain the imbalance in the treatment of pro- and anti-ᶜAlid narrators, followed by an extensive juxtaposition of examples of anti-ᶜAlid narrators who were accepted by Sunni hadith critics with pro-ᶜAlid narrators who were criticised.[36]

The critique of Ibn ᶜAqīl is echoed to a large extent by Aḥmad ibn Ṣiddīq al-Ghumārī, a Moroccan *sharīf* and Sufi shaykh who was one of the most accomplished and prolific hadith scholars of the twentieth century.[37] Al-Ghumārī dedicated an entire work to defending the authenticity of the hadith, 'I am the city of knowledge and ᶜAlī is its gate', which was narrated by Abū al-Ṣalt ᶜAbd al-Salām ibn Ṣāliḥ al-Harawī (d. 236/851), a controversial narrator in Sunni circles and a major source for Imāmī reports from ᶜAlī al-Riḍā.[38] Sunni hadith critics who questioned al-Harawī's reliability did so in part because he narrated uncorroborated (*munkar*) hadiths, and in part because of his Shiᶜism.

Much like Ibn ᶜAqīl, a significant portion of al-Ghumārī's discussion revolves around substantiating a charge of widespread anti-ᶜAlid bias in the Sunni hadith tradition, but in addition to this he adds an extensive discussion aimed at dismantling the standard Sunni doctrines on narrating from innovators. To begin with, he notes that narration from innovators was ubiquitous, even among figures who were theoretically opposed to the practice. He asserts that al-Bukhārī narrated from more than seventy Shiᶜis and that Muslim narrated from an even greater number in his *Ṣaḥīḥ*.[39]

More specifically, al-Ghumārī argues vigorously against the two primary theoretical restrictions on narrating from innovators: that they cannot be accepted if they are proselytisers, or that those of their narrations that lend support to their particular innovation cannot be accepted. With respect to the first restriction, al-Ghumārī argues that the distinction between proselytisers and non-proselytisers is largely arbitrary, since anyone who publicises a doctrine can be considered a proselytiser, and this must include nearly everyone known to be an innovator.[40] With respect to the second restriction, he notes that innovation is a relative category determined by perspective. Sunnis are internally divided, and nearly everyone is guilty of innovation from someone else's perspective. If no one can narrate hadiths in favour of the school to which they adhere, then no one can narrate hadiths at all.[41] Furthermore, according to al-Ghumārī, although this restriction was introduced against the generic category of innovators, its true target was limiting the scope of acceptable pro-ᶜAlid narrations from Shiᶜis. The first scholar to articulate such a restriction, Ibrāhīm ibn Yaᶜqūb al-Jūzajānī (d. *c.* 256/870), was a notorious anti-Shiᶜi. The only considerations that should be taken into account when assessing a narrator's reliability are in fact honesty and accuracy. Considerations of doctrine and sectarian affiliation are largely irrelevant.[42]

It is noteworthy that both al-Ghumārī and Ibn ᶜAqīl weave certain Zaydī authorities who engaged Sunni thought into their works. For al-Ghumārī, some of the strongest historical support for the idea of ignoring sectarian affiliations in assessing narrators comes from Ibn al-Amīr al-Ṣanᶜānī

(d. 1182/1768), a prominent Zaydī scholar who effectively adopted a traditionalist, hadith-based Sunni methodology in theology and law.[43] In another work, al-Ghumārī cites with approval the claim of the tenth-century encyclopaedist Ibn al-Nadīm (d. *c.* 380/990) that 'most of the hadith scholars' were Zaydīs.[44] Ibn ᶜAqīl includes several citations of works by a seventeenth-century Zaydī scholar, Ṣāliḥ ibn Mahdī al-Maqbalī (d. 1108/1696), who also engaged Sunni thought extensively but was somewhat more critical of it than Ibn al-Amīr al-Ṣanᶜānī.[45] Al-Maqbalī directed particular attention to Sunni bias against Shiᶜi narrators in a manner similar to but less systematic than Ibn ᶜAqīl and al-Ghumārī. It is possible that Ibn ᶜAqīl's critique of the Sunni reception of Shiᶜi narrators in fact had its origins in the considerable body of Zaydī work on the subject, although he implies in the introduction to *al-ᶜAtb al-jamīl* that he came to his conclusions through independent research. In any case, the affinity between modern pro-ᶜAlid Sunnis and 'Sunnising' Zaydīs of the early modern period is noteworthy, and this is one of the few instances in which Zaydīs are admitted into the modern conversation on Shiᶜi narrators in the Sunni tradition.

In terms of their historiographical contributions, the aims of Ibn ᶜAqīl and al-Ghumārī are transparently polemical, but their work does alert us to certain biases and key historical turning points in the Sunni hadith tradition. In order to argue convincingly that a millennium of tradition had been misguided, these authors had to identify the points at which things had gone wrong, or, in other words, offer a deconstructive genealogy of tradition before providing it with a new pedigree. Ibn ᶜAqīl alerts us to the biases inherent in the taxonomies of Shiᶜism provided by Mamlūk-era hadith scholars, which became standard reference points for Sunnis, and al-Ghumārī alerts us to the malleable and somewhat arbitrary nature of the discourses on narrating from innovators. Collectively, the efforts of both authors to resurrect the pro-ᶜAlid portion of early Sunni traditionalism shed new light on an otherwise ignored corner of the Sunni past.

Sunni Apologists-cum-Historians

The critiques of the Sunni reception of Shiᶜi narrators surveyed above, from both Imāmī and pro-ᶜAlid Sunni scholars, have given rise to a strand of recent Sunni scholarship that has sought to either elucidate or justify the traditional Sunni approach to the issue. This scholarship consists of an admixture of apologetic, traditional and historiographical tendencies. Nearly all of it has been undertaken by scholars associated with confessional institutions of higher learning, whose intellectual production is often markedly different from that of more traditional ulema. For these scholars, tradition is conceived of less as a dynamic, trans-temporal conversation in which they are simply the latest participants and more as a static object of inquiry, rendering the historiographical questions that it seeks to address somewhat closer to those of Western scholarship. Nonetheless, the break with tradition signified by this style of scholarship is by no means absolute. Formally speaking, it retains significant links to tradition, such as foregrounding discussions of various topics with lexical and technical definitions of key terms, even as it incorporates hallmark characteristics of Western scholarship, such as the literature review. Most importantly, the types of historiographical questions pursued in this scholarship and the answers it provides leave little doubt that tradition is still valued as the historical embodiment of continual divine guidance, and inquiry into it remains aimed more at justification and elucidation than critique.[46] These general observations concerning the relationship of apologetics, tradition and history hold true for the scholarship examined here in varying proportions.

The most explicitly apologetic work by a present-day Sunni on Shiᶜi narrators is that of al-Sharīf Ḥātim al-ᶜAwnī, a scholar of some standing in moderate Salafi circles who is a former professor at Umm al-Qurá University in Jeddah and a prolific author and editor of works on hadith. In a work titled *ᶜAqlānīyat manhaj al-muḥaddithīn fī al-tathabbut min ᶜadālat al-ruwāh* ('The Rationality of the Hadith Scholars' Method of Verifying the Probity of Narrators'), al-ᶜAwnī devotes about one-third of his discussion to the question of narrating from innovators, with particular attention given to Shiᶜis and Nāṣibīs. The overall thrust of his argument is to demonstrate that, in contrast to the assertions of scholars like al-Mūsawī and especially Ibn ᶜAqīl – the primary targets of al-ᶜAwnī's critique – Sunni hadith scholars were both even-handed in their treatment of pro- and anti-ᶜAlid figures, and generally tolerant of differences of opinion that did not lead to deliberate fabrication.[47] He notes, for example, that Sunni scholars not only accepted the narrations of Shiᶜis but cited their opinions regarding narrator criticism, as was the case with scholars like ᶜAbd al-Raḥmān ibn Khirāsh al-Marwazī (d. 283/896). At the same time, scholars like Ibn Ḥajar recognised that the opinions of anti-ᶜAlid critics like Ibrāhīm ibn Yaᶜqūb al-Jūzajānī on Shiᶜi narrators were too biased to be accepted at face value.[48]

Al-ᶜAwnī also argues in favour of the dominant Sunni positions on narrating from innovators, namely, that it is acceptable to narrate from them as long as they are not proselytisers and their narrations do not support their particular variety of *bidᶜah*. These positions, for al-ᶜAwnī, are emblematic of the utmost tolerance, objectivity, impartiality and fairness – all terms that he employs frequently to characterise Sunni hadith critics throughout his discussion. If an innovator is a proselytiser, he is more liable to misinterpret the meaning of a hadith, twist its wording unintentionally, or hide its technical blemishes through obfuscation (*tadlīs*).[49] Likewise, an innovator might unintentionally pass on an unreliable hadith due to his strong desire to support his convictions. Even a good Sunni might fall into this trap, but hadith critics successfully weeded out such anomalous cases. Rejecting the uncorroborated hadiths of innovators is therefore perfectly logical and is paralleled by sound judicial practice, where testimonies of interested witnesses must be rejected under some circumstances.[50]

Although the aims of al-ᶜAwnī's work are unequivocally apologetic, he offers a useful corrective to the bodies of scholarship outlined above, which tend to portray the Sunni hadith tradition as monolithic in its treatment of pro- and anti-ᶜAlid figures and ignore evidence that is not supportive of their critiques. While al-ᶜAwnī's work was framed primarily in apologetic terms and only addresses historiographic questions incidentally, studies by other modern Sunni scholars invert this relationship. Karīmah Sūdānī wrote a dissertation at Algeria University on al-Bukhārī's method of narrating from Shiᶜis in his *Ṣaḥīḥ*, which was subsequently published as a monograph in Riyadh. The work consists of three parts: (1) a discussion of the theoretical problem of narrating from innovators as framed in works on *ᶜulūm al-ḥadīth*; (2) short biographical entries on Shiᶜi narrators in al-Bukhārī's *Ṣaḥīḥ* and an evaluation of the extent of their Shiᶜism; and (3) a survey of their narrations in the *Ṣaḥīḥ*. The first part of the work largely consists of a review of the various theoretical positions on narrating from innovators articulated in Sunni literature.[51] The second part analyses thirty of al-Bukhārī's narrators accused of Shiᶜism. It is here that the apologetic tendencies of the work are most apparent. In the case of certain highly prominent narrators, such as ᶜAbd al-Razzāq al-Ṣanᶜānī (d. 211/827) and Khālid ibn Makhlad al-Qazwīnī (d. 213/828–9?), Sūdānī minimises the significance of their Shiᶜism and ignores altogether the substantial body of anecdotes indicating that they were critical of some of the Companions.[52] In the case of other prominent narrators associated with Shiᶜism, such as al-Aᶜmash (d. 148/765) and Manṣūr ibn al-Muᶜtamir (d. 132/750?), Sūdānī does not even consider the possibility that they may have been Shiᶜis.[53] The overall result of such distortions is that she significantly understates both the presence of Shiᶜi narrators in al-Bukhārī's work and the extent of their dissonance with later Sunni orthodoxy.

The third part of Sūdānī's work is the most historiographically valuable and persuasive. Her unique contribution lies in her detailed analysis al-Bukhārī's narrations from the thirty Shiᶜis included in her study, which includes hundreds of hadiths and is comprehensive enough to shed significant light on al-Bukhārī's method in narrating from Shiᶜis. Sūdānī concludes that al-Bukhārī rarely narrated hadiths that could be construed as supporting Shiᶜi doctrines from Shiᶜis themselves, and even where he did, they were generally corroborated by narrations from non-Shiᶜis.[54] Sūdānī's work is the only comprehensive study of how a particular compiler approached this issue in practice that I am aware of to date, and it strongly suggests that while al-Bukhārī narrated from Shiᶜis extensively, he adopted a highly conservative approach to narrating hadiths related to points of Sunni–Shiᶜi dispute from them. It also suggests that the retrospectively formulated guidelines found in manuals of *ᶜulūm al-ḥadīth* were not entirely divorced from practice, even if the choices of individual authors cannot ultimately be reduced to formulaic rules.

Some scholars have attempted to close this theoretical loophole by introducing further subtle distinctions into the question of hadiths that support innovation. In an article analysing this sort of hadith in the *Ṣaḥīḥayn*, the Jordanian Sunni Jamāl Abū Zāyid attempts to exonerate al-Bukhārī and Muslim from the charge of including these hadiths in their works. In general, Abū Zāyid finds that such narrations from Shiᶜis are corroborated by parallel narrations from non-Shiᶜis. For the few cases where such corroboration is lacking, Abū Zāyid introduces a novel distinction in an attempt to bring the *Ṣaḥīḥayn* fully in line with the theoretical standards of Sunni hadith sciences: an innovated school of thought such as Shiᶜism contains elements that agree with Sunni doctrine and other elements that are truly innovated. The appearance of 'supporting innovation' can thus be chimerical. Hadith critics like al-Bukhārī and Muslim would accept only those narrations that supported the non-innovated portion of an innovated school.[55] Al-Sharīf Ḥātim al-ᶜAwnī likewise argued that certain hadiths only appear to support innovation, but in reality are perfectly consonant with Sunni doctrine.[56] This strained parsing of the concept of innovation suggests an important point. Abū Zāyid and al-ᶜAwnī treat the distinction between non-innovated and innovated doctrines as self-evident (or at least apodictically determined by the choices of authorities like al-Bukhārī and Muslim), but this serves only to highlight the ambiguous and contested nature of innovation itself.

This same point is evident in the work of a Turkish scholar, Muhammad Enes Topgül, whose Master's thesis on Shiᶜi narrators in the Sunni tradition is likely the most comprehensive study on the topic in any language to date and is more deeply engaged with Western scholarship than any of the works surveyed thus far. This study is unfortunately unpublished and written in a language not commonly employed by scholars focused on hadith in Western or Islamic contexts. Like Sūdānī, Topgül approaches the topic largely through the lens of Sunni hadith criticism and includes an extensive survey of the various Sunni doctrines on narrating from innovators.[57] He also includes a comprehensive survey of the various labels and terms applied to Shiᶜi narrators. Here he makes the important observation that key terms of sectarian designation, such as *shiᶜi*, *tashayyuᶜ* and *rāfiḍī* were employed with a high degree of elasticity during the formative period of the hadith tradition and beyond.[58] These insights are fleshed out in a subsequent article, where Topgül demonstrates how geographic and chronological factors led certain hadith critics to accentuate their descriptions of the Shiᶜism of Kufan narrators. Hadith critics from Basra and Syria had a tendency to describe the Shiᶜism of Kufans in relatively harsh terms and later hadith critics, such as Ibn Ḥibbān (d. 354/965), had a greater propensity to describe narrators as *rāfiḍī*s than their third-/ninth-century counterparts.[59]

The bulk of Topgül's study is prosopographical, consisting of brief biographical entries on 201 Shiᶜi narrators. Topgül's study thus surpasses the compilation of any single Imāmī cataloguer surveyed above, although he builds on the works of both al-Mūsawī and al-Ṭabasī. The biographical entries are arranged typologically and chronologically, with the narrators divided into five major categories: (1) extremely inclined towards Shiᶜism (thirteen narrators); (2) inclined towards Shiᶜism (thirty-three narrators); (3) weakly inclined towards Shiᶜism (twenty-four narrators); (4) wrongly accused of Shiᶜism (111 narrators); and (5) narrators of indeterminate status (twenty narrators).[60] What stands out in this typology is obviously the fact that Topgül considers 111 narrators, more than 50 per cent of the narrators he surveys, not to have been Shiᶜis. Unique among Sunni authors, Topgül draws extensively on Imāmī biographical literature in his analysis. His use of this literature is even more comprehensive than that of the Imāmī scholars surveyed above, but it is directed towards very different ends. The primary criterion that determines whether or not a narrator can be properly considered a Shiᶜi is in fact the nature and extent of his incorporation in Imāmī biographical literature, almost irrespective of the extent of his association with Shiᶜism in Sunni literature. (Sūdānī applies the same reasoning in her dismissal of the charge of Shiᶜism from ᶜAbd al-Razzāq, but she does not employ this method systematically.[61]) This is essentially a methodological choice, and one that is supported by a certain logic. As Topgül notes, the terms used to denote Shiᶜism among hadith scholars in Islam's early centuries were elastic and did not necessarily connote sectarian phenomena.[62] However, choosing to make the normative doctrines that eventually settled among Imāmīs the primary historical criterion for evaluating the existence of Shiᶜism in any time period and any milieu entails the dismissal of more than half of the evidence surveyed by Topgül. It also precludes serious consideration of the myriad questions that would arise concerning the type of Shiᶜism observed and described by early Sunni hadith critics, which seems so unfamiliar precisely because of the dominance of the conventional (Imāmī–)Shiᶜi–Sunni binary. With respect to such questions, Topgül allows the taxonomies of early Shiᶜism offered by Mamlūk-era hadith scholars such as Ibn Ḥajar and al-Dhahabī, as well as those of figures from outside the hadith tradition such as (Pseudo-) al-Nāshiʾ al-Akbar, to stand as they are. However, as argued by Ibn ᶜAqīl, these taxonomies are not free of Sunni bias.

Conclusion

At the outset of this survey of Islamic scholarship on Shiᶜi narrators, I posed three questions: (1) what was the extent of Shiᶜi narrators' participation in the proto-Sunni traditionist milieux?; (2) did the taxonomies of Shiᶜism created by medieval Sunni authors accurately reflect the spectrum of Shiᶜi doctrines and affiliations in these milieux?; (3) to what extent did the theoretical positions on narrating from innovators adopted in the Sunni science of hadith accord with the practices of early compilers? This survey demonstrates that on all three points, the body of Islamic scholarship on these narrators significantly advances the state of our knowledge. With respect to the first question, the compilations of Imāmī cataloguers and the study of Topgül give us a sense of how widespread association with Shiᶜism was in the early traditionalist milieux. Sūdānī's survey also gives us a sense of the central role played by some of these narrators in transmitting hadiths in collections that Sunnis would eventually recognise as canonical, even if the results of her survey are truncated by her choice not to consider many of the most prominent narrators associated with Shiᶜism.

With respect to the second question, it is the Sunni critics, Ibn ᶜAqīl and al-Ghumārī, who highlight the subtle biases and tendency towards domestication inherent in the Sunni tradition's reception of Shiᶜi narrators. Al-ᶜAwnī, a Sunni apologist, helps to attenuate the conclusions of these critics by adducing evidence that they ignore in constructing their polemical attacks. With respect to the third question, Sūdānī, Abū Zāyid, al-ᶜAwnī and al-Ghumārī all offer insights that help us to understand the intricate choices made by Sunni hadith compilers as they navigated a nascent discourse on narrating from innovators that would be codified in the genre of *ᶜulūm al-ḥadīth* in later centuries. Sunni authors aiming for the highest standard of authenticity, such as al-Bukhārī and Muslim, seem to have heeded theoretical limitations on narrating hadiths from innovators that support their innovation, without treating such limitations as absolute.

A voice that is noticeably absent from these debates, and which would certainly introduce a complementary perspective if it were present, is that of the Zaydīs. In the early modern period, the topic of Shiᶜi narrators in the Sunni tradition was taken up by several Zaydīs as the Zaydī scholarly establishment in Yemen gradually became more and more engaged with Sunni traditionalist thought. These scholars were critical of the Sunni reception of Shiᶜi narrators, without necessarily attempting to annex their legacy, as has often been the case with Imāmīs. This Zaydī scholarship reverberates faintly into the modern period through the mediation of Ibn ᶜAqīl and al-Ghumārī, but is ignored for the most part by both Imāmīs and Sunnis. I am aware of only one modern Zaydī scholar who has written anything on the topic, and he depends to a large extent, ironically, on the work of Ibn ᶜAqīl, along with earlier Zaydī discussions.[63] One of the major activities that led to the association of certain narrators with Shiᶜism was their support for ᶜAlid rebellions, an activity that became, over time, the hallmark of the Zaydīs. Although support for these rebellions is occasionally mentioned by Imāmīs and Sunnis, it is by and large a blind spot in modern Islamic scholarship, and one that would likely be filled in through the incorporation of a Zaydī perspective.[64]

The fact that neither Imāmīs nor Sunnis substantially incorporate Zaydī literature in their studies is but one indication that their scholarship is aimed primarily at addressing normative questions of orthodoxy and sectarian boundaries foreign to the Western historical tradition. The scholarship surveyed above exists on a spectrum in terms of the relative centrality of historical and normative questions. For scholars like Sūdānī and Topgül, historical questions are primary, although the conclusions reached are shaped by normative commitments. For scholars like al-Ghumārī, Ibn ᶜAqīl and al-Ḥilw, normative questions are primary, but can be addressed effectively only through a re-evaluation of tradition that rests on historical critique. Whatever the particular balance between historical and normative concerns in this scholarship, and wherever individual scholars fall on the spectrum of Sunni and Shiᶜi commitments, we see that the historical problem of sectarian ambiguity is refracted through present sectarian commitments that rest on the assumption of an ahistorical, essentialised meaning of Shiᶜism. For Sunnis, this assumption generally results in the downplaying, discounting and domestication of the sort of Shiᶜism that was an integral, if controversial, component of the proto-Sunni milieu. For Shiᶜis, it leads to a near-total omission of intra-Shiᶜi diversity, whereby anything labelled as Shiᶜism necessarily stands in continuity with Imāmism and lends historical depth to its narrative. The exceptions to these tendencies – Ibn ᶜAqīl and al-Ghumārī on the Sunni side and al-Ḥilw and ᶜAzīzī, Rastagār and Bayāt on the Shiᶜi side – merely serve to prove the rule.

Western historians tend to view sectarian categories as inherently unstable, evolving and perspectival; they serve as so much fodder for our counter-narratives.[65] In spite of this general recognition, there is much to suggest that, at least in certain respects, there is no exit from the sectarian hall of mirrors. In a recent article on al-Nasāʾī, the aforementioned compiler of the last canonical work of hadith recognised by Sunnis, Christopher Melchert labels al-Nasāʾī as a Shiᶜi.[66] Using the term in such a way clearly implies that it need not carry specifically sectarian connotations and can potentially refer to individuals who held characteristically Shiᶜi sentiments or doctrines in spite of otherwise firm Sunni commitments. A contrasting approach is found in the work of scholars like Najam Haider and Wilferd Madelung. Haider defines Shiᶜism as a sectarian phenomenon and views figures that lack a clear sectarian identity as proto-Sunnis, even if they were labelled, for example, as Batrī Zaydīs or Shiᶜis.[67] The problem comes into sharp relief in a dispute between two doyens of the field, Madelung and van Ess, where van Ess characterises certain pro-ᶜAlid Muᶜtazilīs of the medieval period as Shiᶜis while Madelung considers this to be a contradiction in terms. Van Ess's terminological/typological error, Madelung avers, ultimately stems from his belief that Shiᶜism emerged with the assassination of ᶜUthmān, rather than with the succession dispute that took place in the Saqīfah of the Banī Saᶜīdah.[68] Put simply, Western historians whose work focuses primarily on Sunnis, exemplified here by Melchert and van Ess, tend to adopt a maximalist sense of Shiᶜism similar to that adopted by Imāmīs surveyed in this chapter. Western historians whose work focuses primarily on Shiᶜis, exemplified here by Haider and Madelung, tend to adopt a more restrictive sense of Shiᶜism similar to that adopted by Sunnis like Topgül and Sūdānī. We may not set out to valorise particular sectarian narratives over others or to make the normative judgements that divide one sect from another, but our terminological choices and historical judgements ineluctably participate in the continual refiguration of such narratives and boundaries. Ultimately, we can concur with Gadamer that while the ends of the judge and the legal historian are markedly different, there is no absolute distinction between their methods.[69] In the case at hand, the substantive conclusions of one considerably enrich the discussions of the other.

Notes

1. On the Shiᶜi inclinations of al-Nasāʾī and his death at the hands of an angry mob, see Muḥammad ibn Aḥmad al-Dhahabī, *Siyar aᶜlām al-nubalāʾ*, ed. Shuᶜayb al-Arnaʾūṭ et al., 25 vols (Beirut: Muʾassasat al-Risālah, 1981–8), 14:132–3; al-Dhahabī, *Tadhkirat al-ḥuffāẓ*, 4 vols (Beirut: Dār Iḥyāʾ al-Turāth al-ᶜArabī, 1956–8), 2:700–1; Jamāl al-Dīn Yūsuf al-Mizzī, *Tahdhīb al-Kamāl fī asmāʾ al-rijāl*, ed. Bashshār ᶜAwwād Maᶜrūf, 35 vols (Beirut: Muʾassasat al-Risālah, 1982–92), 1:338–9; Christopher Melchert, 'The Life and Works of al-Nasāʾī', *Journal of Semitic Studies* 59 (2014): 403–5.
2. The most explicit argument regarding the substantial historiographical insights yielded by certain normative Islamic scholarship is found in Walid Saleh, 'Marginalia and Peripheries: a Tunisian Historian and the History of Qur'anic Exegesis', *Numen* 58 (2011): 284–313. Behnam Sadeghi also laments the lack of attention among Western scholars to achievements in the field of variant Qurʾānic readings in his article 'The Codex of a Companion of the Prophet and the Qurʾān of the Prophet', *Arabica* 57 (2010): 414–15. His preference for Mehdi Bazargan's chronology of Qurʾānic chapters over the more traditionally accepted chronology of Theodor Nöldeke as the basis for his stylometric analysis of the Qurʾān can also be read as an implicit argument in this regard: Behnam Sadeghi, 'The Chronology of the Qurʾān: a Stylometric Research Program', *Arabica* 58 (2011): 210–99.
3. Christopher Melchert, 'Sectaries in the Six Books', *Muslim World* 82 (1992): 287–95.
4. G. H. A. Juynboll, *Muslim Tradition* (New York: Cambridge University Press, 1983), 179; Eerik Dickinson, *The Development of Early Sunnite* ḥadīth *Criticism: the Taqdima of Ibn Abī Ḥātim al-Rāzī*, Islamic History and Civilization, Studies and Texts, 38 (Boston, MA: Brill, 2001), 102–4; Scott Lucas, *Constructive Critics,* Ḥadīth *Literature, and the Articulation of Sunnī Islam: the Legacy of the Generation of Ibn Saᶜd, Ibn Maᶜīn, and Ibn Ḥanbal*, Islamic History and Civilization, Studies and Texts, 51 (Boston, MA: Brill, 2004), 320–4.
5. See, for example, the discussions found in al-Khaṭīb al-Baghdādī, *al-Kifāyah fī ᶜilm al-riwāyah*, Min dhakhāʾir al-maktabah al-islāmīyah fī rijāl al-ḥadīth (Cairo: Dār al-Kutub al-Ḥadīthah, 1972), 194–210; Abū ᶜAbd Allāh al-Ḥākim al-Naysābūrī, *al-Madkhal ilá Kitāb al-Iklīl*, ed. Fuʾād ᶜAbd al-Munᶜim Aḥmad (Alexandria: Dār al-Daᶜwah, 1983), 49; and Abū ᶜAmr ibn al-Ṣalāḥ al-Shahrazūrī, *Maᶜrifat anwāᶜ ᶜulūm al-ḥadīth*, ed. Nūr al-Dīn ᶜItr (Beirut: Dār al-Fikr, 1986), 114–15. See also Eerik Dickinson's translation of the last as *An Introduction to the Science of Hadith* (Reading: Garnet, 2005), 86–7.
6. Jonathan A. C. Brown, *Hadith: Muhammad's Legacy in the Medieval and Modern World* (Oxford: Oneworld, 2009), 141.

7. Ghassan Abdul-Jabbar, *Bukhari*, Makers of Islamic Civilization (London: I. B. Tauris, 2007), 98.
8. Juynboll, *Muslim Tradition*, 48–9; Melchert, 'Sectaries in the Six Books', 291. For more detail, see the section on 'Sunni Critics', below.
9. Hossein Modarressi, *Tradition and Survival* (Oxford: Oneworld, 2003).
10. Liyakat N. Takim, *The Heirs of the Prophet* (Albany, NY: State University of New York Press, 2006), 163–80; Liyakatali Takim, 'Evolution in the Biographical Profiles of Two Ḥadīth Transmitters', in Lynda Clarke (ed.), *Shīᶜite Heritage* (Binghamton: Global Publications, 2001), 285–99.
11. Cornelis van Arendonk, *Les débuts de l'imamat zaidite au Yemen*, Publications de la Fondation de Goeje, 18 (Leiden: Brill, 1960), 307–19.
12. Amikam Elad, *The Rebellion of Muḥammad al-Nafs al-Zakiyya in 145/762*, Islamic History and Civilisation; Studies and Texts, 118 (Boston, MA: Brill, 2016), 363–73; Amikam Elad, 'The Rebellion of Muḥammad b. ᶜAbd Allāh b. al-Ḥasan (Known as al-Nafs al-Zakīya) in 145/762',in James E. Montgomery (ed.), *ᶜAbbasid Studies: Occasional Papers of the School of ᶜAbbasid Studies, Cambridge, 6–10 July 2002*, Orientalia Lovaniensia analecta, 135 (Dudley, MA: Peeters en Departement Oosterse Studies, 2004), 182–9; Maher Jarrar, 'Ibn Abī Yaḥyā: a Controversial Medinan *Akhbārī* of the 2nd/8th Century', in Nicolet Boekhoff-van der Voort et al. (eds), *The Transmission and Dynamics of the Textual Sources of Islam*, Islamic History and Civilization, Studies and Texts, 89 (Boston, MA: Brill, 2011), 206–9.
13. Jarrar, 'Ibn Abī Yaḥyā'.
14. Najam Haider, *The Origins of the Shīᶜa: Identity, Ritual, and Sacred Space in Eighth-Century Kūfa* (New York: Cambridge University Press, 2011).
15. See Pseudo-al-Nāshiᵓ al-Akbar, *Masāᵓil al-Imāma in frühe muᶜtazilitische Häresiographie*, ed. Josef van Ess, Beiruter Texte und Studien, 11 (Beirut: Franz Steiner, 1971).
16. Josef van Ess, *Theologie und Gesellschaft im 2. und 3. Jahrhundert Hidschra*, 6 vols (New York: Walter de Gruyter, 1991–5), 1:235–98, 334, 2:423–9, 716–19.
17. On the dubious origins of this work, its contents and its reception, see Rainer Brunner, *Islamic Ecumenism in the 20th Century: the Azhar and Shiism between Rapprochement and Restraint*, trans. Joseph Greenman, Social, Economic, and Political Studies of the Middle East and Asia, 91 (Boston, MA: Brill, 2004), 51–81. The authenticity of the work is itself a significant point of dispute between Sunnis and Shiᶜis.
18. Sharaf al-Dīn al-Mūsawī, *al-Murājaᶜāt* (Beirut: Muᵓassasat al-Wafāᵓ, 1983), 52–118.
19. Mūsawī, *Murājaᶜāt*, 118–19.
20. Muḥammad Jaᶜfar al-Ṭabasī, *Rijāl al-Shīᶜah fi asānīd al-sunnah* (Qum: Muᵓassasat al-Maᶜārif al-Islāmīyah, 1420). Although many of these narrators were enumerated among the 'companions' (*aṣḥāb*) of the Imāms, only a handful can be considered to have been Imāmīs *sensu stricto*. Imāmīs, like Sunnis, narrated from figures they considered to hold heretical beliefs, including Zaydīs and Sunnis. See Asma Afsaruddin, 'An Insight into the Hadith Methodology of Jamāl al-Dīn Aḥmad b. Ṭāwūs', *Der Islam* 72 (1995): 25–46.
21. Al-Ṭabasī, *Rijāl al-Shīᶜah*, 15.

22. Muḥammad ʿAlī al-Ḥilw, *Tārīkh al-ḥadīth al-nabawī bayna sulṭat al-naṣṣ wa-naṣṣ al-sulṭah* (Dār al-Kitāb al-Islāmī, 2005), 41–56, and passim (it is noteworthy that the title contains an intentional but largely perfunctory allusion to the work of Naṣr Ḥāmid Abū Zayd, *al-Naṣṣ, al-sulṭah, al-ḥaqīqah*). Al-Ḥilw's particular concern for cases of Shiʿi narrators who were rejected explicitly because of their narrations on ʿAlī's virtues is exemplified by his frequent citation of Jalāl al-Dīn al-Suyūṭī's (d. 911/1505) work on fabricated hadiths, *al-Laʾālīʾ al-maṣnūʿah fī al-aḥādīth al-mawḍūʿah*. From the perspective of Sunni scholars like al-Suyūṭī, these narrators were guilty of narrating *munkar* ('uncorroborated') reports. This was a flexible term that was generally understood to refer to a hadith narrated through a single chain of transmission that was not strong enough to establish it as reliable. At times, however, it was used to express objections to the contents of a hadith. See the discussion of *munkar* reports in Jonathan A. C. Brown, 'How We Know Early Ḥadīth Critics Did *Matn* Criticism and Why It's So Hard to Find', *Islamic Law and Society* 15 (2008): 174–82.
23. Muḥammad al-Ḥusayn Āl Kāshif al-Ghiṭāʾ, *Aṣl al-Shīʿah wa-uṣūluhā* (Beirut: Dār al-Aḍwāʾ, 1990), 83–4.
24. See, for example, ʿAlī al-Ḥusaynī al-Mīlānī, *Nafaḥāt al-azhār fī khulāṣat ʿabaqāt al-anwār* (Iran: n.p., 1414); al-Mīlānī, *Sharḥ Minhāj al-karāmah fī maʿrifat al-imāmah* (Qum: Markaz al-Ḥaqāʾiq al-Islāmīyah, 2007); al-Mīlānī, *Tashyīd al-murājaʿāt wa-tafnīd al-mukābarāt* (Qum: Markaz al-Ḥaqāʾiq al-Islāmīyah, 1997).
25. Ḥusayn ʿAzīzī, Parviz Rastagār and Yūsuf Bayāt, *Rāviyān-i mushtarak: pizhūhishī dār bāzshināsī-yi rāviyān-i mushtarak-i Shīʿah va ahl-i Sunnat*, 2 vols (Qum: Bustān-i Kitāb, 1380). This work was translated into Arabic and revised by ʿAbd al-Amīr al-Wardī, ʿAqīl al-Rabaʿī and Razzāq ʿAbd al-Rasūl under the title *al-Ruwāh al-mushtarakūn bayna al-Shīʿah wa-al-Sunnah*, 2 vols (Tehran: al-Majmaʿ al-ʿĀlamī lil-Taqrīb Bayna al-Madhāhib al-Islāmīyah, 2009). The Arabic edition of the work significantly reduced its scope, including biographical entries on only 115 narrators and omitting the more comprehensive list of shared narrators altogether.
26. ʿAzīzī et al., *Rāviyān-i mushtarak* 1:43–7.
27. For example, compare the entries in the Persian original and the Arabic translation on the 'Batrī Zaydīs' Abū al-Miqdām Thābit ibn Hurmuz (ʿAzīzī et al., *Rāviyān-i mushtarak* 1:156–8; al-Wardī et al., *al-Ruwāh* 1:141–2), Ḥasan ibn Ṣāliḥ ibn Ḥayy (ʿAzīzī et al., *Rāviyān-i mushtarak* 1:226–30; al-Wardī et al., *al-Ruwāh* 1:217–20), and Salamah ibn Kuhayl (ʿAzīzī et al., *Rāviyān-i mushtarak* 1:420–2; al-Wardī et al., *al-Ruwāh* 1:434–6). The publishers of the Arabic edition note that the original 'lacks greater focus on the ecumenical trend.'
28. On Ibn ʿAqīl, see Werner Ende, 'Schiitische Tendenzen bei Sunnitischen Sayyids aus Ḥaḍramaut: Muḥammad b. ʿAqīl al-ʿAlawī (1863–1931)', *Der Islam* 50 (1973): 82–97; William R. Roff, 'Murder as an Aid to Social History', in Huub de Jonge and Nico Kaptein (eds), *Transcending Borders: Arabs, Politics, Trade and Islam in Southeast Asia*, Proceedings/Koninklijk Instituut voor Taal-, Land- en Volkenkunde 5 (Leiden: KITLV Press, 2002), 91–108.

29. Muhammad ibn ʿAqīl al-ʿAlawī, *al-Naṣāʾiḥ al-kāfiyah li-man yatawallá Muʿāwiyah* (Najaf: Maṭbaʿat al-Nuʿmān, 1966); ibn ʿAqīl, *Taqwiyat al-īmān bi-radd tazkiyat Ibn Abī Sufyān* (Najaf: al-Maktabah al-Ḥaydarīyah, 1966).
30. Muhammad ibn ʿAqīl al-ʿAlawī, *al-ʿAtb al-jamīl ʿalá ahl al-jarḥ wa-al-taʿdīl* (Amman: Dār al-Imām al-Nawawī, 2004).
31. Aḥmad ibn ʿAlī ibn Ḥajar al-ʿAsqalānī, *Fatḥ al-bārī bi-sharḥ Ṣaḥīḥ al-Bukhārī*, ed. ʿAbd al-ʿAzīz ibn ʿAbd Allāh ibn Bāz, 15 vols (Cairo: Dār al-Ḥadīth, 1998), 1:613.
32. Ibn Aqīl, *al-ʿAtb al-jamīl*, 30–1.
33. This definition in fact belongs to al-Dhahabī, whose work *Mīzān al-iʿtidāl* is abridged and expanded by Ibn Ḥajar in his *Lisān al-Mīzān*. Ibn Ḥajar, in any case, quotes it here with approval. See Aḥmad ibn ʿAlī ibn Ḥajar al-ʿAsqalānī, *Lisān al-Mīzān*, ed. ʿAbd al-Fattāḥ Abū Ghuddah, 10 vols (Beirut: Dār al-Bashāʾir al-Islāmīyah, 2002), and Muḥammad ibn Aḥmad al-Dhahabī, *Mīzān al-iʿtidāl fī naqd al-rijāl*, ed. ʿAlī Muḥammad al-Bijāwī, 4 vols (Beirut: Dār al-Maʿrifah, 1963), 1:5.
34. Ibn ʿAqīl, *al-ʿAtb al-jamīl*, 31.
35. Ibn ʿAqīl, *al-ʿAtb al-jamīl*, 32–3.
36. Ibn ʿAqīl, *al-ʿAtb al-jamīl*, 33–170.
37. It is likely that al-Ghumārī was influenced by Ibn ʿAqīl's work on the topic. One of his polemical opponents in Morocco noted that he was enamoured of ibn ʿAqīl's work and distributed it to colleagues after his return to Tangier from a sojourn in Cairo. See Muḥammad ibn al-Amīn Būkhubzah, *Ṣaḥīfat sawābiq wa-jarīdat bawāʾiq*.
38. On al-Harawī, see Michael Cooperson, *Classical Arabic Biography: Heirs of the Prophets in the Age of al-Maʾmūn*, Cambridge Studies in Islamic Civilization (New York: Cambridge University Press, 2000), 84–98.
39. Aḥmad ibn Ṣiddīq al-Ghumārī, *Fatḥ al-Malik al-ʿAlī bi-ṣiḥḥat ḥadīth bāb madīnat al-ʿilm ʿAlī* (n.p., 1969), 71.
40. Al-Ghumārī, *Fatḥ*, 63–73.
41. Al-Ghumārī, *Fatḥ*, 52–63.
42. Al-Ghumārī, *Fatḥ*, 73–6.
43. Al-Ghumārī, *Fatḥ*, 68. On al-Ṣanʿānī and his milieu, see Bernard Haykel, *Revival and Reform in Islam: the Legacy of Muhammad al-Shawkani*, Cambridge Studies in Islamic Civilization (New York: Cambridge University Press, 2003).
44. Aḥmad ibn Ṣiddīq al-Ghumārī, *Juʾnat al-ʿaṭṭār fī ṭaraf al-fawāʾid wa-nawādir al-akhbār*, 150, typescript available at: http://k-tb.com/book/Arabi05915, accessed 17 October 2019. Cf. Ibn al-Nadīm, *Kitāb al-Fihrist*, ed. Ayman Fuʾād Sayyid, Silsilat al-nuṣūṣ al-muḥaqqaqah, 4 vols, 2nd edn (London: Muʾassasat al-Furqān lil-Turāth al-Islāmī, 1435/2014), 1:639–40 (*maqālah* 5, *fann* 2).
45. Ibn ʿAqīl, *al-ʿAtb al-jamīl*, 49–51, 167–9. On al-Maqbalī, see M. M. Moreno, 'El-Maqbalī e il Sufismo', *Oriente Moderno* 24 (1944): 7–16.
46. On the kind of relationship to tradition engendered by research practices in Islamic institutions of higher learning, see Muhammad Qasim Zaman, 'Epilogue: Competing Conceptions of Religious Education', in Robert Hefner and Muhammad Qasim Zaman (eds), *Schooling Islam: the Culture and Politics of*

Modern Muslim Education, Princeton Studies in Muslim Politics (Princeton, NJ: Princeton University Press, 2007), 242–68.

47. Al-Sharīf Ḥātim al-ᶜAwnī, *ᶜAqlānīyat manhaj al-muḥaddithīn fī al-tathabbut min ᶜadālat al-ruwāh*, available at: www.dr-alawni.com/books, 128–38.
48. Al-ᶜAwnī, *ᶜAqlānīyat manhaj al-muḥaddithīn*, 119–25.
49. Al-ᶜAwnī, *ᶜAqlānīyat manhaj al-muḥaddithīn*, 105–8. On the practice of *tadlīs* and its various forms, see Abū ᶜAbd Allāh al-Ḥākim al-Naysābūrī, *Maᶜrifat ᶜulūm al-ḥadīth* (Medina: al-Maktabah al-ᶜIlmīyah, 1977), 103–12; al-Khaṭīb al-Baghdādī, *Kifāyah*, 510–27; Juynboll, *Muslim Tradition*, index, s.v. '*tadlīs*'; Brown, *Hadith*, 91, 222–4.
50. Al-ᶜAwnī, *ᶜAqlānīyat manhaj al-muḥaddithīn*, 108–19, 140–7.
51. Karīma Sūdānī, *Manhaj al-Imām al-Bukhārī fī al-riwāyah ᶜan al-mubtadiᶜah min khilāl al-Jāmiᶜ al-ṣaḥīḥ*, Silsilat al-Rushd lil-rasāʾil al-jāmiᶜīyah, 106 (Riyadh: Maktabat al-Rushd, 2004), 41–88.
52. Sūdānī, *Manhaj*, 242–5, 260–2. For evidence of ᶜAbd al-Razzāq's criticism of certain Companions, see, for example, ᶜAlī ibn al-Ḥasan ibn ᶜAsākir, *Tārīkh madīnat Dimashq*, ed. Muḥibb al-Dīn Abū Saᶜīd ᶜUmar ibn Gharāmah al-ᶜAmrawī, 80 vols (Beirut: Dār al-Fikr, 1995–2000), 36:187–9. For Khālid ibn Makhlad, see Aḥmad ibn ᶜAlī ibn Ḥajar al-ᶜAsqalānī, *Tahdhīb al-Tahdhīb* (Beirut: Dār al-Fikr, 1984), 3:101.
53. For reports on the Shiᶜism of Manṣūr ibn al-Muᶜtamir, see, for example, Muḥammad ibn Saᶜd, *K. al-Ṭabaqāt al-kubrá*, 9 vols (Beirut: Dār Ṣādir, 1968), 6:338; Aḥmad ibn ᶜAbd Allāh al-ᶜIjlī, *Tārīkh al-thiqāt* (Madina: Maktabat al-Dār, 1405), 2:299; Abū al-Faraj al-Iṣfahānī, *Maqātil al-Ṭālibīyīn*, ed. Aḥmad Ṣaqr (Cairo: Dār Iḥyāʾ al-Kutub al-ᶜArabīyah, 1949), 145, 148. On Sulaymān ibn Mihrān al-Aᶜmash, see Haider, *Origins*, 221–30; *EIr*, s.n. 'Aᶜmash', by Etan Kohlberg; van Ess, *Theologie und Gesellschaft* 1:237–9.
54. Sūdānī, *Manhaj*, 283–446. Cf. al-Ghumārī, *Juʾnat al-ᶜaṭṭār*, 76, where he notes that al-Bukhārī narrated a hadith including Muḥammad's statement to ᶜAlī, 'You are from me and I am from you' from ᶜUbayd Allāh ibn Mūsá (d. 213/829?), a well-known Shiᶜi. This statement occurs as part of a longer hadith about the treaty of Ḥudaybīyah and was placed by al-Bukhārī in the chapter on *ᶜumrat al-qaḍāʾ* (*al-maghāzī* 44, *bāb ᶜumrat al-qaḍāʾ*, No. 4251) and as a *muᶜallaq* hadith in his chapter on ᶜAlī's virtues (*faḍāʾil aṣḥāb al-nabī* 9, *bāb manāqib ᶜAlī*). Sūdānī mentions the narration in the chapter on *ᶜumrat al-qaḍāʾ* without commenting on its implications for ᶜAlī's virtues (*Manhaj*, 395).
55. Jamāl Abū Zāyid, '*al-Aḥādīth al-muntaqadah ᶜinda al-shaykhayn fī bāb al-riwāyah al-muqawwiyah li-bidᶜat ruwātihā*', presented at Muʾtamar al-intiṣār lil-Ṣaḥīḥayn, Amman, Jordan, 14–15 July 2010, available at: http://www.hadith-turath.org/library/60305#.WQZxOKPMyCQ, last accessed 30 April 2017.
56. Al-ᶜAwnī, *ᶜAqlānīyat manhaj al-muḥaddithīn*, 148–50.
57. Muhammad Enes Topgül, 'Hadis Râvilerinde Şiîlik Eğilimi', Master's thesis, Marmara University, 2010, 17–32.
58. Topgül, 'Hadis Râvilerinde Şiîlik Eğilimi', 58–9, 66–7.
59. Muhammad Enes Topgül, 'Bir Cerh Sebebi Olarak Teşeyyu' (Şiîlik Eğilimi)

Kavramına Tarihsel Bir Bakış,', *Marmara Üniversitesi lâhiyat Fakültesi Dergisi* 42 (2012): 47–76.

60. Topgül, 'Hadis Râvilerinde Şiîlik Eğilimi', 84–337.
61. Sūdānī, *Manhaj*, 242–5.
62. Topgül, 'Hadis Râvilerinde Şiîlik Eğilimi', 58–9.
63. ^{c}Abd Allāh ibn Ḥammād al-^{c}Izzī, *^{c}Ulūm al-ḥadīth ^{c}inda al-Zaydīyah wa-al-muḥaddithīn*, 171–213.
64. For instances of attention to the support of Shi^{c}i narrators for ^{c}Alid rebellions, see Topgül, 'Hadis Râvilerinde Şiîlik Eğilimi', 211; ^{c}Azīzī, *Rāviyān-i mushtarak*, 456.
65. See, for example, the comments of Daniel Boyarin, *Border Lines: the Partition of Judaeo-Christianity*, Divinations (Philadelphia: University of Pennsylvania Press, 2006), 6–7.
66. Melchert, 'Life and Works', 403–5.
67. Haider, *Origins*, 221–30; Najam Haider, *Shī^{c}ī Islam* (New York: Cambridge University Press, 2014), 103–11.
68. Wilferd Madelung, 'Review of Josef van Ess, *Das Eine und das Andere*', *Studien zur Geschichte und Kultur des islamischen Orients* (2004); n.F., 23, 2 vols (Berlin: Walter de Gruyter, 2011), in *Journal of the American Oriental Society* 134 (2013): 531–3.
69. Hans-Georg Gadamer, *Truth and Method* (New York: Continuum, 2004), 321–36.

INDEX

Abān ibn Abī ᶜAyyāsh
  madār, 109–10
ᶜAbbās al-Dūrī, 76
ᶜAbbāsids, 9–10, 19–20, 32, 52, 70, 94, 134, 192, 197
  erection of beacons, 47n
  erection of lighthouse towers, 47n
  erection of milestones, 47n
Abbott, Nabia, 12
Abdak, 58
abdāl, 88n
ᶜAbd al-ᶜAzīz ibn ᶜAbd Allāh al-Uwaysī, 14
ᶜAbd Allāh al-Ḥabashī, 160
ᶜAbd Allāh al-Saᶜd, 163
ᶜAbd Allāh ibn Aḥmad, 60, 74
ᶜAbd Allāh ibn Dīnār, 100
ᶜAbd Allāh ibn Khamīs, 155
ᶜAbd Allāh ibn Salamah
  madār, 109
ᶜAbd Allāh ibn Yazīd, 58
ᶜAbd Allāh ibn Zayd
  and the creation of *adhān*, 42, 44
ᶜAbd al-Karīm al-Wuraykāt
  student of Hammām Saᶜīd, 163
ᶜAbd al-Karīm ibn Abī al-Mukhāriq
  madār, 110
ᶜAbd al-Majīd al-Muḥtasib, 49
ᶜAbd al-Malik ibn Marwān
  and Ibn al-Zubayr, 175–6
  policy on *mawālī*, 25n
  Qurʾān project, 16–17, 19–20
ᶜAbd al-Raḥmān ibn Isḥāq al-Wāsiṭī
  madār, 111
ᶜAbd al-Raḥmān ibn Mahdī, 58
  on Abū al-ᶜĀliyah, 107
  on hadith criticism, 104
  on *madār*, 107
ᶜAbd al-Raḥmān ibn Ziyād al-Ifrīqī
  madār, 111
ᶜAbd al-Razzāq al-Ṣanᶜānī, 28–9, 60, 181
  adhān hadith, 31
  and ᶜAlī's Nabatean heritage, 25n
  possible interpolator of al-Zuhrī hadith, 19–20
  Shiᶜism, 204, 206
ᶜAbd al-Salām Abū Samḥah
  study of *munkar*, 164
ᶜAbd al-Wahhāb, al-Qāḍī, 141
Abdul-Jabbar, Ghassan, 194
Abū al-Ṣalt ᶜAbd al-Salām ibn Ṣāliḥ al-Harawī, 201
ᶜAbdān ᶜAbd Allāh ibn ᶜUthmān, 56, 61
  collector of Ibn al-Mubārak's *al-Istiʾdhān*, 61
Abū Burdah, 100
Abū ᶜAbd Allāh Muḥammad al-Ṣūrī, 74
Abū al-ᶜAbbās al-Sarrāj, 14
Abū al-ᶜAbbās ibn ᶜAṭāʾ al-Ādamī, 77
Abū al-ᶜĀliyah Rufayᶜ b. Mihrān al-Riyāḥī, 61
  as a *madār*, 99, 108
Abū Ayyūb al-Anṣārī, 108, 111
Abū al-Dardāʾ, 2, 67n
Abū al-Ḥasan ᶜAlī ibn Jahḍam al-Hamadhānī, 76
Abū al-Ḥusayn al-Baṣrī
  on hadith contradicting *qiyās*, 139
Abū al-Qāsim al-Junayd, 72
Abū al-Malīḥ al-Ḥasan ibn ᶜUmar al-Raqqī
  possible transmitter to Dāwūd ibn Rushayd, 14–15
Abū al-Malīḥ ibn Usāmah ibn ᶜUmayr
  possible transmitter to Dāwūd ibn Rushayd, 14–15
Abū al-Miqdām ᶜAmr ibn Thābit al-Kūfī

Abū al-ᶜUsharāʾ
  majhūl, 100
Abū al-Walīd al-Ṭayālisī, 1
Abū ᶜAlī al-Naysābūrī, 83
Abū Bakr
  Qurʾān project, 12
Abū Bakr Aḥmad ibn Hārūn al-Bardījī
  on *munkar*, 105
Abū Bakr ibn Abī al-Naḍr, 29
Abū Dāwūd, 29, 57, 73, 76, 83–4, 89n, 157
  on *gharīb*, 113
Abū Dharr, 67n
Abū Ghuddah ᶜAbd al-Fattāḥ
  and al-Albānī, 152, 160
  as a hadith critic, 151, 161
  on Abū Ḥanīfah, 160
  on al-Dhahabī, 162
  on Ibn Ḥajar, 162
Abū Ḥāmid ibn Jabalah, 14
Abū Ḥanīfah, 49–50, 56–7, 64n, 134, 160, 181
Abū Ḥātim al-Rāzī, 83
  on *munkar*, 105
Abū Hurayrah, 1, 103, 110–11, 140, 174
Abū Isḥāq al-Shīrāzī, 133
  as a Shāfiᶜī rationalist, 131
  on rejecting unreasonable Hadith, 132
Abū Isḥāq ᶜAmr ibn ᶜAbd Allāh al-Sabīᶜī
  as a *madār*, 107
Abū Jaᶜfar Muḥammad ibn Abī Ḥātim, 2
Abū Janāb al-Kalbī
  madār, 111
Abū Kāmil, 157
Abū Kurayb Muḥammad ibn al-ᶜAlāʾ, 100
Abū Mūsá al-Ashᶜarī, 100
Abū Naṣr al-Sarrāj, 58
Abū Naṣr al-Ṭūsī, 74
Abū Nuᶜaym al-Faḍl ibn Dukayn, 83
Abū Nuᶜaym al-Iṣfahānī, 11–14, 59–60, 71–5, 80, 83, 90n, 93n
Abū Qilābah, 34
Abū Qudāmah Ḥārith ibn ᶜUbayd al-Iyādī
  discredited by Yaḥyá ibn Maᶜīn, 109
  madār, 109
Abū Rayyah, Maḥmūd, 173
  on Companions, 185n
Abū Ṣāliḥ, 1
Abū Saᶜīd al-Khudrī, 109
Abū Thawr, 57
Abū ᶜUbayd, 11–12
  commencement of Hadith study, 13
  commentary on hadith about taxation, 22n
  explanation of hadith on *awrād*, 16
  ignorance of al-Shāfiᶜī's legal theory, 22n
  interpolation of an *isnād*, 22n
  questionable citation of ᶜUqayl ibn Khālid, 13
Abū Usāmah Ḥammād ibn Usāmah, 100
Abū Wahb Muḥammad ibn Muzāḥim, 56
Abū Yaᶜlá al-Khalīlī
  on *shādhdh*, 105
Abū Yūsuf
  on hadith contradicting inherited tradition, 134, 140
  on hadith contradicting the Qurʾān, 134
  on Sunnah, 134
Abū Zakarīyāʾ al-Naysābūrī, 83
Abū Zayd, Naṣr Ḥāmid, 180
Abū Zayid, Jamāl, 205
Abū Zurᶜah al-Rāzī, 53, 83
  on Ghaylān conversion hadith, 161
adhān
  and an angel, 42
  and Bilāl, 28, 33, 36
  and *būq*, 28, 30–1, 35–6, 38, 41, 46n
  and Christians, 27–8, 31, 33, 35, 40
  and Donner's 'Qurʾānicization' hypothesis, 46n
  and dreams, 28, 36, 38–9, 41–2, 44
  and fire, 28, 33, 35, 47n
  and Jews, 27–8, 31, 33, 35, 41, 46n
  and *nāqūs*, 28, 33, 35–6, 38–40, 47n
  and *qarn*, 28, 30–1, 35–6
  and the Shīᶜah, 32, 42, 44
  and trumpet, 28, 31, 39–41, 46n
  and Zoroastrians, 35
  creation by ᶜAbd Allāh ibn Zayd, 42, 44
  creation by ᶜUmar, 28, 31–2, 36, 44
  diverse treatment of formulae of, 42
  growth and creation of origins-narratives, 27
  modification by ᶜUthmān, 32, 46n
  number of *takbīr*, 34
  origins narratives, 28–9
  pre-history in the Qurʾān, 31
Aḥmad ᶜAbd Allāh, 164
Aḥmad Amīn, 173
  on *matn* criticism, 185n
Aḥmad ibn Ḥanbal, 28–9, 51, 54–5, 57, 60, 72, 75–6, 83–4, 94n
  and Mālik's *ziyādah*, 100
  and *tawakkul*, 59, 67n
  commentary on Ibn Sīrīn and *kitāb*, 23n
  on *gharīb*, 101, 104–5
  on Ghaylān conversion hadith, 161
  on hadith contradicting the Qurʾān, 135
  on Hushaym ibn Bashīr, 101
  on *ijmāᶜ*, 137
  on *munkar*, 104–5
  on *qiyās*, 139
  on *shādhdh*, 101, 104–5
  on comparing hadith transmissions, 103
Ahmed Naim, Babanzade, 173
Aḥmad Shākir, 154, 158, 160
  and *ẓāhir al-isnād*, 159
  on al-Tirmidhī, 162
Aḥwaṣ ibn al-Ḥakīm, al-, 2

ᶜĀᵓishah, 108
Akseki, Ahmet Hamdi, 174
Āl Kāshif al-Ghiṭāᵓ, Muḥammad al-Ḥusayn, 198
Albānī, Nāṣir al-Dīn, al-
and Aḥmad Shākir, 154, 158, 160
and Ḥasan al-Bannā, 155
and Ibn ᶜAbd al-Wahhāb, 155
and *madhhabī* Traditionalism, 167–8n
and Muḥammad Rashīd Riḍā, 154
and Muqbil ibn Hādī al-Wādiᶜī, 159
and Muṣṭafá al-ᶜAdawī, 159
and Muṣṭafá al-Sibāᶜī, 154
and *qarāᵓin*, 158
and revival of hadith sciences, 153, 164
and Saᶜīd al-Burhānī, 155
and Salafism, 159
and Saudi Arabia, 155
and Sayyid Sābiq, 155
and the Muslim Brotherhood, 154–5
and *ẓāhir al-isnād*, 156–8, 164–5
as a modern hadith critic, 151
compared with early hadith critics, 169n
criticism of, 160, 165
criticism of Abū Dāwūd, 157
criticism of al-Mallībārī, 164
criticism of al-Bayhaqī, 157
criticism of al-Dāraquṭnī, 157
criticism of Muslim, 157
development and career, 153–6
influence in the Levant, 155–6
influence in the Arabophone world, 156
method of Hadith criticism, 156
on a judgement by al-Bukhārī and al-Tirmidhī, 157
on ᶜAbd al-ᶜAzīz, 157
on Abū Kāmil, 157
on *ziyādah*, 156–8
Algar, Hamid, 75
ᶜAlqamah ibn Waqqāṣ al-Laythī, 107
ᶜAlī, ᶜIṣām Muḥammad al-Ḥājj, 49–50
ᶜAlī al-Ḥusaynī al-Mīlānī
defence of Shiᶜi hadith transmitters, 198
ᶜAlī al-Riḍā, 201
ᶜAlī ibn Abī Ṭālib, 109, 125n, 175, 194, 197, 199–201, 211n, 213n
ᶜAlī ibn Baḥr, 2
ᶜAlī ibn Sahl al-Iṣfahānī, 77
Aᶜmash, Sulaymān ibn Mihrān al-, 1, 102
and Shiᶜism, 204
élitism in hadith, 25–6n
madār, 107
Amīn, al-, 19, 58
ᶜAmrah, 108
ᶜAmr ibn Dīnār
madār, 107
ᶜAmr ibn Jābir al-Ḥaḍramī
madār, 111
ᶜAmr ibn Thābit, 60, 68n
ᶜAmr ibn ᶜUbayd, 60
Anas ibn Mālik, 28, 34, 109
Arberry, A. J.
on al-Qushayrī, 76
Asᶜad Tayyim
as a student of Hammām Saᶜīd, 163
ᶜĀṣim al-Najjār
publisher of Ibn al-Aᶜrābī, *al-Zuhd*, 73
ᶜĀṣim ibn ᶜUmar ibn Qatādah
madār, 110
aṣḥāb al-raᵓy, 57
Asmandī, al-
on hadith contradicting *qiyās*, 139
Asmarī, Saᶜīd ibn ᶜAlī ibn ᶜAbd Allāh Āl Nāshiᶜ, al-, 69n
ᶜAṭīyah ibn Saᶜd al-ᶜAwfī, 109
awliyāᵓ, 88n
ᶜAwnī, al-Sharīf Ḥātim al-
and the *qarāᵓin* school, 163
apologist, 204
as a Salafi, 163
career, 203
criticism by Dann, 205
disagreement with al-Albānī, 163
on ᶜAbd al-Raḥmān ibn Khirāsh al-Marwazī, 203
on hadith transmission from Shiᶜis, 203, 205
on hadith transmission from Nāṣibīs, 203
versus al-Mūsawī and Ibn ᶜAqīl, 203
Aws ibn Ḍamᶜaj al-Ḥaḍramī, 108
ᶜAynī, al-
on ᶜAbd al-Raḥmān ibn Isḥāq al-Wāsiṭī, 111
on *madār*, 110–11
Ayyūb al-Sakhtiyānī, 66n, 103
Aᶜẓamī, Ḥabīb al-Raḥmān al-, 61–2
ᶜAzīzī, Ḥusayn
engagement with Imāmī literature, 199

Bājī, al- 141
on hadith contradicting *qiyās*, 139
Bakr ibn ᶜAbd Allāh al-Muzanī
madār, 108–9
Barāᵓ ibn ᶜĀzib, al- 140
Barbahārī, al-, 59
Baron, 174
Bayāt, Yūsuf
engagement with Imāmī literature, 199
Bayhaqī, al- 29
on Abān ibn Abī ᶜAyyāsh, 110
on al-Aᶜmash, 110
on al-Haramī ibn ᶜAbd Allāh, 111
on *madār*, 109
Bazdawī, al-
on hadith contradicting *qiyās*, 139
Berg, Herbert
on authenticity deadlock, 3

Bishrī, Salīm al-
  and al-Mūsawī, 196–7
Bīṭār, Muḥammad Bahjah al-, 152
Bonner, Michael
  on Ibn al-Mubārak, 52
Böwering, Gerhard
  publisher of al-Khuldī's *juz*ᵓ, 74
Brown, Jonathan
  good surveyor of hadith science, 7n
  on Muslim's transmitting a Shiᶜi hadith, 194
  on Sufism and hadith, 75
  on Sufism and *isnāds*, 75–7
  on the canonisation of the *Ṣaḥīḥayn*, 71, 80
Bukhārī, Muḥammad ibn Ismāᶜīl al-, 28–9, 32, 34, 55, 83–4, 164
  and *mutābiᶜāt* and *shawāhid*, 104
  canonisation of his *Ṣaḥīḥ*, 71, 80
  combining *adhān* hadiths, 31
  commentary on a hadith, 2, 100
  on Ghaylān conversion hadith, 161
Bukhārī, Muḥammad Saᶜīd ibn Muḥammad Ḥasan Aḥmad, 51–4, 60–1
Burayd ibn ᶜAbd Allāh ibn Abī Burdah, 100
Burhānī, Saᶜīd al-, 155
Būṣīrī, al-, 110–11

Caetani, Leone
  criticism by Ahmed Naim, 173
  criticism by Hatiboğlu, 176
  criticism by Okiç, 174
  translation of his *Annali dell'Islam* into Turkish, 182, 185n
Cevdet, Abdullah, 173
Companions
  Sunni dogma of collective reliability of, 6
Cook, Michael
  on al-Zuhrī and the writing of Hadith, 10
Cornell, Rkia, 76

Daäif, Lahcen, 75
Dār al-Ḥadīth al-Ashrafīyah, 152
Dāraquṭnī, ᶜAlī al-, 72–3, 77–8, 83, 89n, 94–5n
  on Bakr ibn ᶜAbd Allāh al-Muzanī, 108–9
  on *gharīb*, 101–2
  on Jarīr ibn ᶜAbd al-Ḥamīd, 102
  on *madār*, 108
  on *tafarrud*, 102
Dārimī, al-, 15, 29
Dāwūd ibn Rushayd, 14
de Goeje, Michael Jan, 174
Denaro, Roberta, 51–2
Dhahabī, al- 50, 72–4, 78, 80–1, 87–9n, 93n, 95n, 159, 161–2, 175
  on Shiᶜism, 194, 206
Dhū al-Aṣābiᶜ al-Juhanī, 108
Dhuhlī, Abū ᶜAbd Allāh Muḥammad ibn Yaḥyā al-, 83–4

Doğanay, Süleyman
  on common links, 179
  on Western Hadith scholarship, 179
Dozy, Reinhart, 173–4
  Turkish translation of, 182
Dūrī, Riyāḍ Aḥmad Ibrāhīm al-, 50

Elad, Amikam
  on traditionists and rebellions, 195

Faḍālah al-Nasawī, 56
Fasawī, al-, 11, 14, 18

Ghazālī, Abū Ḥāmid al-
  as synthesiser of Sufism and Sunni orthodoxy, 76
  on Hadith contradicting the practice of Companions, 141–2
Ghulām Khalīl, 59
Ghumārī, Aḥmad ibn Ṣiddīq al-
  and Ibn ᶜAqīl, 212n
  and Zaydī authorities, 201–2
  on al-Bukhārī's transmission from Shiᶜis, 201
  on anti-ᶜAlid bias in Sunni hadith, 201
  on Ibn al-Nadīm, 202
  on Ibrāhīm ibn Yaᶜqūb al-Jūzajānī, 201
  on Muslim's transmission from Shiᶜis, 201
  on Ibn al-Amīr al-Ṣanᶜānī, 201–2
Global Assembly for Rapprochement between Islamic Schools
  conference on Shiᶜi hadith transmitters in Sunni hadith collections, 198
Goldziher, Ignaz
  criticism by Goitein, 187n
  in Turkish scholarship, 179
  Muslim discomfort towards, 6
  on ᶜAbd al-Malik and al-Zuhrī, 175, 187n
  on al-Qushayrī, 76
  on al-Zuhrī, 175
  on the authenticity of hadith, 3, 175
  Turkish translation of, 177
Guillaume, Alfred
  Turkish reception of, 178

hadith
  al-jarḥ wa–al-taᶜdīl, 104
  and advocates of the created Qurᵓān, 193
  and dreams, 47n
  and Jabrīs, 193
  and Khārijīs, 193
  and Qadarīs, 193
  and Shiᶜis, 192–208
  authenticity of, 2–4, 6
  common link, 114–16
  contradictory, 3
  contradicting the Qurᵓān, 133
  definition of, 1

development of Western scholarship on, 4
Egypt as a centre of, 3, 183
English names for, 1
gharīb, 101–2, 130
imperfect transmission of, 2–3
iᶜtibār, 103–4
India as a centre of, 3, 183
madār, 106–16, 118n
munkar, 104–6, 130
Muslim (Qurʾānist) rejection of, 3
mutābiᶜ, 103–4
Principle of Dissimilarity applied to, 6
shādhdh, 104–6, 130
shāhid, 103–4
Six Books, 50, 53, 78, 83
source of law, 2
source of Sunnah, 1
source of theology, 2
supplement to Qurʾān, 2
tafarrud, 104–6, 118n, 130
transmission networks, 79–82
Turkey as a centre of, 6, 171–83
use by jurists versus story-tellers, 45
use by jurists versus hadith critics, 131–2
weight relative to Qurʾān and *ijmāᶜ*, 3, 133–7
Western criticism analogous to biblical criticism, 6
writing of, 9–13, 15, 19, 175, 177
ziyādah, 100, 118n, 130
hadith critics, criticism
and *ᶜilal al-ḥadīth*, 152
and the *qarāʾin* school, 163–4
and the *ẓāhir al-isnād* school, 151–60, 164–5
decline of, 152
in the modern Levant, 151
recent Muslim return to, 5
summary of, 5
under the Ottomans, 152–3, 164–5
Hadith folk *see* Traditionalists
Haider, Najam
on the demarcation of Shiᶜis, 195, 208
Ḥafṣ ibn Ghiyāth
and *fard* and *munkar*, 112
Ḥajjāj ibn Muḥammad, 29, 31
Ḥajjāj ibn Yūsuf, al-
involvement in ᶜAbd al-Malik's Qurʾān project, 16–19
Ḥākim al-Nīsabūrī, al-, 73–4, 83
Mustadrak, 109
on ᶜAbd Allāh ibn Salamah, 109
on Abū Isḥāq, 107
on al-Zuhrī, 107
on ᶜAmr ibn Dīnār, 107
on Hishām ibn ᶜUrwah, 107
on *madār*, 107
on *matn* criticism, 130
on *shādhdh*, 105
on Shuᶜbah, 108
on Sufyān al-Thawrī, 107–8
on Yaḥyá ibn Saᶜīd al-Anṣārī, 107
Ḥakīm al-Tirmidhī, al- 77
as a Traditionalist, 94n
Hakkı, İzmirli İsmail
and Turkish hadith studies, 173
Ḥallāj, al-Ḥusayn ibn Manṣūr al-, 75
Hallaq, Wael
on Western and Muslim Hadith scholarship, 143
Hamdan, Omar
on ᶜAbd al-Malik's Qurʾān project, 16
Ḥammād ibn Salamah, 100, 103, 124n
Ḥanābilah see Ḥanbalīs
Ḥanafīs/Ḥanafism, 133
and Ibn al-Mubārak, 56–7
and *matn* criticism, 143
and the Kufan school, 57
in Marw, 66n
on *akhbār al-āḥād*, 132, 137–8
on *ḥadīth al-muṣarrāh*, 140
on hadith contradicting *ijmāᶜ*, 136–7
on hadith contradicting inherited tradition, 140
on hadith contradicting *qiyās*, 138–40
on hadith contradicting *sunnah mashhūrah*, 136
on hadith contradicting the Qurʾān, 133–6
on *mutawātir*, 136
on Sunnah, 137
response to al-Shāfiᶜī on hadith, 135
Ḥanbalīs/Ḥanbalīsm, 133
and hadith specialists, 75
and *matn* criticism, 143
and Sufism, 77
on *akhbār al-āḥād*, 132
on *ᶜamal*, 141
on hadith contradicting *ijmāᶜ*, 137
on hadith contradicting *qiyās*, 138
on hadith contradicting the Qurʾān, 133
on Ibn al-Mubārak and Abū Ḥanīfah, 57
on Ibn al-Mubārak and Sufyān, 57
on rejecting unreasonable hadith, 142
on *tawakkul*, 58
Ḥanẓalah, 1
Haramī ibn ᶜAbd Allāh, al-
madār, 111
Hārūn ibn ᶜAbd Allāh, 29
Ḥasan al-Bannā, 154–5
Ḥasan al-Baṣrī, al-, 94n, 108
alleged introduction of *basmalah* into Qurʾān, 24n
aversion to *awrād*, 16
Ḥasan al-Saqqāf, 160
Ḥasan ibn Sufyān al-Nasawī, al- 61
Ḥasan ibn Yazīd al-Kūfī, 108

Hatiboğlu, Mehmed Said
  and 'Critical Islamic thought', 176
  and the school of Ankara, 182
  criticism of Hurgronje, 176
  criticism of Schacht, 176
  dissertation, 176
  supervised by Okiç, 174
  on Caetani, 176
  on Duncan Black Macdonald, 176
  on *fitan* hadiths, 176
  on Goldziher, 176, 182
  Western influence on, 186
Haythamī, Abū Bakr al-
  on *madār*, 110
Ḥibbān ibn Mūsā al-Marwazī, 56, 61
Hishām ibn ᶜAbd al-Malik
  and al-Zuhrī, 11–12
hadith codification initiative, 11–12, 15–16
Hishām ibn Khālid al-Salāmī, 14
Horovitz, Josef
  criticism by Okiç, 174
  on the Jewish origin of the *isnād* system, 174
  Turkish reception of, 178
Ḥulw, Muḥammad ᶜAlī al-
  on al-Suyūṭī, 211n
  on the evolution of hadith scholarship among Sunnis and Shiᶜis, 197–8
Ḥumayd al-Ṭawīl, 109
Hurgronje, Snouck, 176
Hurvitz, Nimrod
  on *zuhd*, 53
Ḥusayn ibn al-Ḥasan, al-, 50–1, 53, 58, 61–3, 69n
Hushaym ibn Bashīr
  and *fard* and *munkar*, 112

Ibn ᶜAbbās, 111, 140
Ibn ᶜAbd al-Barr
  as a traditionalist Mālikī, 131
  on ᶜAbd al-Raḥmān ibn Isḥāq al-Wāsiṭī, 111
  on *madār*, 109, 111
Ibn Abī ᶜĀṣim, 53
Ibn Abī Ḥātim al-Rāzī, 50, 53, 59–60
  on *al-jarḥ wa-al-taᶜdīl*, 104
Ibn Abī Khaythamah, 11–13, 15, 22n
Ibn Abī Shaybah, Abū Bakr, 29, 44–5
Ibn ᶜAdī al-Qaṭṭān
  on Abū al-ᶜĀliyah, 108
  on Abū al-Miqdām ᶜAmr ibn Thābit al-Kūfī, 101
  on *gharīb*, 101
  on Ismāᶜīl ibn Rajāʾ al-Zabīdī, 108
  on *madār*, 108, 111
  on Saᶜd ibn Saᶜīd ibn Qays al-Anṣārī, 111
Ibn al-Aᶜrābī, Abū Saᶜīd Aḥmad ibn Muhammad ibn Ziyād, 72–3, 75–6, 78, 81–3, 85, 90n
  as chief scholar of Mecca, 73
  biography and works, 73
Ibn al-Ḥājib
  on Hadith contradicting *qiyās*, 139
Ibn al-Humām
  on Hadith contradicting *qiyās*, 139
Ibn al-Jawzī, 74, 129, 143
Ibn al-Madīnī, ᶜAlī, 72
  on Abū Isḥāq, 107
  on al-Aᶜmash, 107
  on al-Zuhrī, 107
  on ᶜAmr ibn Dīnār, 107
  on comparing Hadith transmissions, 103
  on *madār*, 107
  on Qatādah, 107
  on Yaḥyá ibn Abī Kathīr, 107
Ibn al-Mubārak, 83
  agreement with Traditionalists, 57
  and Abū Ḥanīfah, 49–50, 56–7
  and heretics, 59–60
  and Isrāʾīlīyāt, 53–4
  and *jihād*, 52
  and Mālik, 50
  and shift from *qitāl* and *siyar* to *jihād* due to renunciant piety, 52
  and Sufism, 49–50, 53, 58–9
  and Sufyān al-Thawrī, 50, 55, 57
  and *tafsīr*, 60
  and *tawakkul*, 54, 57–9
  and the Khawārij, 59
  and the Murjiʾah, 59
  and the Qadarīyah, 59–60
  and the Sermon on the Mount, 58–9
  and the Shīᶜah, 59–60
  and *zuhd*, 57–9
  as a jurist, 56–7
  as a merchant, 54
  as a traditionist, 54
  authorship and works, 55, 60–3
  collection of doctrine mainly in Marw, 56–7
  disagreement with Rationalists, 57
  Kitāb al-Birr, 49–53, 60–1
  Kitāb al-Jihād, 49–53, 55
  Kitāb al-Zuhd, 49–55, 57–63
  modern Arabic research on, 49
  Musnad, 49–50, 53, 55, 61
  on ᶜAmr ibn Thābit, 60
  recension of *Kitāb al-Zuhd* by al-Ḥusayn ibn al-Ḥasan, 50–1, 53, 58, 61–3, 69n
  recension of *Kitāb al-Zuhd* by Ibn Ṣāᶜid, 63n
  recension of *Kitāb al-Zuhd* by Nuᶜaym ibn Ḥammād, 58, 61–3
  regions of sources, 54–5, 63
  teachers and sources of, 54–6, 63
  transmission from sectaries and heretics, 60
  weaknesses in modern Arabic study of, 49–51
  year of birth, 50

Ibn al-Mulaqqin
on *madār*, 110
Ibn al-Nadīm, 56, 60
on Zaydī Hadith transmitters, 202
Ibn al-Qaṭṭān al-Fāsī
on *tafarrud al-thiqah*, 105
Ibn al-Rāwandī, 58
Ibn al-Ṣalāḥ
as a developer of theory of Hadith science, 143
on *fard*, 102, 105–6
on *gharīb*, 102
on *mutābiʿāt*, 104
on *shawāhid*, 104–6
Western study of, 4
Ibn al-Sharqī, Abū Ḥāmid, 83
Ibn al-Turkumānī
on Abān ibn Abī ʿAyyāsh, 110
on al-Aʿmash, 110
on al-Haramī, 111
on *madār*, 110
Ibn al-Zubayr, ʿAbd Allāh, 175–6
Ibn ʿAqīl
as a Ḥanbalī rationalist, 131
Ibn ʿAqīl, Muḥammad al-ʿAlawī
and Rashīd Riḍā, 199
and Zaydī authorities, 201–2, 207
as a polemicist, 202
criticism of Ibn Ḥajar, 199–201, 206
life and career, 199
on al-Dhahabī, 199, 206
on Ṣāliḥ ibn Mahdī al-Maqbal, 202
on Shiʿi Hadith transmitters in Sunni scholarship, 199, 207
Ibn ʿAsākir, 15–16
Ibn ʿAwn, ʿAbd Allāh, 66n
Ibn Bābawayh, 29
Ibn Ḥajar al-ʿAsqalānī, 49, 41, 51, 60–1, 72, 74, 131, 158–9, 162, 193
and al-ʿIrāqī, 160
as a developer of theory of Hadith science, 143, 159
commentary on *adhān* hadith, 35–6
on Abū Janāb al-Kalbī, 111
on *fard*, 102
on *gharīb*, 102
on Ibn Nāṣir al-Dīn, 166n
on Ibrāhīm ibn Yaʿqūb al-Jūzajānī, 203
on *madār*, 110–11
on Shiʿism, 194, 199–201, 206
Ibn Ḥazm al-Andalusī
on *tafarrud al-thiqah*, 105
Ibn Ḥibbān al-Bustī, 29
on *iʿtibār*, 103
on Shiʿi Hadith transmitters, 205
Ibn Hishām, 29
Ibn Isḥāq, 44
Ibn Jurayj, 29, 44
Ibn Khafīf al-Shīrāzī, Abū ʿAbd Allāh Muḥammad, 76
Ibn Khayr al-Ishbīlī, 61, 73
Ibn Khuzaymah, 29, 78, 83
Ibn Lahīʿah, 53, 60, 63
accused of Shiʿism, 60
Ibn Mājah, 28–9, 83
Ibn Mandah, Abū ʿAbd Allāh Muḥammad, 83
on *gharīb*, 113
on *gharīb* of al-Zuhrī, 113
on *gharīb* of Qatādah, 113
Ibn Masrūq al-Ṭūsī, Abū al-ʿAbbās Aḥmad ibn Muḥammad, 72
Ibn Masʿūd, ʿAbd Allāh, 108, 111
Ibn Nāṣir al-Dīn al-Dimashqī
as a hadith critic, 152
Ibn Nujayd, Abū ʿAmr Ismāʿīl, 72
as a traditionist, 74
biography and works, 74
Ibn Qayyim al-Jawzīyah, 129, 143
on *ʿamal*, 141
Ibn Rajab al-Ḥanbalī
on hadith criticism, 105
Ibn Saʿd, 11, 14, 29
Ibn Ṣāʿid, 63n
Ibn Sīrīn, Muḥammad, 16–17, 103
Ibn Ṭāhir al-Sulamī, 53
Ibn Taymīyah
on *ʿamal*, 141
on *ijmāʿ*, 137
Ibn Ṭūlūn, 166n
as a hadith critic, 152
on Ibn Zurayq, 166n
Ibn ʿUmar, 1, 28–9, 100, 118n, 141
Ibn Zurayq, 166n
as a hadith critic, 152
Ibrahīm, Majdī Fatḥī al-Sayyid, 73
Ibrāhīm al-Nakhaʿī, 108
aversion to ʿAbd al-Malik's Qurʾān project, 16–17
aversion to *kitāb* from the time of ʿAbd al-Malik, 15–17
Ibrāhīm ibn ʿAbd Allāh al-Khallāl, 61
Ibrāhīm ibn Adham, 59
Ibrāhīm ibn Abī Yaḥyá
as a *madār*, 109
Ibrāhīm ibn al-Mundhir, 13–14
Ibrāhīm ibn Muslim al-Hajarī, 111
Ibrāhīm ibn Saʿd
suspicious transmissions from al-Zuhrī, 14
Imām al-Ḥaramayn al-Juwaynī
on hadith contradicting the practice of Companions, 141–2
on *mutawātir* hadith contradicting *ijmāʿ*, 137
ʿImrān ibn Ḥuṣayn, 110

ᶜIrāqī, al-, 160
ᶜĪsá al-Ayyūbī, 50, 64n
ᶜĪsá ibn Abān
on hadith contradicting inherited tradition, 140
on hadith contradicting *qiyās*, 139
response to al-Shāfiᶜī, 135
ᶜĪsá ibn Yūnus, 2
Isḥāq ibn Rāhūyah / Rāhawayh, 51, 57, 83
Islamic law
development of Western scholarship on, 4
Ismāᶜīl ibn al-Ḥusayn al-Maḥāmilī, al-Qāḍī, 74, 83
Ismāᶜīl ibn Khālid al-Aḥmasī, 101
Ismāᶜīl ibn Rajāʾ al-Zabīdī
as a *madār*, 108
isnāds
and classical Hadith scholarship, 178–9
and Sufism, 75–8
definition of, 1
English abbreviations of, 1
fabrication of, 2
in tandem with other methods, 20–1
isnād-cum-matn analysis
Pavlovitch's criticism of, 4
ᶜItr, Nūr al-Dīn
and al-Albānī, 152, 160
as a modern Hadith critic, 151, 161

Jābir ibn ᶜAbd Allāh al-Anṣārī, 111
Jābir ibn Yazīd al-Juᶜfī
as a *madār*, 109
Jamāl, Muḥammad ᶜUthmān, 49
Jarīr ibn ᶜAbd al-Ḥamīd, 102
Jarrar, Maher, 195
Jarrār, Nabīl Saᶜd al-, 73
Jaṣṣāṣ al-Rāzī, al-, 56
on Hadith contradicting *ijmāᶜ*, 137
Jazāʾirī, Ṭāhir al-
and revival of hadith sciences, 152, 164
jihād al-akbar, al-, 53
jizyah, 24n
Junayd, Abū al-Qāsim al-, 77, 94n
and Ibn al-Aᶜrābī, 76
and Ibn Masrūq, 72, 77
and Jaᶜfar al-Khuldī, 73, 78
appearance in dream, 72
Jūraqānī, al-, 143
Juynboll, Gautier H. A.
in Turkish scholarship, 179
on common links, 5, 98, 113
on 'diving' strands, 98
on *madār*, 98
on single stands, 98
on the authenticity of hadith, 3, 46n
on the authenticity of Prophetical taxation provisions, 13
Turkish reception of, 178
versus Muslim scholarship on common links, 114–15
Juwaynī, al- *see* Imām al-Ḥaramayn

Kandemir, Yaşar
as a leader of Turkish Traditionalism, 181
career and approach, 191n
on the reliability of the *Ṣaḥīḥayn*, 181
Karamustafa, Ahmet
on Abū al-Ḥasan ᶜAlī ibn Jahḍam al-Hamadhānī, 76
on traditionist Sufism, 72, 76, 78
Khadījah Muḥammad Kāmil, 73
Khalāf Maḥmūd ᶜAbd al-Samīᶜ, 74
Khālid al-Ḥadhdhāʾ, 34–5
Khālid ibn Maᶜdān, 2
Khālid ibn Makhlad al-Qazwīnī
and Shiᶜism, 204
Khallāl, al-, 58–9
kharāj, 24n
Khārijīs, 59, 193, 199
Khaṭīb al-Baghdādī, al-, 50, 72–4, 80
on hadith contradicting *ijmāᶜ*, 137
on *matn* criticism, 130
on negative judgements of early hadith critics, 104–5
on *raʾy*, 133
on rejecting unreasonable hadith, 133
Khoury, Raif Georges, 51
Khuldī, Abū Muḥammad Jaᶜfar ibn Muḥammad ibn Nuṣayr al-, 72
biography and works, 73
Khuzaymah ibn Thābit al-Anṣārī, 111
Kinberg, Leah, 53
Kırbaşoğlu, Hayri, 181
Kister, Meir
on al-Zuhrī hadith as pro-*mawālī*, 18
on al-Zuhrī versus Umayyads, 11
Turkish reception of, 178
Knysh, Alexander, 73
Koçyiğit, Talât
and Robson, 175
career and influence, 186n
criticism of Goldziher, 175
criticism of Schacht, 186n
on Orientalists, 175
on Western hadith scholarship, 182
Krackowsky, 174
Krymskiy, 174
Kuzudişli, Bekir
criticism of Schacht, 178

Lammens, Henri, 176, 188n

MacDonald, Duncan, 176
on al-Ghazālī, 76
Madelung, Wilferd, 208
Maḥmūd ibn Ghaylān, 29, 31

Maḥmūd Shukrī al-Ālūsī, 155
Mālik ibn Anas, 22n, 29, 44–5, 51, 58, 63, 118n, 181
as a *madār*, 107
inadmissibility of his *gharīb*, 113
on hadith contradicting *ᶜamal*, 141
ziyādah on Nāfiᶜ, 100
Mālikīs / Mālikism, 51, 133
and *ᶜamal*, 140–1, 150n
and *matn* criticism, 143
on *akhbār al-āḥād*, 132
on hadith contradicting *ijmāᶜ*, 136–7
on hadith contradicting *qiyās*, 138–40
on hadith contradicting the Qurʾān, 133, 136
Mallībārī, Ḥamzah al-
and hadith criticism, 163
and the Jordanian hadith movement, 165
and the *qarāʾin* school, 163–5
as a modern hadith critic, 152
as a Salafi, 163
career, 163
criticism of al-Albānī, 163–4
criticism of *ẓāhir al-isnād*, 163–4
Maᶜmar ibn Rāshid, 54–5, 60, 181
and hadith about ᶜAlī's Nabatean heritage, 25n
and the Umayyads, 10
arrival in Yemen, 26n
criticism of, 161
criticism of al-Zuhrī, 21n
possible anti-Umayyad interpolator of al-Zuhrī hadith, 10
possible interpolator of al-Zuhrī's anti-*kitāb* hadith, 20
possible pro-*mawālī* interpolator of al-Zuhrī hadith, 19–20
al-Maʾmūn, 19, 58
Inquisition, 193
Maᶜn ibn ᶜĪsá, 13
Maqbal, Ṣāliḥ ibn Mahdī al-
on Shiᶜi hadith transmitters in Sunni scholarship, 202
Massignon, Louis
on al-Ḥallāj, 75
on Sufism and Hadith, 75
matn
and hadith criticism, 130–1
and juristic criticism, 142–3
and Muslim scholarship, 129, 142
and Western scholarship, 129
definition of, 1
mawālī, 18
role in Islamic learning, 25n
their struggle for equality in the domain of hadith, 9–10, 20
ᶜUmar II's support for, 18–20
Umayyad restrictions upon, 18, 24–5n
Melchert, Christopher
approach to Shiᶜism, 208
Farrell's criticisms of, 71, 77, 93n
on al-Nasāʾī as a Shiᶜi, 208
on Ibn al-Aᶜrābī, 76
on Hadith and Sufism, 70–1, 78
study of sectarian hadith transmitters, 193–4
Mizzī, al-, 13, 60, 74, 78
Modarressi, Hossein
on early Shiᶜi literature, 194
Mottahedeh, Roy, 70
Motzki, Harald, 4
critic of Azami, 8n
in Turkish scholarship, 179
less sceptical than Schacht and Juynboll, 8n
on the importance of assumptions, 3
response to Schacht, 3
Turkish reception of, 178
Muᶜāwiyah, 175
Mughīrah ibn Shuᶜbah, al-, 108–9, 175
Muḥammad al-Bāqir
and hadith contradicting the Qurʾān, 134
Muḥammad ᶜAwwāmah
as a modern hadith critic, 151
Muḥammad ibn ᶜAbd Allāh ibn Muslim, 14
bad reputation, 23n
mutābiᶜāt from al-Zuhrī, 14
questionable attendance of al-Zuhrī's lessons, 14
Muḥammad ibn al-Ḥasan al-Baṣrī, 2
Muḥammad ibn al-Ḥusayn al-Burjulānī, 77
Muḥammad ibn al-Zubayr al-Ḥanẓalī
as a *madār*, 110
Muḥammad ibn Ibrāhīm al-Taymī, 107
Muḥammad ibn Manṣūr al-Ṭūsī, 77
Muḥammad ibn Naṣr al-Marwazī, 57
Muḥāsibī, al-Ḥārith ibn Asad al-, 72
Muqbil ibn Hādī al-Wādiᶜī, 159
Mūsawī, ᶜAbd al-Ḥusayn Sharaf al-Dīn al-
and Salīm al-Bishrī, 196–7
on Shiᶜi transmitters in Sunni hadith collections, 196
Muslim ibn al-Ḥajjāj, 28–32, 34, 55, 83–4, 100
and *mutābiᶜāt* and *shawāhid*, 104
canonisation of his *Ṣaḥīḥ*, 71, 80
selection and categorisation in his *Ṣaḥīḥ*, 104
on Ghaylān conversion hadith, 161
on hadith criticism, 113
on *ziyādah*, 130
Muṣṭafá al-ᶜAdawī, 159
Muṣṭafá al-Sibāᶜī, 154
Muṣṭafá ᶜUthmān Muḥammad, 61
Muᶜtamir ibn Sulaymān, 57
Muᶜtazilīs, Muᶜtazilah, 132
and hadith, 181
and Sufism, 58
on hadith contradicting *qiyās*, 139

Nāfi^c, 29, 118n
Nasā^ʾī, al-. 29, 83
as a Shi^ci, 192, 208, 209n
recording of contradictory hadith, 3
Nāṣibīs, 199, 203
Nawawī, al- 49
on *madār*, 110
non-Muslims under Muslim rule, 40
Nu^caym ibn Ḥammād, 58, 61–3
Nūḥ ibn Darrāj, 101
Nu^cmān, al-, 29

Okiç, Muhammed Tayyib
and Hatiboğlu, 174
and Koçyiğit, 174
criticism of Caetani, 174
criticism of Horovitz, 174
criticism of Lammens, 174
education and career, 174
on al-Zuhrī, 175–6
on Orientalists and Hadith, 174–6
on Sezgin, 174, 177
Orientalists, Orientalism
on hadith, 174–9, 181–2
Orfali, Bilal, 74
Özafşar, Mehmet Emin, 181
Özkan, Halit, 115–16
criticism of Juynboll, 98–9
on *madār*, 98–9, 109
on common links, 98–9

poetry
and Sufism, 72
pious hostility towards, 1–2
Prophet
on taxation, 13
Pseudo-al-Nāshiʾ al-Akbar
and the delineation of Shi^cism, 195, 206

Qāḍī ^cIyāḍ, al-
on *^camal*, 141
on selection and categorisation in Muslim's *Ṣaḥīḥ*, 104
Qarāfī, al-
on hadith contradicting *qiyās*, 139
Qāsimī, Jamāl al-Dīn al-, 155
and revival of hadith sciences, 152, 164
Qatādah ibn Di^cāmah, 108
as a *madār*, 107
aversion to ^cAbd al-Malik's Qurʾān project, 16–17
aversion to *kitāb*, 16–17
Qays ibn Rabī^c, al-
as a *madār*, 109
Qurʾān
and Abū Bakr, 12
and ^cAbd al-Malik and al-Ḥajjāj, 16–17, 19–20, 24n
and the introduction of *basmalah*, 24n
and ^cUthmān, 12, 20
arrangement (*taʾlīf*) of *sūrahs* in, 16–17
early controversy over *awrād*, 16–17
early controversy over diacritics (*naqṭ*) in, 16–17, 19
transformation from ritual object to source of law, 17–18
Qushayrī, al-, 50, 76

Radtke, Bernd
on al-Rūdhbārī's lectures, 74
Rāfi^c ibn Khadīj, 110
Rahman, Fazlur
in Turkish scholarship, 180
Ramaḍān, Sa^cīd, 154
Rastagār, Parviz
engagement with Imāmī literature, 199
Rationalists, Rationalism
versus Traditionalists on *akhbār al-āḥād*, 132
Reinert, Benedikt, 58
Riḍā, Muḥammad Rashīd, 154
riwāyah bi-al-lafẓ, al-
hadith implicitly supporting, 13
rare, 31
Ritter, Hellmut
and Sezgin, 177
Robson, James, 175
Turkish reception of, 178
Rūdhbārī, Abū ^cAbd Allāh Aḥmad ibn ^cAṭāʾ al-, 72
biography, 74
Rūdhbārī, Abū ^cAlī al-, 74

Sābiq, Sayyid, 155
Sa^cd ibn Sa^cīd ibn Qays al-Anṣārī
as a *madār*, 108, 111
Sa^cīd, Hammām
and the Jordanian Hadith movement, 163, 165
and the *qarāʾin* school, 164–5
as a modern Hadith critic, 152
critical edition of Ibn Rajab *Sharḥ ^cIlal*, 163
Sa^cīd ibn Bashīr, 14
Sa^cīd ibn Ziyād
obscurity of, 13, 23n
Salafism
and *madhhabī* Traditionalism, 160–2
and rise in interest in hadith, 165
and Sufism, 160–1
and *ẓāhir al-isnād*, 165
Ṣalāḥ al-Dīn al-^cAlāʾī, 72
Salem, Feryal, 52–4
Sālim, 1
Salmān, 67n
Sāmarrāʾī, Ṣubḥī al-Badrī al-, 61, 69n
Sarakhsī, al-, 56
on hadith contradicting *qiyās*, 139

Sarī al-Saqaṭī, al-, 72
Savant, Sarah
on the limits of Muslim reworking of historical memory, 42
Ṣayrafī al-Shāfiʿī, Abū Bakr Muḥammad ibn ʿAbd Allāh al-, 83
on *ʿamal*, 141
Schacht, Joseph
criticism by Koçyiğit, 186n
criticism by Kuzudişli, 178
Muslim discomfort with, 6
Muslim response to, 3
on common links, 97–8
on hadith authenticity, 3
on spread of *isnād*s, 98
Turkish reception of, 178
Turkish translation of, 177
versus Muslim scholarship on common links, 114–15
vindication by Pavlovitch on spreading *isnād*s, 22n
Schoeler, Gregor, 51
on al-Zuhrī and the writing of Hadith, 10
on Maʿmar interpolating a hadith from al-Zuhrī, 10
on the nature of early Islamic books, 52–3
on ʿUmar II's Hadith project echoing earlier Qurʾān projects, 12
Turkish reception of, 178
Şentürk, Recep
on Ibn al-Aʿrābī, 75, 78
on hadith transmission networks, 79–80, 82
on Sufism and hadith, 75, 78
on the canonisation of the *Ṣaḥīḥayn*, 80
Sezgin, Fuat, 61, 68–9n
and Okiç, 174
and Ritter, 177
and the Faculty of Theology, Ankara, 177
and Turkish military coup, 177
criticism of Goldziher, 177
on the writing of Hadith, 177
Shāfiʿī, al-, 51, 57, 105, 122n
acceptance of Mālik's *ziyādah*, 100
date of his *Risālah*, 22n
influence on Islamic legal theory, 135, 150n
on *ʿamal*, 141
on hadith, 134–5
on *ijmāʿ* contradicting Sunnah, 137
on *munkar*, 105–6
on *shādhdh*, 105–6
on Sunnah, 134–5
response to Abū Yūsuf, 134
theory of Qurʾān and Sunnah, 22n
Shāfiʿīs, Shāfiʿism, 133
and *matn* criticism, 143
on *akhbār al-āḥād*, 132
on *ʿamal*, 141
on hadith contradicting *ijmāʿ*, 137
on hadith contradicting *qiyās*, 138
on hadith contradicting the Qurʾān, 133
on *qiyās*, 139
on rejecting unreasonable hadith, 132–3, 142
on Sufism, 75
Shaqīq al-Balkhī, 58–9
Shāṭibī, al-
on hadith contradicting *qiyās*, 139
Shiʿis, Shiʿism
ʿAlid rebellions, 193, 195
and Imāmī scholarship, 196
and the *adhān*, 32
hadith transmitters, 192–3
in Sunni hadith collections, 192–4
rebellions against Umayyads and Abbasids, 192
Western scholarship on Shiʿi Hadith transmitters, 193–6
Shuʿayb al-Arnaʾūṭ, 151
Shuʿbah ibn al-Ḥajjāj, 1, 26n, 57
as a *madār*, 108
on hadith criticism, 104, 113
shuʿūbiyah, 19, 25n
Sibṭ ibn al-ʿAjamī, 152
Sobieroj, Florian, 76
Sprenger, Aloys, 174, 176
Sūdānī, Karīmah, 204
Suddī, al-, 108
Sufism, 58
and hadith, 75
and hadith specialists, 70–1, 76, 82
and *isnād*s, 75–8
and opposition to hadith, 74, 76
and the Ḥanbalis, 75, 77
inward moral attitude, 71
Sufyān al-Thawrī, 50–1, 55–9, 63
and ʿAbd Allāh ibn ʿAwn, 66n
and Ayyūb al-Sakhtiyānī, 66n
and Kufan Shiʿism, 66n
and rationalism, 66n
and the Basran school, 66n
and the Kufan school, 57
as a *madār*, 107–8
Sufyān ibn ʿAbd al-Malik, 56
Sufyān ibn ʿUyaynah, 15, 59, 83, 111
al-Sulamī, Abū ʿAbd al-Raḥmān, 71–2, 74–7, 80, 82, 88n, 91n
Sulaymān ibn Arqam
as a *madār*, 110
Sulaymān ibn ʿAbd al-Malik
not associated with a hadith project, 16
Sulaymān ibn Ṭarkhān al-Taymī, 61
Sulṭān al-ʿAkāylah
as a student of Hammām Saʿīd, 163
Sunnah
as revelation, 22n
authority equal to Qurʾān, 12
in the thinking of al-Shāfiʿī, 22n

Sunnis, Sunnism
  and anti-ᶜAlid trends, 199
  and hadith transmission, 70
  and Muᶜtazilīs, 132
  and Shiᶜi hadith transmitters, 192–4, 199–206
  and Shiᶜism, 59
  and Sufism, 70
  and philosophers, 132
  authoritative collections, 2
  pro-ᶜAlid Sunnis, 192
  self-definition, 132
  Sunni consensus, 133
  theology, 2
  view of history, 51–2
Suyūṭī, al-, 61, 153
  on fabricated hadith, 211n

Ṭabarānī, Abū al-Qāsim al-, 73, 78, 83
Ṭabarī, al-, 175
Ṭabasī, Muḥammad Jaᶜfar al-
  and the distinction between Imāmism and Shiᶜism, 198
  on Shiᶜi transmitters in Sunni hadith collections, 197, 210n
Ṭaḥāwī, al-
  as a traditionalist Ḥanafī, 131
Takim, Liyakatali
  on Imāmī narrators, 194–5
Ṭayālisī, al-, 29, 57, 83
Tilimsānī, al-
  on hadith contradicting *qiyās*, 139
Topgül, Muhammad Enes
  and al-Ṭabasī, 205
  and Imāmī biographical literature, 206
  and Mūsawī, 205
  on Shiᶜi hadith transmitters in Sunni scholarship, 205–7
  on the delineation of Shiᶜism, 205–6
traditionists
  and common links, 97
  and Sufism 70–82
  as *ḥuffāẓ*, 72
  English meaning of, 1
Traditionalists, Traditionalism, 131
  hegemony in hadith, 181
  summary of, 5
  versus jurisprudents on hadith, 5
  versus rationalists on *akhbār al-āḥād*, 132
Tirmidhī, al-, 28–30, 51, 55–6
  and *gharīb*, 99–101
  on *ziyādah*, 130
Turkey
  and Faculties of Theology, 172–3, 184n
  and hadith, 6, 171–83
  and hadith debates, 173, 177, 179–83
  and Westernisation, 171–2, 182–3, 185n
  under the Ottomans, 171–2
  under the Republic, 172–4, 182
Turkish Modernists / Modernism
  and Hatiboğlu, 176–7
  and Kırbaşoğlu, 181
  and Orientalists on hadith, 179, 181
  and the Sunnah, 180
  and Western hadith studies, 182–3
  based in Ankara, 179, 186n
  criticism of the *Ṣaḥīḥayn*, 181
  name of, 190n
  on hadith, 180–1
  versus Traditionalists, 179–80, 182
Turkish Qurʾānists / Qurʾānism (*Kur'ancılar*), 180
  and Edip Yüksel, 190–1n
  on Sunnah, 180
Turkish Traditionalists, Traditionalism, 173
  based in Istanbul, 173
  name of, 190n
  on 'historicalists', 179
  on prophetic medicine, 180
  on the authority of the Sunnah, 180
  on the Faculty of Theology in Ankara, 186n
  versus Modernists, 179–80, 182

ᶜUbayd Allāh ibn Mūsá, 1
ᶜUbayd Allāh ibn Walīd al-Waṣṣāfī, 109
Ugan, Zakir Kadiri
  and Islamic modernists, 173
  and Orientalists on Hadith, 173–4, 182–3
  and Turkish hadith studies, 173
  on Abū Hurayrah, 174
  on Goldziher, 174
  on the Companions, 173–4
ᶜUrwah ibn al-Zubayr, 108
ᶜUmar (II) ibn ᶜAbd al-ᶜAzīz
  and al-Zuhrī, 11
  hadith codification initiative, 11–12, 15–16
  policy on *mawālī*, 18–20, 25n
  similarities between his hadith project and earlier Qurʾān projects, 12
ᶜUmar ibn al-Khaṭṭāb, 107
  family of, 13, 22n
  role in creation of *adhān*, 28, 31–2, 36, 44
ᶜUmar ibn Thābit al-Anṣārī, 108
ᶜUmārah ibn Khuzaymah, 111
Umayyads, 9–11, 13, 15–20, 21n, 25n, 32, 94n, 175–6, 187n, 192, 197, 199–200
  and al-Zuhrī, 10, 21n, 175–6
  and *mawālī*, 18, 24–5n
  and the Qurʾān, 16–18
  and the writing of hadith, 9, 11, 13, 15, 19
  and ᶜUmar's *sunnah*, 46n
ᶜUqayl ibn Khālid, 13
  possession of al-Zuhrī book, 22n
  preference for transmission from memory (*ḥifẓ*), 22n
uṣūl al-fiqh

and hadith criticism, 129
initial Western focus on, 4
ᶜUthmān al-Nahdī, 109
ᶜUthmān ibn ᶜAffān
abolition of tower houses, 35
modification of *adhān*, 32, 46n
Qurʾān project, 12, 20
ᶜUthmān ibn ᶜAṭāʾ al-Khurāsānī, 108

van Arendonk, Cornelis
on the Zaydī Imāmate in Yemen, 195
van Ess, Joseph
and Pseudo-al-Nāshiʾ al-Akbar, 195
on Shiᶜi hadith transmitters, 195
on the demarcation of Shiᶜis, 208
versus Madelung, 208

Wahb ibn Munabbih, 54
Wahb ibn Zamᶜah, 56
Wakīᶜ ibn al-Jarrāḥ
on *zuhd*, 67n
al-Walīd ibn ᶜAbd al-Malik
not associated with a hadith project, 16
al-Walīd ibn Muslim, 14
problems with transmission from al-Zuhrī, 15
Wāqidī, al-14
Watt, William Montgomery
Turkish translation of, 177
Wellhausen, Julius
Turkish translation of, 177

Yaḥyá ibn Abī Kathīr
as a *madār*, 107
Yaḥyā ibn Maᶜīn, 83
on Abū Qudāmah Ḥārith ibn ᶜUbayd al-Iyādī, 109
on *gharīb*, 101
on Nūḥ ibn Darrāj, 101
Yaḥyā ibn Saᶜīd al-Qaṭṭān, 83
Yaḥyá ibn Saᶜīd ibn Qays al-Anṣārī, 101
as a *madār*, 107
Yaᶜqūbī, al-, 175
Yüksel, Edip, 190–1n
Yūnus ibn Yazīd al-Aylī, 54–5
Yūsuf ibn Asbāṭ
on *zuhd*, 67n

zandaqah, 58
Zayd ibn al-Ḥawārī al-ᶜAmmī
as a *madār*, 110
Zaydīs, Zaydism
and Sunni hadith, 207
and Sunnising, 202, 207
in Shiᶜi scholarship, 207
in Sunni scholarship, 207
Zaylaᶜī, al-
on *madār*, 110
Zuhrī, Ibn Shihāb al-, 44, 108
acquiescence in ᶜAbd al-Malik's Qurʾān project, 17
and ᶜAbd al-Malik ibn Marwān, 15, 175–6
and the hadith of ᶜUthmān's Qurʾān project, 20
and the Umayyads, 9–20, 21n, 175–6
and trial topos, 13
as a *madār*, 107
false ascription of pro-*mawālī* hadith to, 19
growth or retrojection of his isnad, 13
hostility towards *mawālī*, 18–20, 25n
negative reaction to al-Ḥajjāj and ᶜAbd al-Malik's Qurʾān project, 10, 17–18
on the writing of hadith, 9, 175
pro-*mawālī* hadith, 9–10, 18
reinterpretation and reformulation of his anti-*kitāb* hadith, 20
whether he was coerced by Hishām, 12–13

EU representative:
Easy Access System Europe
Mustamäe tee 50, 10621 Tallinn, Estonia
Gpsr.requests@easproject.com

www.ingramcontent.com/pod-product-compliance
Lightning Source LLC
Chambersburg PA
CBHW070348240426
43671CB00013BA/2439
* 9 7 8 1 4 7 4 4 4 1 8 0 3 *